RARITAN VALLEY
COMMUNITY COLLEGE LIBRARY
NORTH BRANCH, NEW JERSEY

Presented by

Lewis M. Ostar

BRISTOL

BRISTOL
AN ILLUSTRATED HISTORY

Charles Oxley

The Crowood Press

First published in 1990 by
The Crowood Press Ltd
Gipsy Lane, Swindon
Wiltshire SN2 6DQ

© The Crowood Press Ltd 1990

All rights reserved. No part of this publication may be reproduced or transmitted in any form or by any means, electronic or mechanical, including photocopy, recording, or any information storage and retrieval system without permission in writing from the publishers.

British Library Cataloguing in Publication Data

Oxley, Charles
    Bristol
    1. Bristol Cars, History
    I. Title
    629.2222

ISBN 1 85223 377 X

Typeset by Chippendale Type Limited, Otley, West Yorkshire.
Printed in Great Britain by BAS Printers Limited, Over Wallop, Hampshire.

Contents

	Acknowledgements	7
1	The Whites of Filton	9
2	The Brothers	15
3	Postwar Developments	21
4	The Type 400 Goes Into Production	27
5	A Change of Direction	
	Type 401 Saloon	39
6	Where Did They All Go?	61
7	The Odd One Out	
	Type 402 Convertible	68
8	Evolution	77
9	The Heavenly Twin	
	Type 403 Saloon	80
10	From Little Acorns	
	The Development of the Bristol Engine	94
11	The Almost Car	
	Type 404 Coupe	105
12	An American's Dream	
	The Arnolt-Bristol	118
13	How the 2-litre Bristols Were Made	130
14	Big Brother	
	Type 405	133
15	The Loner	
	Type 406E	145
16	The End of a Line	
	Type 406 Saloon	148
17	The Bristol Racers	164
18	The Thief of Time	180
19	The Shape of Things to Come	184
20	The Big Red Lump	
	The Chrysler Engine	186
21	The Pioneer	
	Type 407	192

22	Second Edition	
	Type 408 Saloon	203
23	Great Expectations	
	Type 409 Saloon	211
24	Evolution Not Revolution	
	Type 410	216
25	Advice to a Potential Buyer	
	Type 407–411 Models	223
26	Family Favourites	
	Type 411	230
27	In Pursuit of Perfection	245
28	From A to Zagato	
	The 412 Series	251
29	Sleeping Beauty	
	Type 603	266
30	The Paragons	
	The Brigand and the Britannia	277
31	The Club	287
32	The Others	
	Bristol 2-litre Engines	297
33	A Very Private Company	307
	Bibliography	314
	Index	315

Acknowledgements

Serious research is not easy on a small island like the Isle of Man lacking specialist library facilities, and I am grateful to the many members of the Bristol Owners' Club, and others, who have been so generous in their assistance.

I would also wish to acknowledge, with thanks, the permission given to me by the Editor of *Autocar and Car* magazine, Bob Murray, to reproduce drawings that appeared in back numbers, and which can be so useful when describing some especially idiosyncratic method of operation or design.

Club members have sent me their photographs and slides, sometimes the only examples extant, and I wish to thank them all. They include: Jack Addenbrooke, David Allen, Paula Bicknell, Stefan Cembrowicz, David Crownshawe, Bob Charlton, Ray Cross, Geoffrey Herdman, John Howden-Richards, Glynnis Iles, John Juliffe, Dick Peacock, Bill Robinson, Hunter Rogers and Ian Tonkin.

I would also like to thank David Crownshawe and Eric Storey for the help given me regarding certain technical points, and for reading the relevant chapters in draft. I am grateful to Raymond Victor Williams, for photographs, and a very clear description of the methods used when building the Bristol racing engines.

The useful Spotter's Guide, supplied by Theo de Rose, has been extended to cover the current range of models. The separate guide showing distinguishing features of the Type 412 range was specially devised by Lawrence Cook, and I would like to thank him for it.

Finally I would like to record my appreciation of the help given me by Mr Anthony Crook. He read the manuscript at the galley proof stage, as a friendly gesture, not as an endorsement, and his observations and advice have been most valuable. I am extremely grateful.

1
The Whites of Filton

The First Attempt

The time, a summer's day in 1942; the place, a small airfield in the west country; and the group of men standing on the runway were a team of technicians, seconded from the Filton factory of the Bristol Aeroplane Company.

Their task had been to assist the Company's chief engineer, Sir Roy Fedden, in the construction of a prototype on which a Bristol motor car might be based when the war was over. The design was by Fedden, and included many innovations; a chassis with all-round independent suspension, a rear axle incorporating the gearbox, and an engine of radial type, using sleeve valves.

It was not until the car was finished and testing on the runway began that problems arose, the driver complaining of excessive oversteer. With hindsight, it is probable that the cause was the positioning of the engine, in the tail and high above the gearbox. Fedden, however, insisted that the basic design was right, and that the problem could be solved with minor adjustments. Much time and effort was devoted to various palliatives which were all unsuccessful, and the team's early enthusiasm waned. Most of them were Bristolians, and longed to return to their much-bombed city, yet the tests went on.

The new modifications were checked and approved, and the driver was given the signal to start his engine, and to make another run. As the car gathered speed, all appeared to be going smoothly, until, without warning, it swerved off the runway, careering across the grass until it hit an obstruction. It collided with such force that the car was wrecked, and the driver severely injured. The project was abandoned, and Fedden left the Company's employ.

One might ask why, during a war that was not going well, the chief engineer should have been given a task of such a long-term peacetime nature. The answer lies in a much earlier period of the Company's history, in 1918, when it was still called the British and Colonial Aeroplane Company.

The Innovators

A phenomenon of the late Victorian and Edwardian periods was the appearance of a new type of businessman, more interested in supplying services, or items of an ephemeral nature, than the solid goods on which Britain's prosperity had been based.

In Birmingham, the brothers George and Stanley Cadbury had made a fortune from the very large-scale manufacture of confectionery, devoting much of their wealth to the creation of a model village for their employees at near-by Bournville. At Birkenhead the Lever brothers 'built an empire out of soap', and also cared for their staff in a most enlightened fashion, by creating a new town at Port Sunlight. In Bristol, another pair of brothers, George and Stanley White, indulged in discreet philanthropy and pioneered the use of the electric tram to provide a cheap and reliable urban transport system.

In 1903, the Wright brothers had made the first recognised flight by a heavier-than-air machine, at Kitty Hawk in North Carolina, and had come to Europe in 1908, to sell licences for their designs. One was purchased in the following year by the French firm of Maurice Farman, who then built an aeroplane, known as the 'Longhorn'.

At the annual general meeting of the Bristol Tramways Company, held in February 1910, the

Chairman, Sir George White, Bt, gave his report and stated: 'I may tell you that for some time past, my brother and I have been directing our attention to the subject of aviation which is one hardly ripe for practical indication [sic] by such a company as the Bristol Tramways Company, but yet seems to offer promise of development at no distant date, so much so that we have determined personally, to take the risks and expense of the endeavour to develop the science, from the spectacular and commercial or manufacturing point of view.'

I have before me a copy of the minutes of the first board meeting of the British and Colonial Aeroplane Company. It is dated 25 February 1910, and shows Sir George White, Bt, as chairman, and the five original shareholders as members of the White family, either directly or through marriage.

It would be interesting to speculate on the cost of the factory that was built at Filton, on the northern outskirts of Bristol, and how the work force was recruited and trained; for just five months later, on 29 July, the first Filton-built aeroplane made a successful maiden flight from Larkhill. It was described as 'an improved version of the "Longhorn"', and was known as the Bristol 'Boxkite'. It was a large machine, by contemporary standards, with its 50hp le Gnome rotary engine set behind the pilot and passenger; and the tail section, with its twin rudders, connected to the rest of the biplane's fuselage by four metal tubes without any covering.

To modern eyes it would seem both ponderous and primitive, yet it soon established a sound reputation for safety and reliability. Many of the young men who joined the newly formed Royal Flying Corps (RFC) and Royal Naval Air Service (RNAS) received their initial flying training on 'Boxkites'.

Of necessity, the early models were by foreign designers, such as the 'Monoplane' by Pierre Prier in 1911, and the 'Military Monoplane' by Henri Coanda a year later. In 1914, the post of Chief Aircraft Designer was created at Filton, and Captain Frank Barnwell was appointed. He was to hold that position

This is Sir George White's garage. Mr E Chivers (Sir George's mechanic) is on the right.

until 1938, and was responsible for a series of successful designs, the first of which, known as the 'Scout', was displayed at the Olympia Aero Show in 1914.

Details of other Barnwell designs are shown in the chart at the end of this chapter, but I feel mention should be made here of just one of them – the Bristol 'Fighter'. In 1916, the RFC was suffering heavy casualties for lack of a plane that could match the performance of the enemy machines, and work began at Filton to rectify the situation. It came into service early the following year, and soon proved its worth. A two-seater, with pilot and observer sitting back to back, attacks from the rear being defended by a machine gun on an adjustable mounting.

It was an 'unforgiving' aircraft, but, in the hands of an experienced pilot, was both powerful and manoeuvrable, and rugged enough to withstand severe punishment and still return to base. Its new feature was the engine, no longer an oil spattering rotary, but a Vee-12 cylinder liquid-cooled design by Rolls Royce. The engines used by Filton were built under licence, by Brazil–Straker, at their works at Fishponds in Bristol; the power developed from an initial 150hp to an ultimate 275hp. The total number built is not known, but 500 were supplied to Filton in the five months of June–October 1918.

Between the Wars

In November 1918 an Armistice was signed, and hostilities ended; contracts for war planes were cancelled, and the Filton directors were faced with a hugely expanded work force with little obvious employment until a peacetime demand for aircraft emerged. In the manufacture of wooden fuselages and wings, considerable skill was required, and this talent was now used to make bodies for private cars and commercial vehicles; and so the firm survived.

In 1920, the name was changed to the more familiar Bristol Aeroplane Company, and, after much pressure by the government, the engine-makers, Cosmos, were acquired. This firm had absorbed Brazil–Straker, and so, indirectly, Filton had not only gained the services of Roy Feddon and his team, but

Evolution of the Bristol Aeroplane Company

1910	British & Colonial Aeroplane Company founded. 'Zebra' plane a failure. July: 'Boxkite' maiden flight at Boxhill. November: First foreign order – 8 Boxkites to Russia.
1911	Foreign design 'Monoplane'.
1912	Foreign design 'Military Monoplane'.
1914	Captain F Barnwell appointed Chief Aircraft Designer. First 'Scout' design.
1916	Bristol 'Fighter'.
1918	Captain Cyril Uwins appointed Chief Test Pilot.
1920	Company changed name to Bristol Aeroplane Company Ltd and Cosmos Engineering acquired with the Fedden design team.
1921	'Jupiter' aero-engine in production.
1922	'Lucifer' 3-cylinder engine for light aircraft. 'Cherub' light 2-cylinder aero-engine developed from home generator design. 'Racer' designed for a maximum speed of 220mph but was a failure due to wing-flexing.
1924	'Brownie' failed as a light aircraft boom did not occur.
1933	Type 123 – last Bristol biplane. Type 133 – new style monoplane.
1934	Type 138A – for high altitude study – first flown by Uwins, at 50,236ft in September (used 'Pegasus' aero-engine).
1937	World record at 54,252ft for Flight Lieutenant Adam on 30 June.
1936	'Mercury' aero-engine – later used by Fighter and Bomber Command 25 June – Blenheim fighter-bomber maiden flight by Uwins.
1937	Blenheim entered RAF service.
1939	17 July – Beaufighter maiden flight.
1940	Beaufighter entered RAF service.

Total production of aero-engines by the Bristol Aeroplane Company Ltd was 104,000 (as well as many thousands of aircraft).

1945	Directors minuted a decision to 'enter the quality car market'.
1946	Car Division established at Filton.
1947	Series production of Type 400 Bristol began.

also his designs for the Lucifer, Jupiter and Mercury engines.

Rolls-Royce had insisted that experience gained from building the Falcon engine under licence should not be used for a similar in-line design, and because of this all three of the new engines were of the radial type. The Lucifer was the smallest, being a three-cylinder, air-cooled unit, built at Filton during 1922–

A Chronological Record of the Bristol Car

1910	British & Colonial Aeroplane Company Ltd, established with factory at Filton.
1920	Name changed to Bristol Aeroplane Co. Ltd Cosmos Engineering acquired, and with it Roy (later Sir Roy) Fedden plus design team.
1942	Sir Roy Fedden designs prototype for Bristol car – prototype oversteers, crashes, driver injured: Fedden leaves Company.
1945	Bristol Board decision minuted to enter quality car market and to acquire manufacturing rights to established design to form its basis. Approached by H J Aldington, who demonstrates Type 327 Frazer Nash-BMW, encouraged to visit BMW, Munich, ostensibly to recover car wrecked in Hamburg GP of 1939. Actually to begin negotiations for transfer of the rights to 326, 7 and 8 BMWs to BAC. Negotiations successful and second visit to Munich by HJ, to obtain data on which prototype Bristol made.
1946	First Filton-made engine on test bed – satisfactory, and fitted to 327 FN-BMW as mobile test bed for 20,000 miles – no problems. Short-run contracts negotiated with Pininfarina and Touring of Milan.
1947	January – Type 400 exhibited at Geneva Motor Show – well received despite high price. Polish Rally won outright, third in Monte Carlo Rally (first British car to finish). Class wins in Mille Miglia and Giro de Sicilia.
1948	Type 401 – aerodynamic saloon body very successful.
1949	Type 402 – convertible: a relative failure and estimated twenty-one built in twelve months.
1953	Type 403 – improved 401 with 100A engine – a success. Type 404 – short chassis with new style body, no trace of BMW origins left – estimated fifty-one built to 1955. Arnolt-Bristol – using short chassis, BS1/2 engine & 403 gearbox; railed to Turin, where Bertone bodies fitted and sold in Chicago for less than half the price of 404. Type 450 racers competed at Le Mans (disaster) and Reims (class win), and broke records at Montlhéry race track in autumn. Type 220 chassis built and tested (project authorised previous year) over 51,000 miles.
1954	Type 160 engine built and tested – approved. Project re-numbered 240; time wasted on attempts to make satisfactory automatic transmission. Comet air disaster occurred.
1954	Type 405 saloon and drophead (latter's body built by Abbotts of Farnham). 450 racers class win and team prize Le Mans, class win at Reims.
1955	450 racers class win at Le Mans, but due to Levegh crash, Reims cancelled. Team disbanded. Directors ordered the racers to be destroyed but one example now owned by T A D Crook.
1956	Car Division became wholly owned subsidiary company of Bristol Aeroplane Co. Ltd. As result of Comet disaster, all development projects cancelled – end of 220/240 project, and Bristol designed automatic transmission never achieved.
1957	Type 406E (2.2-litres) for export only. Following year Type 406, anounced for general sales.

1924, mainly for light civil aircraft and trainers. With an original rating of 100hp, it finally developed 140hp though its production was limited.

By contrast, another Fedden design, the Jupiter, was to enjoy a long and successful career, with thousands being built at Filton, and many more by the holders of licences in some seventeen countries. The Jupiter was a nine-cylinder radial, air-cooled unit, with power ratings from 290–595hp, and it was used by seventy different types of aircraft. Other Fedden designs are shown in the chart accompanying this chapter, but it is relevant to mention one here. Called the Centaurus, it was Fedden's masterpiece dating from 1938. To obtain maximum power in as small a space as possible, it was a two-row air-cooled radial design, and to simplify routine maintenance, sleeve valves replaced the more common poppet valves. Its rating was from 2,000–3,300hp, and it was used for both civil and military aircraft.

By 1939 the Bristol Aeroplane Company was recognised as the world's largest maker of aircraft and aero engines, and it was typical of the Company that despite the bias by some personnel at the Air Ministry in favour of the biplane, it very quickly put into production a monoplane that proved to be faster than any machine then in RAF service. It used as its basis a seven-seater commercial design, though its crew was to number only three – pilot, navigator and wireless operator/air gunner. Called the 'Blenheim', it was first flown on 25 June 1936, by the Company's chief test pilot, Captain Cyril Uwins. As skilled an administrator as he was a pilot, he became the Assistant Managing Director 1947–1957, and the deputy Chairman 1957–1964.

The Blenheim was an all-metal twin-engined monoplane, with a bomb load of 1,000lb and a range of 1,000 miles, being later extended to 1,900 miles. During the winter of 1940–1941, it was the backbone of the RAF's night-fighter squadrons, and later served in Fighter, Bomber and Coastal Commands, over Europe and in the Middle East. Yet by 1942, it had become obsolescent, and was relegated to the role of trainer until the end of hostilities. A total of 4,500 Blenheims were built, mostly at Filton, though some were also made by Rootes and A V Roe.

Another twin-engined machine was built by the Bristol Aeroplane Company. Known as the Beaufighter, it was first produced as a private venture, using the wings, undercarriage and tail section from an earlier plane, the Beaufort. Its armament consisted of four cannon and six machine guns, and it still had enough power to carry the newly developed interceptor apparatus known as 'radar'. It entered service in August 1940 as a night-fighter.

A year later its function changed to that of fighter-bomber in the Middle East, with a bomb load of 1,000lb. In 1943, equipped with torpedoes, it joined Coastal Command, for low level attacks on enemy shipping. Finally, using rockets, it played a decisive part in the Burma campaign. Some pilots perfected such a stealthy approach that the plane gained the enemy nickname of 'Whispering Death'.

1960 Bristol Aeroplane Company joined Vickers Ltd and English Electric Ltd, to form British Aircraft Co. Ltd, later British Aerospace. The car-making subsidiary seemed doomed. Saved when Sir G White and T A D Crook bought 'Bristol Cars', and the light engineering division from Bristol Aeroplane Co. Despite change in ownership, the cars continued to be made by the same staff and in the same premises within the BAC complex.

The 406 was the last model to be fitted with Filton-made Bristol engine and gearbox.

1961 The Type 407 was announced. It was the first Bristol to be fitted with Chrysler engine and Torqueflite automatic transmission. Chassis modified to fit large Vee-8 unit, bodywork basically that first seen on the 406E.

1963 Type 408 – quite similar to 407, used same No. 313 engine: capacity 5,130cc.

1965 Type 409 – quite similar to 408, but used No. 318 engine: capacity 5,211cc.

1967 Type 410 – quite similar to 409, and used No. 318 engine: capacity 5,211cc.

1969 Type 411 appearance subtly different. Engine was No. 383 and capacity now 6,277cc with compression ratio 10:1.

1971 Type 411 (Series 2) mechanical details similar to 411.

1972 Type 411 (Series 3) used No. 383 engine, capacity 6,227cc, but compression ratio 9.5:1.

1973 Sir George White retired, and T A D Crook became the sole proprietor.
Type 411 (Series 4) similar to Mark III, but used No. 400 engine, capacity 6,556 and compression ratio 8.2:1

1975 Type 411 (Series 5) generally similar to 411 (4), price increased to £12,587 (the original Type 411's price was £6,997).
Type 412 – marks the beginning of the third generation of Bristol models. Appearance utterly different using convertible coachwork by Zagato. Engine as on 411(5).

1976 Type 603S and 603E – beautiful saloon cars, reminiscent of the 403 – 'S' type fitted with engine No. 360 with capacity of 5,898cc; the 'E' type used No. 318 of 'only' 5,211cc capacity, and both models had compression ratio of 8:1.

1977 Type 603S2 Basically similar to 603S – but price raised to £27,995, compared with £19,660.

1980 Beaufighter – first Bristol with a name and not a number. Appearance deceptive as looked not unlike the 412, but many detail differences and engine turbocharged.

1982 Brigand and Britannia appeared; both shared same saloon body – only mechanical difference was the fact that Brigand was turbocharged, and Britannia normally aspirated.

The Beaufighter, Brigand and Britannia remain in production.

Prices shown in Autocar *and* Motor *dated 18 April 1990*
a) Bristol Beaufighter   £93,462
b) Bristol Brigand   £93,462
c) Britannia   £87,450

Note: The cars are now produced in a purpose-built factory at Bracken Industrial Estate, Concorde Road, Patchway, Avon. It is still within sight of the Filton runway. There is no dealer network; the spares and service depot is at The Baltic Centre, Great West Road, Brentford, Middx. TW8 9BT (081 568 8998).
The showrooms and offices are at 368/370 Kensington High Street, London W14 8NL (071 603 554/5/6).

A side view of the disguised Bristol prototype. Note scanty bodywork, flimsy mudguards and chained spare wheel.

When hostilities ended, the Bristol Aeroplane Company, at Filton and its various other factories in the West Country, had built 104,000 engines, and many thousands of aircraft.

Postwar Developments

It has been estimated that some fifty per cent of all private housing in England and Wales was either destroyed or seriously damaged by enemy action during World War II. In 1945, the newly elected Labour government gave housing a top priority, and this gave the Bristol directors a means of employing their greatly expanded labour force, pending new peacetime designs. New skills had been learned in the fabrication of all-metal air frames, and these were now used to make simple bungalow-style dwellings. Soon nicknamed 'prefabs', they proved very popular, and so well designed and made that a few remain in use to the present day. Later, much larger models were made at Filton, for use as temporary schools, hospitals and offices.

The Bristol directors were aware that such products were likely to be phased out as soon as more permanent construction began, and in June 1945, less than a month after the end of hostilities in Europe, their decision to enter the quality car market was minuted. After the unfortunate Fedden experiment however, the prototype would be based on an existing model, with a known performance and a good reputation. It would be necessary for the manufacturing rights of such a model to be transferred from the original manufacturers, which might prove to be difficult, complicated and expensive.

Yet the Bristol history is full of coincidence, and, as will be related in the following chapter, one of these was to solve the directors' problem.

2
The Brothers

The Frazer Nash

Though he had obtained effective control of AFN Limited in early 1929, it was not until March the following year that Harold Aldington completed the move from the old factory in Kingston-upon-Thames to the Falcon Works in Isleworth. His younger brother Donald was already with him, and later they were joined by the eldest brother, William. Since their various gifts and abilities were complementary, they formed a formidable trio. Harold, or 'HJ' as he much preferred to be called, was their acknowledged leader; William's skills as a publicist enabled him to take over the production of publicity material and advertisements (and even 'letters to the editor', for woe betide anyone daring to criticise the Frazer Nash). Donald was the utility player, almost as good a driver as HJ, and able to cope with the day-to-day problems of running the factory.

In appearance HJ was slim and lanky, and with his tweed coat, pipe and spectacles he might have been mistaken for the house master of a public school. In fact, behind his ready grin and avuncular manner was a very different person; hard and ambitious, yet also possessing the gift of friendship. He had seen how time and money had been wasted in the old factory, making one-off specials for Archie Frazer Nash to race. Once in control, he concentrated on making cars to sell. While aware of the value of sporting successes, he was unwilling to spend company funds on achieving them. Instead he was able to persuade customers to enter their cars in quite major events, often with himself as co-driver or team manager.

In a very short time, he moved the image of the company up market, no longer a crude cyclecar, but rather an exclusive sports model that appealed to young men, often with enough money and time to compete in such long-distance events as the Alpine Rally. In 1934, HJ entered a trio of privately owned Nashes for this event, with himself as manager, and with a fourth car, which would compete for the top individual award. The cars combined a very good power/weight ratio with the unique chain-drive transmission, and HJ was confident that the team award would be gained. When the results were declared, to his chagrin, it was a trio of BMW Type 315/1 open two-seaters that were declared the winners, with his own team the runners-up.

During the trial, he had inspected the German cars as well as he was able, and realised that he possessed neither the finance nor the facilities to bring his own cars up to the standards they had achieved. By comparison, the Nash was crude, with suspension so harsh that only the flexing of the chassis gave much relief over poor surfaces, and the steering lock was very limited. The BMW's suspension was independent on the front wheels, with light accurate steering and a small turning circle, allowing the driver to pick his path over poor surfaces, minor irregularities hardly seeming to exist.

The BMW Connection

HJ instructed his elder brother to write to the German company, suggesting some arrangement that would permit AFN Limited, to build BMWs, under licence, in Britain. The tone of the letter gives the impression of having come from a much larger and more important firm than was actually so. Reference is made to an 'experimental model' which would be fitted 'with an orthodox transmission system, independent springing etc'. It would be cancelled if the licence was granted. It seems doubtful that such a model existed.

In its reply dated 30 October 1934, BMW suggested a meeting, at which HJ's businesslike approach evidently impressed the Director-General, Franz Josef Popp, for in a letter dated 13 November he offered AFN Limited a one-year contract, for the import and sale in Britain of certain BMW models. The offer was accepted with the contract to take effect from 31 December 1934.

To protect itself, should the year's trading show a loss, the German company insisted on a banker's guarantee. Lacking the funds, HJ persuaded a young, wealthy and enthusiastic Frazer Nash owner, A F P Fane, to provide the necessary capital, in exchange for a twenty per cent interest in AFN Limited. Matters moved swiftly thereafter, with a number of BMWs, some complete and others with only the engine and chassis, arriving at the Falcon Works, to be sold in right-hand-drive form, and badged as Frazer Nash-BMWs. Bodies, where necessary, were designed and fitted by local coachbuilders.

HJ was admired by the Germans for his driving ability, as well as his qualities as a businessman, and he became a frequent and trusted visitor at the Munich headquarters and at the car factory, located in Eisenach, Lower Saxony. It was there in 1936 that HJ heard of a new model, the 328, that was to prove so superior to its rivals that it might be termed 'the standard by which other sports/racing cars were judged'.

A Winning Combination

The key to the success of the new BMW was its engine, developed from an earlier 2-litre unit, but giving more than fifty per cent extra power. It was this new engine that was to become the basis for all those used in the first-generation Bristols during 1946–1961.

As a mark of its superiority, it was usual for the 328 BMW to compete, even in major events, in full road-going order, with wings, windscreen and spare wheel. Yet it proved wellnigh invincible against rivals

A photograph of a 1938 Type 328 BMW. Note the knock-on wheels and twin grilles.

A photograph of a 1938 Type 328 Frazer Nash BMW. Very similar to the above, it is a right-hand drive model. (Both above photographs taken at Speed Hill Climb, on Isle of Man, September 1989.)

racing stripped of such encumbrances. In 1936, HJ persuaded BMW to include in its team for the French Grand Prix one car painted in British Racing Green, and shown on the programme as a 'Frazer Nash-BMW'. It was driven by HJ and A F P Fane, but was retired because of failed engine mountings.

Fane soon showed his extraordinary skill with the German cars, winning the 2-litre class in the 1937 Eifelrennan, gaining a similar victory in the 1938 Mille Miglia, and, in the same year, making the fastest time of the day in the Grossglockner Hill Climb. It seems likely that had the war not intervened Fane would have followed the example of Richard Seaman, and have been given the opportunity of joining the Mercedes works team that then dominated the European Grand Prix.

In the spring of 1937, Bill Aldington arranged for the Royal Automobile Club (RAC) to observe an

The Three 'Generations' of Bristol Models: 1946 Onwards

In production From	To	Model	Type	Original price inc tax	Estimated production	Engine(s)
1946	1950	400	Saloon	£2,373.14.6	475	85, 85A, B, C
1948	1953	401	Saloon	£3,213.3.4	605	85A or 85C
1949	1950	402	Convertible	£3,213.3.4	21	85A or 85C
1953	1955	403	Saloon	£2,976.2.6	275	100A
1953	1955	404	Coupe	£3,542.15.10	51	100B or 100C
1953	1954	Arnolt-Bristol	2-seater	$3,995[a]	142	BS1 Mark 2
1954	1958	405	Saloon	£3,188.12.6	297	100B2
1954	1958	405 Drophead	Drophead	£3,188.12.6	43	100B
1957	–	406E	Saloon	Export only	1	110
1958	1961	406	Saloon	£4,493.17.	178	110[b]
1961	1963	407	Saloon	£4,259.18.7		313[c]
1963	1965	408	Saloon	£4,459.6.3		313
1965	1967	409	Saloon	£4,849		318
1967	1969	410	Saloon	£5,673.1.10		318
1969	1970	411	Saloon	£6,997		383
1970	1972	411 (2)	Saloon	£7,537		383
1972	1973	411 (3)	Saloon	£7,688		383
1973	–	411 (4)	Saloon	£8,973		400
1974	1975	411 (5)	Saloon	£12,587		400
1975	1980	412	Convertible	£14,584		400
1976	1977	603S	Saloon	£19,660		360
1976	1977	603E	Saloon	£19,359		318
1977	1982	603S2	Saloon	£27,995		360
1980		Beaufighter	Convertible	£37,999.16		360
1982		Britannia	Saloon	£46,843.32		360
1982		Brigand	Saloon	£49,827.09		360

[a] Price quoted was for basic 'Bolide' model; 'de Luxe' cost $4,645, and the 'Coupe' (only 3 made) cost $6,390.
[b] There was also a 110S engine, fitted to the Zagato 406 coupe, some Zagato 406 saloons and the short-chassis experimental Bristol: 406 SP1.
[c] This engine, and the rest of the units fitted to the second and third generation of Bristol models, were by Chrysler; the first generation were all made by Bristol.

Basic Data – First-Generation Bristol Cars – Models 400–406

Type	Year	UK price when first built.	Engine No.	Capacity (cc)	Comp. ratio
400	1946	£2,373.14.6	85, 85A, 85B, 85C	1,971	7.5:1
401	1948	£3,213.3.4	85A, 85C	1,971	7.5:1
402	1949	£3,213.3.4	85C, 85A	1,971	7.5:1
403	1953	£2.976.2.6	100A	1,971	7.5:1[a]
404	1953	£3,542.15.10	100B 100C	1,971	8.5:1
Arnolt	1953	$3,995	BS1(2)	1,971	9.0:1
405	1954	£3,188.12.6	100B2 100B[b]	1,971	8.5:1
406	1958	£4,493.17.0	110	2,216	8.5:1

Type	Length	Width	Height	Weight (lb)	Max. speed (mph)	Fuel consumption (mpg at 60mph)
400	15'3"	5'4"	4'11"	2,580	90+	26
401	15'11½"	5'7"	5'	2,700	95–100	26
402	15'10½"	5'5"		2,632	95	26
403	15'11½"	5'7"	5'	2,788	104	24
404	14'3¼"	5'8"	4'7¾"	2,290	110	20–25
Arnolt	13'11"	5'8"	3'8"	2,120	108.7	16–24
405	15'9¼"	5'8"	4'9½"	2,712	105	24
406	16'4"	5'8"	5'	3,010	100+	20–24

Year – Chassis Nos 001 and 002 (saloons) and 003 and 004 (convertibles) were built in 1946, but are regarded as 'test driving chassis' and 'prototypes' respectively.

Engine – A very few *Type 400s* were fitted with the Type 85 engine with single Solex carburettor. Only a handful used the Type 85B with triple SU instruments and a 'sports' camshaft. Most early examples were fitted with the Type 85A with triple SUs and standard camshaft. Very few *Type 401* cars used the 85A engine, the majority were fitted with the 85C. All the Type 402 cars used either the 85A or the 85C engine as original fitting.

[a] The last few *Type 403* cars used the higher compression ratio of 8.5:1. Some earlier cars were converted to this ratio by Anthony Crook Motors Limited.

Though there was a choice of engines for the *Type 404* car, very few buyers opted for the 100C unit.

[b] Most preferred the 100B which was standard on the 405 convertibles.

The BS1(2) engine was peculiar to the *Arnolt-Bristol* with a 'sports' camshaft, producing 130bhp @ 5,500rpm.

In addition to the standard 110 engine fitted to the Type 406 cars, there was also the 110S which was fitted to the short-chassis Zagato coupe and a very few Zagato 406 cars. It used a compression ratio of 9.0:1, a 'sports' camshaft and a tuned Abarth twin-pipe exhaust system, and produced 130bhp @ 5,750rpm.

Basic Data – Second- and Third-Generation Bristol Cars – Models 407–Britannia

Type	Year	UK price when first built	Engine No.	Capacity (cc)	Comp. ratio
407	1961	£4,259.18.7	313	5,130	9.00:1
408	1963	£4,459.6.3	313	5,130	9.00:1
409	1965	£4,849	318	5,211	9.00:1
410	1967	£5,673.1.10	318	5,211	9.00:1
411	1969	£6,997	383	6,277	10.00:1
411 (2)	1970	£7,537	383	6,277	10.00:1
411 (3)	1972	£7,688	383	6,277	9.50:1
411 (4)	1973	£8,973	400	6,556	8.20:1
411 (5)	1975	£12,587	400	6,556	8.20:1
412	1975	£14,584	400	6,556	8.20:1
603S	1976	£19,660	360	5,898	8.00:1
603E	1976	£19,359	318	5,211	8.00:1
603S2	1977	£27,995	360	5,898	8.00:1
412S2	1978	£34,968	360	5,898	8.00:1
Beaufighter	1980	£37,999.16	360	5,898	8.00:1
Brigand[b]	1982	£49,827.09	360	5,898	8.00:1
Britannia	1982	£46,843.32	360	5,898	8.00:1

Type	Length	Width	Height	Weight (cwt)	Max. speed (mph)	Fuel consumption (mpg)
407	16'7"	5'8"	5'00"	32	122	19.5
408	16'1½"	5'8"	4'11"	32	122	16–20
409	16'1½"	5'8"	4'11"	31½	122	15–21
410	16'1½"	5'8"	4'11"	31½	128	12–16
411	16'1½"	5'8"	4'9½"	33¼	138	13–17
411 (2)	16'1½"	5'8"	4'9½"	33¼	138	13–17
411 (3)	16'2½"	5'8"	4'9½"	33¾	138	14–18
411 (4)	16'2½"	5'8"	4'9½"	33¾	138	15–20
411 (5)	16'2½"	5'8"	4'9½"	33¾	138	15–20
412	16'2½"	5'9½"	4'8½"	33¾	140[a]	12.2–16.7
603S	16'1"	5'9½"	4'8¾"	35.1	140[a]	15–20
603E	16'1"	5'9½"	4'8¾"	35.1	130	17–22
603S2	16'1"	5'9½"	4'8¾"	35.1	140[a]	15–22
412S2	16'2½"	5'9½"	4'9½"	33¾	140	14
Beaufighter	16'2½"	5'9½"	4'8½"	34½	150[a]	14–20
Brigand[b]	16'1½"	5'9½"	4'8½"	34½	150[a]	14–20
Britannia	16'1½"	5'9½"	4'8½"	34½	140[a]	15–22

[a] Estimated maximum speed
[b] Turbocharged engine

hour's run of a 328 BMW at Brooklands race track. The driver was the journalist S C H (Sammy) Davis, and a distance of 102.226 miles was covered. In the advertising matter written by Bill Aldington, the impression was given that the car, in full road trim, was a standard model. In fact it was one of the three special racers, and imports of the standard 328 did not begin until later that year.

As the sales of the Frazer Nash-BMWs increased, so those of the 'real' chain-drive Nashes declined, until in 1938 just two were made, and in 1939 a solitary car was sold. The total production of these very unusual cars during the period 1930–1939 is estimated at only 170, yet many still exist, cherished by their owners. They support such events as the Alpine Rally, as 'forays' to the areas where the very same cars once competed.

In addition to the BMW cars, AFN Limited were also importing the fine flat-twin motorcycles, and the Steib sidecars to which they were often attached. HJ also obtained a licence to sell the four-seater aeroplane known as the Messerschmitt 'Taifun' Bf 108, ordering one for demonstration purposes. It arrived in June 1939.

The War and AFN Limited

HJ had already qualified as a pilot, and flew the new aircraft as much as possible, even including a flight to Frankfurt. Once war was declared in September, private flying ceased, and the Taifun was soon commandeered by the Air Ministry. It was flown to the Royal Aircraft Establishment at Farnborough, in Hampshire, where it was given a very detailed inspection. The reason was that much of the design was similar to the German fighter known as the Messerschmitt Bf 109, later to become an all too familiar sight in the skies of southern Britain.

It seems strange that so shrewd a businessman as H J Aldington should not have taken precautions to diversify the products. He did not do so, and, now that all German imports ceased, the three brothers agreed to seek some wartime use for the Falcon Works. Bill would remain as caretaker, and transfer the remaining stock to a safer area. He proved to be an excellent negotiator, first obtaining a contract from the War Office for the training of drivers and mechanics, and later with the Admiralty, when the works was given the official name of 'HMS Victory V'. Ratings were trained to become engine-room artificers, and Aldington was commissioned as a lieutenant in the Royal Naval Volunteer Reserve.

The two younger members of the family joined the Royal Army Ordnance Corps, later transferring to the newly-formed Royal Electrical and Mechanical Engineers, usually known as REME. As might have been anticipated, HJ gained accelerated promotion, to the rank of Lieutenant-Colonel. His younger brother became a captain on the supply side of the regiment. Later in the war, he was involved in a car accident, and was injured so badly that he was invalided out of the Army, later becoming an A.I.D. inspector based in the Bristol area.

On learning of the interest by the board of the Bristol Aeroplane Company in building a car, he informed HJ. The latter, aware that the future of AFN Limited was bleak, requested Donald to arrange for him to demonstrate a Frazer Nash-BMW to the Bristol directors.

3
Postwar Developments

Demonstration and Travel

H J Aldington was a very experienced demonstrator, and put the borrowed car though its paces, to show its combination of speed, comfort and excellent suspension. Though nothing in the way of a formal agreement was reached, he felt that the directors recognised that the car represented the basis for the type of Bristol they wished to build, provided manufacturing rights could be acquired from BMW. HJ was prepared to act as the intermediary, and made plans to renew his German contacts with as little delay as travel restrictions permitted.

With his elder brother, he managed to reach Frankfurt, in a Dakota aircraft of the Royal Canadian Air Force, both men in the uniforms of their respective services. The reason given for their German visit was to recover the white 328 BMW that HJ had crashed in the Hamburg Grand Prix of 1939. The car had been left for repair, and he persuaded the American authorities to allow his brother and himself to continue by staff car to Munich. Meanwhile he had learned that the BMW Director-General, Franz Josef Popp, was imprisoned on war charges at Stadelheim gaol, and obtained authority to visit him, though a time limit was set of half an hour.

HJ found Popp in a very pessimistic mood, not just because of his personal predicament, but because the entire car making operation, at Eisenach, was now within the Russian zone of occupation. He saw little hope of his company ever regaining control, and raised few objections to the proposed take-over by the Bristol Aeroplane Company of the pre-war BMW 326, 327 and 328 models. While in the Bavarian capital, HJ was able to meet some of the other former executives, and was shown a BMW that was not the one he was seeking. In fact his 328 had long been broken up, and the white car he now saw was one of the later and very special racers that had dominated the short-course Mille Miglia of 1940. HJ accepted the car as his own and arranged to drive it back to Britain.

With the British registration numbers of the 328 now stencilled onto the other car, the Aldingtons set off for the Falcon Works, though they ended up at the wrong end of a tow rope when the BMW's sump was damaged. HJ's report to the Bristol board was encouraging, and specially picked staff at Filton now began preliminary work on what would become a new Car Division. Further discussions took place with the directors of AFN Limited, and on 16 July a major shareholding in the latter was acquired by Bristol.

'Under New Management'

To administer the company, and to represent the Bristol interests, a new board of directors was appointed, with HJ and his younger brother Donald plus, as Bristol nominees, George White and Reginald Verdon-Smith. It was further agreed that HJ should function as managing director, and Verdon-Smith as the chairman. Board meetings would be held either at the Falcon Works, or at the Arlington Street London office of Bristols, or at Filton.

It is not always realised that even firms as large as the Bristol Aeroplane Company remained subject to government control as regards the products that were to be made, and it was not until September 1945 that it was announced that the company was free to undertake projects of its own. With the

POSTWAR DEVELOPMENTS

A two-tone Type 327 on right, with late Type 403 Bristol on left. Note single bumper.

support and approval of the War Reparations Board, the BMW rights were transferred, and H J Aldington requested that an official visit to the headquarters of the German company should be arranged. The real purpose would be to collect all the documentation, manuals, blue prints, drawings, etc. – essential for the production of a prototype Bristol car. However, the visit was approved because it was considered important for experts to inspect the high altitude test plant, used during the war by the very advanced BMW aero engines.

The visit was a success, and the party returned with a mass of material, which included a 2.5-litre car engine. Though only partially developed, it already produced 120bhp, and HJ urged the Bristol directors to substitute it for the 328 engine, on which to base the Bristol unit. The latter was nearing the end of its development life, whereas the 2.5-litre still had much room for improvement. But the view of the Bristol board was that the new car should go into production without delay, and a fully developed engine would be preferable. Had HJ's advice been taken, the later history of the marque might have been very different.

The basic idea was for AFN Limited to concentrate on a sports model, and for Filton to deal with a saloon version, and also to supply spare parts for the pre-war Frazer Nash-BMWs. Engines for both models would be the responsibility of the Engines Division at Filton. Though by the standards of aero engineering progress was quite satisfactory, HJ began to complain, and was impatient that major decisions still had to receive final approval by the directors at Filton.

Relations between the two sets of AFN directors tended to become strained, with minor differences usually settled by uneasy compromises. The root cause was the completely different attitudes of HJ and George White. The former had little practical experience of anything but small-scale car manufacture. The largest number of chain-drive Frazer Nashes produced annually was only thirty-nine, in 1934, and he seemed unable to comprehend the sort of time scale between a design drawing and the fabrication of the part itself.

George White had been trained in a very different atmosphere, in a factory where the units of production were measured by the thousand, and was familiar with the techniques by which such results were achieved. He was also aware that all the finance was being provided by the Bristol Aeroplane Company, and that actual costs were heavier than anticipated.

The Bristol-Engined Bristols – Basic Data

Type	Year	UK price when first built	Engine No.	Capacity (cc)	Comp. ratio
400	1946	£2,373.14.6	85, 85A, 85B, 85C	1,971	7.5:1
401	1948	£3,213.3.4	85A, 85C	1,971	7.5:1
402	1949	£3.213.3.4	85A, 85C	1,971	7.5:1
403	1953	£2,976.2.6	100A	1,971	7.5:1, 8.5:1[g]
404	1953	£3,542.15.10	100B, 100C	1,971	8.5:1
Arnolt-Bristol	1953	$3,995[a], $4,645[b], $6,390[c]	BS1(2)	1,971	9.0:1
405	1954	£3,188.12.6	100B[d], 100B2[e]	1,971	8.5:1
406E	1957	–	110	2,216	8.5:1
406	1958	£4,493.17.0	110	2,216	8.5:1

Type	Length	Width	Height	Weight (cwt)	Max. speed (mph)	Fuel consumption (mpg)
400	15'3"	5'4"	4'11"	2,580	'over 90mph'	26 @ 60mph
401	15'11½"	5'7"	5'	2,700	95+	25 @ 60mph
402	15'10"	5'5"	–	2,632	95	25 @ 60mph
403	15'11½"	5'7"	5'	2,788	104	24 @ 60mph
404	14'3¼"	5'8"	4'7¾"	2,290	110	20–25
Arnolt-Brsitol	13'11"	5'8"	3'8"	2,120	108.7	16.5–24
405	15'9¼"	5'8"	4'9½"	2,712	105	24 @ 60mph
406E	16'4"	5'8"	5'	2,548[f]	–	–
406	16'4"	5'8"	5'	3,010	'over 100mph'	20–24

[a] 'Bolide' sports/racer model
[b] 'De Luxe' 2-seater sports model
[c] 'Coupe' closed model
[d] Used only on the convertible model with bodywork by Abbots of Farnham
[e] Used only on the saloon model with Filton bodywork
[f] Estimate only
[g] This higher compression rate was used on last few examples as standard

The Chrysler-Engined Bristols: Basic Data

Type	Year	UK price incl. tax	Engine No.	Capacity (cc)	Comp. ratio
407	1961	£4,259.18.7	313	5,130	9.00:1
408	1963	£4,459.6.3	313	5,130	9.00:1
409	1965	£4,849	318	5,211	9.00:1
410	1967	£5,673.1.10	318	5,211	9.00:1
411	1969	£6,997	383	6,277	10.00:1
411 (2)	1970	£7,537	383	6,277	10.00:1
411 (3)	1972	£7,688	383	6,277	9.50:1
411 (4)	1973	£8,973	383	6,277	8.20:1
411 (5)	1975	£12,587	400	6,556	8.20:1
412	1975	£14,584	400	6,556	8.20:1
603S	1976	£19,660	360	5,898	8.00:1
603E	1976	£19,359	318	5,211	8.00:1
603S2	1977	£27,995	360	5,898	8.00:1
Beaufighter	1980	£37,999.16	360	5,898	8.00:1
Brigand	1982	£49,827.09	360	5,898	8.00:1
Britannia	1982	£46,843.32	360	5,898	8.00:1

Type	Length	Width	Height	Weight (cwt)	Max. speed (mph)	Fuel consumption (mpg)
407	16'7"	5'8"	5'	32	122	19.5
408	16'1½"	5'8"	4'11"	32	122	16–20
409	16'1½"	5'8"	4'11"	31.5	122	15–21
410	16'1½"	5'8"	4'11"	31.5	128	12–16
411	16'1½"	5'8"	4'9½"	33.25	138	13–17
411 (2)	16'1½"	5'8"	4'9½"	33.25	138	13–17
411 (3)	16'2½"	5'8"	4'9½"	33.75	138	13–17
411 (4)	16'2½"	5'8"	4'9½"	33.75	138	15–20
411 (5)	16'2½"	5'8"	4'9½"	33.75	138	15–20
412	16'2½"	5'9½"	4'8½"	33.75	140	12.2–16.7[a]
603S	16'1"	5'9½"	4'8¼"	35.10	140	15–20
603E	16'1"	5'9½"	4'8¼"	35.10	130	17–22
603S2	16'1"	5'9½"	4'8¼"	35.10	140	15–22
Beaufighter	16'2½"	5'9½"	4'8½"	34.50	150	14–20[b]
Brigand	16'1"	5'9½"	4'8½"	34.50	150	14–20[c]
Britannia	16'1"	5'9½"	4'8½"	34.50	140	15–22

[a] The weight includes driver, passenger and full fuel tank
[b] The Beaufighter is turbocharged
[c] The Brigand is turbocharged

Prices of the Current Series (*Autocar & Motor* 18 April 1990)

A. *Bristol Beaufighter Turbocharged Convertible*   £93,462
B. *Bristol Brigand Turbocharged Saloon*   £93,462
C. *Bristol Britannia Saloon*   £87,450

A BMW Type 327, side window raised and hood in its bag, behind a late Type 403 Bristol.

He was confident that the first Filton-built engine would be ready for testing by May 1946, and this was confirmed when, on the test bed, it produced 85.4bhp compared with the 80bhp of the standard BMW unit on which it was based.

With a rather 'milder' camshaft, the engine was fitted into a Type 327 Frazer Nash-BMW belonging to Reginald Verdon-Smith, and the car then became a mobile test bed, covering some 20,000 miles, and the new engine gave no problems. Much of this mileage was done with HJ at the wheel, including several visits to Italian coachbuilders. He was of the opinion that these firms were far superior to their British equivalents, not only as regards design, but also in the speed with which the work was accomplished.

The Italian Influence

If HJ had had his way, it seems likely that the new models would have had Italian bodies, but George White was quietly adamant. An open clash was avoided by making small numbers of chassis/engines available both to the Touring firm of Milan and to Pininfarina of Turin. Meanwhile, work proceeded on five sports models, though it was intended that the bodywork for fifty more would be produced on a commercial scale, at Filton.

With the new engine tested and approved, work on the chassis continued. It was based on the 326 BMW, using transverse leaf springs for the front suspension, and torsion bars at the rear. In typical British motor trade fashion, the prototype was tested with a heavily disguised body, though already rumours were circulating, encouraged by various 'leaks' of information as to the progress of the new models. It would seem these probably came from the Falcon Works, and yet even such basic matters as a name or a badge had still not been resolved.

At Filton, with the chassis tested and approved, only the bodywork remained to be finalised, and when this was done it was seen to be quite different from the Autenrieth coachwork of the BMW Type 327, which it had been thought would form the basic bodywork. It was rather angular, and to modern eyes has a much more 'dated' appearance than the smooth elegance of the BMW. Yet it was to prove surprisingly aerodynamic, and may have contributed rather more to the sporting successes of the early Bristols than is sometimes realised.

All models produced by Bristol up to 1957. From left to right: the Type 405 drophead coupe, the Type 405 saloon (1955–58), the Type 404 coupe (1953–55), the Type 403 saloon (1953–55), the Type 402 convertible (1949–50), the Type 401 saloon (1948–53), the Type 400 (1947–50) and the Type 450 Racer (1955).

A total of seven sets of parts had been made at the prototype stage, of which two were used for the test vehicles, one was kept in reserve, and the remaining four were used on the first of the 400 series. Chassis Nos. 1 and 2 became saloons, while 3 and 4 were clad with convertible coachwork. It had been originally expected that 250 of each type would be made at Filton, but in fact only these two dropheads were produced. One is now in the United States, the other the cherished possession of a member of the Bristol Owners' Club.

The Car Division had now come into being, and work began on the manufacture in series of the Type 400 Bristol car.

4
The Type 400 Goes Into Production

Early Days

It was an odd convention by which a new model car was officially launched at a Motor Show, even though for months past detailed descriptions had appeared in the motoring press.

In its issue of 6 November 1946, *Motor* stated: 'The combination of 85bhp with . . . low weight enables outstanding performance to be realised. It is obvious that the new Bristol can start life with unusually strong claims to be entitled a car of the first order'. Yet it was not until January 1947 that the

The first standard Bristol ever made, taken against the background of the then headquarters of the Bristol Aeroplane Co Ltd, at Filton near Bristol, 1946.

THE TYPE 400 GOES INTO PRODUCTION

This is said to be the best photograph ever taken of a Type 400 with convertible body. It was built in 1946, is chassis No. 3, and only one other example was made, now in America. Note the Vee screen, filler cap just behind the hood bag, and the way the furled hood 'rides high'. Note the tubular rear bumper; on most of the Type 400 saloons, this is replaced by a much sturdier, girder-type bumper.

Bristol was exhibited – at the Geneva Motor Show. It was received with enthusiasm, despite the very high price in Britain of £2,373 14s 6d, for it was realised that here was a truly exceptional vehicle.

Not only was it built of the best materials then available, by the famed Bristol Aeroplane Company, and to aero-engineering standards, but its basis was the BMW that had gained such a formidable reputation for excellence in the period immediately before World War II. To the experienced motorist, its comfort, good road manners and comparative economy must have appealed, while for the sportsman, here was a car with an all-round performance including a maximum speed of 94mph, and acceleration that could propel it from rest to 50mph in just 13.5 seconds; exceptional by contemporary standards for a fully equipped 2-litre saloon model.

The car's appearance was not overly exciting, for it had an upright stance, lacking the subtle curves of the Type 327 BMW, and its glazed area was small. Though described as a 'close-coupled two-door saloon; four-seater', the accommodation in the rear was not generous as regards leg room, though the bench seat was quite comfortable.

A full specification will be found at the end of this section, and the 9ft 6in wheelbase was to become traditional; the sole exceptions among the 2-litre models being the Type 404 and the Arnolt-Bristol, on

THE TYPE 400 GOES INTO PRODUCTION

Side view of one of the two Type 400 Bristols with convertible bodywork. Despite its age, it is always maintained in immaculate condition, and attracts attention wherever it goes.

which a shorter chassis was used, offering a wheelbase of only 8ft ¼in. Another feature that became traditional was the massive separate chassis, the frame of deep box section, with a strengthening 'tray', and large tubular cross-members at its midpoint.

The main part of the frame ended some 15in ahead of the rear axle. For the standard saloon, two light pressings extended rearwards, to act as body supports. Much of the car's admirable handling may have been due to the fact that it had 'a wheel at each corner'. For the specialist coachwork, by such firms as Pininfarina and Touring, where the tail section extended well beyond the rear wheels, a longer type of light pressing was used to cope with the extra body-hang.

The location of the rear axle and rear suspension

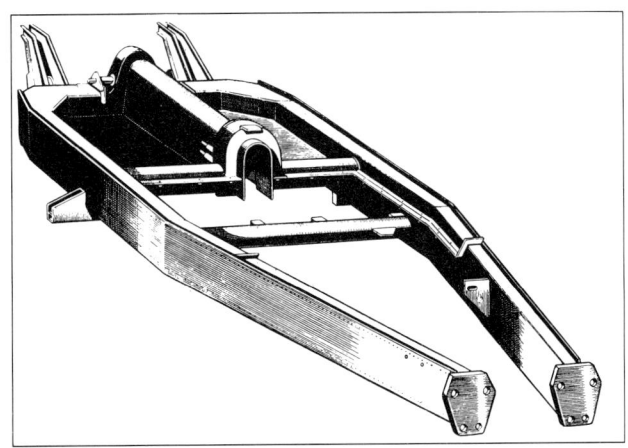

The separate frame is deep box-section, with large tubular cross-members. The complete front suspension is bolted onto the front of frame, while light pressings provide support for the body at rear. (Type 400).

was complicated since neither leaf spring nor torque tube was used. To locate the axle and to enable power to reach the rear wheels, a short triangulated link was used, with its apex on the top of the bevel box housing, and terminating with two swinging bearings, mounted on the ends of the frame. This ingenious solution to a difficult problem proved light, simple and reliable. Rear suspension was by a single arm on either side of the car, connected to a torsion bar, each 59.4in long and 0.805in in diameter. The anchorage was remote, taking the form of a splined member approximately in the centre of the frame.

Front suspension employed a transverse leaf spring and a pair of upper wishbones. The hydraulic shock absorbers were of piston type, and, on the majority of the Type 400s, of Bristol manufacture. They were excellent, but not easy to set up, and it was not until they were about to be phased out that a special rig for this purpose was used. On some of the late examples, the shock absorbers were by Newton and Bennett, much cheaper to buy, and rather more substantial.

Though few reports mention it, the body used a basic structure of seasoned ash and spruce that was steel covered. The two doors were timber-framed, and it is important to keep the two drain holes clear, or woodrot would result. Only the bonnet, door-sheathing and boot lid used light alloy, yet with a dry weight of 22cwt the car was not unduly heavy. Seats were upholstered in finest Connolly leather, and made in-house.

The gearbox was unusual in that it had a centre bearing, with the casing split for assembly purposes. As the offtake shaft was internally splined, and the propeller shaft was mated to it, the enclosed splines were oil lubricated. The rear axle looked after itself, and the front suspension and steering box relied on the Enots One-shot pedal-operated system, so that maintenance was very simple. There were only four points where attention with a grease gun was necessary. These were one at either end of the propeller shaft, and one each for the brake and clutch pedal shafts. Many Type 400s were exported to Australia, and this ease of maintenance may have been a contributory reason for their popularity. A local modification was a steel 'cage' to strengthen the rear

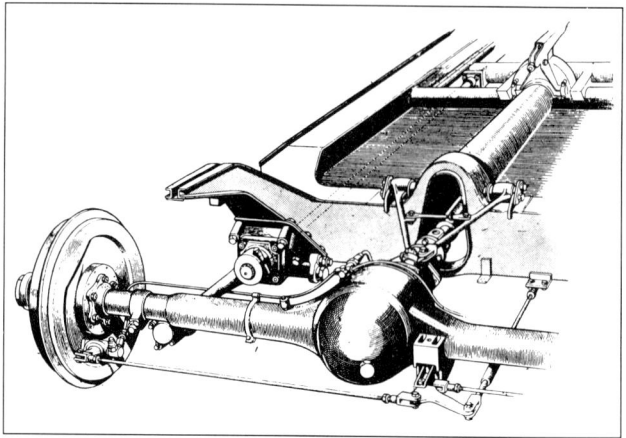

Rear suspension details of Type 400 model. Springing medium is torsion bars coupled to rear axle by shackle links. Driving torque and lateral location are dealt with by a triangulated link mounted on top of bevel housing, as shown.

The independent front suspension. Direction is provided by a rack and pinion gear, while suspension is provided by a transverse leaf spring, grooved so as to reduce weight. (Type 400).

axle, and, thus fitted, the cars saw extensive service in the outback, often on cattle stations and far from a garage.

As engine details will be dealt with in a separate chapter, I will only mention here that on the 400, four types were used: the basic being the Type 85 which employed a single Solex carburettor. Then there were the 85A and 85B, both using triple SU instruments, but the B being fitted with a more sporting camshaft. The 85C was fitted with three Solex

THE TYPE 400 GOES INTO PRODUCTION

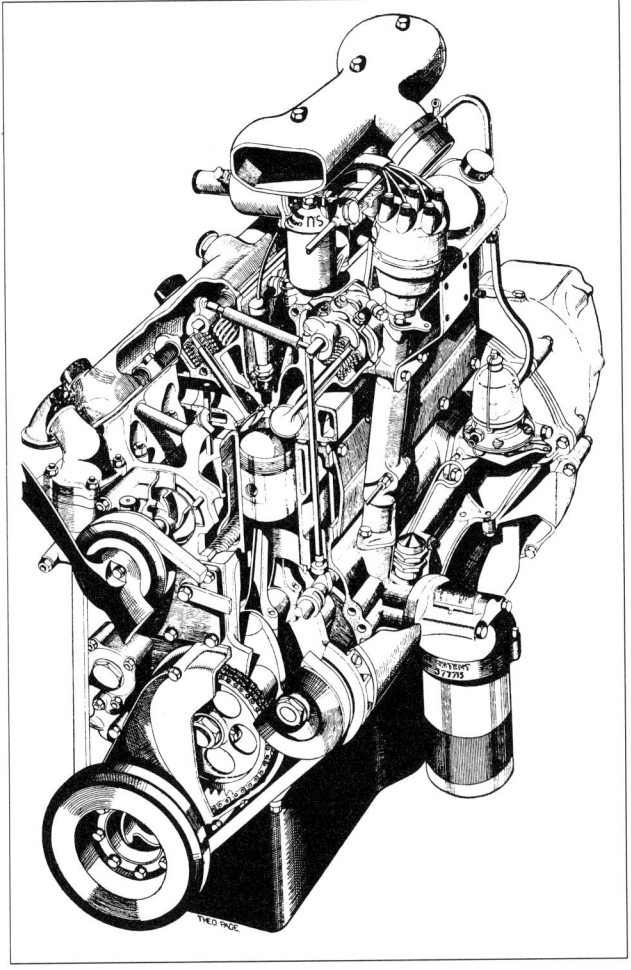

The early Type 85 Bristol engine. The inclined overhead valves and direct down-draught induction system give the unit its excellent performance (by contemporary standards). There is a temperature stabiliser on the side of the cylinder block, a feature that was discontinued on later 85C engines.

carburettors, and this system was used by all the later Bristol 2, and 2.2-litre models.

Equipment was to a very high standard and included a full set of instruments, with speedometer, tachometer, oil and water temperature gauges, oil pressure gauge, a cigarette lighter and a clock. Where the 85A or 85B engine was used, an SU auxiliary starting carburettor was fitted, with an additional control on the dashboard. Instrument needles were white, as were the markings on the black-faced dials, making for very easy reading. Though an HMV radio was standard, the heater was fitted as an extra.

The headlamps were praised for their power, and also their dipped beam, and the seating position gave the driver a good view of the way ahead. Unlike all later 2- and 2.2-litre models, the steering wheel was of the three-spring-spoke type, with telescopic adjustment. The brakes were praised for their efficiency, with drums of 11in (27.94cm) diameter. The foot brake used the Lockheed hydraulic system, and the handbrake operated via rods and cables, with the lever of the racing 'fly off' type.

The dashboard of one of the only two Type 400 Bristols made in 1946 with convertible bodywork. Note the comprehensive display of instruments, the three spoked wheel, organ type accelerator and gear lever knob. The small lever in the 'Vee' of the screen operates the semaphore type turn indicators.

A front view of a Type 400 Bristol. Note twin grilles and Bristol roundel; also the lockable handles on each side of the bonnet.

THE TYPE 400 GOES INTO PRODUCTION

A Type 400 taking part in the Norwich Union Classic Car event at Silverstone, May 1986. Note the non-standard turn indicators either side of the number plate.

A rear view of a Type 400 Bristol. Here the spare wheel is secured under a shaped metal cover on the boot lid, an indication that this is a late example.

33

MODEL: 400	Date: 1946–1950
Wheelbase	9ft 6in (2m 89cm)
Front Track	4ft 4in (1m 30cm)
Rear Track	4ft 6in (1m 37cm)
Overall Height	4ft 11in (1m 49cm)
Overall Width	5ft 4in (1m 83cm)
Overall Length	15ft 3in (4m 66cm)
Weight	2,580lb (1,170kg)
Tyres	5.50 × 16in
Engine Type	85A
Number of Cylinders	6
Bore	66mm
Stroke	96mm
Capacity	1,971cc
Gearbox	Bristol 85C
Ratios	1st: 16.8 2nd: 8.47 3rd: 5.06 4th: 3.9 Reverse: 13.4
Brakes	Footbrake: Lockheed hydraulic on all 4 wheels Handbrake: Cable and rod operating from central lever on rear wheels only
Suspension	
Front	Independent transverse leaf springs
Rear	Longitudinal torsion bars with telescopic dampers

Distinguishing Series 1 and 2

Potential buyers of used models often ask how they can tell which series a car may represent. The very earliest examples were fitted with tubular bumpers of a delightfully aesthetic shape, but giving little protection. The replacement found on the majority of 400s is much more substantial, and some owners of the early examples had them fitted later. The rear window on the earlier cars was flush glazed, but on the later version a hinged type with perspex instead of glass was used, and was operated by a chain link mechanism. However, some owners of the early cars complained of stuffiness in hot weather (or warm climates), and had their rear windows modified.

The one feature that can be trusted as indicating to which type the car belongs is the method of stowing the spare wheel. On early examples it is within the boot, in a vertical position, with the lid being hinged at the top. On later cars, the spare is mounted externally on the boot lid, which is hinged from the bottom. There should be a shaped metal cover over the wheel, and, though this is sometimes missing, it was original equipment when the car was built.

A Type 400 competing in Driving Tests, organised by the Bristol Owners' Club in April 1988. The wing mirrors are non-standard.

===== THE TYPE 400 GOES INTO PRODUCTION =====

The Type 400, with convertible bodywork, setting out to defend its holding of the 'Elite' Trophy ('best car'), won at the 1988 Concours of the Bristol Owners' Club. It was successful at the 1989 event too. Its chassis is No. 3, and only one other example was built.

An immaculate Type 400 Bristol, waiting to be judged in a Concours organised by the Bristol Owners' Club. Note the orifice for the lifting jack on side valance, hole for starting handle in centre of bumper, and small streamlined wing lamps.

A pre-flight discussion. Behind the helicopter, one can see a Type 400 Bristol.

Some owners fitted later type engines to their cars, and some fortunate buyers of used examples have discovered their new purchase boasts a 100A or a 100B unit. In the Workshop Manual however, owners with very early engines – the 85, 85A and 85B units – are warned not to attempt to modify them to later specifications, which can impose an extra strain for which they were not designed.

No less than four different exhaust systems were used while the Type 400 was in production:

1. On what are termed pre-production cars, with chassis Nos. 1–10, the system was such that in the event of damage it was recommended that the 'whole exhaust system should be replaced by the twin entry system'.
2. On early production cars with chassis Nos. 11–25, a four-piece system was used, which in case of damage should be scrapped and replaced with the twin entry system.
3. On cars with chassis Nos. 26–125, the system 'has separate down pipes which connect with double-entry single-outlet oval-section "Burgess" silencer fitted in the centre section unit'. The rear pipe of the latter 'connects with the tail-pipe unit which is cranked to pass over the rear axle. An extension pipe is fitted to the rear end'.
4. On cars with chassis Nos. 126 and upwards, the system is similar to (3), except that there is a 'new type tail-pipe which passes beneath the back axle. No extension pipe is fitted.'

Purchasing a Used Type 400 Bristol

Since timber was used extensively, woodrot in the bodywork can occur, though it appears less common than on some later models. If the car is in a small closed garage, a smell likened to pear drops or some types of nail varnish is a simple means of identifying its presence. To eradicate rot can be a very expensive business, so beware! Worn leather upholstery can often be restored, using the various Connolly preparations, but if it is very dry or perished renewal may be required, at a cost of at least £1,000. Dull paintwork can usually be brought back to a reasonable state, using one of the branded 'cutting' compounds.

Brakes, both foot and hand, should be tested on a straight and level road, and with enough application by the driver to be able to determine the efficiency of the system, and to discover whether there is a tendency to pull to one side. The handbrake should be able to 'hold' the car on a reasonable incline. Remember that the lever is of the fly-off type.

Although the alloy body parts will not rust (bonnet, boot lid and doors), they can be subject to electrolytic action unless well insulated from the steel body parts. Naturally the latter should be inspected for rust, and the king-pins checked for wear, which can be expensive to cure. Check the Enots One-shot lubrication system, by giving the

THE TYPE 400 GOES INTO PRODUCTION

A Type 400 undergoing a 'ground-up' restoration. Note doors and windows have been removed.

A trio of Bristols: a Type 400 on the right, a Type 410 in the centre and a late Type 403 on the left. Note non-standard turn indicators and spot lights on the Type 400.

auxiliary pedal a gentle push. If an obstruction is felt, beware, for this can mean that vital suspension parts lack lubrication, including the steering box. The steering wheel should be moved, with front wheels straight, and if it can be shifted more than half an inch before movement to the front wheel begins, there is wear, which needs inspection.

The wheels are of the ventilated disc type, and on early cars were inclined to crack at the boss, especially if the retaining bolts were nipped too tightly. Many owners of these cars exchanged their wheels for the later, stronger type, but all five road wheels should be checked for cracks, or over-painting to conceal them. The tool roll should be checked too, as it is important that the special jointed plug spanner is included. The tiny 10mm plugs are buried deep between the valve chests, and can be damaged if the incorrect tool is used. A very useful auxiliary can be made from a wooden dowel, a piece of rubber tubing and a small magnet. If, as often happens, a plug is 'lost' while being removed or fitted, the magnet will locate it and facilitate recovery. Without it, such an operation can be hot and messy.

All the 2- and 2.2-litre Bristols have an aperture for a starting handle, and the would-be purchaser should make sure the handle is included. With it, the engine can usually be persuaded to start, even if the battery is very flat. Without it, a visit by the local garage tow-car can be expensive . . .

It is sometimes claimed that the Type 400 was the best made of all Bristols, and a surprising number have survived in reasonable condition. Until recently prices were very low, but are now rising fast, especially for examples in Grade A condition. If one is tempted to buy a car 'for restoration', this can be a long and very expensive business, though most spare parts are still available from the makers.

5
A Change of Direction

Type 401 Saloon

Despite its success, the Type 400 was not without its critics, mostly from countries that had escaped the devastation of the war. The demand was for a bigger, roomier model possessing some luxury, yet still with a general performance which was above average.

MODEL: 401 Saloon	Date: 1949–1953
Wheelbase	9ft 6in (2m 89cm)
Front Track	4ft 3.75in (1m 31cm)
Rear Track	4ft 6in (1m 37cm)
Overall Height	5ft (1m 52cm)
Overall Width	5ft 7in (1m 70cm)
Overall Length	15ft 11.5in (4m 86cm)
Weight	2,700lb (1,255kg)
Tyres	5.50 × 16in or 5.75 × 16in
Engine Type	85C
Number of Cylinders	6 in-line
Bore	66mm
Stroke	96mm
Capacity	1,971cc
Carburettors	3 Solex 32BI Controls interconnected
Gearbox	4-speed and reverse
Ratios	1st: 16.8 2nd: 8.47 3rd: 5.5 4th: 3.9 Reverse: 13.4
Brakes	Footbrake: Lockheed hydraulic Handbrake: Cable and rod operation on each rear drum
Suspension	
Front	Independent transverse leaf springs
Rear	Longitudinal torsion bars

When the Type 401 was launched towards the end of 1949, it was obvious how seriously the criticism of the 400 had been taken, and its successor was to become the most popular of all Bristol models, with an estimated 605 cars produced between 1949 and mid-1953. Its original price in Britain, inclusive of Purchase Tax, was £3,213 13s 4d, a very large sum then, yet demand continued until it was succeeded by the 403 which had many improvements and a more powerful engine.

The 401 was a handsome car, with flowing lines quite different from those of the rather 'square-rigged' look of the 400. Unlike the latter, there was considerable body overhang, but it was treated in such a subtle fashion that the car looked much longer and lower than its predecessor. In fact at 15ft 11½in it was 8½in longer, and at exactly 5ft, was actually one inch higher. The streamlined appearance of the 401 was enhanced by a complete lack of excrescences; even the door locks were recessed and of aero 'button' type, and designed by Bristol and made in-house. That the sleek looks were also efficient was proved when the Motor Industry Research Association conducted a comparative study into the drag coefficients of 118 vehicles of many types. The Bristol 401 was placed fifth.

The Car's Exterior

Though it appeared ultra-modern, the design had been seen in 1939 on a Type 328 BMW and also on an Alfa Romeo 25SS.

Cutaway drawing of Bristol 401 model. Note spare wheel stowage in tray below boot, also extensive drilling of side members. Note tubular roof supports to which alloy panels were 'wrapped' with hessian material between alloy and steel, to prevent electrolytic action.

A prototype saloon body on a Type 401 Bristol engine/chassis. Note the heavy looking double front bumpers, and ultra long and narrow twin grilles.

A prototype body on a Type 401 Bristol engine/chassis. Its looks are much improved with the removal of the heavy-looking double bumpers.

On the Bristol stand at the 1948 Geneva Motor Show, there had been two cars with Touring bodies, and, though handsome and eye-catching, I felt there was a basic lack of harmony between the somewhat angular front section of the body and the very curvaceous rear.

It came as a relief, when the 401 commenced series production, to note the alterations achieved by the Filton design staff. Gone was the high and narrow radiator shell, with its twin grilles that emphasised the car's BMW origin. Now the shell was smaller and better proportioned, and though there were still two oval grilles they now merged with the front apron in a more harmonious fashion.

On the original design, the twin front bumpers gave the car a heavy, somewhat Teutonic appearance, but with the new single alloy bumpers the whole look was lighter and more modern. Made of aluminium, they appeared to be integral with the body, but in fact were attached to the chassis by long steel supports, sandwiched between rubber blocks. The design was by Alex Moulton, whose rubber suspension was to be used in the Issigonis-designed revolutionary Austin and Morris Mini car. The rubbers were intended to save or reduce body damage in the event of a slight accident, but I did not find them effective.

Because of its long-term experience with aircraft manufacture, the Bristol Company appreciated the advantages offered by the new method of body building, and used it in the manufacture of its cars. In essence it consisted of first welding to the chassis a series of shaped steel supports, to which were clinched the alloy body panels. The two metals

An original photograph of the prototype body by Touring of Milan, mounted on a Type 401 Bristol engine/chassis. With its heavy-looking double bumpers and high yet narrow grilles, the front of the car is less pleasing than its curvaceous rear section.

A CHANGE OF DIRECTION

The original Type 401 Bristol saloon with bodywork by the Italian coachbuilders Touring of Milan

Bristol 401 – Registration number KHU 924

The car was purchased from Bristol Cars Ltd by Mr R D B Robinson.

Mr Robinson is an engineer, and carried out various modifications:
1 He removed front and rear bumpers as he felt they gave the car a 'heavy nose-down effect'.
2 He made an addition to accommodate the reversing lights.
3 He added a 'tapered stainless steel piece' which fitted under the bumper down to the number plate
4 He fitted new slimmer-type bumpers, of two-piece type, leaving a space for the number plates, fore and aft.
5 He had the whole car resprayed in a much lighter colour.

The effect of the above alterations and modifications was to give the car a much lighter appearance, with its good proportions and smooth lines, and, though the long narrow radiator grilles were unchanged, they appeared to merge into the rest of the body, so that the 'nose heavy' look was completely gone. Mr Robinson kept his car for many years, approving of its excellent roadholding and performance, the latter outstanding for such a large car with an engine of only 2-litre capacity. However, when he saw the 406Z saloon, with a Zagato four-seater saloon body mounted on a Type 406 Bristol chassis, he 'succumbed to temptation', and the 401 was sold.

Since acquiring his 406Z, Mr Robinson has carried out various modifications including:
1 Fitting Minilite alloy road wheels.
2 Installing three Weber carburettors in place of the standard Solex instruments. He states: these have 'transformed the performance . . . and the fuel consumption appears to have greatly improved'.

Since he considers the 406Z to be far too precious for ordinary 'bread and butter' motoring, Mr Robinson uses what he calls 'a Robinsonised Mini Clubman estate'. His modifications include:
1 Cooper 'S' front suspension and brakes, with servo.
2 Larger road wheels (12″ × 5″), with 155×70×12″ tyres.
3 New body, zinc sprayed for protection against rust.
4 Metro bumpers mounted on 'rubber blocks away from body'.
5 Engine fitted with Piper 567 camshaft, head gasflowed, combustion chambers balanced, giving 65 bhp at the wheels. Fuel consumption averages 40 mpg.

Having ridden in both the 406Z and the Mini Estate, I have been most impressed by the quality of the ride as well as the overall mechanical performance.

A prototype body on a Type 401 engine/chassis. It looks high and angular beside the Ferrari on its right.

A side view of the prototype 401 Bristol with saloon bodywork. Modern single bumpers have been fitted, and they suit the car's lines well.

A rear view of the saloon body on a Type 401 chassis/engine. Note the twin lights set into the oblong panel between the split bumper. Now a handsome car.

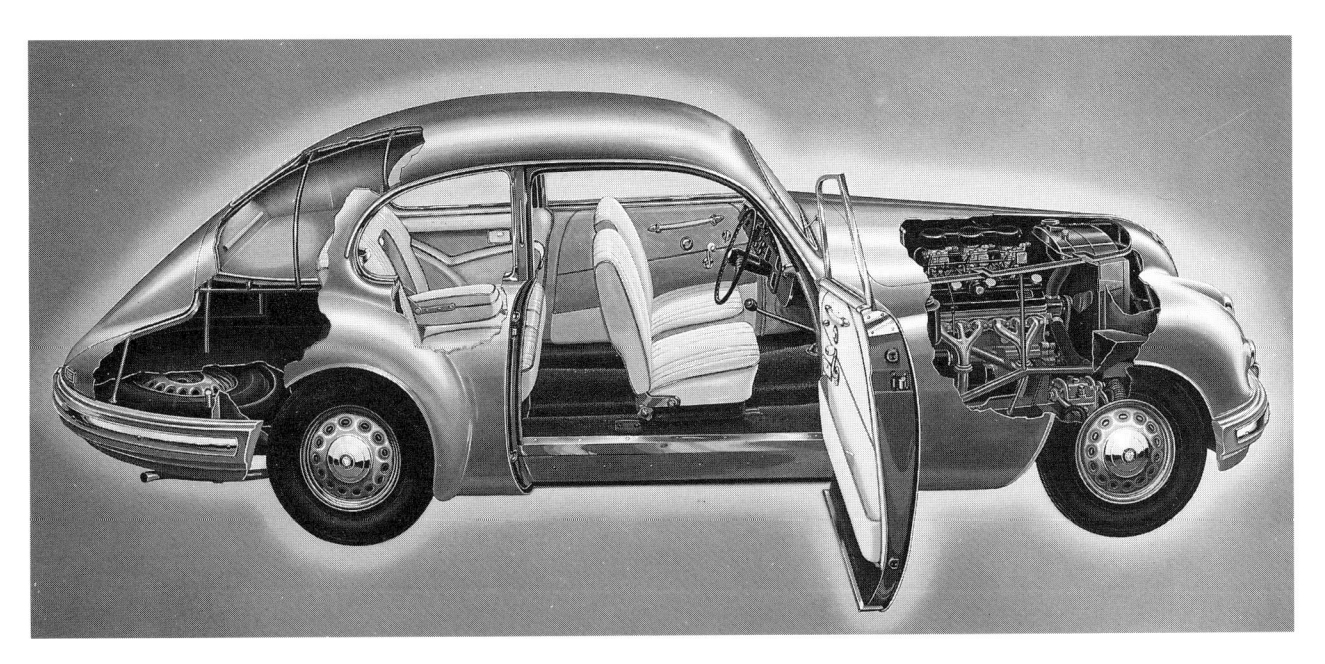

Cutaway drawing of the Type 401 Bristol. Note the roof construction using alloy panels 'clinched' to steel supports.

were insulated from one another by wrapping the supports with a hessian material. A number of the early Type 401s suffered from electrolytic action between the bumper blades and their supports. The probable reason was a breakdown in the insulation, and later examples appeared much less prone to this problem. By contrast, the insulation between body panels and steel supports seemed most effective.

A car built to Bristol aircraft standards had to be assembled with absolute accuracy, and jigs of considerable complexity were designed and made at Filton. With these, it was possible for the mechanic to check his work as it progressed; at the same time building a master-jig, stage by stage. This enabled the inspector to check the accuracy of the entire body, and, when passed, to dismantle the master-jig piecemeal, handing the component parts to his assistant through the empty door apertures.

The technique described resulted in a body that was light in weight, yet extremely strong. This was noted by J Eason Gibson in his report on a very early 401, when he quoted a ratio of 3.2bhp per cwt, which was exceptional by contemporary standards. He added that 'this enabled high gear ratios to be used, with the result that the theoretically safe cruising speed is as high as 78.6mph'.

On cars with chassis numbers up to and including No. 1005, the shock absorbers, or dampers, were of Bristol manufacture. From chassis No. 1006, these were replaced by bought-out items made by Newton and Bennett. At the same 'break', a new gearbox, the BW.CR/5, replaced the Type 85C which was used previously. The initials denoted that the new box possessed synchromesh by Borg Warner, and that the gear ratios were closer, as shown below:

	The 85C	*The BW.CR/5*
First gear	16.80: 1	14.00: 1
Second gear	8.47: 1	7.12: 1
Third gear	5.50: 1	5.05: 1
Top gear	3.90: 1	3.90: 1
Reverse gear	13.40: 1	11.22: 1

Note: A freewheel was fitted to bottom gear on both gearboxes.

It might seem logical that the above changes denoted the end of the first series cars, but this was not the case, according to the records maintained by the Chief Registrar of the Bristol Owners' Club. Both chassis 1005 and 1006 are shown as belonging to the series 896/1022, made in 1951–1952, the notation beside them reading '2nd series no Ridge body'. It is the presence of this 'ridge' along the lower edges of wings and doors that is generally used to establish to which series a particular 401 belongs. On this basis, and again using data supplied by the Chief Registrar, the break appears to come at chassis Nos. 695 (with 'ridge') and 801 (without 'ridge'). The numbers in between, Nos. 701–721, represent the entire estimated production of the Type 402 Bristol with convertible coachwork. No chassis Nos. 696–700 are shown in the Register, but there is a note: 'Transition body restyle'.

The brakes on the 401 were operated by foot pedal on all four wheels, using the Lockheed hydraulic system, and by hand lever on rear wheels only. With drums of 11in diameter, there was ample lining area, but to bring the car to a complete stop very heavy pressure on the brake pedal was required. On my own 401, after a near accident, I fitted a Girling servo, and this has solved the problem completely.

Though in general the roadholding was judged to be excellent, by contemporary standards there was some tendency to oversteer when taking bends at speed. This was probably due to the rear overhang, plus the positioning of the fuel tank low down in the tail, and the stowing of the spare wheel in a tray beneath the boot.

J W E Banks carried out a number of experiments with his own 401 during his competitive career, and found a significant improvement in handling resulted from repositioning the fuel tank rather higher and nearer the centre of the car. A similar position was chosen for the Type 405 model, some five years later.

A potential purchaser of a 401 Bristol had the choice of two engines – either the 85A or the 85C. The power output was 80bhp @ 4,200rpm and 85bhp @ 4,500rpm respectively.

It would appear that many of the early 401s and the 402 convertibles were fitted with the 85A unit, but one can never be certain, as Bristol owners tend to 'modernise' their cars. In my own case, I fitted a much later 100B engine, taken from a short-chassis 404. Allied with the servo it gave the car a most exhilarating performance.

A 401 in good mechanical condition, and using the 85C engine, should be capable of exceeding 100mph on a slight downgrade. A maximum on the level of 97.8mph was recorded by Eason Gibson on a very early example, fitted with the 85A unit. Fuel consumption varied with driving methods and speed, but averaged 22–24mpg. With a tank holding fifteen gallons, plus two in reserve, a reasonable driver could expect to cover some 350 miles before switching to the reserve.

In 1949, when the 401 was launched in Britain, petrol was still in short supply, and syphoning from the tank of a parked car was very common. Perhaps this was one reason why the new Bristol had a filler cap protected by a spring-loaded flap, controlled from within the car. Similar internal controls applied to bonnet and boot, and there were twin toggles within the latter, which had to be operated to obtain access to the spare wheel.

Unlike the 400, the spare wheel on the 401 was stowed in a shaped metal tray, quite separate from the boot. In the event of a puncture, wheels could be changed without interfering with the luggage. This was a boon on a rainy night, or in a country where 'light fingers' were almost the rule. It was important to note that both toggles should be operated at the same time, otherwise there was a danger that the lowering mechanism might be damaged. Unless correctly lubricated, the latter could become very stiff, and even reach a stage where the tray was almost immovable, just at the time when its contents were needed.

The Enots One-shot system was used to lubricate the front suspension and steering box. The rear axle looked after itself, so that the only points requiring use of a grease gun were one each on the brake and clutch supports, and two on the propeller shaft.

In Australia, when I asked owners why they had chosen a 401 Bristol, many replied that this very simple maintenance had appealed to them. The

Almost twins! On the left is a Type 401, and next to it a 403. While body and chassis are quite similar, the 403 has a new engine – the 100A, producing 100bhp @ 5,000rpm. The 401 had the 85C engine producing 85bhp @ 4,500rpm.

majority lived in the outback, far from the nearest garage, yet found their cars suitable and reliable enough to cope with very rugged conditions. Some owners fitted their cars with a 'cage' over the differential, protecting it when traversing especially rough tracks or fording shallow or dried-up river beds. All spoke warmly of the model's practicality. As one grazier put it: 'She may have the looks of a high-born lady, but underneath she's got the heart of a tigress'.

I was reminded of this when I read a report by *Autocar* in its issue of 7 March 1952, which read: 'The car has the feel of a thoroughbred, it is light and lively, and seems to know what is expected of it.'

The Car's Interior

The glazed area of the 401 was generous by contemporary standards, and as a result the interior was very light and airy. The two doors were wide, and the lower edges were high enough to avoid problems when parking close to a kerb, a difficulty that was to bedevil the drivers of the four-door Type 405 saloon.

As on the 400, the instrumentation on the 401 was comprehensive, the individual instruments being set across the dashboard, with the rev counter and speedometer in front of the driver and the front passenger respectively – an ideal arrangement when touring. On very early examples, the dashboard is of

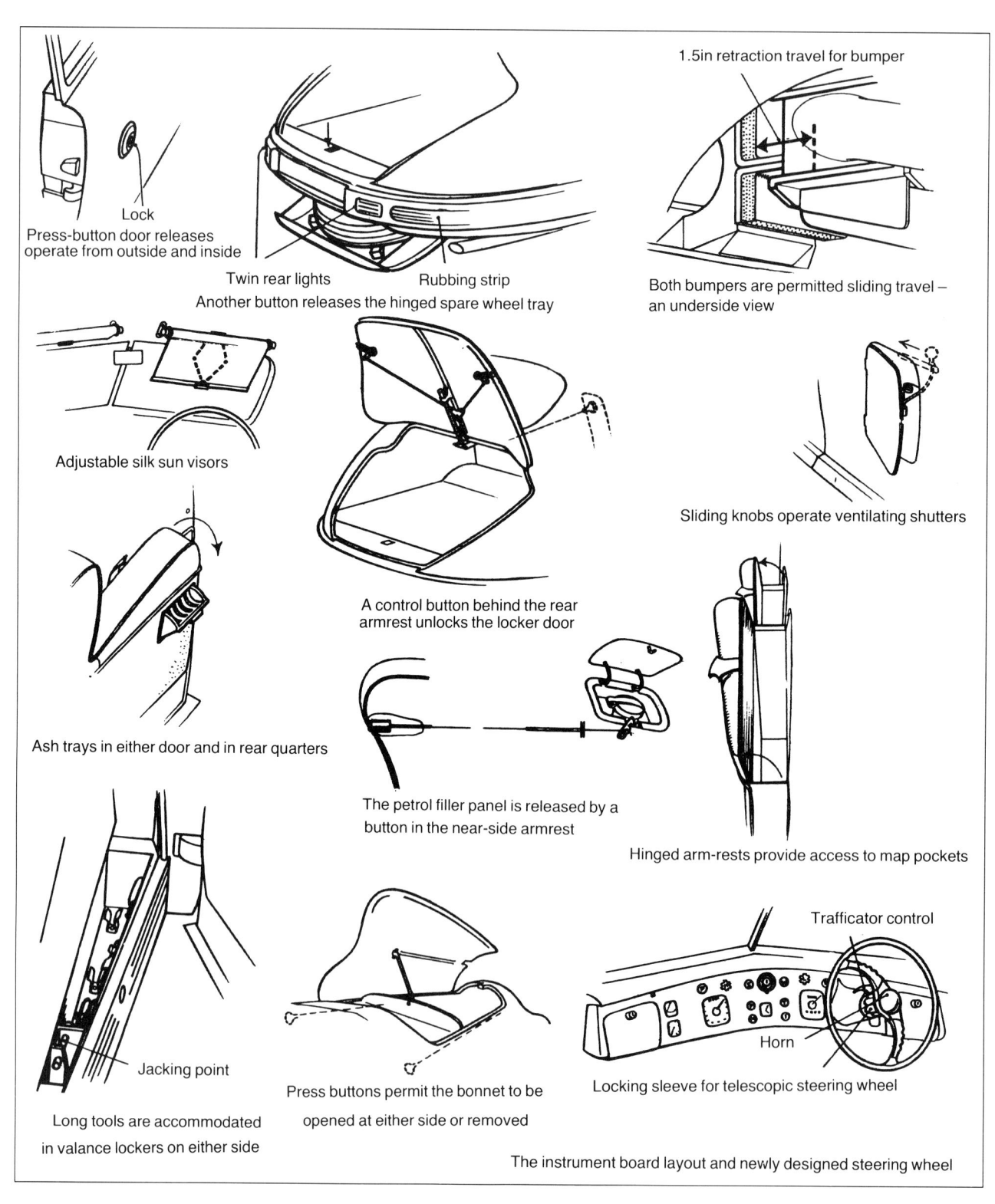

Some of the details that helped make the Type 401 Bristol 'a most desirable car for home or overseas' (Autocar, 26 November 1948).

Tufnol, but this was soon replaced by solid wood, usually walnut, though I know of one where it was of rosewood. In case of need, it was quite simple to remove the dash, to gain access to the wiring of the instruments.

In addition to the rev counter and speedometer, there was also a clock, ammeter, oil pressure gauge and a combined oil/water temperature gauge. Separate switches controlled ignition, lighting, demisting, screen wipers, roof and dash lights, the fuel reserve, and, on later examples, the trafficators. Push-pull controls adjusted ignition and engine speed. There were also warning lights for 'high beam' headlights, and to warn the driver when the fuel reserve was in use.

A typical Bristol touch was to give knurled edges to controls that had to be turned, and plain edges for those to be pulled in or out.

The trafficators were of the semaphore type, recessed into slots in the slender roof pillars just to the rear of the two wide doors. On early examples the control was by a small metal toggle set just under the steering wheel; on the later cars there was a switch set into the centre of the scuttle. This was extended to overlap the dashboard, so that at night there would be no windscreen reflection from the illuminated instruments.

The horn button was in the centre boss of the big steering wheel. Made by Bluemel especially for Bristols, the wheel was to remain in use on all future models, up to and including the 410. It had two wide spokes or 'wings', leather-covered to match the trim, and with useful finger grips. On early examples the steering column could be adjusted for length telescopically, but on the later cars a bolt was used to secure the column in one of three alternative positions.

Side view of a Bristol 401 saloon. The semaphore trafficators are housed in slots set into the door pillars.

When not in use, twin sun visors were rolled up and stowed just above the top of the windscreen. They could be pulled down as far as the scuttle top, and if a car had to be left in the sun for long periods a noticeable reduction in interior heat resulted. Made of a stiff felt-like material, constant tension was maintained by means of ingenious metal 'lazy tongs'.

A most unusual feature on the 401 was the provision of a roller blind for the flush-glazed rear window. Controlled by a cord just above the driver's head, it prevented the headlight beams of a following car from penetrating the car's interior.

On the 401, the Leverol seat mechanism was used, enabling the driver or the front seat passenger to select the most comfortable leg length. When a rear passenger was entering or leaving the car, the front seat could be slid forward, and then pushed back to lock securely in the original position.

The rake of the front seats was adjusted by means of a four-lobed wheel, one of which was set low on either side of the seat. One chose the lobes on which the seat rested, to give the most comfortable angle, making sure both were on the same lobe. Otherwise there was a danger of damage through distortion.

Though often described as a four-seater, the 401 provided comfortable accommodation for a driver and four average-sized passengers. The rear squab included a recessed armrest, for use when there were only two passengers in the back. If there was a third, the armrest was pushed back out of the way.

With its cavernous boot and seventeen-gallon fuel tank, the 401 was an ideal car for long-distance touring. In countries, like some in the Near East, where the petrol was of very low octane rating, by the intelligent use of the manual ignition control on the dashboard, pinking could be greatly reduced.

At a time when ergonomics was a word almost unknown in the motor trade, the seating on the 401 was praised for its comfort. The front seats were very large, and, though recently I read two reports that criticised them for alleged lack of side support when cornering at speed, I must confess that over a considerable mileage I never found this a problem.

There were plenty of places where small items could be stowed – two lockable compartments at either end of the dash, large pockets in the backs of the front seats and other pockets in the doors. The latter were so arranged that maps or the invaluable Michelin guide could be carried upright and ready for use. The headlining was light in colour, and made of a man-made material that could be wiped clean with a damp cloth.

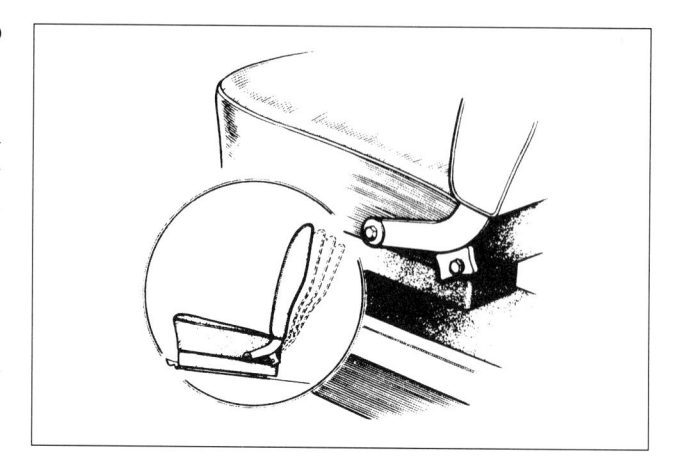

Shows simple but effective seat adjustment. (Type 401).

All the upholstery was in top-quality leather, cut, fitted and sewn in-house on machines of varying ages. One was said to have started life at Filton when the original company, the British and Colonial Aeroplane Company, was founded in 1910.

The floor was covered in good pile carpet with an underlay, which tended to damp out what little vibration there was, so that driver and passengers could progress in almost complete mechanical silence, except at very high speeds, when some noise from the complicated valve gear could be heard.

As *Autocar* in its already mentioned report put it: 'The Bristol is in a class of its own'.

Comparison of First and Second Series

As mentioned earlier, it is the 'ridge' or 'tumble home' that is probably the most reliable and obvious way for a potential purchaser to determine if a Bristol belongs to the first or second production series. A car with the 'ridge' along the lower edges of wings

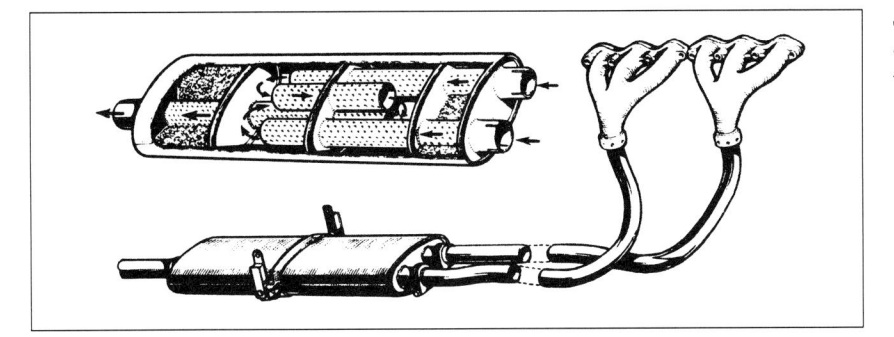

Shows new exhaust system using Burgess silencer – see cutaway drawing. (Type 401).

and doors belongs to the earlier series; if the sides are quite smooth, then it is later.

A less obvious difference is the treatment of the instrumentation. On earlier cars the individual instruments are recessed, but on later examples they are set flush to the wooden dashboard.

On most 85A and some early 85C engines, an internal oil cooler was located in a chamber on the right-hand side of the cylinder block. It did not prove efficient, and was not fitted to later 85C units. An alloy blanking plate covered the aperture, but was

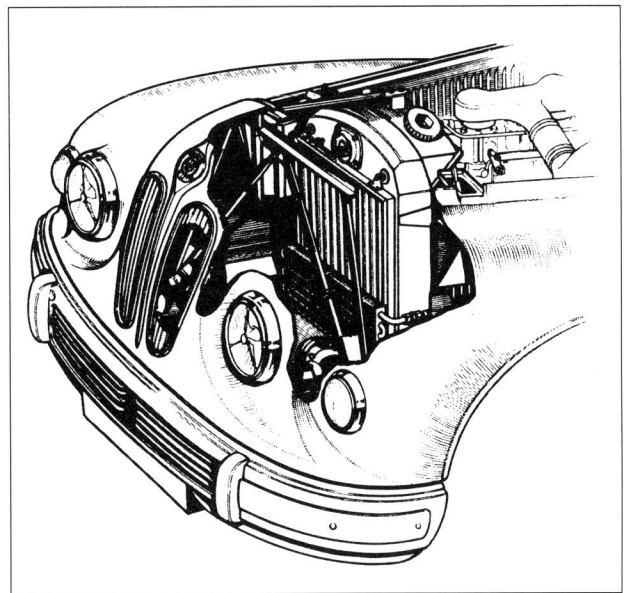

Shows new type oil cooler located ahead of water radiator. (Type 401).

found to be subject to deterioration. A brass replacement plate became available, its Spare Part No. CPS 235. After so many years, it seems unlikely any of the alloy plates are still in service, but it is a point a potential buyer might bear in mind.

Over the years, I have been a judge at a variety of Concours, yet I cannot remember having seen a Type 401 with the three SU carburettors that were original equipment on the 85A engine. Instead triple solexes were used.

But the mere substitution of triple Solexes did not, as some owners appeared to believe, bring their engines up to full 85C specifications. At one time it was not uncommon to find all sorts of modifications

This gives details of improvements of tail section of the later 401 models including: new type road wheel, counterbalanced support to boot lid, and modified tail pipe. Lid uses similar construction technique as rest of body – tubular steel supports and alloy panel.

made with this end in view. Cylinder heads were 'shaved' to give a higher compression ratio, and one man actually fitted the extremely expensive 'sports' camshaft to his 85A unit.

Yet the Workshop Manual advises strongly against such attempts, stating:

> 'IMPORTANT: For reliability this engine is best maintained at its original specification of 80bhp @ 4200rpm. It is not comparable with later Bristol engines, and it cannot be made to reliably perform the same. Materials for later engines are of higher grade, the crankshaft is larger and also fitted with balance weights. Connecting rods are splash fed giving greater strength, and tappets and push rods are lightened. Therefore it is not practicable, neither is it recommended, that the 85A engine should be upgraded.'

To any new owner seeking a higher performance from his early 401, I would suggest he attempts to find a later engine, a 100B or 100B2 perhaps, that can be substituted, and which will give him the results he wants. One word of warning though: the linkage on early 401s is such that if a later type of gearbox is fitted to them some clutch adjustment may be required.

Non-Bristol Bodywork (Type 400 cars)

Of an estimated production of 475, only *five* examples had bodies not made within the Filton works. Taking them in chassis order, they were:

1. *Chassis No. 102*: a very pretty convertible body by Pininfarina.
2. *Chassis No. 151*: a wood-framed estate body, built by a Hereford firm.
3–5 *Chassis Nos. 186, 412 and 482*: these were 'used' chassis that were fitted with new saloon bodies by Zagato. They were commissioned on the orders of Anthony Crook Motors, Hersham, Surrey, and not by the Bristol Aeroplane Company.

The judges confer. A Type 401 Bristol saloon at a Concours organised by the Bristol Owners' Club. Note the widely opening 'handed' bonnet top. The direction indicators are non-standard.

A CHANGE OF DIRECTION

A side view of a rare Type 401 Bristol with bodywork by Zagato. Note the 'Z' motif in the abrupt change of direction of the ridge from scuttle to rear window.

A semi-front view of a Type 401 Bristol with saloon bodywork by Zagato. The direction indicators, either side of the plain air intake, are standard. Note the air duct in the bonnet.

The rear view of a Type 401 Bristol, with saloon coachwork by Zagato. Note the simple rear-lamp treatment, very wide rear window, and simple bumper with wraparound protection of wings.

Type 401 cars fitted with non-Filton-made bodies were:

1–4 *Chassis Nos. 207, 218, 219 and 220*: were all given saloon coachwork by Touring of Milan.
5–7 *Chassis Nos. 208, 212 and 216*: had convertible bodies by Pininfarina.
8 *Chassis No. 211*: was fitted with a drophead coupe body by University Motors.
9 *Chassis No. 892*: had a saloon body made by Gebr. Beutler, Thun, Switzerland.
10 *Chassis No. 895*: was fitted with a convertible body, by Riverley Motors or Richard Mead? (see below)
11 *Chassis No. 1023*: shown in the BOC register as: 'Rebodied: make unknown'.

Only three of the four chassis shown under (1) above have been positively identified, and it seems likely that one was merely a prototype.

The three chassis shown under (5) above followed the general lines of the solitary Pininfarina-bodied Type 400 (chassis No. 102). With hood lowered, the cars resembled open four-seater sports cars, the hood under its tonneau cover being stowed flush to the top of the rear body. Except perhaps for its twin-paned windscreens, the cars are quite timeless, and all were owned by BOC members.

The chassis shown under (8) above, had a rather heavy-looking drophead body by University Motors, who at that time were mainly known as MG specialists. With the hood lowered, it was quite handsome, and the two wide doors were fitted with windows which were operated by electric motors housed

On a standard Type 401 Bristol saloon. The wheels are of alloy and are non-standard.

in the lower section of the trim. It too, was once owned by a BOC member, but its whereabouts since he sold it are unknown.

The chassis shown under (9) above was considered very modern, with its Beutler saloon coachwork. It was exported to Sri Lanka, but now forms part of the collection of that arch-Bristol enthusiast, Brian May of Solihull. To modern eyes it looks very dated, with its imitation 'portholes' along its bonnet sides, but at least it is still whole, and May says one day he may restore this unique example of Swiss coachbuilding in the 1950s.

Side view of a Beutler-bodied Type 401 saloon. Though now awaiting restoration, it was a handsome vehicle when made in the late 1940s. Typical contemporary 'touches' are the 'port-holes' on the side, and the rear wheel 'spats'.

A front view of a Type 401 Bristol with saloon bodywork by Beutler. It is in need of a complete restoration. Note the absence of a front bumper, the single grille, and horizontal air inlets inset into the front apron.

A close-up shot of nearside mid-section of a Type 401 with Beutler saloon body. Note the semaphore type trafficator set into the door pillar, and the ingenious sun visor. Tension is maintained by means of a form of 'lazytongs', and it is most effective.

The present owner, Mr Brian May, shows the size of the boot of his Type 401 saloon with Beutler saloon bodywork. Unlike the standard 401, the spare wheel is stowed inside the boot.

On a Type 401 Bristol with saloon body by Beutler. This 17-inch two-spoked wheel by Bluemel was the standard fitment on Models 401-10, made between 1948 and 1969.

The last two chassis shown under (10) and (11) are enigmas. Originally, I had been informed that Chassis No. 895 had been a Type 401 saloon, that its body was destroyed by fire, and that a new convertible body had been designed and built for it by Richard Mead at his coachworks at Hockley Heath, West Midlands. However, subsequently I was told that the car was to have been one of three new 401s to be built by Riverley Motors, on the instructions of Messrs Bradburn and Wedge, who in the fifties were very active Bristol agents. Unable to identify the other two chassis, I searched through back numbers of the BOC Bulletin, and found a reference in the issue for Autumn 1978.

It consisted of a report of a conversation by a BOC member with Richard Mead, and took place at a Prescott Hill-Climb event. Mead stated that the car had been supplied by Filton 'complete with the body up to the A-frame which rose to just above the front screen; doors and seats were fitted but not trimmed'. He went on to describe how he had been approached by 'a young chap from River Motors in the Midlands' who 'seemed out of his depth over a commission to build a drophead 403'. Though it was a 401, not a 403, there are enough similarities in this reported conversation to suggest the chassis was probably No. 895.

Finally there is Chassis No. 1023, fitted with a saloon body the origin of which remains a mystery. It is stated that the car is fitted with an 85C engine No. 1924, that its car number was 101/3/422 and that it was once owned by a N J Dowrick. An engineer, he gave the car an eight-blade cooling fan, and altered the ignition with a dual contact distributor. When approached, the London coachbuilders Park Ward denied all knowledge of the car, while extensive enquiries to senior Filton personnel were also fruitless.

With its huge oval air intake, it is said to resemble a Lancia more than a Bristol, but from photographs it does not appear quite as ugly as has been suggested. It had a shallow carburettor duct on the bonnet top, large rear quarter lights and a squarer rear section than the standard 401 body. Its registration number was EVG 500, so one day the puzzle may be solved. I certainly hope so.

With a weight disadvantage of 120lb compared with the Type 400, and still with the latter's 85A or 85C engine, the new model hardly seemed likely to continue the sporting tradition established by the earlier model. In fact in acceleration from 0–60mph, and in maximum speed, the new car was superior, though it was the 400 that recorded the slightly better fuel consumption:

Acceleration (0–60mph)
Type 400 – 19.1 seconds (*Autocar*: 9 January 1948)
Type 401 – 16.4 seconds (*Motor Sport*: January 1953)

Maximum Speed
Type 400 – 95.7mph (*Motor*: 19 May 1948)
Type 401 – 97.0mph (*Autosport* 1 August 1952)

Fuel Consumption
Type 400 – 22-26mpg (*Autocar* Road Test No. 1343)
Type 401 – 22.7mpg (*Autocar* Road Test No. 1458)

Note: Many owners of Type 401 Bristols have claimed that their cars were capable of at least 100mph. The speedometers of these cars were unusually accurate, and therefore to reach such speeds it seems probable that the needle of the rev counter must have been near or just over the 5,000rpm mark.

Sporting Achievements

Like its predecessor, it was not long before the 401 was competing successfully in major motor sport events.

In 1951, the Touring Class in the Cannes Rally of the Sun, and also the Dutch Tulip Rally were won by 401s. In 1952, another Bristol was runner-up in the Tulip Rally, while both individual and team awards were gained in the one-hour races for saloon cars that the Daily Express newspaper organised at the Silverstone circuit for several years.

Probably the most convincing proof of the 401's stamina was given by Mr T A D Crook, a dyed-in-the-wool Bristol enthusiast, who later became sole owner of the Company.

Here a Type 401 Bristol saloon is showing its paces in a hill climb. The model continued the sporting tradition that began with the Type 400 Bristols.

A Type 401 Bristol saloon with Zagato bodywork, in side view; competing in a speed hill climb.

A picture of a Type 401 competing in the seventh Rally of the Sun, 1953. The car is still owned by a member of the Bristol Owners' Club, and has competed in Club events.

In 1950 he drove a standard model 401 from Caterham in Surrey to the Montlhéry circuit, with an airlift from Lympne to Le Touquet, and including a brief visit to the Paris Motor Show. Then, under official observation, he covered 104.78 miles in one hour from a standing start, with a best flying lap at 107mph.

He then drove back to Caterham, with an airlift across the Channel, the entire 'visit' having taken just under the twelve hours that it had been estimated would be sufficient. The only alterations made to the car were a slightly higher rear axle ratio, and racing tyres.

Press Reactions

In general, press reaction by the motoring journals was very favourable, though one drew attention to the firm's aeronautical background. In *Autocar* report No. 1458, it was stated: 'It was remarked by a Company representative: "To increase the cabin ventilation, air flow can be increased by opening the rear quarter lights." The Bristol has a cabin, while other cars have a passenger compartment.'

William Boddy, Editor of *Motor Sport*, has a formidable reputation as a fearless critic of modern cars, but he often wrote very favourably about the cars from Filton. In his road test of a 401 in January 1953, he stated: 'The fascinatingly complete equipment and the craftmanship evident in the specification and construction are truly refreshing in this age of standardisation and chromiumed tin shrouds. This, indeed, is the car for the connoisseur. It can only be modesty on the part of the Bristol publicity boys which has prevented them from quoting as the 401's slogan: "The Best Car in Britain".'

Perhaps the ethos of the car was best summed up in the *Autocar* Road Test No. 1458, which stated: 'The Bristol is expensive, but it gives the experienced driver the strongest impression that the purchaser is getting for his money, a car that is really something, with a fine performance, an "atmosphere" in detail and in road behaviour, that belongs to only a select few cars, and with highly practical equipment of a nature not found in many modern cars of lower price.'

With reports such as I have quoted, no wonder the Type 401 was the most popular of all the 2-litre Bristols, with an estimated total production of 605 cars from 1949 to mid-1953.

Hints for Intending Purchasers

I will not repeat the advice contained in the chapter on the Type 400 Bristols, which I hope may be helpful. Instead I will emphasize the new points that a potential purchaser might remember, when he views a used example.

Semi-front view of a Type 401 Bristol saloon. The nearside quarter light is open.

The Type 401 Bristol. Note twin radiator grilles reminiscent of pre-war BMWs.

Shock Absorbers

If they are the Bristol type of lever damper fitted to the early examples, test by leaning heavily on wings and boot. If there is excessive movement, replacements may be necessary.

Under-Chassis

If possible, have the car up on a lift, and check the condition of the chassis, especially the front suspension. After many years of use on salt-laden winter roads, rust may be present.

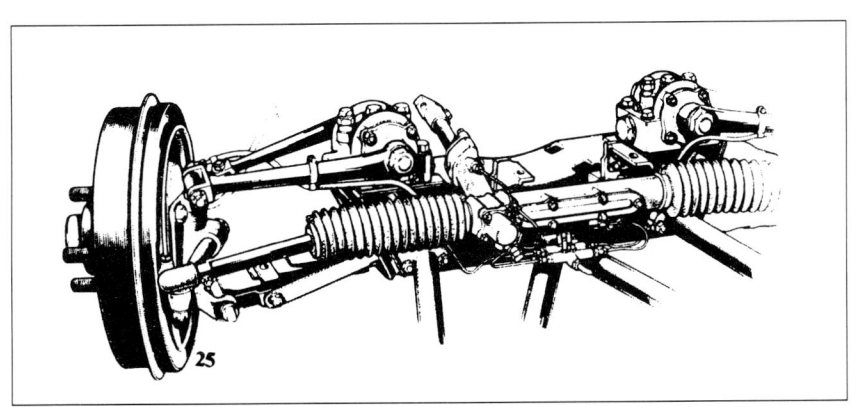

Brakes

If it is an early model, test the foot brake to see whether excessive pedal pressure is required. In many cases though, previous owners may have fitted a servo to reduce such pressure.

Upholstery

Examine closely, not only for tears or amateurish repairs, but also to determine if the surface is very dry, whether it can be saved by generous use of a cream 'feeder', or if it will have to be re-covered. If

Shows complete independent front suspension for late Type 401.

so then this should be taken into account when a price is being negotiated. The cost of such work is now very high, probably well above the £1,000 mark.

Paintwork

The alloy bodywork makes it essential that if a respray will be necessary only a firm specialising in such work should be selected. Unless the body surface is brought right down to the 'metal' and then 'pickled' correctly, it is very likely that the new paint will start to 'lift' in just a few months. Such work is not cheap, and should also be taken into consideration when a price for the car is discussed.

Electrolytic Action

This should be borne in mind. The danger sign is a deposit of fine white powder on the surface of the bumper blade.

Generally

Insist on a test drive of sufficient length for water and oil temperatures to have reached a reasonable level: at least 40 degrees centigrade for the engine oil, and at least 60 degrees centigrade for the water. Do not be impatient, because on a cold day this may require some distance. Use the interim period to observe the rev counter and speedometer needles – do they progress round their respective dials in a smooth and regular fashion, or do they 'swing'? This is usually a sign of a worn or dry cable, rather than a mechanical fault.

Once the oil and water are hot, check the engine's tickover in neutral, and, of course, the oil pressure at low revs.

For the rest, rely on your own common sense – are the tyres worn, and if so, are the treads on the tyres on one side more worn than on the other? Do the brakes 'pull' to one side when applied hard? Is there any sign of 'fading' if they have been used frequently – as when descending a long steep hill? Did the engine start from cold, and if so did it fire immediately, or was there any sign of misfiring or spluttering: any of which are signs of possible wear in the carburettors?

Above all, realise the car must be at least thirty-five years old, so do not judge it as you would a car built rather more recently.

6
Where Did They All Go?

At the Classic Car Shows, where the Bristol Owners' Club (BOC) usually has a stand, one of the questions that is often posed concerns the Bristols that were exported during the late forties and early fifties.

In this period, the phrase 'export or die' was more than a catch phrase for the British industrialist, for he was aware that future supplies of raw materials depended on his success as an exporter. Those firms unable to satisfy government departments on this score found it increasingly difficult to obtain the items required for their own manufactures, and many faced ruin for this reason. But there were some small firms that did succeed. The story is told of AFN Limited, which made a formal request for further supplies, on the grounds that the previous year it had exported fifty per cent of the cars it had made. This was literally true, for though its total production had amounted to just two vehicles, one had been sold to the then Shah of Persia.

Export Problems

The regulations were enforced very strictly, and even a firm as large as the Bristol Aeroplane Company had to conform. At a time when its order book for aircraft was almost empty, much reliance had to be placed on the ability of the infant Car Division to provide not only cash flow, but the export credibility which was so vital for obtaining further supplies of raw materials.

The initial problem for the Export Manager, was to

A Type 401 Bristol Saloon about to leave for a Continental holiday.

A Bristol Type 401 with a saloon body, by an unknown coachbuilder.

appoint agents to sell the cars in the various countries considered as possible markets. The car was new and very expensive, and it lacked any pre-war track record on which a potential agent might rely as indicating the likely volume of sales, and the subsequent commission that might accrue.

As war-torn Europe gradually reached some degree of normality, the governments of countries with their own motor industries were urged to rush through legislation aimed at protecting the home market. This took many forms: in some cases a blanket refusal to issue the necessary import documentation; in others a very limited quota was agreed; while in a third category were countries that no longer made cars but still possessed excellent coachbuilders. One such was Switzerland and, with true Swiss logic, it was agreed that chassis, engine and transmission might be imported, but that the bodywork had to be made locally, by such firms as Graber or Gebr. Beutler of Thun. Even countries without much in the way of previous car manufacturing experience were unwilling to allow the importation of complete cars, and some, like Denmark, insisted on what became known as the 'CKD Technique'. This meant that only the components might be imported, with all assembly work performed by a local labour force.

In Belgium a somewhat Gilbertian situation prevented the importing of complete Bristol cars. There were no governmental prohibitions, but the agent claimed to have suffered from poor British workmanship pre-war, and insisted on all bodywork being made by local coachbuilders such as the famous Belgian firm Van den Plas. By contrast, in Sweden, another free import market, the agent was a real Bristol enthusiast, and indeed his optimism for the new make was such that he was sure he could sell them by the hundred. According to the data on which Appendix A is based, Swedish sales totalled three cars: one Type 400 and two Type 401 Bristols.

One of the many depressing features of the period was the way in which the British Empire was dwindling. Hardly a week seemed to pass without a small ceremony, usually at midnight, with the bugles blowing, and the Union Jack being hauled down for the last time. It soon became obvious that what were termed the 'emergent nations' wished to demonstrate their newly-granted independent status by showing a preference for non-British goods, and it was to the 'old dominions', namely Australasia, Canada and South Africa, that exporters now turned their attention.

With the assistance of the Chief Registrar of the Bristol Owners' Club, I have compiled Appendix A annexed to this chapter, showing the countries to which the early Bristols were exported, by numbers and percentage share. It should be emphasised that there were many gaps in the data supplied, so that the table is more of a random sample than an absolute statistic. On the other hand, it does indicate the general trend, and shows that between them Australia and New Zealand took by far the largest numbers of Type 400 and 401 models.

Neither Canada nor South Africa proved to be large importers, the former having its own car industry at Windsor, Ontario, plus proximity to the huge American plants at Detroit and Willow Run.

The Importing Countries

The Type 400

It would appear that in the period 1947–1950 a total of sixty-nine Type 400 Bristols were exported. The majority (forty-nine or 71.4%) were imported by Australia, after which the numbers fell – Belgium being in second place with just four cars (5.8%). The United States came third, with three cars (4.3%), and France, South America (probably Brazil) and South Africa were equal fourth with two cars each (2.9%). The following countries each imported one car, or 1.4% of the total: Holland, Malta, New Zealand, Saudi Arabia, Sweden, Switzerland and West Germany.

The Type 401

Using the same source of information, it would seem that in the period 1949–1953 ninety-one Type 401 Bristols were exported. Again it was Australia that took most of them – sixty-two or 69.1% of the total. New Zealand was second with ten cars (10%).

A Type 401 with cabriolet body by Pininfarina. Only six examples were made, and they are much sought after as their lines are timeless and they are practical and comfortable cars.

A Bristol Type 401, with convertible bodywork by Richard Mead. The lines are well balanced and there are quarter lights, unusual on a convertible.

A convertible body that looks similar to an example by Richard Mead, but it has not been positively identified.

Holland was third with four cars (4.4%). The following countries each imported two cars, or 2.2% of the total: Canada, South Africa, Sweden and the United States. Single cars (1.1% each) were sent to the Bahamas, Belgium, France, Japan, Kenya, Sri Lanka and West Germany.

If at first sight these figures appear less than impressive, it should be remembered that series production of the Type 400 only got into its stride in the middle of 1947, declining in 1950 when the Type 401 succeeded it. Though some of the latter model were made during the previous year, it was not until both 400 and 402 models were phased out in 1950 that full production was achieved. By mid-1953 it too had been superseded, by the Type 403.

At the Filton factory, weekly output rarely exceeded three cars, so that the total of 160 vehicles could represent slightly more than a full year's production. The spread of the importing countries reflects credit to the Sales Division for having penetrated so many markets with a new make lacking any previous record.

Appendix B to this chapter shows the cars imported by Australia in the period 1947–1986 by numbers and percentages. In addition to the original Type 400 and 401 Bristols, there are later arrivals, and also models in the 402–411 range. Finally, the table includes AC and Cooper cars with Bristol engines.

The state that imported most Bristols and Bristol-engined cars in the period covered by Appendix B was Victoria, with 104 vehicles (39%) of practically all types. By contrast New South Wales, in second place with 57 cars (21½%), imported fewer of the later models. Rather surprisingly, South Australia was third with 34 cars (12¾%), and New Zealand a very close fourth with 31 cars (12%).

Imports fell sharply after the above, with the Australian Commonwealth Territory and Western Australia, equal fifth, each with six cars (2¼%). This might suggest that the tremendous developments in the Perth area may have occurred when the Bristol was no longer regarded as such an exceptional car, and when the competition was much greater. The remaining states, by import numbers and percentage

Semi-front view of a Type 401 Bristol saloon. Note the lower horizontal grille between the bumper, directing cooling air to the sump or oil radiator if fitted. The direction indicators below head and road lamps are non-standard.

share, were: Queensland five cars (2%); Tasmania four cars (1¾%); and the Northern Territory three cars (1¼%).

To reconcile the totals, two general categories were included: 'Wrecked' with nine cars (3%), and 'No Data' with six cars (2¼%). The first is small, and indicates how many of the early cars are still roadworthy, while the second reflects credit on the care with which the Australian data was compiled. The Australian climate is a contributory factor in the astonishing survival of much older cars, and I recall seeing such long obsolete makes as Essex, Hupmobile and Packard, mostly in excellent working condition.

Appendix B also includes examples of the AC–Bristol and Cooper–Bristol. There are nine of each (3%), and some are unique. They include the Brabham 'Bobtail' which was built by Jack Brabham at the Cooper Works in Surbiton, Surrey, and which he drove to victory in the 1955 Australian Grand Prix. Other one-offs include the exotically named 'Dowidat Spanner Special', and the 'Warrior Bristol' which was said to have done well in a Macao Grand Prix. Such cars are cherished, and maintained in immaculate condition by their owners.

It is hoped that the information contained in this chapter may be of interest, showing as it does the extent of market penetration by Bristol in the early postwar period, even though in many cases actual numbers of cars exported were very small. I wish to express my thanks to Bob Charlton (BOC) and Ian Tonkin (BOC of Australia) for providing the data used in this chapter.

APPENDIX A

Bristol Type 400 and 401 Models Exported in the Period 1947–1953

Type 400 model 1947–1950			Type 401 model 1949–1953		
Country	Number of cars	Percentage of total	Country	Number of cars	Percentage of total
Australia	49	71.4	Australia	62	69.1
Belgium	4	5.8	Bahamas	1	1.1
France	2	2.9	Belgium	1	1.1
Holland	1	1.4	Canada	2	2.2
Malta	1	1.4	France	1	1.1
New Zealand	1	1.4	Holland	4	4.4
Saudi Arabia	1	1.4	Japan	1	1.1
Sweden	1	1.4	Kenya	1	1.1
Switzerland	1	1.4	New Zealand	10	10.0
South Africa	2	2.9	South Africa	2	2.2
South America	2	2.9	United States	2	2.2
United States	3	4.3	West Germany	1	1.1
West Germany	1	1.4	Sweden	2	2.2
			Sri Lanka	1	1.1
Total	69	100%	Total	91	100%

Note: This table was prepared from information supplied by the Chief Registrar of the Bristol Owners' Club, and not from official sources. Since there are gaps in the Club's archives, it is possible that other Bristol cars were also exported. Bristol Cars Ltd point out that chassis numbers are allocated to a chassis *frame* and not to a completed car. The company further states that it has never been its policy to quote the number of models made, nor to whom or where they were sold. It is not possible therefore to make any reliable estimate.

APPENDIX B

Distribution of Bristol and Bristol-Engined Cars in Australasia 1947–1986

Model	ACT	NSW	N. Ter.	Q'land	S. Aust.	Tas.	Vict.	W. Aust.	N.Z.	**Sub-total**	Wrecked	No Data	**Total**
400	1	10	–	2	22	2	40	1	2	**80**	1	1	**82**
401	1	25	–	2	4	1	20	1	13	**67**	4	3	**74**
402	–	–	–	–	1	–	2	–	–	**3**	–	–	**3**
403	1	12	1	1	1	–	20	3	4	**43**	3	1	**47**
404	–	2	–	–	–	–	2	–	1	**5**	–	1	**6**
405 Sal.	–	1	1	–	4	–	8	1	1	**16**	1	–	**17**
405 D/H	–	1	–	–	–	–	–	–	–	**1**	–	–	**1**
406	2	–	–	–	1	–	1	–	3	**7**	–	–	**7**
407	–	–	–	–	–	–	1	–	–	**1**	–	–	**1**
408	–	–	–	–	1	–	1	–	–	**2**	–	–	**2**
409	–	–	–	–	–	–	–	–	1	**1**	–	–	**1**
410	–	–	–	–	–	–	1	–	–	**1**	–	–	**1**
411	–	1	–	–	–	–	3	–	1	**5**	–	–	**5**
Sub-total	5	52	2	5	34	3	99	6	26	**232**	9	6	**247**
AC Bristol	–	3	1	–	–	–	4	–	1	**9**	–	–	**9**
Cooper-Bristol	1	2	–	–	–	1	1	–	4	**9**	–	–	**9**
'Wrecked'	–	–	–	–	–	–	–	–	–	**–**	9	–	**(9)**
'No data'	–	–	–	–	–	–	–	–	–	**–**	–	6	**(6)**
Total	6	57	3	5	34	4	104	6	31	**250**	9	6	**250**
Percentage	2¼	21½	1¼	2	12¾	1¾	39	2¼	12	**94¾**	3	2¼	**100**

Abbreviations: ACT = Australian Commonwealth Territory; NSW = New South Wales; N. Ter. = Northern Territory; Q'land = Queensland; S. Aust. = South Australia; Tas = Tasmania; Vict. = Victoria; W. Aust. = Western Australia; N. Z. = New Zealand.

7
The Odd One Out
(Type 402 Convertible)

In retrospect, it seems ironic that though the Type 401 saloon was the most popular of all the 2-litre Bristol cars its stable mate, the 402 convertible, was the reverse. It was in production for only the twelve months (1949–1950), during which time it has been estimated that only twenty-one examples were built.

Many reasons have been advanced for the 402's seeming inability to generate sales, the most common being that its dashboard shook, that its doors flew open on corners, and that its hood mechanism was far too complicated. A sociologist advanced his own theory that its nickname of 'Hollywood Special' caused resentment at a period of acute austerity in Britain, and when America was regarded by many as the 'Promised Land'.

The price of the car was rarely advanced as a reason for its lack of success, for in Britain it cost the same as the 401; £3,213 13s 4d, including Purchase Tax.

Legend has it that the 402 resulted from the efforts of two young Filton engineers, armed with hacksaws, who decapitated a scrapped 401 saloon. I have heard the story so often that recently at a club dinner I was determined to get the facts from one of the men supposed to have done the deed. He said the convertible version of the very popular saloon model 'was an evolutionary process' involving the Filton designers. As for the hacksaw story, he shook his head and informed me that 'by that stage in my career, I had long ceased to have anything to do with hand tools'. Those are the facts, but I've a feeling the story of the 'Hacksaw Twins' will continue to be believed . . .

Although I have never owned a 402, I was able to borrow one for sufficient time to gain a fair idea of its good and bad points. Despite a considerable mileage in the hands of several owners, the car was in good mechanical condition, and would start on the first press of the button.

Road holding was inferior to my 401, but this may have been due to worn shock absorbers. These were

MODEL:	402 Convertible	Date:	1949–1950
Wheelbase		9ft 6in (2m 89cm)	
Front Track		4ft 3.75in (1m 31cm)	
Rear Track		4ft 6in (1m 37cm)	
Overall Width		5ft 5in (1m 64cm)	
Overall Length		15ft 10in (4m 82cm)	
Weight		2,632lb (1,194kg)	
Tyres		5.50 × 16in low pressure	
Engine Type		85C	
Number of Cylinders		6	
Bore		66mm	
Stroke		96mm	
Capacity		1,971cc	
Carburettors		3 Solex 32B.1	
Brakes		Footbrake: Lockheed hydraulic on all 4 wheels. Handbrake: 'Fly-off' type on rear wheels only. Freewheel on first gear.	
Suspension			
Front		Independent transverse leaf spring	
Rear		Torsion bars	

A photograph of a fine example of the Type 402 Bristol convertible, which had just won its class in the annual Concours of the Bristol Owners' Club, hence the cup!

of the early type, made in-house at Filton, and when badly worn were not effective. The hood mechanism was complicated to stow, but simple to erect. No doors flew open on bends, and the scuttle shake was about what one might expect in a car lacking the stiffening of a full saloon body.

I was surprised at the lack of sun visors in a car presumably aimed at countries with good climates. According to the Workshop Manual these could be fitted – as an extra. However, no mention was made about the possibility of fitting a heater – perhaps it was not deemed appropriate on a convertible. I feel, though, that its omission may have been a contributory factor to the model's lack of success.

With the hood erected, I felt like a horse in blinkers, but with it down the forward visibility was improved, though the nearside front wing could not be seen from the driver's seat. Braking was adequate, but if the car had been mine I would have fitted a servo, as pedal pressure was excessive to bring the car to a complete standstill. I would also have replaced the shock absorbers, have added sun visors, and if possible, a heater. The leather on the dashboard had deteriorated, and needed re-covering with some man-made material, impervious to the weather.

The 402 featured the same internal controls as the 401, making it difficult to open the bonnet, boot lid or filler cap from outside the car. But a determined thief with a sharp knife can gain ready access to the interior of a soft-topped vehicle, and can usually start the engine without the ignition key. Because of this

The Type 402 4-Seater with Convertible Body

Procedure for raising hood

1 Tilt backrest forward.
2 Remove side cushions, first releasing the press studs at top and bottom of each.
3 Detach cant rails from their stowage, and erect them in their slots on the shut pillar.
4 From inside the car, push fully down the ivory pivot pin knobs on each side.
5 Pull the hood forward by the screen rail, bearing down on the rail to ensure that it clears the body.
6 Standing in the car and holding the hood still folded at its centre, lift it with a smart upward jerk. The hood pivots will be heard to snap into position.
7 Partially extend the hood by raising the hood screen rail upward to its full extent, whilst the rear hoodstick rests on the deck panelling. Engage the slots in the rear hoodstick with the hooked studs on the car deck panelling behind the rear seats, and at the same time pull the screen rail of the hood forwards over the car.
8 Engage the spigots with the holes in the screen pillars (automatically depressing the spring-loaded plungers which normally close these holes) and lock the hood in position by the three toggles which engage with hooks on the screen pillars.
9 Ensure that the sides of the hood are tucked into the rain channel of the cant rails on either side.
10 Engage the five press stud buttons aft of the door on either side.
11 Replace the side cushions and backrest.

The Tonneau Cover – when using it to cover the rear seat, first place the tonneau rail across the car in the fixings provided on the door rear pillars and fasten the cover down with the straps provided which are fitted to the heel-board of the rear seats. When not in use, the tonneau cover is stowed in the luggage compartment.

Procedure for lowering hood

1 It cannot be *emphasised too strongly* that the first step must be to release all the five press button studs on either side. Attempts to lower the hood with these fasteners secured will result in *serious damage*.
2 Tilt the seat backrest forwards and remove the side cushions, first releasing the press studs at the top and bottom of each.
3 Disengage the three toggle fasteners from the windscreen pillars and fold hood back.
4 Ensure that rear hoodstick is disengaged from the hooked studs on the car body.
5 Standing in the car, close the hood up from front to rear until the frames are approximately vertical and support it centrally.
6 Pull each pivot pin knob inwards and turn it a quarter turn, so that the engraved stroke on the knob is vertical. This locks the pivot pins out of engagement with their upper location holes.
7 Still holding the folded hood centrally, allow it to drop to the full extent of the slots on either side.
8 Bearing downwards on the centre of the hood screen rail, keep the hood clear of the body decking and push it gently back into its stowed position.
9 Raise each of the pivot pin knobs a few inches either side and 'unlock' each knob by turning it until the engraved stroke is horizontal.
10 Remove cant rails and stow.
11 Replace the side cushions and backrest.

The Cant Rails – are provided to give full protection for winter conditions. They need not be erected when the hood is in temporary use.

To see one Type 402 is a rare event, but to see two such fine specimens together is practically unheard of! Note how much better this model looks with the hood stowed.

risk, whenever I had to street park my borrowed 402, I used a 'Krooklok', as affording some extra protection. It is a sturdy steel device with two crooks, one to go under the clutch pedal and the other over a steering wheel spoke. With the car left in bottom gear, it would have been almost impossible to tow away.

Technical Details

The 402 shared a chassis, engine, gearbox, suspension and transmission with the 401, so that one's attention naturally centred on the convertible body. From the scuttle forward, it was virtually the same as the saloon, but the tail treatment was utterly different. From just behind the rear compartment, it curved over the boot lid to merge with the bumper in a very graceful fashion. A central chromed strip ran down the centre of tail and boot lid, and was ornamented with a Bristol roundel badge, similar to those on the nave plates of the road wheels.

Unlike the Type 400 and 401 models, both of which were made in two series, the 402 cars were all built in a single run, their chassis numbers being consecutive: Nos. 701–721. Even so, there were some small differences; in particular, the very early examples had plated bumpers with ribbed rubbing strips of white rubber superimposed. On later examples, the bumper blades were coloured to match the bodywork, with a wide chromed rubbing strip, the rear one recessed for the tail lights. On some cars there were small adjustable ventilators set into the lower front wings, but these were omitted on other examples.

The potential purchaser of a new 402 was offered a choice of engine; either the 85A or the 85C both of which used Solex instruments. *Motor* reported (24

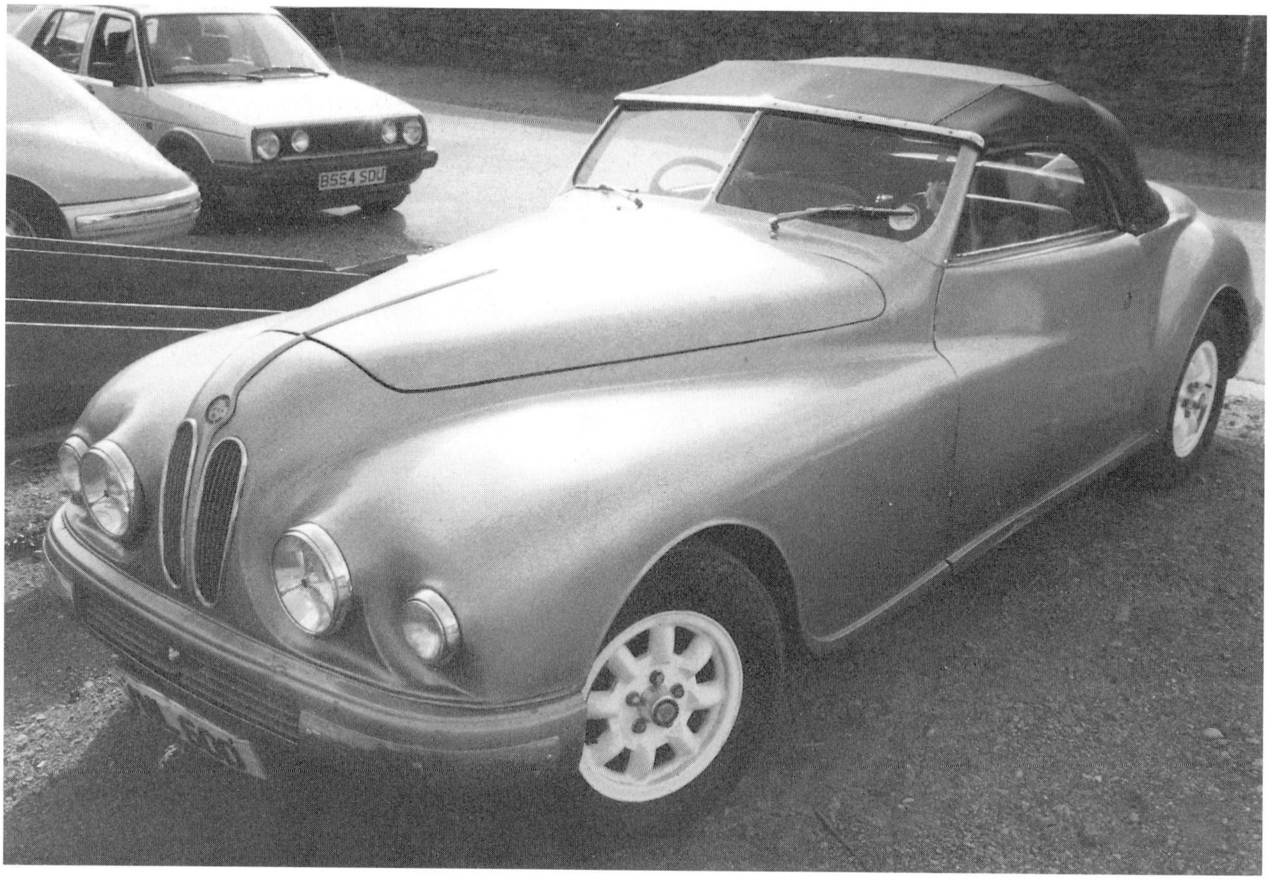
BS54 SDU

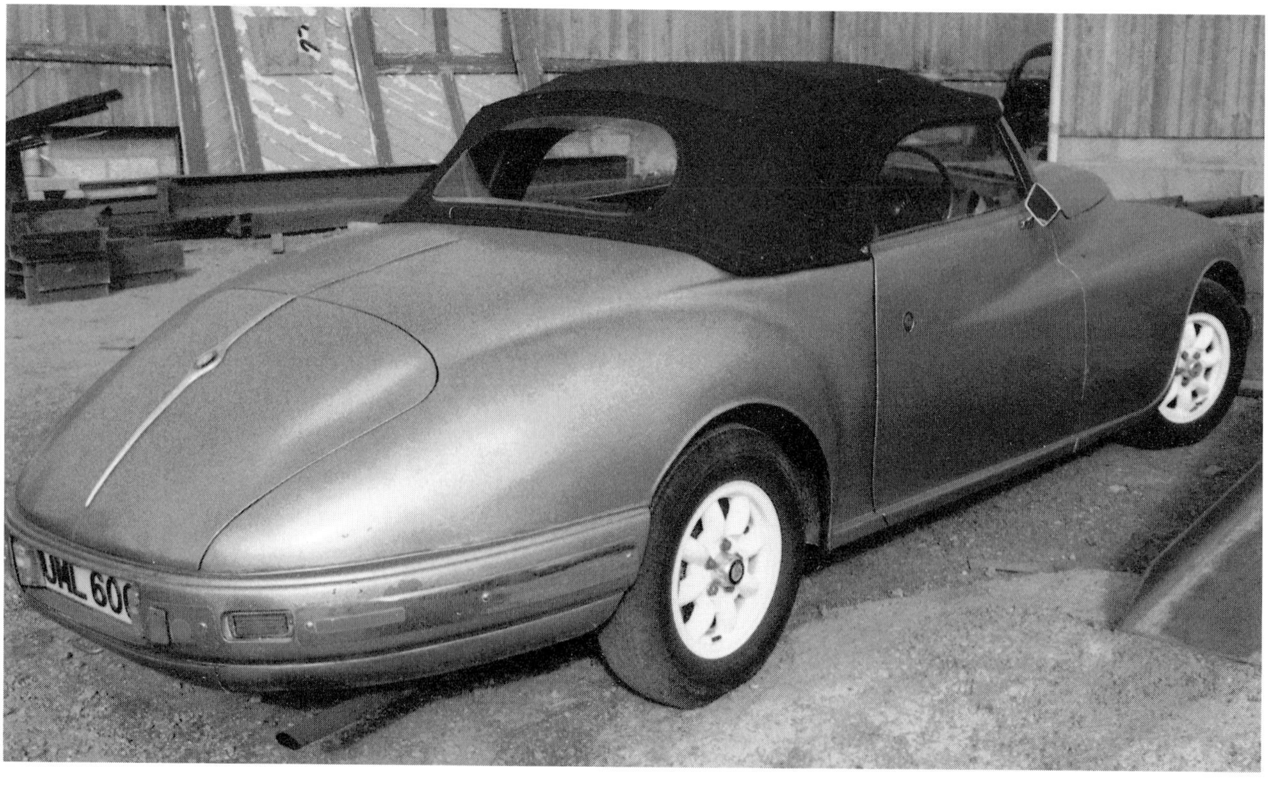
UML 60(

Three-quarter-front view of a Type 402 convertible Bristol, hood erected. The wide ridge or 'tumblehome' on lower edge of sides and doors indicates that this is an early car.

Left above: Front view of a Type 402 convertible Bristol. Only twenty-one examples were made in the twelve months 1949-1950, making it the rarest of all 2-litre Bristols.

Left below: Rear view of a Type 402 Bristol convertible, showing the long tail, with curved boot lid, and Bristol 'roundel' inset. The rear bumpers are of the early type, with the rear lights inset into them. The spoked road wheels are non-standard and so is the mirror.

November 1948): 'Alternative manifolding arrangements are available . . . the most favoured version being a triple down-draught layout quoted as giving 85bhp @ 4,500rpm'. This corresponded to the power output of the 85C unit.

Mention was made in the same report of the 'very smooth contours' of the 402, with the hood erected. However, from the wind-roar at speed that I encountered, I doubt that the convertible would have compared favourably with the saloon as regards aerodynamic efficiency.

The trafficators were of semaphore type, and were recessed into the upper section of the body just to the rear of the two wide doors. I felt they were rather too vulnerable under modern driving conditions, and would have preferred trafficators of the flasher type to be substituted.

The standard gearbox on the 402 was the 85C fitted to the earlier Type 401 cars, with a freewheel on bottom gear. It was excellent except for the wideness of its ratios, and had the car been mine I would probably have fitted it with a BW.CR/5 box-with closer ratios (see page 43).

In a report contained in *Motor* dated 24 November 1948, it was stated: 'The alternative convertible body is notably handsome, having the rear seat set slightly further forward than on the saloon, but is nevertheless a genuine four-seater'. Based on my own experience, I feel this is a trifle over-generous. So much space was required for the hood and its mechanism that leg room in the rear seats was limited, and the width of the seat only just adequate for two normally sized adults. While I felt the car might function as a four-seater for short journeys, I doubt its suitability for a fortnight's touring holiday, four up.

By contrast, the space for luggage in the boot was the same as on the 401 saloon, and, like the latter, had the spare wheel in a separate metal tray under the tail.

Hints for Intending Purchasers

A potential buyer should bear in mind the age of the vehicle under inspection, and accept that after some forty years of often hard use there are bound to be some signs of normal wear and tear. But there are still good examples to be found, and one such was recently sold to an Australian who was delighted to have located a 402 that was quite immaculate, and with a very low mileage. That was an exceptional case, and it is more usual to find one that will need replacements or restoration.

The lower edges of the doors and wings of the 402 have the ridge also seen on 400 and early 401 cars. Often referred to as the 'tumble home', it is typical of the difficult period when the car was made, a time when materials were perhaps of lower quality. It has been my own experience that such cars are more prone to electrolytic action than later models. Unless there is good insulation between the bumper blades (alloy) and their supports (steel), damage may occur, and, unless checked, the entire blade will slowly disintegrate so that, as one owner put it, 'they look more like Gruyere cheese than bumpers'.

It is not often realised that a small amount of timber was used in the 402's construction. The wood is steel-sheathed and butt-welded to the front door pillars and extends into the latter, with a light alloy shell secured over the steel sheathing by means of wood screws. I have been unable to ascertain how the two types of metal and the timber were insulated, but the only case of serious deterioration I have known occurred when a 402 was left to rot in an open field.

A standard feature of the 402 convertible was the provision of a cover that could be used to conceal the hood in the stowed position, to protect the rear compartment when unoccupied, or to clip over the entire tonneau if the car was being parked for a short period.

A potential purchaser of a 402 would be well advised to check that the cover is still usable, that its material is sound and that the fasteners still function correctly. If a cover is unused for a lengthy period, it tends to shrink, and it is very easy to tear a fastener away from the surrounding material, which can be expensive to patch and repair. Similarly, the hood should be checked for weak spots where the material has chafed. Finally the hood should be erected and lowered, to show up any weakness in the actual mechanism, as well as demonstrating to the buyer how both tasks are best performed. But if there is

THE ODD ONE OUT

Rear view of a Type 402 Bristol convertible. The spare wheel is carried in a separate tray under the tail and it can be seen in the lowered position, with the spare beside it.

A rather distant view of a Type 402 Bristol convertible; space in the rear compartment is limited because of the quite complicated hood mechanism.

evidence of neglect, beware, for it is extremely difficult to find a craftsman willing and able to tackle the restoration or replacement of what is now an obsolete design.

The law of supply and demand applies to cars just as it does to other objects of value. Over the past year or two, the convertible-bodied model has become very popular, and prices have escalated accordingly. This being so, and bearing in mind that some of those original twenty-one Type 402s will have been written off through accidents or other causes, a potential purchaser must be prepared to pay a substantial price, even for a car requiring a fair amount of restoration. On the other hand, once such a car is in a really good condition it can represent both a very acceptable road vehicle and a steadily improving asset.

I think the appeal of a 402 was summed up by *Motor*: 'Attractive as the cars are in a showroom or on a brief demonstration run, we have seen enough . . . to say confidently that big mileages will render owners ever more appreciative of their inbuilt quality.'

8
Evolution

One of the advantages of building motor cars in very small numbers is the ease and speed with which modifications or improvements can be incorporated in a model while it is still in full production. During World War II, the Bristol Aeroplane Company had followed a policy of continuous development so that one basic model might go through a variety of series or marks, each showing detail improvements. A typical example was the Beaufighter, of which no less than ten different versions were made.

When car production began in 1946–1947, it was logical for the new Car Division to continue the same policy of discreet development, which was applied to each model regardless of the actual total made. Thus the short-chassis Type 404 coupe appeared in three mini-series, although the estimated production in the period 1953–1955 was only fifty-one.

The Type 401 as an Example

As an example, the Type 401 has been chosen, because it was made over an unusually long period (1948–1953) and also because its estimated production of 605 cars was much the biggest of any of the early Bristol models.

Internal Changes

Probably the most important alteration was the introduction of liners in the cylinder block. These were of the dry type inserted into the bores under pressure. The alloy of which they were made had been developed for the Bristol Centaurus aero-engine, and was called Brivadium. It had remarkable wear resistance, and on many Bristols, using engines fitted with these liners, a mileage exceeding 200,000 is not unusual, with the bores showing negligible wear. If liners do have to be replaced, they are simply pressed out, new ones fitted, and the same pistons and rings continue in use. It might also be mentioned that the Type BSX racing engines were not considered to be fully run in below 8,000 miles, and were not deemed to have attained peak condition until 20,000 miles had been covered.

The opportunity was taken, when the liners were introduced, to drill additional water holes in the cylinder block. This improved the cooling of the block, which depended on thermosyphonic action, in contrast to the alloy cylinder head, where water circulation was by pump.

A slight flutter had been detected as the plunger uncovered the relief passage in the oil pump. This was cured by using additional holes that were uncovered progressively, thus relieving excessive pressure evenly.

Bristol owners living in hot climates sometimes reported oil temperature readings that were abnormally high. In many cases, a simple air scoop fitted under the oil sump was the answer. But an oil radiator became available, as an extra, for owners who preferred this method of keeping their oil temperature at a lower level. From personal observation in Australia, I found that even with this extra the temperatures of both oil and water were often much higher than those recommended as the safe maxima. The engine remained unaffected, but it was worrying at the time.

The 2-litre Bristol engine could have a rasping exhaust note at high revs, which was considered incompatible with the image of a luxury saloon. It would have been relatively easy to have used a proprietary system that subdued the exhaust noise, at the expense of creating excessive back pressure.

Careful research revealed that a periodic effect occurred under certain conditions at the Y-junction, where the twin downpipes from the separate exhaust manifolds united into a single pipe that led into the silencer. The cure was to continue the twin exhaust pipes into a new type Burgess silencer, made specially for the Bristol engine.

Complaints by some owners that engine fumes were entering the interior of their cars resulted in a series of practical tests to discover the cause. To do this, a car whose engine had been given an excessive dose of upper cylinder lubricant was driven along the so-called 'Brabazon Straight' at Filton, which is 1¼ miles in length. Observers in a following Bristol were able to see that the exhaust fumes were not being dispersed by the air stream, as might have been anticipated. It was reasoned that this indicated that the single tail-pipe from the silencer was discharging the exhaust gases into a low pressure area behind the tail. A complete cure was effected by altering the outlet pipe so that the gases were now discharged at an angle to the tail, and were then dispersed by the car's air stream.

Complaints were also investigated from owners who claimed that excessive heat and engine fumes were penetrating into the interiors of their cars. A cure was effected by the use of a modified bulkhead, and by shrouding the brake and clutch pedals.

When some customers reported clutch operating difficulties, a detailed investigation found the cure in a new release block for the Borg and Beck clutch, of the coppered-carbon type.

The original gear lever was of a very hard material, and complaints were received by some drivers who found it uncomfortable. A new type, made of softer material, was introduced. Not only did this meet with drivers' approval, but it was found to eliminate a slight noise (likened to a sizzle) that sometimes occurred on a car that had covered a considerable mileage. The opportunity was taken at the same time to introduce a new type of seal to the clutch and brake pedals, to make doubly sure that engine fumes were prevented from entering the car.

As a result of practical experience gained with a Bristol competing in the Italian long-distance classic known as the Mille Miglia, a new way of securing the rear axle casing to the banjo was introduced. Hitherto studs had been used and had given no trouble, but, as a precaution, bolts were now substituted.

The rack and pinion steering of the Bristol was often praised for its accuracy and lightness, but it too was improved with a new type of steering arm. The transverse leaf spring eye was modified at the same time. Steering geometry was improved when traversing rough roads and the master spring suffered wide deflections.

At Filton, a special test rig was used in which the master springs of the independent front suspension were checked for deflection. Dual hydraulic rams were used with the suspension unit bolted into place. Steel discs of appropriate weight replaced the road wheels for this test. Though it was considered most unlikely there was a possibility of a master spring breaking after considerable mileage or poor maintenance, and as a precaution a safety link was now introduced. At the same time, the front end attachment plate for the entire suspension unit was strengthened, and the removal of the front shock absorbers was simplified.

A standard fitment on the Type 400, and some of the 401 and 402 cars, these shock absorbers were extremely effective, but at the same time quite delicate. Some owners complained that, when traversing rough ground, with the shock absorbers with working hard, there was some noise. The matter was investigated, and improvements introduced. They included a new type of recuperating valve and spring, the modification of the valve seat, and facing the disc with the man-made material known as Tufnol.

Oil leakage sometimes occurred when the shock absorbers had been in use over many thousands of miles, and new improved oil seals were introduced to prevent this.

My own car had suffered from this problem, and it was disconcerting to return to it, after being parked in hot sunshine, to find long streams of oil from one or more shock absorbers.

External Changes

Reference has been made to breakages that had occurred to some of the road wheels on early model Bristols. The resultant complaints were passed on to the makers, Dunlop. It was a lengthy process before a satisfactory compromise material was developed. It combined flexibility with strength, and the problem was solved.

The handbrake lever was unusual in that it was of the 'fly off' type, more common to racing cars than luxury saloons. Originally fitted with a single ratchet, later cars were fitted, as a safety measure, with a modified double ratchet system.

On Bristol cars, the upholstery is of finest Connolly hide, cut and stitched in-house. When it was found that the original pleated seats soon attracted dirt which was very hard to remove, a simplified design was introduced, in which pleating was reduced to a minimum.

When first introduced, the aero-style button door locks on the Type 401 model could only be operated by an occupant within the car, via a hole cut in the trim. Some owners complained that this was not only inconvenient, especially if a passenger was unfamiliar with the car, but the actual operation of the lock was far too stiff. Tests were made, and a new pattern of lock developed that was easier to operate, with the inner button now flush with the trim, and not within it.

By contemporary standards, the original recessed headlights of the Type 401 Bristol were quite adequate for night driving. However, when the Lucas P770 lamps became available they were considered to be so superior that they became standard equipment on the later cars. With these long-range headlights, driving was a real pleasure at night on the relatively traffic-free roads of those days.

Not every driver has the foresight to keep an electric torch in his car. Yet its absence, when suffering a puncture or other mishap at night, can be a most unpleasant experience. To obviate such a possibility, an inspection lamp was introduced, together with a socket into which the cable could be plugged. The latter was of sufficient length to allow the light to be used at any point within a short radius of the car's exterior. The socket had a secondary advantage since it could also be used, with a suitable charger, to keep the car's battery up to strength, if it was being used only occasionally.

Continuous Development Policy

It is hoped the foregoing will give some indication of the care and interest taken at Filton when owners sent in their complaints, and the improvements and modifications that resulted. Much space was devoted by Jack Channer, in a lecture he gave to the Bristol Owners' Club in 1975, on what he called the 'fix' or 'cure' methods used when he was the Bristol suspension specialist, and parts of his talk will be given in a later chapter.

The policy of continuous development pursued by Filton contrasts strongly with the attitude common to many large scale car makers. In volume production, the original model is continued unchanged until a new model is introduced incorporating the various modifications and improvements, which are then advertised as reasons for buying a new car.

When seeking a good used Bristol, it is often worth while to try to find a car made towards the end of a run. For example, a Type 401 built in the first half of 1953 often includes many of the features of the 403 that succeeded it. Similarly, the last of the latter model may have improvements incorporated into the 405.

Bristol owners tend to remain faithful to the marque, confident that over the past forty years each model has incorporated lessons learned from the earlier cars. I think this feeling is well described in an extract from John Bolster's report on a 401 that appeared in the August 1952 issue of *Autosport*: 'It was one of those journeys that live long in the memory, and whether you regard the Bristol as the most sybaritic of sports-cars, or as a luxurious magic carpet with an incidental turn of speed, the result is such de luxe transport for five people and their luggage, as one never thought that a car of only two litres could provide'.

9

The Heavenly Twin

The 403 Saloons

I was standing in the car park admiring my 403 Bristol when Hugh joined me.

'Is that your new car?' he asked; when I nodded, he looked puzzled. 'But it's just like your last one,' he said, 'same colour, same shape – same everything.' He frowned and added: 'I know if I'd just spent thirty thousand Swiss francs* on a car, I'd want everyone to know it was new.'

I watched him march off, and then turned back for a little more gloating.

The Type 403 came into series production in mid-1953 and, as Hugh had observed, its body was virtually the same as its very popular predecessor, the 401. But as *Autocar* remarked in its issue of 13 May 1953: 'If a car is built according to results obtained from wind tunnel tests, it is unlikely that a different result would be obtained from subsequent tests. The Bristol 401 was built as a result of wind tunnel tests, and consequently the 403 is almost identical in general appearance'.

To a casual observer, the only external differences between the two models were a silvered radiator grille, the numerals 403 on body sides and boot lid, and Bristol roundels in red, instead of the traditional yellow.

In fact there were substantial differences between the 401 and 403, some reflecting lessons learned in the development of the BS series of racing engines. Many of the other changes had been incorporated in the 401s built in the first half of 1953, which is why I have advised potential buyers to seek such late examples.

*The original cost of a 403 in Britain was £2,976 2s 6d (£237 less than a 401)

MODEL: 403 Saloon	Date: 1953–1955
Wheelbase	9ft 6in (2m 89cm)
Front Track	4ft 3.75in (1m 31cm)
Rear Track	4ft 6in (1m 37cm)
Overall Height	5ft (1m 52cm)
Overall Width	5ft 7in (1m 70cm)
Overall Length	15ft 11.5in (4m 86cm)
Weight	2,788lb (1,265kg)
Tyres	5.75 × 16in
Engine Type	100A
Number of Cylinders	6 in-line
Bore	66mm
Stroke	96mm
Capacity	1,971cc
Carburettors	3 Solex 32B1
Gearbox	4-speed and reverse
Ratios	1st: 14.0 2nd: 7.12 3rd: 5.05 4th: 3.90 Reverse: 11.22 Freewheel on 1st gear
Brakes	Footbrake: Lockheed hydraulic Handbrake: Cable and rod operating on rear wheels
Suspension	
Front	Independent transverse leaf spring with Newton and Bennett telescopic shock absorbers
Rear	Longitudinal torsion bars. Newton and Bennett telescopic shock abosrbers

Cutaway drawing of the Type 403 Bristol saloon.

Side view of Type 403 Bristol saloon. Note nave plates have roundels. Also the semaphore type trafficators, inset into the door pillar.

Close-up shot of grille and bonnet of a Type 403 Saloon. The 'roundel' is in red. Only the 403 and 404 Bristols used it; the rest of the 2 and 2.2-litre standard models used yellow.

The New Engine

Known as the Type 100A, it developed 100bhp @ 5,000rpm, compared with the 85bhp @ 4,500rpm of the 85C engine fitted to many 401s. Usually, credit for this power increase is given to the new camshaft, the lobes of which provided a valve timing of 15:65:65:15. While such an overlap did help to give the new car such an exhilarating performance, other engine changes had been made, some quite small, but all aimed at increased power.

The alloy cylinder head, with its six hemispherical combustion chambers, had been redesigned to provide space for larger inlet valves of 39mm (1.54in), and the valve springs were 'packed' so that valve bounce would occur at exactly similar engine speeds.

To cope with the higher performance, there was a new sump of 12 pint capacity, compared with the 8½ pints of the 85C unit, and a Hoburn-Eaton oil pump

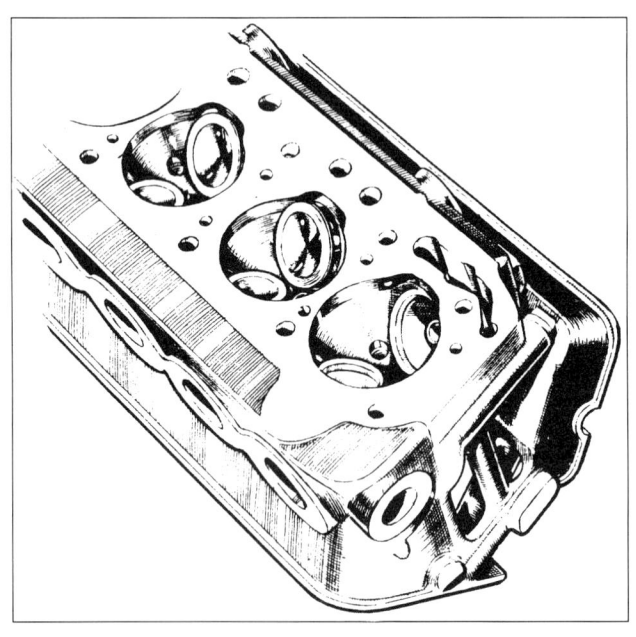

Shows 100A cylinder head with larger valves. (Type 403).

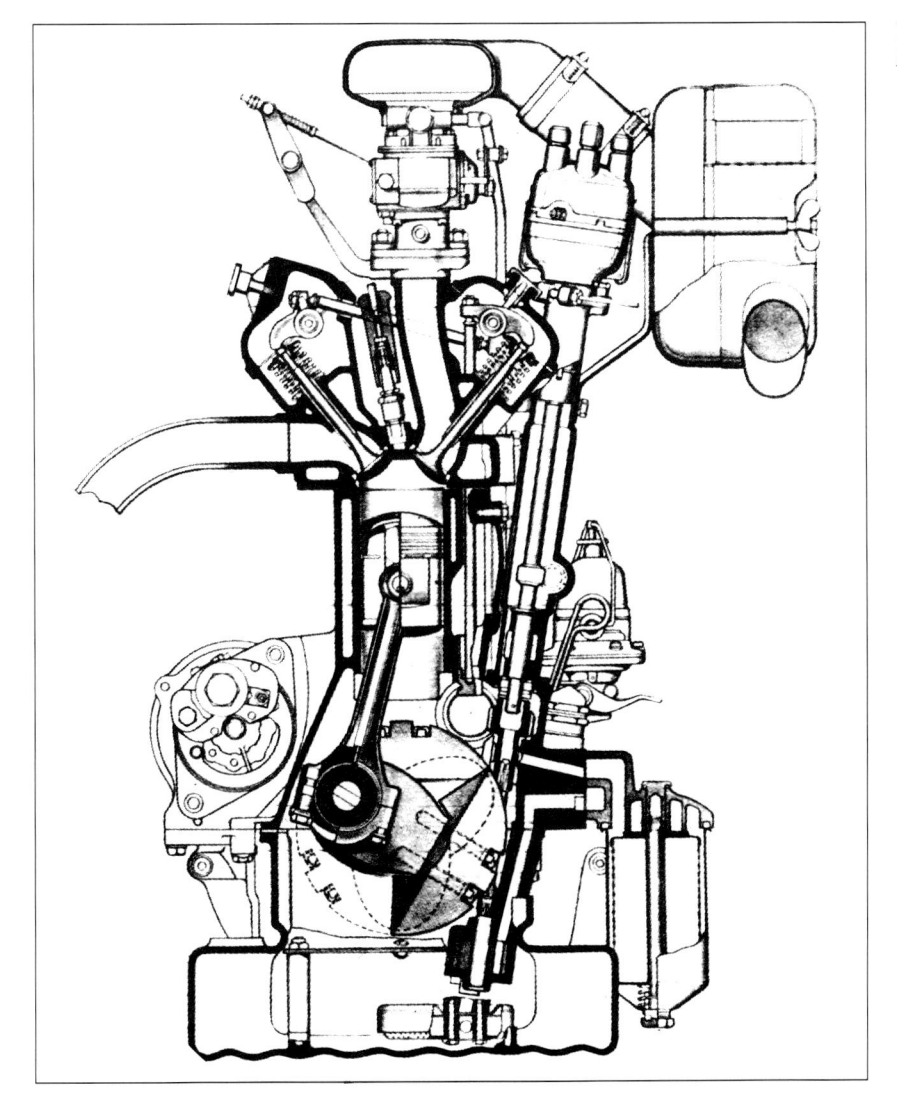

The 100A engine as fitted to the Type 403 Bristol.

was fitted, with a capacity of 195 gallons/hour @ 3,000rpm. This compared with only 130 gallons/hour on the earlier engine. Oil from the pump passed through drillings in the cylinder block, firstly through a filter of the full-flow type, and then back through further drillings to the main gallery; a relief valve being positioned between pump and filter.

Additional drillings then took oil to the main bearings, and also, through offset holes in the crankshaft, to the big-end bearings. Oil reached the gudgeon pins via the big-end bearings and the connecting rods.

With the complex valve gear used on the 2- and 2.2-litre Bristol engines, there was a considerable reciprocating mass at high engine speeds. On the BS series, experience had been gained in ways of lightening the valve gear, and this was also used on the new 100A unit. The skirt thickness of the piston-type tappets was reduced, and a groove 0.15in in width was cut in the lower portion. To prevent oil being trapped at the tappet base, radial drillings connected with these grooves. To save more weight, the rocker adjusting screws, which were of the cup type, were redesigned.

The noise made by the Bristol valve gear at very high revs has been likened to 'a Paisley knitting floor on a busy afternoon', and the reductions achieved in

Front view of Type 403 Bristol saloon. The horizontal grille between bumpers directs air to cool oil sump. Note Vee screen and wipers.

Shows 100A crankshaft with bolt-on counterweight. (Type 403).

the reciprocating mass by the methods described above proved effective.

On the 100A engine, a new method was used for attaching balance weights to the nitrided crankshaft. The weights were placed on either side of the two intermediate bearings, and on the inside of the front and rear main bearings. The big-end bearings were hollow, to reduce weight, and a torsional vibration damper was fitted to the front of the crankshaft. The latter was balanced statically and dynamically.

In its main design, the new engine did not differ materially from the old. The cylinder block and crank chamber were of cast iron, and to reduce the height of the engine the latter ended at the centre line of the crankshaft. On the side, the bores were water-jacketed almost completely, but only for some 2½in on the inlet side. This was to allow sufficient space for the insertion of the tappets. The dry liners, inserted under pressure into the cylinder bores, were of Brivadium, the ultra-hard alloy steel developed for the mighty Centaurus aero engine. A small yet practical detail was the cutting of two slots at the foot of the bores, so that connecting-rods might be raised, allowing pistons and their compression rings to be fitted without affecting the crankshaft.

The crank chamber was divided into three sections by the webs supporting the two (inner) main bearings, the crank being of the four-bearing type. On the 100A engine, the diameter of these main bearings was increased to 64mm (2.12in), compared with the 50.8mm (2in) of the 85C unit. The bearings were of the copper lead steel-backed type, and the journals were nitrided.

The gearbox known as the BW.CR/5 was fitted to the last 401s, and was standard on the 403s. As on the earlier 85C box, bottom gear included a freewheel, allowing it to be engaged without using the clutch – a boon in an emergency. Except for the top gear, all ratios were higher, even reverse, which in some cases could cause problems, especially in very hilly regions. However, for fast driving under normal conditions, the new box was a great improvement, and in his report on the 403 (*Autosport* – 28 August 1953) John Bolster reported speeds of 60mph in second gear, and a rousing 85mph in third. He gave a maximum of 104mph in top gear, though in some other reports speeds as high as 107mph were mentioned.

Some critics felt the box was over-stressed by the extra power transmitted through it, but by far the most common weakness was in the freewheel design. If a driver accelerated from a traffic light in bottom gear, then raised his accelerator foot for an instant, and slammed it down again, the freewheel could literally burst. It did not happen often, but when it did most drivers realised that this was a feature that required rather more care, and that a 'traffic light Grand Prix' could be expensive.

On the 403, two 'Layrub' universal joints were fitted to the Hardy Spicer propeller shaft, tending to reduce snatch at low road speeds, when perhaps a change down to a lower gear might have been advisable.

One of the few points on which the Bristol 401 was criticised was its braking. This was not because of any inadequacy as regards its 11in diameter brake drums or the area of its linings, but rather that far too great a pedal pressure was required to make a crash stop. On the 403, the actuating mechanism was redesigned, to reduce the pressure on the foot brake, and the cast iron drums were replaced by the

Bristols in France. In immediate foreground two late Type 403 Bristols; next is a '405' saloon and at the far end a '603'.

Alfin ribbed type in which aluminium was bonded to iron, improving thermal conductivity. The brake pedal ratio was increased from 3.5:1 to 4.6:1.

The Alfins were fitted to all four wheels originally, and it was soon discovered that they were almost too efficient, later cars having them on the front wheels only. It is said that some owners of the earlier cars were quite happy to exchange their rear Alfins with owners of 401s – with a slight cash adjustment.

Some very fast drivers had criticised the 401 for a tendency to oversteer, and this had been virtually eliminated on the 403. This was due in part to new damper settings, but much more resulted from the fitting of an anti-roll bar to the front suspension. The transverse front spring was protected from road dirt by gaiters, and, as on the earlier cars, the front

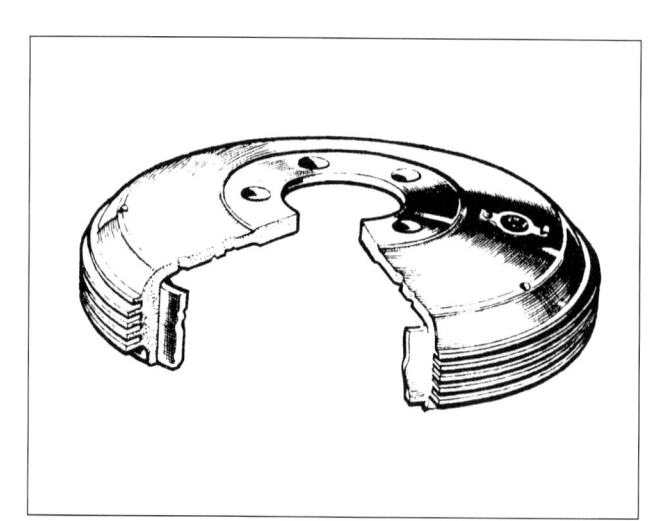

Alfin light alloy brake drum with bonded cast iron liner.

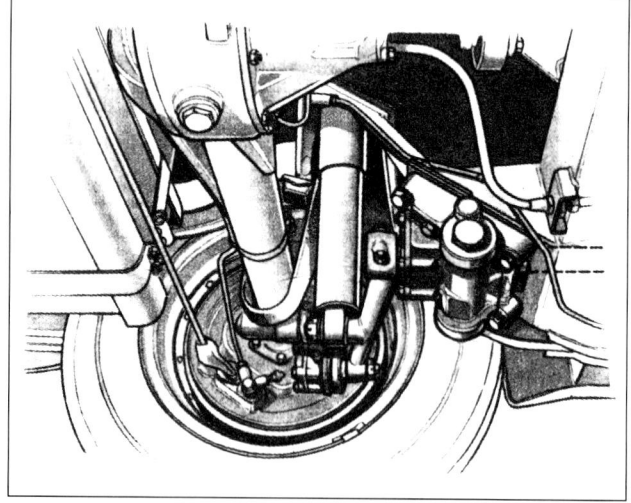

Shows rear suspension of 403.

Shows front suspension with new anti-roll bar (Type 403). Note safety link in case main spring breaks.

suspension and rack and pinion steering box were lubricated automatically by the Enots One-shot system. A prod on the auxiliary pedal every ninety miles or so ensured that oil was fed to each moving part of the suspension, but care is necessary to ensure the absolute purity of the oil used. It is contained in a brass reservoir clamped to the bulkhead, and includes a fine-mesh filter.

The heating and cooling system fitted as standard to the 403 was superior to that used on the 401. I had tested the latter in the heat of an Australian summer and the depths of a Swiss winter, and found it unsatisfactory on both counts. But on my 403 it was very different; but I may have been fortunate. One owner complained bitterly that almost no heat was coming through those bronze aerodynes. He said:

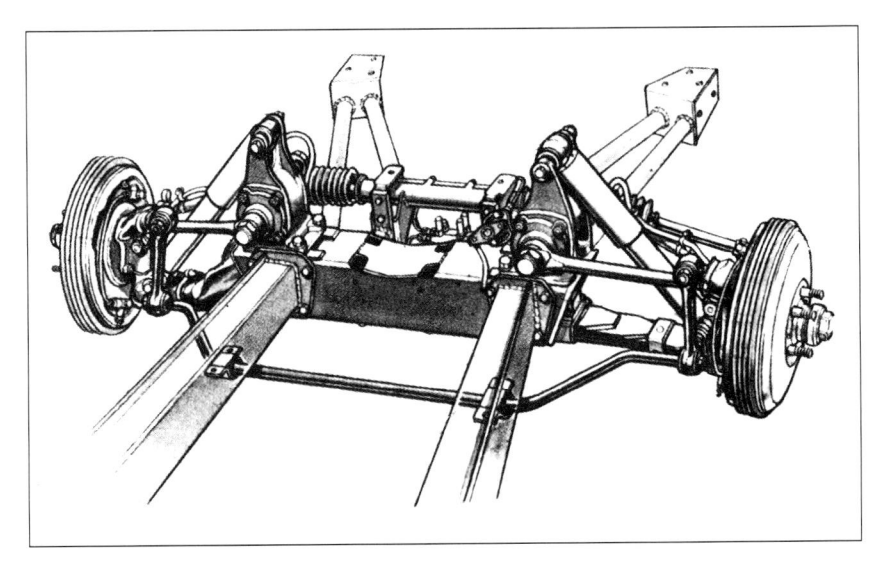

Independent front suspension of the 403, with new anti-roll bar.

A Type 403 Bristol saloon in Paris, with the Eiffel Tower as background. Note push button door lock, '403' numerals on bonnet and exceptionally aerodynamic bodywork.

'Pulling to pieces the heater plumbing, I found the hot water tap hardly opened at all. It was a simple job to turn off a bit of brass from the ferrule, and another – smaller – from the spindle. The result is greenhouse temperatures; if you want them'.

Other Improvements

The 403 had numerous small differences when compared with its predecessor. For example, there was now a light in the boot, a boon when reaching one's goal at night in pouring rain, with a load of luggage to be removed.

The socket for the trickle charger had been moved to a position where it was accessible from either side of the car. In a narrow garage this could be most useful, if one wished to keep the battery charged when the car was used infrequently.

In the tool kit of my own car there was a small armoured inspection lamp, with a reel of flex long enough to reach any exterior spot on the car. It was

On a standard Type 403 Bristol saloon. These wheels are the late type, of stronger, more flexible pressed steel, and were made by Dunlop.

provided with a hook so that it could be hung in a convenient spot, a feature I blessed when changing a wheel at night. In the Upper Savoy region of France there were still plenty of farm horses, and their enormous horse-shoe nails could penetrate the stoutest tyre.

A small yet very useful improvement on the 403 was the mounting of the pinion bearing in the steering box on an eccentric bush. This simplified fine steering adjustment, with two large bolts holding it securely in position.

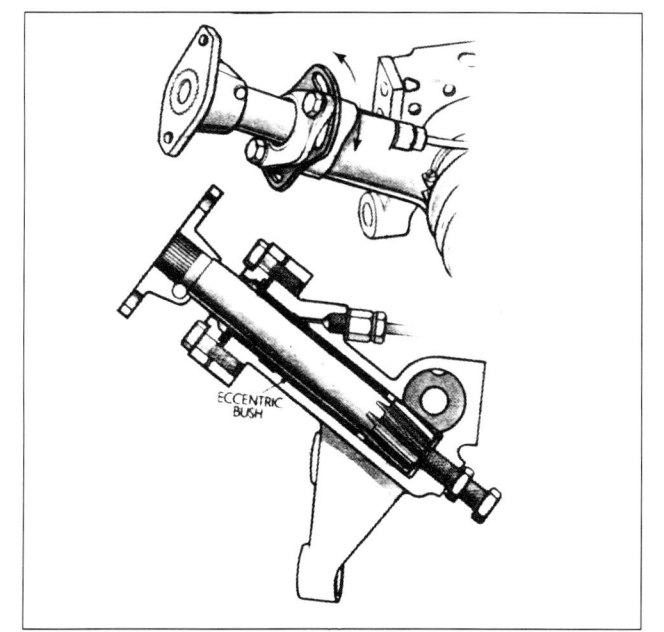

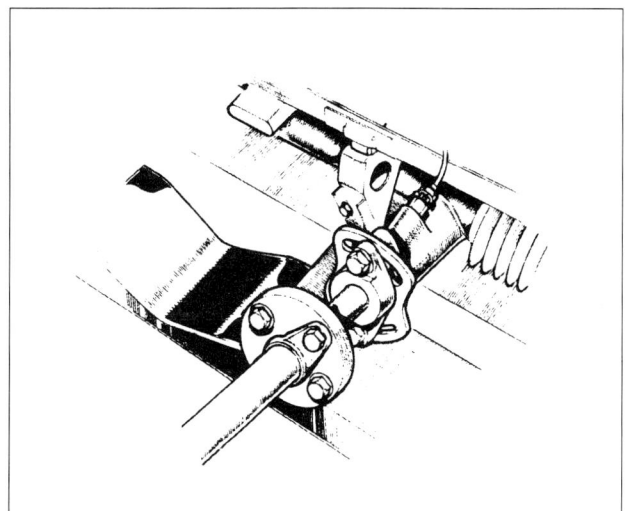

Both show details of the location of pinion on 403 steering box to permit fine adjustment for taking up wear in rack and pinion steering (Type 403).

Tail view of Type 403 Bristol saloons. Note the numerals on the two examples nearest camera. Beyond them is a Type 401, and then an early '400'. Note flap over filler cap.

Though the single bumper blades at front and rear appeared similar to those on the 401, the material was of a quality that virtually eliminated that old failing – electrolytic action between the alloy blade and the steel attachment to the chassis.

A feature that was criticised by some was the increased use of bought-out items, and the fact that the forward section of the floor, scuttle and toeboard were now made of aluminium-faced plywood, instead of the Tufnol on earlier cars. But it was light, immensely strong – and much cheaper. Upholstery continued to be made of top-quality leather, over Dunlopillo, making accommodation extremely comfortable.

My 401 had been the Geneva Show model, and with a 100B engine and gearbox, and a Girling servo, had served me well over some years. Yet even so I found the 403 to be the better car. There was no single point, but rather the whole vehicle seemed tauter and 'more of a piece'. The brakes were superb, easy to operate and progressive, while the centre-mounted handbrake would hold the car on the steepest slope.

The gear change was firm and definite, yet the long lever could be whipped from one gear to another so easily that, with such a responsive engine, there was perhaps a temptation to use it more than was strictly necessary. John Bolster must have felt the same, for he wrote: 'I employed the gearbox to the full, generally engaging top speed at around 70mph . . . my continuous use of that delightful lever did nothing to mar my passengers' enjoyment of the built-in radio'.

As on the 401, the bonnet, filler cap and boot lid were all controlled from within the car, and there was still the excellent and unusual rear roller blind and the ingenious cloth visors for the windscreen. In fact it seemed to me that here indeed was what one might have termed the 'definitive Bristol'. A good basic design had been improved in so many subtle ways that they all added up to a truly fine car.

I feel I cannot do better than to quote the words used by John Bolster when he said: 'The Bristol car has such a world-wide reputation for quality that one can hardly believe that the first model, the Type 400, was not produced until 1946 . . . Now the 403 has put the Bristol very high indeed among the world's best cars, and as an extremely fast machine of immense refinement and superb handling qualities, it is probably unique'.

A Supercharged Type 403 Bristol

After some forty years of neglect, the use of a supercharger in a motor car is again attracting some attention. In part I feel this may be due to the success of the highly complicated Lancias, that have proved the winners in so many major events, using engines that were both turbo- and supercharged.

In the immediate pre-war period, supercharging was widely used as a relatively cheap and simple method of increasing a car's performance, and there were plenty of MG Type J2 open two-seaters that used a blower, often of the Arnott type.

The reasons for the decline of interest in the supercharger may have included the common belief that of itself a supercharger can cause a car's fuel consumption to increase out of all proportion to the extra performance gained. More recently, it may have been due to the rise of the turbocharger, believed to confer most of the blower's advantages, while also actually reducing fuel consumption.

That it was quite possible to supercharge the six-cylinders of the Bristol 2-litre engine was well known; after all, that arch-exponent of Bristol engined racers, Anthony Crook, had driven such cars with success in a number of events.

It came as no great surprise, therefore, to read an account of a blown Type 403 Bristol in the issue of *Autocar* dated 30 April 1954. The supercharger was of Arnott manufacture, and the object of the conversion was stated to be to improve the car's acceleration, without impairing its quite reasonable fuel consumption. For this reason, the maximum blower pressure was a very modest 2½lb per square inch.

A major alteration was to replace the triple Solex carburation system with a single Zenith instrument of the 36 VHG type. It was mounted between the front of the engine and the radiator header tank, and connected to the supercharger via a water-heated induction pipe. An unusual feature was that the belt-driven blower ran at engine speed.

The petrol-air mixture passed through a pipe of 1½in diameter to a distribution centre, connected directly to the three inlets on the cylinder head where the triple Solexes would have been. For safety reasons the system incorporated a blow-off valve.

There was a separate lubrication system for the supercharger, by means of a 'Drok' reservoir, with the oil entering the blower from the rear. Consumption was given as approximately one gallon of oil per 4,000 miles. Though tappet adjustment might have been affected adversely by the various connecting pipes, the sparking plugs remained reasonably accessible, so long as the special jointed Bristol spanner was used.

Unlike the pre-war superchargers, the Arnott was stated to be almost silent, except at high revs with the car stationary, as, for example, during engine tuning. But starting from cold appeared unaffected, if the normal routine was followed. An unusual feature was the removal of the standard 2-bladed alloy cooling fan, and as a result some over-heating was experienced in heavy traffic. Once out on the open road however, the water temperature remained steady at 80 degrees centigrade.

Very little difference in the car's performance was noticed below 2,000rpm, but when accelerating hard in second gear, from 3,500rpm onwards, the power increased rapidly, and this continued, with 80mph achieved in third gear without difficulty. The car would go from zero to 60mph in 14.4 seconds, and from rest to 80mph in 25.9 seconds. In third gear, it would accelerate from 50mph to 70mph in just 9.2 seconds. Such a performance by a 2-litre engine in a car weighing some 25cwt would seem useful for overtaking in modern traffic conditions.

Fuel consumption remained relatively modest, and was stated to have averaged 20mpg, though on a long journey including both dense traffic and high-speed open-road motoring a very creditable 22.2mpg was achieved. The engine was happy at 30mph in top gear, and would pull away from 18mph, without judder or transmission 'snatch'.

From the description, it would appear that the fitting of such a supercharger to a 403 Bristol might be well worth while. And how much would it cost? I have no idea, for the experiment took place over thirty-five years ago, when the installation cost approximately £100.

On a 'Dual Control 403'. Just a joke, since the nearer wheel is only being held and is not connected to a steering column!

Hints for Intending Purchasers

I would commend the choice of a 403 Bristol because, like many other long-term drivers of Filton-made cars, I feel it is the model that somehow typifies the entire series of 2- and 2.2-litre models at their best.

It must be borne in mind, though, that the estimated production over the period, mid-1953–1955, was only 275, and so many of these were exported that it may be far from easy to locate a specimen in Britain. Recently I met a man who had advertised for eighteen months without success.

As in the case of the 401, I would advise the potential purchaser to look for one of the later examples. These can be recognised by the little parking lights mounted on the front wings. I found them most useful as aiming spots when parking, as the nearside wing cannot be seen from the driver's seat.

Some of these later cars have the higher compression ratio of 8.5:1, but some earlier engines were modified, by Anthony Crook Motors, then of Hersham in Surrey.

There should be no fear of electrolytic action between alloy bumper blades and steel supports, and unless very badly maintained – or neglected – most 403s seem to remain in excellent condition almost indefinitely.

A Type 403 Bristol saloon, with helicopter. The car is an early example, without the wing lights of later cars. Note push-button door lock, numerals on bonnet and 'logo' on side.

Three-quarter front/side view of a Type 403 Bristol saloon. Note wing lights (indicating this is a late example) and the numerals at far end of bonnet. Other similar numerals were on the boot lid.

The advice given to the reader in earlier chapters should be observed, both on the mechanical side and as regards the condition of paintwork and upholstery. But I have found most owners of these cars to be genuine enthusiasts, who keep their cars in top condition, and are loath to dispose of them.

Though it may be a long wait, keep looking, and sooner or later fortune will smile on you, and you will find the car you are seeking.

10

From Little Acorns

The Development of the Bristol Engine

The first Bristol 2-litre engines were based on the pre-war Type 328 BMW unit, though the materials which were used were of higher quality, and the assembly was by mechanics trained to aero-engineering standards.

Type 85 engine

This was the first series production Bristol engine and was of the straight six-cylinder type, with a capacity of 1,971cc. The bore and stroke dimensions were 66mm x 96mm, and the combustion chambers were hemispherical. The cylinder block was of chrome iron, the aluminium cylinder head having Brimol valve inserts, and bronze inserts for the 10mm sparking plugs. The latter were by KLG, and were of P TEN L 50 type, set vertically between the two valve chests.

The dimensions of the inlet and exhaust valves were 36mm (1.425in) x 33mm (1.3in) respectively, and they were set at an included angle of 80 degrees. Inlet valves were operated by a set of vertical pushrods, but the exhaust valves required an additional set of short pushrods, contained in tubes across the top of the engine, with bell cranks to change the movement from vertical to horizontal, to operate the valves. The camshaft was driven by a duplex chain from the crankshaft, and was carried by four pressure-fed bearings.

A single Solex dual-port down-draught carburettor was used, of the AAPI type.

The engine was water-cooled, with positive pump circulation to the cylinder head, and a fan belt-driven from the forward crankshaft pulley.

The ignition was by coil and distributor, the latter being skew-driven from the camshaft. Distributor, starter, dynamo and battery were of Lucas make, and the fuel pump, by AC, was driven from the camshaft.

Pistons were of forged aluminium, with three compression and one scraper ring, and a central oil feed to the gudgeon pins. Connecting rods were of forged steel, and the crankshaft was nitrided, balanced statically and dynamically, and fitted with a rubber-bonded torsional vibration damper. The four main bearings were of the lead-indium shell type, and steel-backed.

The original compression ratio was 7.4:1, later increased to 7.5:1, and power output was 75bhp @ 4,200rpm.

The Type 85A Engine

The Type 85A engine was similar to the Type 85 unit, except for the carburation. Three SU instruments of D2 type were used, the fuel-air mixture entering the hemispherical combustion chambers direct, and not via an induction manifold. Breathing or aspiration was extremely good.

The later 85A engines were fitted with cylinder liners of the dry type which were to become standard on all subsequent Filton-made engines. The camshaft was similar to that used in the Type 85 engine. It gave the following valve timings:

Type 85A engine – an offside view – fitted to early Type 400s and some 401s. Note the triple SU carburettors.

a) Inlet valve opens 10 degrees BEFORE the dead centre.

b) Inlet valve closes 50 degrees AFTER bottom dead centre.

c) Exhaust valve opens 50 degrees BEFORE bottom dead centre.

d) Exhaust valve closes 10 degrees AFTER top dead centre.

This camshaft is known, for obvious reasons, as the 10:50:50:10 type. A temperature equaliser, mounted within the cylinder block, proved a failure and was not used on later engines.

With a compression ratio of 7.5:1, output was 80bhp @ 4,200rpm.

The engine was fitted to many Type 400 and some early Type 401–402 cars, through triple Solex carburettors were fitted.

The Type 85B Engine

The Type 85B engine was similar to the 85A unit, except that a more sporting camshaft was fitted.

The engine produced 85bhp @ 5,000rpm, but few were chosen; to date I have indentified less than half a dozen examples.

Type 85B – a nearside view; note accessible battery and coil.

Type 85B – an offside view; note individual adjusting rods for triple carburettors.

Type 85B – an offside view; note wiper motor on left, the oil reservoir for the Enots 'One-shot' lubrication system and 'pancake' air filters.

The Type 85C Engine

The Type 85C engine was similar to the Type 85A except for the substitution of three Solex carburettors for the triple SU instruments of the earlier unit. On very early engines, a blanking plate sealed off the aperture in the cylinder block where a temperature equaliser would have fitted.

Using a compression ratio of 7.5:1, power output was 85bhp @ 4,500rpm. It was fitted to the majority of the very popular Type 401 saloons.

Type 85C – a nearside view, note 'banjo' air cleaner and 'slanted' battery securing rods.

Type 85C – an offside view; note twin three-port exhaust manifolds.

Type 85C – an offside view; note the matt finish of the rocker box cover.

Type 85C – a nearside view; note accessible battery and coil, jointed plug spanner.

The 100A Engine

The 100A engine unit was peculiar to the Type 403 introduced in mid-1953.

It included a number of changes compared with the 85 series. A new camshaft giving valve timings of 15:65:65:15 was used, also a stepped oil sump of greater capacity. Inlet valves were larger, the diameter being 39mm (1.54in), and main bearings were also bigger at 64mm (2.12in). Valve gear was lightened, to reduce reciprocating masses at high revs.

The standard compression ratio was 7.5:1, when the output was 100bhp @ 5,000rpm. However, some owners had their engines converted by Anthony Crook Motors to a higher ratio of 8.5:1, and this was standard on the last few 100A engines made at Filton.

With an estimated production of 275 Type 403 cars made in the period mid-1953–1955, the 100A is relatively rare, and engines from scrapped cars are eagerly sought by owners of earlier Bristols.

Type 100A – a nearside view; note the non-standard finish to the rocker box cover and 'pancake' air filters.

The 100B Engine

In October 1953 a short-chassis coupe, the Type 404, was launched and potential customers were given a choice of engines, of which the 100B was one. Later it was to become the standard engine of the Type 405 convertibles, and was also used on some of the Ace and Aceca models built by AC Cars Limited, of Thames Ditton in Surrey.

The exhaust manifold differed from any earlier catalogue Bristol, a single six-port exhaust manifold and big bore exhaust pipe being used, instead of the twin three-port manifolds, two-pipe exhaust system used on the 85/100 series engines.

With a camshaft similar to that of the 100A, the output of this engine was 105bhp @ 5,000rpm.

The 100B2 Engine

The 100B2 engine was basically similar to the 100B, but a new camshaft was fitted giving valve timings of 36:72:72:36. It was the standard engine in the Type 405 saloons.

The exhaust system reverted to the earlier twin-manifold, twin-pipe system. Output of the 100B2 unit was 105bhp @ 5,000rpm.

Type 100B2 – a nearside view; note standard dynamo and circular air cleaner. This engine was only fitted as standard to the Type 405 saloon.

The 100C Engine

The 100C engine unit was the alternative to the 100B engine for buyers of the little 404 coupe, and its performance was high by contemporary standards.

The engine combined a more sporting camshaft giving valve timings of 40:80:80:40, with a higher compression ratio of 9:1. Very few were chosen by 404 owners, some of whom appeared to equate high power output with frequent gear-changing and unreliability. This was not true but full power tended to come in at around the 3,000rpm mark, making the performance at lower engine speeds less impressive. The engine produced 125bhp @ 5,500rpm.

Type 100C – an offside view. A very rare engine and fitted only to a handful of Type 404 coupes. It produced 125bhp at 5,500rpm.

The FNS Engine: First Series

Like the 100D2, the FNS engines were made for another car manufacturer, AFN Limited of Isleworth. The three initials stood for Frazer Nash Specification and not, as is often supposed, either 'F N Special' or 'F N Sports'.

It was based on the earlier 85A engine, but triple Solex carburettors replaced the three SU instruments. The ignition was fitted with a Delco–Remy–Hyatt twin contact distributor, with a Holset viscous damper on the crankshaft. With a compression ratio of 8.5:1, the output was 110bhp @ 5,250rpm.

The 100D2 Engine

The 100D2 engine was one of the only two standard Bristol engines never fitted to Filton-made cars. It was built specially for AC Cars Limited and though the owners, the brothers Hurlock, drove a very hard bargain the engine proved powerful and reliable. It was fitted to Ace and Aceca models.

The essential difference between this unit and the 100C is that the triple Solex carburettors incorporated accelerator pumps. The power output of the engine was 128bhp @ 5,750rpm.

Type 100D2 – a nearside view; note the corrugated hose to the radiator, red fan, oil filler cap on right and the 'pancake' air filters. It is fitted to an AC Bristol 'Ace' open two-seater.

Type FNS – an offside view. This engine was made by Bristol only for use on the Frazer Nash sports/racers. It produced 126bhp at 5,000rpm. Note the knock-on perforated disc road wheel.

The FNS Engine: Second Series

This second series engine was similar to the first series units, except for an increase of 0.15in on the inlet ports, resulting in 26.5 per cent greater port area. An oil sump of greater capacity was fitted and compression ratio was 9.5:1. The output was 126bhp @ 5,500rpm.

The Type 110 Engine

The Type 110 engine was the first Bristol engine to exceed 2-litres in capacity. With the increased bore and stroke ratio of 68.89mm x 99.64mm (2.7in x 3.92in), the swept volume of the engine was 2,216cc (135cu in).

A camshaft giving valve timings of 36:72:72:36 was used, as on the 100B2 engine, and the compression ratio was 8.5:1. Main bearings were of 64mm (2.12in) diameter, and the crankshaft was fitted with a Holset viscous damper.

The engine was used for the much heavier Type 406 Bristols, and on some 'Greyhound' models made by AC Cars Limited. Also on a few of the Type 406Z saloons, with coachwork by Zagato. The output was 105bhp @ 4,700rpm, the same as the 100B2 unit, but was achieved at lower engine speeds. Torque was much improved, making it more suitable for a heavier and more luxurious Bristol.

Type 110 – an offside view. This is the only Bristol engine with a capacity of 2.2 litres, and was fitted to the Type 406 saloon as standard and also to some AC 'Greyhound' saloons and 406Z models. The example shown here was fitted to a restored Type 400 Bristol.

The Type 110S Engine

The Type 110S engine was a very powerful, high-revving engine, with a camshaft giving valve timings of 40:80:80:40, as used on the 100C and 100D units. Very few 110S engines were made, and they were fitted to the 406Z coupe and a few 406Z saloons (the 'Z' denoting coachwork by Zagato). Some may also have been fitted, to special order, on the 'Greyhound' saloon cars made by AC Cars Limited. It would have been logical for the unique short-chassis Bristol 406/SP1 to have used this engine too. With a special twin-exhaust system by Abarth, the output was 130bhp @ 5,750rpm.

The Type 160 Engine

Though a number of prototypes were made and tested very thoroughly on the test bed, the Type 160 engine never went into series production. It differs considerably from the other Filton-made engines, both as regards capacity and valve actuation.

The bore and stroke ratio was 83mm x 92mm (3.27in x 3.62in), giving a capacity of 2,987cc (18cu in). The design was the classic twin-camshaft, with drive by chain. The distributor was driven by a skew-gear from a front-mounted shaft. The crankshaft was fitted with a viscous vibration damper. Though triple Solex carburettors were retained, they were now of the twin-barrel type. The output was 140bhp @ 5,500rpm.

NOTE: Before the cancellation of the 220/240 project, the engine capacity was enlarged to 3.6 litres, and with petrol of a higher octane value there was a significant increase in power. At that time, in the later Fifties, the only fuel available from the pumps was probably the equivalent of two star grade.

With the ill-fated 220/240 project aborted, the Type 160 was the last Bristol-made engine. The later cars, commencing with the Type 407 saloon, were all fitted with Chrysler engines of varying style and capacity.

The Development of the BS Series of Bristol Racing Engines

In 1948, the International Automobile Federation introduced a new racing category. Known as 'Formula 2', it applied to cars with supercharged engines not exceeding 500cc cylinder capacity, or 2,000cc if normally aspirated. A number of small British firms were interested in competing in the latter class, but could not afford the cost of making and developing their own engines.

In Britain the only maker of racing engines for sale to other car firms was Alta, owned by Geoffrey Taylor, with a workshop near the Kingston bypass. The engine was famed for its power and strength, but the total made was less than twenty, and Taylor was unable to increase his production to meet the new demand.

A 2-litre Bristol engine was used for experimental purposes at Filton, and run under laboratory conditions. Using a compression ratio of 7.5:1 and a camshaft merely described as 'of super sports type', the power developed on the test bed was 122bhp @ 5,500rpm. Next, camshafts of varying degrees of overlap, with fuels of differing octane values, were used with the same engine, and power readings taken. With a compression ratio of 9.5:1 and a higher quality fuel, 145bhp were produced @ 5,750rpm. Maintaining the same compression ratio and fuel, but with a milder profiled camshaft, power dropped to 137.5bhp at the same engine speed.

Motor sport in Britain is a small world, and when rumours of what was being achieved at Filton began to circulate, some of the smaller firms realised that here might be the solution to their engine problem. Early enquiries came from John Cooper of Cooper Cars Limited and Leslie Johnson of ERA Limited.

Type BS – a nearside view; note 'pancake' air filters. This engine was produced in a variety of types for use by other makes, including Frazer Nash, Cooper, Kieft, Lister and Lotus.

Type BS – an offside view. This engine is fitted to a Cooper Bristol, note the very special six port manifold with six separate exhaust pipes. There are no air filters, but when racing, special air 'straighteners' were used, to improve gas flow.

The latter was working on a new 'G' type of very advanced design, and felt the Bristol unit might do as a stop-gap until his own engine, based on that of the air-cooled racing Norton motorcycle, was ready.

Encouraged by the obvious demand, the Bristol directors agreed to put the experiments onto a commercial basis, and with typical caution preferred to use the initials BS for 'Bristol Sports', when it might have seemed more logical to use BR for 'Bristol Racing'. BS type engines were allocated distinguishing marks and numbers, even when detail differences were very small, as shown below.

The Type BS1 Engine

The bore and stroke ratio was 66mm x 96mm (2.6in x 3.78in), and the engine capacity 1971cc. Better quality petrol was then available, and the compression ratio was 8.5:1, with the camshaft giving valve timings of 40:80:80:40. Diameters of inlet and exhaust valves were 39mm (1.54in) and 33mm (1.3in) respectively. The crankshaft was fitted with a Girling viscous damper, with a chain drive to the camshaft. The crank (Part No. 331970) was not suitable for a Holset damper. A cooling scoop was fitted to the oil sump.

The valve gear was lightened and each combustion chamber measured and adjusted to equalise compression ratios. The valve springs were 'packed' so that valve-bounce occurred at the same engine speeds. The sump capacity was nine pints, with a Hoburn–Eaton large-capacity oil pump fitted. The Delco–Remy–Hyatt twin-contact distributor was used and driven by skew-gears from the camshaft. The resulting power output was 132bhp @ 5,750rpm.

After Mike Hawthorn's meteoric performance at the 1952 Easter Meeting at the Goodwood circuit, he sent his engine back to Filton for further development, and the following action was taken:

a) The compression ratio was raised to 9.5:1, the flywheel was lightened and the valve seats reshaped.
b) An alloy pulley was fitted to the water pump drive.
c) An extended air duct was developed, soon nicknamed 'Mike's elephant trunk'. It was more sophisticated than it appeared, incorporating 'air straighteners' or deflectors, and a gain of 4 more brake horse power resulted.

The resulting power output was 149.8bhp @ 5,750rpm.

The Type BS1/SC and BS1A/SC engines were similar to the Type BS1, but crankshaft No. 332580 was used, with smaller main bearings of 2in diameter. It was known as the 'short nose' type.

The Type BS1A engine was again similar to BS1 but the compression ratio was raised to 9.5:1. Some owners had the cylinder heads skimmed to give 10:1 ratio, and each engine was tuned to customer's individual requirements. No power output data is available.

The BS1 Mark 2 engine was peculiar to the Arnolt–Bristol cars, two-seater sports/racers, with Bertone bodywork. Full flow oil filter and Vokes air filter were fitted with an oil sump capacity of 8½ pints. The camshaft gave valve timings of 40:80:80:40, and the compression ratio was 9:1. The power output was 130bhp @ 5,500rpm.

The BS1 Mark 3 engine was similar to BS1 except that the Girling viscous damper was fitted to the crankshaft, and the carburettor butterfly valves were streamlined. The crank was of the short-nose type, Part No. 332580, and there were twin rocker-box breather pipes. Engine parts were polished and balanced, and there were no balance weights on the crankshaft. The oil sump was of the sports type, and an oil filter was not fitted. The power output was 142bhp @ 5750rpm.

The BS1A Mark 3 engine was similar to BS1 Mark 3, but a Delco–Remy–Hyatt twin-contact distributor was fitted and engine parts were polished and blended. Oil filter, starter, dynamo, torque bracket, and air cleaner were not fitted. The power output was 148bhp @ 5,750rpm and compression ratio 10:1.

The BS4 Mark 1 Engine

This was similar to BS1 Mark 3, but the crankshaft might be fitted with either Girling or Holset viscous damper. Crank was part No. 332580, and a gear-driven camshaft was available to special order. Twin rocker-box breather pipes and new anti-surge baffles were fitted in the sump. No oil filter was fitted. Ports were polished and blended and the compression ratio was 9:1. The power output was 142bhp @ 5,750rpm.

The BS4 Mark 2 engine was similar to BS4 Mark 1, except an oil filter *was* fitted. A gear-driven camshaft fitted and side-mounted magneto or distributor drive by bevel gears from the front were available to special order. The Delco–Remy–Hyatt twin-contact distributor and Lucas starter and dynamo were fitted. The compression ratio was 9:1. The power output was 142bhp @ 5,750rpm.

The BS4A Mark 1 engine was similar to BS4 Mark 1 except that the compression ratio was raised to 11:1 and the power output was 155bhp @ 6,000rpm.

The BS4 Mark 2 engine was again similar to BS4 Mark 1, except that an oil filter was fitted. The Delco–Remy–Hyatt twin-contact distributor was fitted, and a magneto was available to special order. Neither starter nor dynamo were fitted. The camshaft was driven by gears, and the distributor driven by bevel gears from the front. The compression ratio was 9:1. The power output was 155bhp @ 6,000rpm.

The BS4A Mark 2 was similar to BS4 Mark 2 except that it was fitted with new pistons giving a compression ratio of 10.5:1. It had a jockey pulley as a belt-tensioner. The camshaft was driven by gears, and the distributor driven by bevel gears at the front. Air cleaner, starter, dynamo, and engine torque brackets were not fitted and side magneto drive to special order. The power output was 155bhp @ 6,000rpm.

The BSX Engine (Known by some as the BCE and BS5)

This engine was peculiar to the Type 450 Bristols that competed in the Le Mans Twenty-Four Hour and the Reims Twelve Hour races in 1953–1955. It was basically similar to the BS4A Mark 2, but the compression ratio was reduced to 9.2:1 as cars competing in the French events were limited to fuel of low octane value.

Inlet valve diameter was 39.6mm (1.56in) and triple Solex carburettors were fitted with twin chokes, accelerator pumps and air straighteners. The butterfly valves were streamlined. The Delco–Remy–

Hyatt twin-contact distributor was used, and the dynamo and starter were of Lucas manufacture. The exhaust system was altered in 1954 to 'six into three' pipes, and in again 1955 to 'six into three into one' pipes.

Special cooling arrangements were made, with a second pump to circulate water to the block as well as the cylinder head, the latter being of the 'twelve port' type. The crankshaft was polished and connecting rods were peened.

As raced in 1955, the engine developed 155bhp @ 6,000rpm, but later, using fuel of higher octane value, and an increase in compression ratio, 170bhp was produced at 7,000rpm.

The decision of the Bristol directors to withdraw from the racing scene after the disastrous accident at the 1955 Le Mans race ended the hope of a new hyper-sports car, with an engine based on the developed BSX unit.

The BSX was the last Filton-built engine to be fitted to a Bristol chassis, but details of the Type 160 engine, of a quite different design, follow.

Though the engine was subjected to rigorous and extensive testing on the Filton test-bed, it was never road-tested, as the automatic transmission system had not been finalised when the project was finally aborted.

The Type 160 Engine

This unit was to have powered a new generation of Bristol models, and the story of the ill-fated 220/240 Project is told in a later chapter.

The main features of the engine included a bore and stroke ratio of 83mm x 92mm (3.27in x 3.62in) giving a total engine capacity of 2,987cc. The complicated valve gear, a feature of the 2- and 2.2-litre Bristol engines, was replaced by a classic twin-overhead camshaft design. The compression ratio remained low, as the only available fuel was of poor quality during the early design stages. Triple Solex double-choke carburettors were used and the crankshaft was fitted with a viscous damper. The camshaft, chain-driven from the latter, powered the distributor by means of a skew-drive. Starter, dynamo and distributor were all of Lucas manufacture. The power output was 140bhp @ 5,500rpm.

The capacity was later increased to 3.65-litres, and using fuels by then available, of higher octane value, a considerable increase in power resulted. A number of prototype engines were made in this larger capacity, but could only be checked on the test-bed, as the automatic transmission system was never completed. All later Bristol models were fitted with Chrysler engines and Torqueflite transmission.

11

The Almost Car

Type 404 Coupe

The story of the short-chassis coupe known as the Bristol 404 is a curious one, for it did not follow the logical development of the 400–403 series, but was actually the brain-child of Jack Channer, then a member of the Filton design staff, who gained a formidable reputation as one of the world's most respected suspension specialists.

He had a very inquiring mind, and often stayed long after normal working hours, pondering on some problem of design that often involved a suspension aspect. During one such session, it occurred to him that it would be feasible to shorten the standard 9ft 6in Bristol chassis, and still maintain its well-tried suspension system, using transverse leaf springs at the front, with torsion bars at the rear.

Channer completed his drawings, but found little interest at senior level, and it was not until about two years had passed that Sir George White authorised the construction of a prototype.

When completed, the car had a grim, almost menacing air, with its three fins, two sweeping back from the rear wings, while the third, a huge shark-like affair, was fixed to the roof. The little car was promptly nicknamed 'The Bomb', and after thorough testing without the upper fin was put into series production, its official description being: 'Bristol 404 two-door two-seater saloon with *very* small rear seats in the tail. Ash frame with light aluminium panelling. Heater standard: radio extra. Built on special short chassis'.

MODEL: 404 Saloon	**Date:** 1953–1955
Wheelbase	8ft 0.25in (2m 44cm)
Front Track	4ft 4.36in (1m 33cm)
Rear Track	4ft 6in (1m 37cm)
Overall Height	4ft 7.75in (1m 41cm)
Overall Width	5ft 8in (1m 72cm)
Overall Length	14ft 3.25in (4m 35cm)
Weight	2,290lb (1,039kg)
Tyres	6.00 × 16in
Engine Type	100B or 100C
Number of Cylinders	6
Bore	66mm
Stroke	96mm
Capacity	1,971cc
Carburettors	3 Solex 32BI
Gearbox	BW CR7 Bristol 4-speed and reverse
Ratios	1st: 14.08 2nd: 7.12 3rd: 5.04 4th: 3.90 Reverse: 11.27 Freewheel on 1st gear
Brakes	Footbrake: Lockheed hydraulic on all wheels by tandem master cylinder. Handbrake: Cable and rod operated by central lever on rear wheels only
Suspension	
Front	Independent transverse leaf spring with direct acting telescopic dampers; anti-roll bar
Rear	Longitudinal torsion bars with direct acting dampers

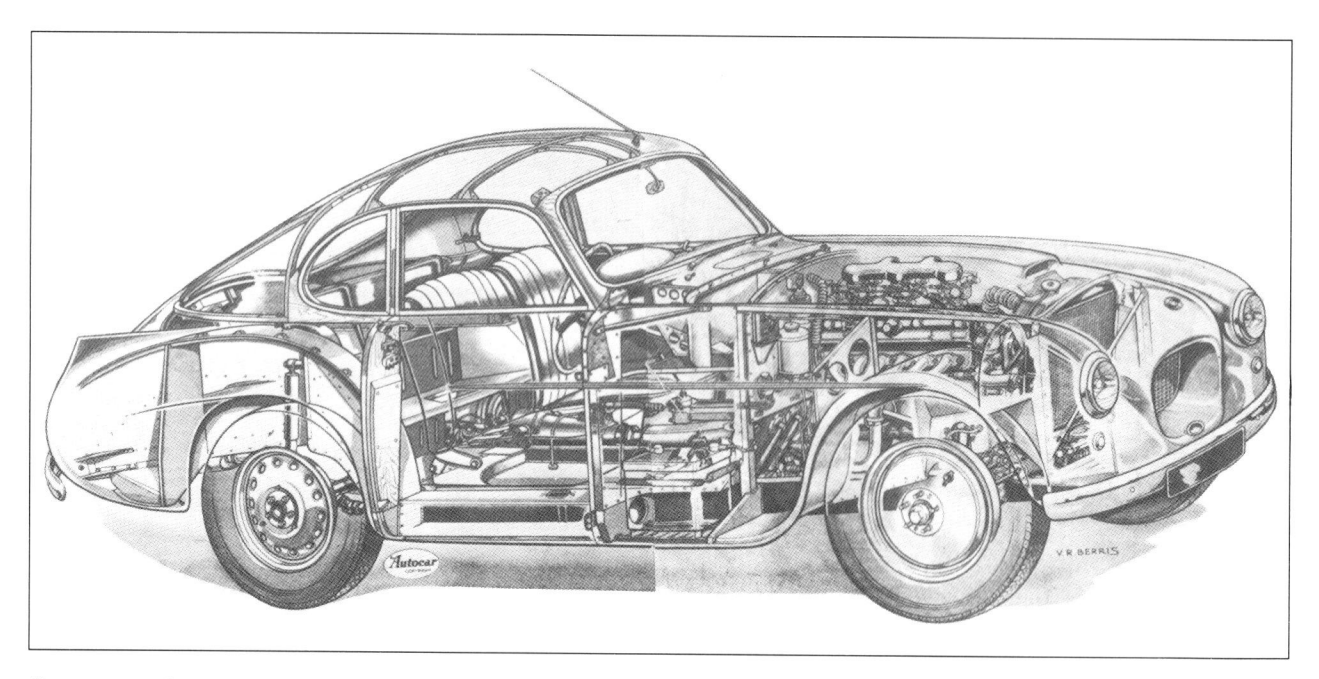

Cutaway drawing of Type 404 coupe; note single six-port exhaust manifold, and neat remote gear lever.

'Beside the river'. A Type 404 Bristol. Note large air duct in bonnet.

Side view of a Type 404 Bristol. Note vestigal 'fin' on rear wing. The '404' was in production from late 1953 until 1955.

First Appearance

The new model was exhibited at the Earls Court Motor Show in the Autumn of 1953, and it attracted considerable attention. The last vestiges of similarity to the pre-war BMW cars had gone, and the radiator air-intake of aero type was said to have been based on those used on the Brabazon airliner.

There was no roof-fin, but those on the rear wing tops were retained, in a vestigial form. For the rest, the series production cars were very similar to 'The Bomb', though now they were more generally known as 'The Businessman's Express'.

I have often been told of the dislike of Sir George White to the new model, and, according to one version of the tale, he would not even drive a 404 unless 'a huge fin was riveted to the roof'. Sir George was a businessman, and I hardly feel he would have wanted to advertise his own misgivings in such a very obvious fashion. What is certain is that he liked, whenever possible, to test every new model, and so it seems probable he did drive 'The Bomb' himself – shark fin and all!

It may be, however, that he preferred the longer chassis, and this view would seem to be supported by the alacrity with which a contract was concluded with the late Harold 'Wacky' Arnolt.

The latter was anxious to sell a Bristol-based car from his Chicago headquarters, at a price far lower than for a standard Filton car, and the end-result will be described in the following chapter. Suffice it to say that 142 short chassis were sold to Arnolt, plus a special engine known as the BS1 Mark 2. Channer referred to this incident when he said: 'You will remember the Arnolt-Bristol, which was bodied by Wacky Arnolt on a cheaper version of the 404 chassis. We used up the surplus 11-inch brake drums and "A" links, etc., on these chassis, and so usefully cleared stocks.'

Because of the short length of the new chassis frame, just 8ft ¼in, there was no need for two intermediate cross members. Instead, a single cross member of tubular type was welded to the frame's side members, some 3ft 7in from the attachment points of the front cross member. The latter was attached to the side members by four bolts each side. The complete front suspension and steering unit was supported by the cross member, with the transverse leaf spring inside the box section, like the Type 403 saloon.

As on the earlier models, rear suspension was by torsion bars, their anchorage points being attached to the centre cross member. The method of attachment was simplified, thus saving weight.

Body Building Methods

It must have been an unwelcome surprise for members of the old guard of Bristol owners to discover that the all-metal construction of the 401–403 cars had been discontinued, and that the main body framing of the 404 was a complete structure of steel, light alloy, and timber. This was built in three stages as follows:

1. Lightweight frames were welded to the main chassis frame, to support the scuttle structure. This consisted of a suitably braced bulkhead with twin side plates forming the inner panels for both the spare wheel and battery compartments.
2. A sub-frame, suitably braced by diagonal cross members, connected the horizontal members running forward from the scuttle. These were fastened to the light alloy wing valances, which in turn held the supports for the aluminium body panels.
3. The two front side panels and the body panels were then welded up to form a complete unit, before being attached to the framework. The body panels were hinged, to provide stowage space for the spare wheel (nearside), and battery and other electrical items (offside).

The rear wheel arches also gave support for the main body structure, being riveted to form a light yet solid construction. The rear body panels depended on light alloy girders attached to the inside of each wheel arch.

To save weight, the floor section of the tail was composed of a honeycomb paper core, faced with plywood with a thin lower panel of metal. The result

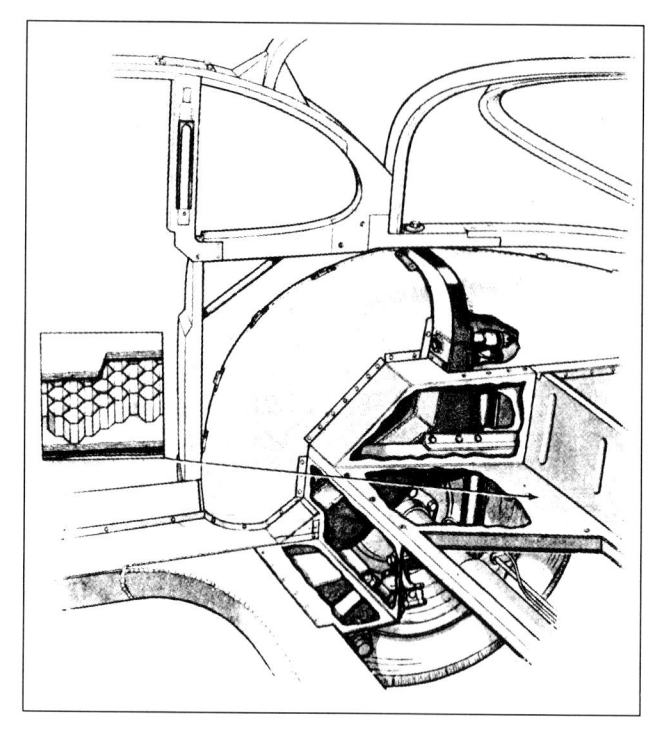

Showing composite use of steel, alloy and wood in 404 body frame.

Showing short chassis frame used on the 404 coupe.

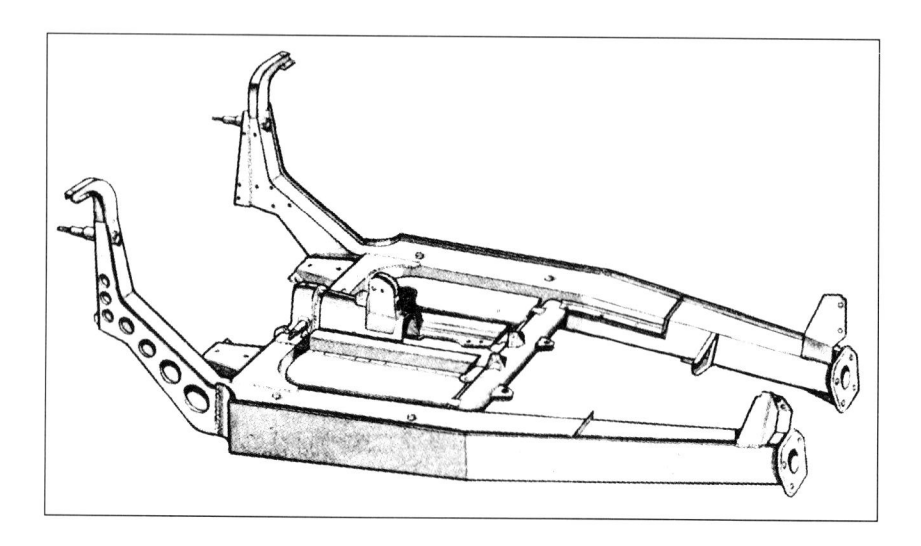

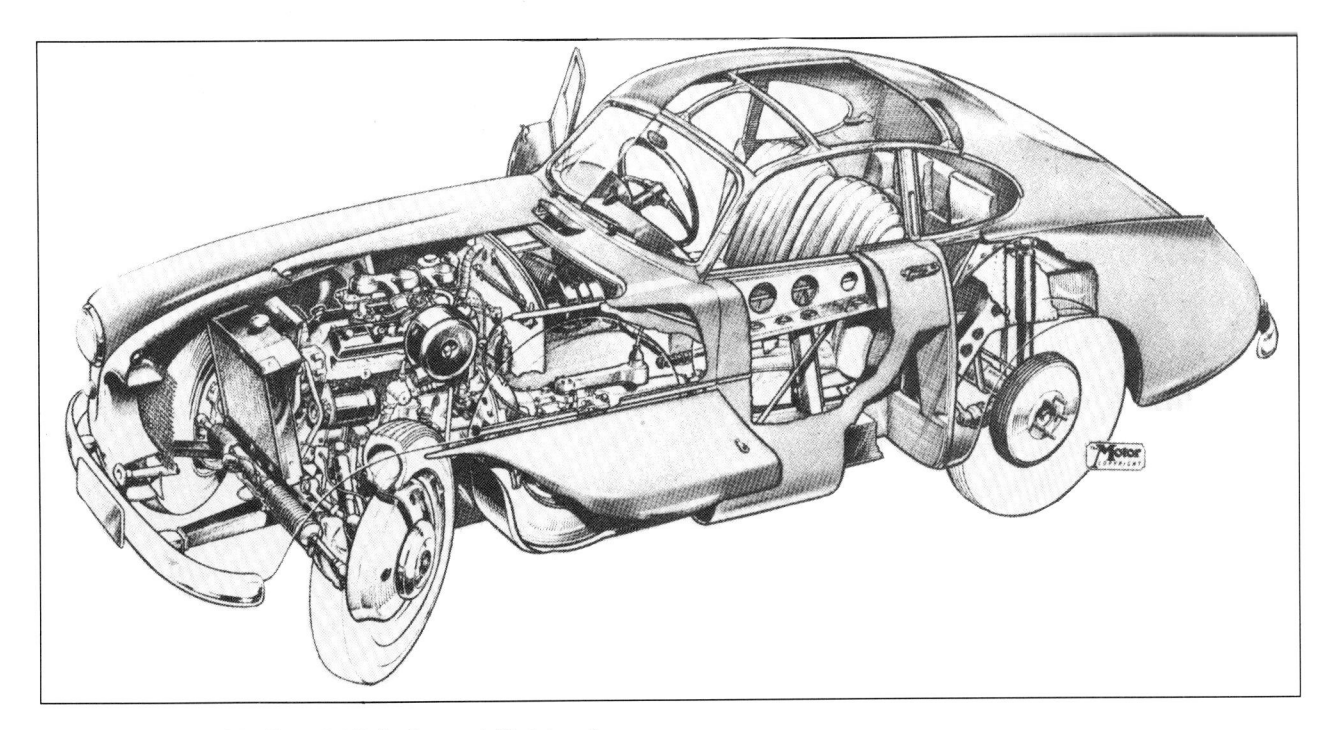

Cutaway drawing of the Type 404 Bristol; note drilled door frame.

was much stronger than one might have expected, and the main body panels were protected by a quickly detachable stoneguard.

In the workshop manual, the upper body structure is referred to as a 'canopy' – a good description for a very complex design. The timber used was principally ash, the whole framework being built as a unit, and attached to the main body frame via sockets at both ends of the door apertures. The outer faces were then covered with felt, prior to the attachment of the alloy body panels.

Internal Details

The interior of the car was fully trimmed, and a comprehensive display of instruments was housed in an oval pod or console just ahead of where the steering column would be located. The scuttle was extended rearwards, to prevent windscreen reflection at night from the illuminated instruments. For safety, the scuttle top was well padded, and there was a foam rubber crash pad on the passenger's side.

The 404's driving compartment. The instruments are all grouped in a cowled panel in front of the driver. There is a grab handle on the passenger's side, and hand brake and new remote gear lever are conveniently placed.

On a Type 403 Bristol Saloon. The steering column was adjustable. Note the needle of the speedometer is on the 100mph mark.

The front seats were upholstered in fine leather over Dunlopillo, fully to usual Bristol standards, but the two little jump-seats in the rear compartment were poorly padded, and more akin to stools of repentance than adult seating for more than a very short journey.

Access to the tail could only be gained by using the hinged squab, so that all luggage had to be stowed by going via the car's interior. In practice, this was far from easy for anything more substantial than a overnight bag.

So far as I am aware, the only 404 that possessed an opening boot lid belonged to J W E Banks, whose experiments with a 401 while competing in major sporting events had helped to improve its road holding. He insisted that his 404 should have a boot lid similar to those fitted as standard on the Type 405 saloons and dropheads. This entailed modifying the filler cap arrangements.

As mentioned above, the filler cap of the 404 was normally located on the exterior (centre) of the tail. To gain access to the cap, a control had to be operated just aft of the pull-up handbrake lever. A spring-loaded panel then clicked up, and refuelling could begin.

The trafficators were of semaphore type, housed in the slim panels between the wide doors and the side windows. The Bristol roundels on nave plates, bonnet and boot were in red, as on the 403 all the other 2-litre models used yellow.

The stowage of spare wheel and electrics under wing flaps is a feature that has continued to be used up to the latest Brigand and Britannia models. Not only does this result in a large uncluttered boot, but in the case of a puncture the wheel can be changed without moving the luggage. On the offside, there is a good airflow that appears beneficial to the battery and to the other electrical items housed there, while weight distribution is much improved.

Though the estimated number of 404s made is only fifty-one, there were no less than three different methods used to secure the wing flaps. On very early examples this was accomplished by means of a cable release from within the car, on intermediate cars it was by a square section carriage key, while the rest relied on up-and-over toggles which were quite effective, but collected dirt.

Each 404 was equipped with a substantial detachable tool box, with separate shaped sections for each item. The bonnet was opened by cable release, the knob being set in the centre of the lower dashboard. Under its protective flap, the fuel cap was of the quick-release type, not unlike those used on the drophead version of the 405.

Close-up nearside of Type 404 Bristol. Note the semaphore type trafficator inset into door pillar, also the 'ordinary' door handle. The sprung steering wheel and door mirror are non-standard. On right, note telescopic bonnet stay, and 'pancake' air filters below.

Front view of a Type 404 Bristol. Note the 'flamethrower' road lamp in air intake; also auxiliary lights inset into apron and the direction indicator lights. On the early examples there were semaphore type trafficators, inset into the door pillars.

Gearbox and Engine Details

The 404 Bristol used the BW.CR/7 gearbox, and some critics felt it might be overstressed by the power of the new engines that could be fitted to the little car. No trouble was experienced, however, possibly because so few owners chose the more powerful 100C unit.

For most Bristol enthusiasts, the most obvious, and enviable, feature of the gearbox was the very neat remote control. Gone was the wand-like lever, know affectionately as the 'porridge stirrer', used on the earlier models. Now there was a black metal extension, attached to the top of the gearbox, and teminating in a small chromed lever with a soft rubber knob. It was located, as the old motoring manuals would have put it, 'easy to the hand', and the selectors worked so smoothly that it could be moved from one gear to another, just using the thumb and a finger.

Needless to say, many owners of earlier Bristols approached the Spares Manager at Filton to ask whether they could fit a similar remote control to their own boxes. The answer was yes, though I found, when I had such a conversion on my early Type 401, that some selector adjustment was necessary, before the desired action (likened by one satisfied user to pushing a warm knife through a slab of butter) was achieved.

As mentioned above, potential purchasers of a 404 could choose between two new engines. For those who just wanted a good reliable prime-mover, the obvious choice would have been the 100B, with a power output of 105bhp @ 5,000rpm. For the few more interested in motor sport, the 100C would probably have had more appeal, as a very healthy 125bhp @ 5,500rpm was extracted from the 1,971cc straight-six cylinder engine.

Both units shared a compression ratio of 8.5:1 and an exhaust system quite different from that of earlier Bristols. The latter had used twin three-port exhaust manifolds, feeding into two pipes of modest dimensions. By contrast, the new engines had single six-port manifolds, with a pipe of big-bore dimensions. This change may have been due to the lessons Filton had learned in developing the BS series of racing engines, and it is significant that the Type 450 Bristols that competed in the Le Mans Twenty-Four Hour and Reims Twelve Hour races in 1954 used similar manifolds.

Three-quarter front view of Type 404 Bristol. Note plated orifice for starting handle above bumper, 'flame thrower' road light inset into air inlet, and auxiliary lamps inset into apron.

THE ALMOST CAR

Racing at Goodwood in 1954. The registration number 'MPH 100' suggests that the car may have been driven by Mr Anthony Crook.

Though the 404 did not have the sporting successes of the earlier models, here is a rare shot of a 404 competing at a Sprint Meeting held at Curborough in April 1977. No nave plates.

The increased power of both the 100B and 100C engines was in part due to the better-quality fuels that were now available, increasing the compression ratio to 8.5:1. But in the case of the 100C unit most of the credit is usually given to the camshaft.

Of much more sporting type, it gave valve timings of 40:80:80:40. A viscous damper was fitted to the crankshaft, and the valve springs were packed to ensure that valve bounce occurred at similar engine speeds. The combustion chambers were polished, and each engine was very carefully assembled. Why so few owners chose them is not known, but one reason may have been a fear that so highly tuned a unit might be intractable at low speeds, and that much more gear changing would be necessary.

On my Type 405 drophead, the engine was to full 100C specification, and I found it quite flexible, though it was better to change down a gear as soon as the road speed began to fall on a steep incline.

Much thought had obviously been lavished on the braking system. The dimensions of the front drums had been increased to 12in, with a width, (also increased), of 2¼in. Special Alfin drums were fitted, of bell shape, to dissipate as much heat as soon as possible under heavy braking.

By contrast, ordinary cast iron drums were used on the rear brakes, the dimension being 11in diameter and 1¾in in width.

Early Type 404 cars (up to chassis No. 2028) were fitted with a twin master cylinder system, a feature discontinued on the later examples. While it was probably true that a vehicle weighing just 2,290lb (compared with the 2,788lb of the 403) needed only one master cylinder, for safety reasons the original system would have seemed preferable.

Non-Bristol Bodywork

So far as I am aware, the only 404 with a non-Bristol body was the drophead example by Abbotts of Farnham. For a while it was owned by a member of the Bristol Owners' Club, and I was able to test it very briefly. With the hood lowered, it was a most delightful little car, but with it erected the interior soon got hot and rather stuffy.

A three-quarter front/side view of the only Type 404 Bristol with drophead body by Abbotts of Farnham. Its lines are very smooth and pleasing, but the Vee screen gives it a dated air.

The general performance and road holding were good, though to check its performance I would have preferred the opportunity of a much longer test period. I felt it a pity that the coachbuilders had fitted a twin-paned windscreen as it rather dated the car. Though a little better than the spartan rear seats of the standard 404, space was still limited, and a smaller boot might have been wiser. On so short a wheelbase, adequate accommodation for four adults was probably impossible.

Personal Experience

I was able to borrow a late model 404 for long enough to assess its good and less good features.

To me, the lack of an opening boot was very poor design, but the strength of my opinion may have been due to the struggle I had to persuade a large suitcase through the nearside door, over the front seats, and past the hinged-down rear squab. This was bad enough, but when I had to extract the thing, in pouring rain, it was far worse.

The other feature I disliked was the rear 'seating'. I put the word in quotation marks, because really those two thinly padded benches were far too small and uncomfortable for adults, on anything but a very

Front view of Type 404 Bristol, with bonnet raised. Note road lamp in air intake; this was an 'extra' on early examples, but a standard fitment on later cars; also fog/spot lights inset into apron.

brief trip. I realised this when I collected two boys from school, prior to their summer vacations. They were hefty fellows, and from their squirmings, and occasional grunts it was obvious that they did not enjoy the experience.

Generally speaking, the car's road manners were far better than I had expected. There was a hint of vagueness at high speeds on a straight, well surfaced road, and a slight choppiness on a poorer surface. I have to admit I was probably affected subconsciously by memories of two other short-chassis cars, both of which had overturned on top of me. They were Ulster Tourist Trophy Austins, and on a road that was less than smooth speeds much above 65mph could pose problems.

For the rest, I found the car snug and comfortable;

Three-quarter rear view of a Type 404 Bristol. Note the flap over the fuel cap just above badge on tail. Next to it (left) is a late Type 403 Bristol saloon.

the brakes were good, even though I would have preferred the twin master cylinders of the first series cars. The engine, a 100B, started at first press, and even on a very hot day showed no signs of temperament or overheating. The fuel consumption averaged about 23mpg, including some fast journeys as well as suburban motoring. The official range was 20–25mpg.

At night, on long solo drives, it was very comfortable, the heater worked, and so did the radio, which was an extra. The big road light, standard on the later cars, was very helpful, and though placed in the centre of the air intake it did not seem to affect the cooling.

To sum up, I was favourably impressed, but at an original price in Britain of £3,542 15s 10d (inclusive of Purchase Tax) I felt it over-priced.

Why So Few?

In the period late 1953–1955, the estimated production of the 404 was only fifty-one, the second smallest of all the 2-litre Bristols. Why this should have been is a difficult question to answer. I once posed the same query to Michael Arnolt, whose father had had so much success with the Arnolt-Bristol. He thought for a moment, and then replied, 'I guess that little puddle-jumper was way ahead of its market.'

I think that probably is the answer, rather than the usual moans about its price or the alleged shortcomings of its 8ft ¼in wheelbase. In 1953, Britain's economy was just beginning to revive, and I think that had the car been launched just a little later – in the 'You've never had it so good' era – it might have

On the right is a three-quarter side/front view of a Type 405 saloon Bristol and on the left a Type 404 coupe Bristol. From scuttle forward, they are almost identical, though the 404 is shorter.

had the success it deserved. Using the 100C engine, some examples might have continued the sporting tradition of the earlier Bristols. For me, the game little 404 will remain 'the almost car' that promised so much, yet failed to make the grade.

Of course, since it was built in tandem with the far more popular 403, perhaps the production facilities at Filton were really insufficient for two such different designs. I still feel, however, that it could have had a future, if the timing had been more fortunate.

Considering how few were made, there were an astonishingly large number of reports in the motoring journals, most of them extremely favourable to the 404. Of them all, I feel the following quotation sums up the little car very well indeed. It is by John Bolster, and he said:

> 'The Bristol is an expensive car, but it gives that indefinable feeling of quality that only big money can buy. The upholstery and interior trim, the walnut dashboard with its array of accurate instruments, the excellent finish of every little detail – all these things make this vehicle worth its price to the man who must have the best. I am sure that with the competition camshaft fitted, this car would be in that very select band of machines that can exceed a timed 120mph. For a long fast journey à deux, the 404 is a magic carpet indeed!'

Hints for the Intending Purchaser

The last 404 was built in 1955, and it would be interesting to know how many still survive. A comparatively large number were exported, and others must have been destroyed in accidents, or through neglect. Recently I heard of one in the Midlands and went to see it. It was out in a field, with neither engine nor gearbox, with one door rotting on the ground, and the rear frame and body sections rusted completely through. I spent some time examining the poor thing; even the chassis was past salvaging, and all the trim was missing together with the lamps and instruments. It was a wasted journey, but what really saddened me was that such a lovely little car should have come to such an untimely end.

I mention this incident because so often I have people writing to me asking if I can help them find a 404 'in any condition whatsoever'. Few seem to realise the tremendous cost of restoring a vehicle these days, even one still with its engine and transmission, and in far better condition than the one I have described.

In many cases, I feel it might be wiser to set your sights rather lower, and settle for an earlier model, a Type 401 perhaps. It may lack the glamour of a 404, but it will provide you with excellent motoring, and still not cost the earth. Hurry though, for Bristol prices are rising fast.

To those for whom it is a '404 or nothing', I would just say: please remember the advice given in earlier chapters, and also be prepared to pay a very large sum indeed for any 404 that is in a reasonable condition.

Remember too, that there is quite a lot of timber in the bodywork, so that any smell resembling pear drops is a warning that wood rot is present. Danger areas are around the windscreen and rear screen, and where the timber canopy meets the metal bodywork at the rear.

Finding such a car is largely a matter of luck, though, obviously, having plenty of friendly contacts can be of immense assistance. So I will end this chapter with good wishes that you may succeed, but at the same time I must tell you that I doubt your chances are very bright.

12

An American's Dream

The Arnolt-Bristol

Had Jack Channer not designed the little 'Bomb', it seems unlikely that there would ever have been an Arnolt-Bristol. The story of the latter is an odd one, for it is centred on one man, Stanley Harold Arnolt.

A big, powerfully built man, usually wearing a ten gallon hat and cowboy boots, he might have been a Texas cattle baron or an oil man from Oklahoma. In fact he came from the Middle West, and was a very shrewd businessman. It was typical of his personality that he liked his nickname of 'Wacky' (a word that might be taken as meaning foolish or irresponsible), precisely the opposite of his own far-seeing and deliberate approach to life.

Leaving Wisconsin University at the height (or depth) of the Great Depression, he gained practical experience to augment his engineering degree, and obtained the rights to a small marine engine. Soon after the Second World War began, he realised that America was bound to be drawn into the conflict, and that there would be a demand for the sort of small general-purpose craft for which his engine was ideal. Packing a bag, he visited Washington, returning with a large contract to supply them to the United States Navy.

By the end of the war, Arnolt had become a successful industrialist, and in a very short period built up a commercial empire that included such seemingly disparate elements as tubular furniture, car accessories, a Mexican coconut plantation, newspapers, boat building, and car distribution.

During a visit to Italy in 1952 Arnolt met Nuccio Bertone, head of the Italian coachbuilders, Carrozzeria Bertone of Turin. After seeing the near-empty works, he realised that orders and finance were lacking, and after driving a very hard bargain, emerged as Vice-President.

Cars were both a business and a hobby to Arnolt, and after buying a small MG in 1949 he had established himself as an importer of European models, with premises in East Street, Chicago, as S H Arnolt Incorporated.

Though he sold 'prestige' makes, such as Aston Martin and Bentley, he did not neglect the humbler end of the market, and was especially proud of having secured a bank loan (allegedly unsecured) for $1,000,000, with which he purchased 1,000 Morris Minors, the biggest overseas order ever secured by the British Motor Corporation. Not long afterwards, he became the latter's distributor for the whole of the American north-west.

It was typical of his logical yet opportunist methods that he arranged for Bertone bodies to be fitted to the chassis of MG Midgets, for sale in America as 'Arnolt-MGs'. Both sedan (closed) and convertible models were made, a hundred each, and, by very efficient costing, they sold for only $2,995 f.o.b. Chicago. This was far lower than for any other imported car with Italian coachwork, and they found a ready market.

The Watt Meeting

Arnolt hankered after a 'real' car bearing his name, and the possibility of realising this dream came in April 1953. While visiting the International Motor

Show, held that year in New York, at the Grand Central Palace, he met James Watt, the sales manager of the Bristol Aeroplane Company. The Englishman was not sanguine of being able to sell a new short-chassis model, the 404, which was to be launched in the autumn. At an American price of $6,750, he considered it far too expensive.

The possibility of equipping the Bristol short chassis with a suitable engine and a Bertone body was mentioned during discussions with Arnolt. He warmed to the idea, and even spoke of an initial order of 250 units, which served as a basis for tentative agreement. As usual, Arnolt drove a hard bargain, insisting that the price per completed car should not exceed $4,500.

According to an account that appeared in *Motor* magazine, in its 3 February 1954 issue, Watt lacked the authority to enter into such a contract, but regardless of whether or not this was so, his action seems to have been approved. He was authorised to visit the Bertone works and to commence the preliminary negotiations.

Arnolt was already in Turin when Watt arrived on 27 April, and the two men, plus the local directors, studied the chassis drawings brought by Watt, and discussed the conditions on which the project would be based. There would be a weight limit for the body of 450lb, it should be of open sports/racing type, and there should be two doors. Only the bonnet and boot lid would be of alloy; the rest of the bodywork would be of steel. It has been suggested that this was because the American panel beaters, who might have to effect repairs, were more accustomed to working in steel. Another reason may have been the need to give a very firm line to the high-peaked front wings. Before Watt left for home, agreement was reached, so that the Bertone designers might commence work.

Matters were now moving fast, and on 11 May 1953 a meeting was held at Filton at which Arnolt scaled down his original estimate to just 142 chassis-engine units. They would be packed three to a wagon, and legal possession would be taken on Arnolt's behalf, at the rail-siding adjacent to the Bristol factory. The units would go across the Channel by rail ferry, and, after the Bertone bodies were fitted at Turin, would be shipped to Chicago for sale. Agreement was reached on all points of substance, both parties appeared well satisfied, and a formal contract was signed.

Arnolt had realised his dream of marketing his own make of car, while at Filton the opportunity was taken, as Jack Channer put it, 'to use up the surplus 11 inch brake drums and "A" links, etc, on these chassis, in readiness for the 406 change'.

Prototypes

The momentum did not slacken after Arnolt's visit, and by the end of May 1953 the first prototype chassis was on its way to Italy, to return complete with stark 'Bolide' bodywork, ready for extensive road-testing. A month later, on 30 June 1953, a second prototype was despatched, to have a 'de luxe' body fitted.

It had been planned to exhibit the second proto-

MODEL: Arnolt-Bristol Bolide	
Date: 1953–1954	
Wheelbase	8ft 0.25in (2m 45cm)
Front Track	4ft 3.86in (1m 32cm)
Rear Track	4ft 6in (1m 37cm)
Overall Height	3ft 8in (1m 9cm)
Overall Width	5ft 8in (1m 70cm)
Overall Length	13ft 11in (4m 20cm)
Weight	1,988lb (902kg)
Engine Type	BS1/2
Number of Cylinders	6 in-line
Bore	66mm
Stroke	96mm
Capacity	1,971cc
Carburettors	3 single-throat Solex 32BI
Gearbox	Bristol 4-speed and reverse
Ratios	1st: 11.4 2nd: 7.12 3rd: 5.04 4th: 3.9 Reverse: 11.3
Brakes	Lockheed hydraulics
Suspension	
Front	Transverse spring and A-arms
Rear	Rigid axle longitudinal torsion bars

type on the Bristol stand at the 1953 Earls Court show. This was in the autumn, and the new car arrived at 6pm on the Press Day, having come direct from the Bertone works. There was barely time for a wash and polish.

In August 1953, a Bristol representative named John Geddes was sent to Turin, in case major alterations to the chassis might have been found necessary when the bodywork was fitted. Despite the speed with which the whole project had been accomplished, there was only a slight adjustment in the rake of the steering column, necessitated by the shallowness of the bodywork. It was also agreed that a locally made fuel tank should be used and that the headlights should be Italian. No major problems had been encountered, and series production could commence.

The Arnolt-Bristol's Appearance

The 'Bolide' and 'de luxe' models were basically similar, differing mainly in the equipment supplied. They were attractive, distinctive and sporting. Despite the height of the Bristol engine, an optical illusion was created by the manner in which the high-peaked front wings merged with the small square radiator cowl and were flanked by the inset headlights.

A wide and shallow duct set into the curved bonnet top directed air to the triple Solex carburettors, and the frontal aspect was very pleasing. This was especially so in the case of the 'de luxe' model with its divided bumper blades and full-width windscreen with wipers. There was a quickly detachable hood and side curtains too, making it a practical road car.

The 'Bolide' tended to be more of a fun car, without a hood and with only a low-set vestigial screen without wipers. Out on the West Coast, with its fine climate and excellent highways system, the little car sold well, and some still survive.

The coupe which completed the range was less of a sports car, with a well-proportioned hard top, and tall narrow ventilators set into the body sides. On at least one example the standard bolt-on wheels had not been used, and pierced discs with knock-on hubs were substituted.

Arnolt favoured lightness rather than a highly tuned engine, for giving *his* car a sporting performance. Yet despite his cost-cutting, the unit fitted was the BS1 Mark 2 and it proved to be fast and reliable, with a modest fuel consumption, making it ideal for long-distance events. Petrol of good quality was available in America, so that the compression ratio

A three-quarter front/side view of standard Arnolt-Bristol 'Bolide' sports/racer. Note narrow air duct in bonnet feeding air to the triple Solex carburettors.

View of a cockpit of Arnolt-Bristol. Note left-hand drive, with four-spoked spring steering wheel. The handbrake is between the seats. Note also door and grab handles.

A close-up view of the tail of an Arnolt-Bristol open two-seater. Note Arnolt logo on boot lid and deep-set rear lights; also push-button lid catch and twin exhaust pipes.

A front view of an Arnolt-Bristol. Note the very neat grille and inset headlights, simple bumper and bonnet air duct. The wing mirrors are non-standard.

Building the BS1 Mark 2 Engines Used on the Arnolt Bristols

I am indebted to R V Williams for the following details of engine construction. Williams was at Filton in 1953–1955 which coincided with the Bristol works racing team – he was also concerned with the building of the Type BSX units used in the cars that competed in 1954 at the Le Mans Twenty-Four Race and later at the Reims Twelve Hour Race.

Workshop foreman: Ted Conibere
Inspectors: Ron Lear, George Pruett, Jimmy Morris
Engine builders: Alfie Freke, Bill Rose, Fred Reid, Ray Williams (Specials were built by Bernard Tamplin, and customers included Horace Gould, a long-term Cooper-Bristol driver)

The BS1 Mark 2 engine

After building many Bristol engines to the 100A specification, Williams described the BS1 Mark 2 engine as being 'similar to the 100A, but it was rather lighter, and was fitted with a different camshaft'. This was the 'sports' camshaft giving valve timings of 40:80:80:40, the oil sump was lighter than the standard item, and he did not think the crankshaft was fitted with the big damper. This may have referred to the Girling viscous damper, used on the BS1 engines.

Cylinder heads were surfaced by hand on a large plate, and the ports were worked very carefully. The combustion chambers were also worked with great care, calibrated and gas-flowed. To reduce the reciprocating mass at high engine speeds, the rocker gear was lightened and balanced. This was accomplished first by grinding, and then by polishing to a high finish. The dimensions of the valves were larger than the standard items, and the valve seats were very carefully prepared, using an angle grinder. The result is described as 'a knife-edge seat which, in turn, improved the breathing'.

Crankshafts and connecting rods were received already shot-peened and polished, to reduce the danger of cracking through fatigue. Williams describes them as 'a joy to behold'. He adds that he believed the cranks had no bolt-on balance weights. All bores were measured very carefully, 'and A, B, C pistons were fitted accordingly'. Air filters were of the pancake type on the BS1 Mark 2 engines.

could be 9:1, and the camshaft gave valve timings of 40:80:80:40, to produce 130bhp @ 5,500rpm. A Vokes full-flow oil filter was fitted, yet the sump was of only 8½-pint capacity, possibly to keep the height of the engine as low as possible. So far as I am aware, no lubrication problems were encountered.

The gearbox was the BW.CR/5, as used on the standard Type 403 Bristol saloon. Despite the extra 30bhp of the Arnolt engine, the gearbox proved reliable, though the long whippy gear lever was sometimes criticised as not compatible with the car's racy appearance. Some members later fitted the remote 'shifter' standard on the 404–406 Bristols. Others made up their own alternatives with a ball joint, twin rods and a much shorter gear stick.

The Arnolt-Bristol weighed only 2,120lb with full fuel tank, compared with the 2,290lb of a 404 with

Details of Engines Built for Arnolt-Bristols by R V Williams

Engine No.	Chassis No.	Model	Its Ultimate Fate
BS1 Mark 2/202	404–X/3001	De Luxe	Unknown
204	3002	Bolide	Unknown
205	3004	De Luxe	Retired
208	3003	Bolide	Unknown
213	3017	Bolide	Unknown
214	3012	Bolide	Still roadworthy – now located in Connecticut, USA
215	3016	Bolide	Unknown
217	3013	Bolide	Still roadworthy – now located in California, USA
220	3015	Bolide	Unknown
221	3019	Bolide	Still roadworthy – now located in Maryland, USA
206	3005	Bolide	Still roadworthy – now located in Texas, USA
209	3009	Bolide	Retired

It is good to know that a few of these carefully assembled engines are still in Arnolt-Bristols cherished by their owners. The Bolide was the very Spartan sports/racer model, the De Luxe being rather more civilised, with hood and full-width windscreen.

A side view of an Arnolt-Bristol with hood erected. Note the knock-on road wheels.

A three-quarter side/front view of an Arnolt-Bristol with hood 'up'. Note the footwell ventilator, tiny headlamps (non-standard), and wide door.

only five gallons aboard. It was anticipated that the 11in brake drums fitted to the Arnolt would be adequate. Under racing conditions, however, fading problems were to be encountered.

When the three-model range of Arnolt-Bristols first became available, 'f.o.b. Chicago', the basic 'Bolide' cost $3,995; a 'de luxe' was $4,645; and a coupe was $6,390. Prices rose in 1956 to $4,250 and $4,995 for 'Bolide' and 'de luxe' respectively. No new price was shown for the coupe, but, as only three were said to be made, possibly all had already been sold. Recently there has been news of a possible fourth coupe, but this has yet to be confirmed.

The first standard models arrived in Chicago in March 1954, and despite a warehouse fire destroying twelve cars, sales were very promising. At the end of the racing season, the 'E-modified championship' of the Sports Car Club of America was shared between an Arnolt-Bristol driven by an aptly-named Fred Wacker and a Frazer Nash driven by Ted Boynton, also with a Bristol engine.

Despite a complete lack of racing experience,

A close-up view of front of an Arnolt-Bristol. Note the twin headlights and small spot lights, also inset direction indicators. The high peaked wings are of steel.

Tail view of an Arnolt-Bristol, with hood erected. Note large rear window, up-and-over catch for boot lid, and inset rear lights.

A fine three-quarter front/side view of a de luxe model Arnolt-Bristol. Note the split bumper, high peaked (steel) wings, Arnolt badge, neat grille and headlights; also 'buried' trafficators.

A three-quarter side/front view of the very rare Arnolt-Bristol fixed head coupe. Note the special knock-on perforated disc wheels and 'pop up' headlights. Also the footwell ventilator. The three examples made are all still roadworthy.

Arnolt not only entered a team of three 'Bolides' for the 1955 Sebring Twelve Hour Race, but insisted on being one of the drivers. Arnolt's faith in his cars was fully justified, with a first, second and fourth in the class for production cars with engines not exceeding 2 litres capacity.

Arnolt, who had shared a car with a very fast driver from Chicago, named Bob Goldich, finished in second place. The team lost time fitting fresh brake shoes, but 'fade' continued to be the Arnolt's one weakness.

The Sebring Twelve Hour Race of 1955

The Sebring Circuit is situated in mid-Florida and has a lap distance of approximately 4.85 miles. As its name suggests, the race was for a period of twelve hours, starting at 10am, so that the last five hours would be run in darkness. The circuit was flat, but had an acute bend just before entering the main straight, a feature that tested the brakes. The surface was quite abrasive and several tyre changes were necessary, unless the driver had a very smooth style.

Entries were of very high quality, including such drivers as Carol Shelby, Phil Hill and Phil Walters of America, the Franco-American Harry Schell, Pietro Taruffi of Italy, and Mike Hawthorn, Stirling Moss and Lance Macklin, of the United Kingdom. The cars matched the high quality of the drivers and included Allard, Arnolt-Bristol, Austin-Healey, Ferrari, Jaguar, Kurtis-Lincoln, Maserati, Morgan, Mercedes-Benz, O.S.C.A., M.G., and Porsche.

In most respects the race was run on lines similar to those used in the Le Mans Twenty-Four Hour Race. Two drivers were accredited to each car, driving alternately, and they were also responsible for any repairs or adjustments during the race. A third person could assist them for refuelling only, and all spares, tyres, petrol and oil were held in the replenishment pit of each car.

Stanley Harold Arnolt had entered three Arnolt-Bristol 'Bolides', specially prepared and tuned by the mechanics at his headquarters at Warsaw, Indiana.

The team manager was Walter Inai, the chief mechanic being Juan Lopez. The team livery was a pure white body, with dark blue stripes extending from bonnet to boot. In addition to the standard headlights, there were also two Lucas road lights set low in the nose of each car.

The Arnolt Drivers

To captain the team, Arnolt had persuaded Rene Dreyfus to forsake his famous New York restaurant, and return to motor racing after a very long absence. Dreyfus had been France's champion Grand Prix driver in 1939, and much valuable publicity resulted from his selection.

The six-man team was composed of the following:
Car No. 58 – Rene Dreyfus with Bob Grier
Car No. 59 – 'Wacky' Arnolt with Bob Goldich
Car No. 60 – John Panks with Ernie Erickson
A fourth Arnolt, Car No. 54 – had been entered privately by John Norwood.

As at Le Mans, the drivers, at a given signal, sprinted to their cars, started their engines, and moved out onto the circuit. There was a total of sixty-five cars, each with a second driver to take over later.

A blistering pace was set, and retirements were numerous. However, the Arnolt-Bristols circulated without incident, though tyres were changed as the abrasive surface wore them, and brakes were found to be subject to fade, when used under racing conditions.

The three cars kept to a top speed in the region of 113mph, and Panks's car was timed at 116mph along a special flying kilometre strip. Brakes shoes had to be changed, as well as tyres, slowing the cars considerably. When the race ended at 10pm, the winners were Mike Hawthorn and Phil Walters in a Jaguar entered by Briggs Cunningham, the runners-up were Phil Hill and Carol Shelby, sharing a Ferrari, third place going to a Maserati driven by the Spear and Johnston duo.

In the class for production cars with engines not exceeding 2-litre capacity, the Arnolt driven by Panks and Erickson was the winner. Arnolt must

A view of the showroom at Warsaw, Indiana, of S H Arnolt Inc. In the background (left), one of the works team of long-distance racers can be seen, and in the centre is a chassis and engine. The nose of another team car can just be seen on right.

have been delighted with his second place in the car he shared with Bob Goldich, while Rene Dreyfus, with Bob Grier as his co-driver, was fourth. The privately entered Arnolt of John Norwood, also finished.

Despite maintaining speeds of about 113mph for twelve hours, the average fuel consumption of the three Bristol engines was only 21.6mpg. It was modest thirst, coupled with utter reliability, that made the Arnolts so successful in long-distance events.

As Arnolt once remarked, 'The longer the race, the better we like it'.

The First Season

After such an encouraging beginning, the rest of the year was something of an anti-climax. However, some success was achieved in minor events, mostly in the vicinity of Warsaw, Indiana, where Arnolt's original marine engine plant had been established, and which now served as his racing headquarters.

He did not begrudge the large amount his team was costing, but went racing in the grand manner, with his cars immaculate in their white and blue livery. So impressive was their whole presentation that they might have been competing in a major Grand Prix, rather than the small-capacity production class in which they were actually entered.

It must have been some consolation when two of the team finished in second and third places at the 1956 Sebring Twelve Hour Race, though Arnolt, who again shared a car with Bob Goldich, had been forced to retire with damaged steering after a slight accident.

For the 1957 Sebring Twelve Hour Race a full

works team was entered, but little attempt appears to have been made to solve the braking problems.

Once again Arnolt's co-driver was Bob Goldich, and when he was about to take over for his stint at the wheel Arnolt warned him that the brakes were grabbing to one side. The driver from Chicago was the fastest driver in the team, and knew he would have to make up some of the distance lost by Arnolt. He set off at a blistering pace. No-one appears to know exactly the subsequent sequence of events. He may have been blinded by the low rays of the setting sun, or he may have underestimated his speed as he approached an acute bend. Whatever the reason, he applied his brakes hard, the car swerved to one side and overturned.

Without an anti-roll bar or even a safety harness, Goldich was dead before the car could be removed. The race was not stopped, and an Arnolt driven by Durbin and Cook finished fourth in its class. It would seem doubtful that this was of much consolation to Arnolt himself, who was well aware that had he driven for one more lap the accident might have happened to himself.

The Last Season

It was not until 1960 that another Arnolt works team competed at Sebring. It consisted of one 'Bolide' and two cars with special alloy bodies and long-distance fuel tanks. One of these, shared by Max Goldman and Ralph Durbin, won its class, and, with the others in fourth and sixth places, they gained the team prize. By now, all the 142 standard cars had been received from the Bertone factory, and most had been sold.

Though no fresh orders were placed, there remained an excellent spares and service depot at Warsaw, Indiana. Arnolt's seeming loss of interest in his racing team has been ascribed to several causes. Perhaps there had been some delayed reaction from his narrow escape at Sebring; possibly the enormous costs were becoming too much; or it may simply have been that, having accomplished all his objectives, motor racing had lost its savour.

After all these years, I doubt we shall ever be certain, for in Chicago, on Christmas Eve 1963, Arnolt died. He does not appear to have trained a successor, probably thinking there was plenty of time. Lacking his leadership, his empire soon began to crumble, and less than a decade later all that remained was the single factory in Warsaw, Indiana, where his career had begun in 1939.

The Arnolt-Bristol Registry

It says much for the personality of the little British-Italian-American sports car that some thirty-five years after the last Arnolt left the Bertone works there is still a flourishing club called the Arnolt-Bristol Registry, devoted to the twin purposes of keeping as many cars on the road as possible and having a little organised motor sport too.

The Registry is fortunate in having Lee Raskin as its Editor and 'spark plug', ready to devote much of his scanty free time to keeping the membership informed of events, and, of course, to editing the magazine. Close contact is maintained with the Bristol Owners' Club, and when in 1987 Lee visited England the Club's Oxford Group did its best to make him feel welcome.

A Registry event that attracted plenty of support was the visit to Sebring, to celebrate the thirtieth anniversary of that splendid first appearance of the works team back in 1955, when first, second and fourth places were secured in class. What is sometimes forgotten is the very long period when the little cars remained competitive, after all works support had ceased.

Well into the 1960s successes were still being gained, from engines that, on paper, were now outclassed by more modern machinery. A first, third and sixth in class were secured at Sebring, and also the team award. At the Bridgehampton circuit on Long Island, New York, an Arnolt won its class, and there were other victories at Corpus Christi, Louisville and Waterford, as well as in Canada.

In the United States, as in Britain, motor sport enthusiasts now organise events enabling cars built in the so-called post-war Golden Age to become competitive again. The movement has gained sufficient

An Analysis of Arnolt-Bristol Owners – 1986

A The United States	Coupe	De Luxe	Bolide	Total
California	2	6	6	14
New York	1	1	4	6
Florida	–	1	4	5
Indiana	–	3	2	5
Massachusetts	–	–	4	4
Illinois	–	1	2	3
Maryland	–	2	1	3
Wisconsin	–	1	2	3
Colorado	–	1	1	2
Connecticut	–	1	1	2
Maine	–	1	1	2
Oregon	–	1	1	2
Vermont	–	1	1	2
Delaware	–	–	1	1
Iowa	–	–	1	1
Kentucky	–	–	1	1
Missouri	–	1	–	1
North Carolina	–	1	–	1
Ohio	–	1	–	1
South Carolina	–	–	1	1
Tennessee	–	–	1	1
Texas	–	–	1	1
Virginia	–	–	1	1
Washington State	–	–	1	1
Sub-totals	3	23	38	64

B Outside USA	Coupe	De Luxe	Bolide	Total
United Kingdom		1	2	3
Europe		2	–	2
Switzerland		1	1	2
Canada		–	1	1
France		–	1	1
Sub-totals		4	5	9

C Miscellaneous	Coupe	De Luxe	Bolide	Total
Destroyed		–	1	1
Lost in Chicago Fire		7	3	10
Fate unknown		21	33	54
Wrecked		2	2	4
Sub-totals		30	39	69

Summary

Sub-total	Coupe	De Luxe	Bolide	Total
A	3	23	38	64
B	–	4	5	9
C	–	30	39	69
	3	57	82	142

Notes:
1. In fact there were twelve Arnolt-Bristols involved in the Chicago Fire, but two, a coupe and a de luxe model, were subsequently rebuilt.
2. In a letter to the Editor of the Arnolt-Bristol Registry in 1986, John Panks (who won his class in the 1955 Sebring Twelve Hour race) reported seeing an Arnolt-Bristol Bolide when visiting Queensland, Australia. He was informed by a mechanic carrying out an oil change that the car had been brought from the United Kingdom, by an immigrant. The man added that:
  a) The mileage was 85,000 miles.
  b) The car received minimum attention, but remained sound.
  c) The owner 'drives it like hell'.

This analysis is based on data provided by Mr Lee Raskin, the Editor of the Arnolt-Bristol Registry magazine, and I would like to thank him for his assistance.

support to boast its own organising body: the Vintage Sports Car Club of America, which runs a full calendar of meetings and events.

This has enabled owners of Arnolt-Bristols to go racing again, and, judging by the information contained in the Registry magazine, full advantage is being taken of this opportunity. Such events have included Summit Point, West Virginia, where that great Arnolt-Bristol enthusiast, John Schieffelin, gained a good second place behind a Ferrari. In the 1983 season, he competed in three other vintage events, his only maintenance being one change of lubricating oil, plus a thorough engine check by his mechanic, Mike DiCola.

Some 3,000 miles to the west, the Monterey Historic Automobile Races took place, with three more Arnolt-Bristol owners enjoying some healthy competition, as they had done at another Western event in Laguna Seca. The 1982 race had been won by an Arnolt-Bristol, driven by Bill Watkins.

The little cars have proved to be great survivors, probably because of their simple construction that makes routine maintenance such an easy and straightforward matter. Many of the cars have had the advantage of having spent most of their lives in a dry climate, and others have been thoroughly restored by their enthusiastic owners.

I was looking through a list of some seventy Arnolt-Bristol owners, and marvelled at the variety of modifications they had made. Few were in any way revolutionary, the most major being the introduction of a bigger engine – Chevrolet, Ford or Pontiac, or else a Bristol engine of another type, such as the 100D2 that was standard on the AC 'Ace' sports two-seater.

Naturally brakes have received attention, some owners fitting disc-type replacements, some preferring the Alfin bonded alloy/iron drums, while others have changed from the standard wheels to the wire variety, to promote more effective cooling.

Anti-roll or anti-sway bars have been fitted to some cars; different types of headlamps, too; the basic 'Bolide' has been given a hood and side curtains; and the remote 'shifter' is quite common. Oil coolers appear to be unusual, and in only one case have I noticed the fitting of a ski rack. Not one of these cars is less than thirty-five years old, yet they still generate enough enthusiasim for owners to spend time, effort and money in keeping them roadworthy, and in some cases competitive too.

13

How the 2-litre Bristols Were Made

I have often noticed the surprise, sometimes tinged with disbelief, when I explain to people that in the past forty years the average weekly production of Bristol cars has rarely exceeded three. This is easily the smallest of any recognised British manufacturer. The philosophy of the Company was described by *The Autocar*, in its issue of 7 December 1951, as 'one of idealism tempered with a shrewd appreciation of what is practical'.

In an attempt to reconcile such seeming contradictions, I shall try to describe the various procedures used at the Filton factory, in the construction of a Type 405 Bristol saloon. This very popular model was in series production from 1954 until 1958, during which time it has been estimated that 297 saloons were made, plus another forty-three chassis with convertible bodies by Abbotts of Farnham. I will concentrate on the closed version, commencing with the manner in which the chassis frame and the body components were assembled.

Structure

The chassis frame was light yet strong, and was formed of box section members braced by cross-members and a steel floor. In the early assembly stage, the boot section was attached as a composite structure, using both steel and aluminium. Next came the shaped steel tubing, to be welded to the chassis as the basis for the body. And then the laminated wood framing was added for the upper part of the bodywork.

To ensure absolute accuracy in assembly, each component had its own jig, with a complex master-jig to be used as they were attached to one another. This was quite normal in aircraft production, but was most unusual in the British motor industry. Jigs were also employed in the production of the four doors, which were made of both steel and alloy.

The exterior of the body was composed of light alloy panels, with two separate jigs for the front and rear sections; the latter being fitted together at the foot of each windscreen pillar. In service this is a vulnerable point, and some slight flexing is essential, if cracking is to be avoided. It was accomplished by means of an unfastened lap joint, which is both simple and effective. The gauge of the alloy varied with the stress to which it would be subjected.

With the hanging of the doors, the car's main structure was complete, and, using special casters, the assembly was pushed to the Hardware Bay. Here the windscreen and window frames, door handles and locks, the ventilating catches and similar details were fitted. In tailor's parlance, this was a trial fitting, to make quite sure that adjustments would not be required at a later stage, when paintwork might be damaged.

Engine

As the newly formed Car Division expanded, so its responsibilities increased. Originally the car engines were made by the Engines Division, but now there was an Erecting Section within the Car Division to build the units, though components were still supplied by the Engines Division. Each unit was assembled by one man, a mechanic trained to aero-engineering standards. This was a very different approach from the anonymity of the average Midlands factory, where the 'Friday car' was far from uncommon.

The crankshaft was balanced both statically and dynamically to exceptionally fine limits, and the flywheel and every other rotating component received the same meticulous attention. The six connecting rods were exactly matched, with the mechanic removing a minute quantity of metal where necessary to form a 'set'. To give some idea of the limits imposed, the maximum difference in weight between all six rods should not exceed two dram, or the equivalent of one-sixteenth of an ounce avoirdupois.

The camshaft was checked for cracks and hardness, and Filton applied such tests to every lobe of every camshaft. The six hemispherical combustion chambers of the cylinder head were polished, and then the ports were profiled, polished and matched to their carburettor inlets or exhaust manifolds. The object of this was to allow the gases to flow smoothly, and thus increase efficiency.

Seating the valves was done with extreme care, and when all else had been completed a final check was made, and, using a burette, the capacity of each chamber was measured exactly, adjustments being made where necessary. This ensured that within very fine limits all six chambers shared a common compression ratio.

It was typical of the Bristol attention to detail that the threads of all nuts, bolts and other threaded components were checked for conformity with the appropriate standards. A profilometer was used for these checks.

When erection was complete, the engine was inspected, and any faults remedied. This was a rare occurrence, and would require a second inspection. When his engine was passed, the mechanic was required to complete a written statement, to the effect that he was satisfied with the engine. Only when he had signed this statement did his responsibility for it cease.

Most of the men took a personal interest in the engines, long after installation and delivery. I recall an occasion when my own 405 drophead was at Filton, having its carburettors synchronised. Its bonnet was raised, and a passing mechanic glanced down at the little brass plaque on the rocker box. He must have noticed its number for, stopping, he jerked a thumb down at it, grinned and said, 'You've got a good one there, I built her'.

As with the engine and gearbox, there was a personal responsibility for the assembly and testing of the entire front suspension unit. When completed, the whole unit was checked on a special rig fitted with twin hydraulic rams.

The entire steering and suspension unit was attached rigidly to it, and each half could then be moved at a known controlled speed through any part, or the whole, of its travel. At the same time, it was possible to operate the steering, so that the effects of suspension movement on the steering geometry could be checked.

Another device measured the camber of the road wheels, at all positions of both steering and suspension. This test was applied to every production unit, and any inaccuracy adjusted. It was not passed by the inspector until spring loads and camber characteristics, as well as the steering geometry of the steering and suspension, all met the required standards.

Paintwork

Applying paint to an alloy body is a very skilled business because such metal is liable to instantaneous oxidation when exposed to the atmosphere. Yet it is essential that the necessary degree of cleanliness is achieved, to provide the key that will stop the paint flaking in service. This is done in three stages; first, to degrease the outer surface, then to treat it with a deoxidising agent, and lastly to wash the latter off, in order that the resultant phosphate coat may provide the necessary key.

The body was then oven-dried and spray-painted with a primer coat, and left overnight to dry. Next morning a stopper was applied, followed by two brushed coats of filler, and was again left to dry overnight. After being rubbed down and inspected, two coats of cellulose filler were applied by spray.

The assembly was left for several days, to harden after which a further inspection took place, and any defects were remedied. Only when all the latter had been checked and passed were five coats of cellulose, in the appropriate colour, applied by spray, after which it was left to harden overnight.

The next day the new paint was flatted, and another two coats of the cellulose sprayed on. After standing overnight, the work was inspected for ripples,.which would be easily visible after polishing. Only when all defects had been remedied was the assembly passed for the completion of the car.

Trim

All upholstery was designed and made in-house, and the science of ergonomics was used to good effect, with all seating being exceptionally comfortable, even for very long journeys. Using the finest leather, great skill was shown by the specialist staff. All the piping was in leather, all pockets and door pulls were hand-sewn. The door pulls were given a herringbone design, handsome in appearance, and providing a secure grip. The headlining was made of a material coated with PVC, which was both practical and attractive. It resisted stains, though it was susceptible to cigarette smoke, and some misguided owners used petrol and even paint thinners as cleaning agents, but little lasting harm resulted. All carpets were of top quality, usually Wilton, with an underlay. Dunlopillo served a similar purpose under the leather upholstery.

On test

At last, with the body completed and engine, gearbox and suspension installed road testing could begin.

Initially the test driver took the car for a run of such length and duration that even the most obscure faults came to light. For example, it might be noted that the engine was running at a higher temperature than was considered normal. In such a case, the car was returned to the Car Division, where the fault would be investigated and remedied, before a second test took place. If during that the original fault persisted, or another was discovered, the same process of test and treatment continued until all faults were cured. Such an extensive exercise was very rare, not only because of the inspections at various stages of the assembly, but also because of the real interest taken by the staff in their tasks.

While the cars were being road-tested, 'slave' seats and floor coverings were used, and only after such testing was completed in satisfactory fashion were these items actually allocated to each particular car fitted. Even after these had all been added, there was a final road test, and it was only after it was passed by a very experienced inspector that the car was returned to the factory for cleaning, polishing and general titivation, before being delivered to the doubtless impatient customer.

One particular owner arrived at Filton to collect his new Type 405, and, while waiting, was taken on a brief tour of the assembly area. On his return, his car was ready in all its pristine beauty. He stared at it for a long time, and then remarked: 'Now I know why you cost me so much, and after seeing the way you've been built, I don't begrudge a penny'.

14
Big Brother

Type 405

When the Type 405 saloon was exhibited on the Bristol stand at the 1954 London Motor Show, it was obvious that the all-metal body construction, used on the 401–403 models, had been abandoned in favour of the composite metal and timber techniques first seen on the little 404 coupe. From the scuttle forward, the new model resembled the latter very closely.

Purchasers of the new model had a choice of bodies – a four-door saloon or two-door convertible.

Three-quarter side/front view of Type 405 saloon Bristol. Note the very large rear screen, the bonnet air duct, road light in air inlet, and the very harmonious lines of the car.

General layout of the mechanical components of the Bristol 405. Note the position of the fuel tank, right behind the rear seat squab to keep the weight of the tail as low as possible.

The 405 Saloon

Despite its very modern, almost futuristic, appearance, the new saloon was not without its critics, and not just because wood had been used in its construction. It was the first and only Bristol ever built as standard with four doors, and was criticised on three counts. Firstly the doors were deemed to be too small to render entry or exit either easy or dignified; secondly the thickness of the rear doors restricted the usable passenger space, so that the car was strictly a four-seater; and thirdly the bottom of the doors was so low that to park by a moderately high kerb could mean that they were impossible to open.

To make matters worse, the centre tunnel, over the Hardy Spicer propeller shaft, was so high and broad that each rear passenger could only gain access from one side. To have to step out into heavy traffic in a busy street was neither wise nor popular.

Despite such criticism, the 405 saloon was an immediate success; indeed, having first been exhibited at the Paris Show in October, there was already a full order book when it was shown in London shortly afterwards. Buyers appeared intrigued by its very unusual appearance, with a frontal aspect that was likened to various other objects, including a dragon's snout, and a fighter aircraft. In fact the air intake, like that of the 404, was modelled on those of the ill-fated Brabazon giant airliner.

Three-quarter front/side view of Type 405 Bristol saloon. Note air duct in bonnet, front bumper with overriders and headlights inset into front wings with turn indicators below. The various auxiliary lamps were non-standard.

BIG BROTHER

Three-quarter front/side view of a 405 saloon Bristol. The large lamp set into the air inlet was standard, but not the mesh stone guards.

MODEL: 405	Date: 1954–1958
Wheelbase	9ft 6in (2m 89cm)
Front Track	4ft 4.5in (1m 33cm)
Rear Track	4ft 6in (1m 37cm)
Overall Height	4ft 9.5in (1m 46cm)
Overall Width	5ft 8in (1m 72cm)
Overall Length	15ft 9.25in (4m 80cm)
Weight	2,712lb (1,230kg)
Tyres	5.75 × 16in
Engine Type	100B2
Number of Cylinders	6
Bore	66mm
Stroke	96mm
Capacity	1,971cc
Gearbox	Bristol BW CR11
Ratios	1st: 15.24 2nd: 7.71 3rd: 5.46 4th: 4.22 Reverse: 12.20 Overdrive: 3.28 Freewheel on 1st gear
Brakes	Footbrake: Lockheed hydraulic on all 4 wheels Handbrake: Cable and rod operating from central lever on rear wheels only
Suspension	
Front	Independent transverse leaf spring hydraulic telescopic dampers, anti-roll bar
Rear	Longitudinal torsion bars with telescopic dampers

Many writers spoke of the 405's 'lean and hungry look', and its whole appearance suggested speed, in a most uncompromising fashion. Yet its interior was fully up to Bristol standards, with thick Wilton carpets, and a fitted underlay, while the upholstery incorporated hand-sewn Connolly hides over Dunlopillo.

The chassis of the 405 reverted to the traditional 9ft 6in wheelbase of the 400–403 models, but now at the rear there was a strong riveted section with the dual functions of supporting the lightweight body and forming the luggage boot. The latter was of 17cu ft capacity, unusually large for a car with such modest overall dimensions.

An ingenious new feature was the way additional luggage room was gained by using the hollow space on the inner side of each rear wing as a pannier. These were large enough to hold a small soft case, but to me their real use was to accept items too wide to go into the boot in any other way. I recall carrying a huge roll of carpet in this fashion, wedged from one pannier to the other. I have to admit, though, that this very considerable extra weight did make the car rather tail happy.

A small and typically thoughtful detail was the way in which the rear doors overlapped the wheel arches. On a wet and muddy day, when a door was opened, the passenger found a clean space on the upper

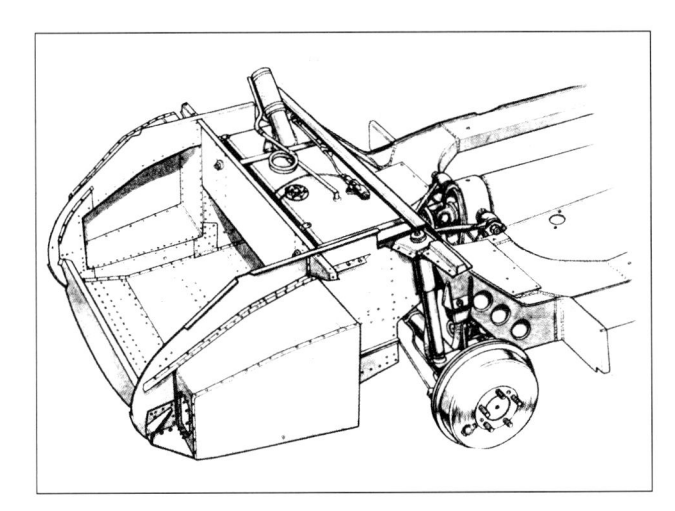

Details of the rear section of the Type 405 Bristol saloon.

A side view right to left. Note the slight 'bulge' aft of front wheel arch indicating stowage of spare wheel under hinged panel. On the rear side just aft of the door can be seen the circular flap with lock, protecting the filler cap. The road wheels are the standard pierced disc type, with nave plates showing the Bristol roundel.

surface of the wing, enabling entrance or exit to be accomplished without soiling his clothes.

As on the 404, the spare wheel, with its wheel brace, was stowed under a hinged flap on the nearside front wing, with the battery, windscreen washer bottle, and servo if fitted, under a similar hinged flap on the offside. Beside the battery was a ladder with all the car's fuses, which could facilitate inspection and repair of an electrical fault.

I have never understood why so obvious a way of carrying the spare should remain unique to Bristol, and it is still a feature of current models. Not only does such a position increase the boot capacity, but, if a puncture occurs, wheels can be changed without even opening the boot lid, and weight distribution is also improved. Additionally, since it is in such a cool and well ventilated position, the battery usually has a very long and useful life.

As on the 404, timber (usually ash) is present in the surrounds to front and rear screens, while the alloy top and side panels are supported by a wooden canopy, much longer than the little coupe's, and with additional cross-bracing.

Timber is also present in the boot lid and its surround, a spot that seems quite susceptible to rot, and yet is often ignored when a potential buyer inspects a used example. More obvious is the area adjacent to the windscreen, and I have seen terminal cases in which only a little dust remains to prove that a wood surround was ever present. Restoration is possible, but it tends to be a long and costly business. I have heard of a new process involving the use of plastic by injection that sounds promising. The heavy timbers used in the stowage space in both front wings might appear extremely vulnerable, out in the open and often covered with mud thrown up by the front wheels. Yet I have not heard of a case of rot there, and can only conclude that good ventilation and well-seasoned material is the probable reason.

As on the 404, a comprehensive collection of instruments is housed in a console or pod just ahead of the 17-inch Bluemel steering wheel which is adjustable.

Main switches and controls are situated on the dashboard, while the minor items, such as the heating quadrant, are in a sort of mini-dash below. On the 405, the speedometer was often criticised for its 'extreme optimism', as one motoring journalist put it. This was most unusual on a Bristol, but probably explains the stories that circulated about the ease with which the cars could exceed the 'ton', according to their very satisfied owners.

With the proliferation of motorways, it had become desirable for the new Bristol to possess a fifth gear, to allow high cruising speeds without overstressing the engine. The Laycock de Normanville overdrive unit was the perfect answer. Not only did it reduce engine speed in fifth gear by 22 per cent, compared with the normal top of earlier models, but it fitted just behind the gearbox, in the space formerly occupied by the very long tail extension.

The overdrive was controlled by a small toggle on the dash, just to the right of the steering wheel. To bring it into operation, the little lever was pushed upwards when fifth gear was engaged. To change down, one could just push the toggle back to its original position, but this could result in a slight transmission jerk that I disliked. So, instead, it was my practice just to nudge the neat little remote gear lever towards neutral, and then ease it back. This ensured a smooth change down into fourth gear, while the toggle dropped, ready for use when next required.

The overdrive is well designed and extremely

A Type 405 Bristol saloon – side view – taken at night, with the Clifton Suspension Bridge in the background.

strong, though I recall an occasion when a nasty whine began when the car was in neutral, with the engine running. I telephoned the service manager at Filton, and was told: 'It may be nothing at all, or it might mean a total failure in the next few miles'. Cold comfort when I was just about to take my daughter back to university after the summer vacation!

So I left the Bristol with an expert for a complete check and used my other car, loaded to the gunwales, for the long trip to Scotland. Rather foolishly, I had instructed the expert to replace any bearing not 100 per cent perfect. He took me literally, and several bearings were renewed, though, as he told me rather smugly: 'The wear is so slight, you'd best keep 'em for spares'.

A new Bristol engine was fitted to the 405 saloon. Known as the 100B2, its power output was identical with the 100B used on the 404, i.e. 105bhp @ 5,000rpm. It reverted to the twin three-port exhaust manifolds of the Type 85 engines, with two narrow-bore pipes to the silencer. The camshaft was slightly more sporting, giving valve timings of 36:72:72:36, and it proved powerful and surprisingly frugal, with a fuel consumption of 24–25mpg at reasonable road speeds.

Unlike the 401–403 cars, which had their fuel tanks at the extreme rear of the body, on the 405 it was set well forward and higher, just behind the rear seat squabs. The filler cap was protected by a hinged flap with a substantial lock.

The moving of the spare wheel to its new position, and the re-siting of the fuel tank, improved the handling of the car, even when compared with the excellent 403. It was unaffected by strong cross-winds, and there was little trace of the oversteer that some critics had detected in earlier models. On my own car, I felt there was a slight vagueness in the steering above the 85mph mark. It only evidenced itself on a long straight well-surfaced road, when the car seemed very gradually to veer, regardless of the camber. It was never enough to be serious, yet I knew it was present, which, I suppose, helped keep me alert on the long solo trips of those days. The steering geometry and suspension were checked, but the cause was never found, and I have met other 405 owners with a similar problem.

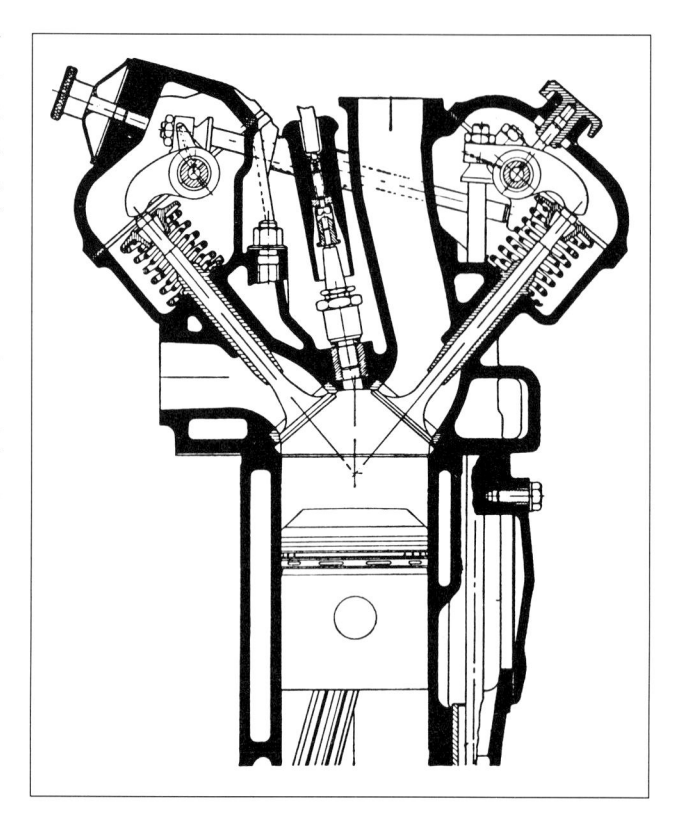

Shows details of the 100B cylinder head as used on 405 saloon.

The beautifully engineered aero-style button door locks of the 401–403 series were replaced on the 405 by mass-produced handles from an outside source. This aroused considerable criticism, but by that time the aircraft side of the Company was far too busy for highly skilled staff to be employed on such tasks. In fact the new handles were quite adequate, though the locks were not nearly as thief-proof.

The door hinges were of solid brass, and tremendously heavy, but I have known very few cases where a Bristol door has dropped to such an extent that serious remedial action was necessary.

The bonnet was controlled from a knob in the centre of the lower dashboard, and the fuel tank had its own lockable panel. The wing flaps were secured by up-and-over toggles, and the boot lid had a lock set into its centre lower edge as standard.

In practice I found the latter quite ineffective, and on more than one occasion an over-eager hall porter only had to give the handle a hard pull, for the lid to open, with the hasp of the lock still in position. In the end, I replaced the original plain handles with two incorporating additional locks, and these proved quite effective.

The cable controlling the bonnet can break, and it can be a very tricky operation to persuade the bonnet to open. After suffering such an experience, I attached a long piece of cobbler's twine to the lock, leading it back to a convenient bolt head under the dash. Needless to say, this back-up was never required, but it was there – just in case.

While on the subject of back-up, the 405 has a solenoid switch under the bonnet. It is positioned immediately in front of the Enots One-shot oil reservoir. Should the dashboard starter button fail, all that is required is to lift the bonnet with the ignition on, then press the black top of the solenoid switch, and the engine should start. Though this procedure can be irksome, on a hot day in heavy traffic if the engine stalls it is much better than having to use the long starting handle which is usually tucked away in some inaccessible position in the boot.

As on the 404, the heater unit was much simpler than the complicated system used on the 401–403 cars. It was fitted behind the engine bulkhead, with the controls in a quadrant under the dash. These could be set so as to draw cooling air into the car's interior. This was necessary in hot weather, when the car could become uncomfortably stuffy. The main cause was probably the very large glazed area of the wrap-around rear screen, a feature that may account for the saloon's nickname of 'The Bristol Glasshouse'.

The heater box incorporated a small radiator and control flaps, with water being supplied from the main radiator, via a control valve. The resultant hot air not only warmed the car's interior but also provided the necessary heat for the demisting and defrosting system of the windscreen.

The blower unit was positioned just to the rear of the main radiator, and operated by a lower lever on the dashboard quadrant. I did not find it very effective, and in the instruction manual it states: 'If additional air flow is desired, open the rear quarter lights to suit requirements'. I have always thought that this stuffiness in warm weather was the probable reason for my daughter's sudden susceptibility to car sickness. This became so severe that, on medical advice, the car was sold and a 405 convertible acquired.

I found the saloon an excellent car for long-distance motoring, but less satisfactory in urban traffic, despite the ability to see the near-side front wing, an impossibility on the 401–403 series. But those low-set doors posed problems when stopping at a kerb of more than average height. This, combined with the stuffiness already mentioned, made it less suitable for carrying passengers on business, as well as the fact that entry and exit from the rear compartment was not nearly as easy as on the earlier two-door models.

But those are my personal views, and many other owners praised their cars to the skies, for their virtues of high speeds, good road-holding and frugal fuel consumption. To be fair, I think my feelings may be clouded by subconscious comparison between the saloon and drophead versions of the same model.

The 405 Convertible

The body was made, in collaboration with the Bristol Aeroplane Company, by the long-established firm of E D Abbott Limited. The practice was for a supply of engines and chassis to be held at the coachworks in Farnham, Surrey, until a firm order was received from Bristols, when a body would be made and fitted.

The combination of simplicity and proportion resulted in a car that was handsome and yet practical. Its appearance was quite timeless, except, perhaps, for the vestigial fins on the tops of the rear wings, a feature shared with the saloon version. Often, when abroad, I would be asked its origin, and my answer that it had been made in England, sometimes met with polite scepticism. Surely it must have come from the drawing board of some celebrated Italian designer . . .

Unlike the saloon version, the 405 drophead had two wide doors and, using the Leverol mechanism in the front seats, the rear compartment was easily accessible. The boot had an area of 17cu ft, as on the

A French entry in the annual Concours of the Bristol Owners' Club. The car is a Type 405 Bristol, with convertible body by Abbotts of Farnham. With the hood erected, it was very warm and comfortable. The auxiliary lamps below the front bumper were non-standard.

A scene at the annual Concours of the Bristol Owners' Club, held on 3 September 1989, at Clifton Downs, Bristol. In the foreground is an immaculate Type 405 Bristol convertible, with the cup awarded as 'best in class' on the bonnet.

saloon, including the same pannier design in the rear wings. The boot lid was of steel instead of alloy, with a spring-loaded strut at one side to facilitate loading. However, the centre lock was as ineffective as the saloon's, and additional locks were set into the handles for security.

While the front seats were extremely comfortable, the same could not be said for those in the rear compartment. Made in one piece, and with a hump in the centre, the usable space was far from generous for two adults. The high propeller cover made it impossible, with the hood up, to move over from one side to the other, and unless the front seats were set well forward leg room was restricted. While it sufficed for short trips, it was hardly suitable for a touring holiday for four adults.

I noticed no hint of scuttle shake, probably because of the long experience of Abbotts as makers of excellent convertibles. The data from official sources indicate that the drophead was 48lb heavier than the saloon version, which could indicate the amount of extra material deemed necessary to compensate for the lack of a hard top, with its structural stiffness.

The hood was of double-texture material, and was lined. It was simple to raise or lower, and could be coped with single-handed, though in practice an assistant could be very useful. The front section was secured to the windscreen surround by three up-and-over toggles, and, single-handed, it was not easy to clip them down virtually simultaneously. Having two pairs of hands simplified matters considerably, and

This Type 405 Bristol convertible is being judged, hence the opened wing flap on offside. Immediately below can be seen the battery, and there is also a 'ladder' containing all the fuses, greatly facilitating identification in case of need. The fog/spot lamps are non-standard.

avoided the risk of cracking the windscreen if only one or two clips had been secured straight away.

Since the hood was fully lined, the car was almost as snug as a saloon in cold weather, yet when the sun shone I was always tempted to drop the top and revel in the unseasonable pleasures of al fresco motoring. The main snag on such occasions was the need to insert the hood into its bag-cum-tonneau cover. Again an extra pair of hands saved time and effort. Several 405 drophead owners I know just pull their hoods back and drive away, but I was always aware of what might happen if a strong gust of wind caught those folds of hood material, and preferred to be safe rather than sorry.

When fully fitted, the cover extended right over the entire tonneau. It was secured by a very large number of 'lift-the-dot' fasteners, each with its own little peg, screwed into the body. On a bright autumn day, with the cover flush with one's shoulder, and the road streaming ahead between the poplars, a long Continental journey was a joy rather than a business necessity.

The 405 drophead version was fitted with the Type 100B engine, standard on the little 404. As on the latter car, a single six-port exhaust manifold directed the gases to the silencer via one large-bore pipe. The exhaust system was unique to the 405 convertible, and there is a special section in the Workshop Manual, with part numbers.

Some examples of this rare model have had their exhaust systems modified, with non-standard silencers, and tail pipes that extend beyond the tail. The correct position is just to the rear of the offside back wheel. To facilitate restoration to the car's original specification, since the Workshop Manual for the 404/5 models is now almost unobtainable, here is a full list of the necessary parts, each shown with the number of items required.

Three-quarter side/front view of a white Type 405 Bristol convertible, with hood raised. The slight 'bulge' just aft of the front wheel arch indicates where spare is stowed, under a hinged flap. Note the quick-action filler cap set high, behind hood; also the 'fin' on wing.

Quantity	Details	Part No.
1	Ring nut	404–1–29003
1	Down pipe	405–1D–29001–1
1	Bracket	405–1D–29001–7
17	Nuts ¼" BSF brass	
17	Locknuts BSF brass	
1	Coupling pipe	405–1–29001–2
3	Pipe clips	NS. 10491
3	Bolts	FB 105/2BD
3	Washers 5/16"	plain
3	Spring washers	AGS 585/E
1	Centre pipe	405–1D–29001–3
1	Exhaust Pipe & silencer	405–1D–29001–10
1	Silencer clips – bottom	405–1D–29001–9
1	Silencer clip – top	N. 716062
1	Reinforcing Plate	N. 716068
16	Bolts	FB104/BD
1	Mounting Rubber	405–1D–29001–9
1	Clamping plate	404–II–29037
8	Washers ¼"	plain
1	Chromed Sleeve Tail pipe	400–II–29039
1	Jubilee clip	Size 2A

To cure a flat spot for which some 100 series engines were criticised, there were minor differences between the centre Solex carburettor and the inner and outer instruments: this applied to ALL Type 404s and 405s to chassis No. 4058.

Centre Carburettor	Inner and Outer Carburettors
Choke 26	Choke 26
Main jet 120	Main jet 115
Correction jet 190	Correction jet 200
Pilot jet 45	Pilot jet 45
Air bleed 1.0	Air bleed 1.2
G. A. jet 2.0mm	G. A. jet 2.0mm
G. S. jet 95	G. S. jet 95
Emulsion tube No. 10	Emulsion tube No. 10
Needle valve 1.5	Needle valve 1.5

From Type 405 chassis No. 4059 onwards all three carburettors were similar:

Choke	26
Main jet	115
Correction jet	200
Pilot jet	45
Air bleed	1.0
G. A. jet	2.0mm
G. S. jet	95
Emulsion tube	No. 10
Needle valve	1.5

The crankshaft of the 100B2 engine was fitted with a viscous vibration damper, and it is important, if an engine change is contemplated, to realise that an engine fitted with a viscous damper will not fit any Type 404, or any Type 405 with a chassis up to and including No. 4051. From chassis No. 4052 onwards, the front chassis cross-member and the front spring attachment were redesigned to give the necessary clearance for the damper.

'Brimol' valve inserts are fitted to the alloy cylinder head and are extremely durable. If a buyer of a used 405 finds that renewal is imperative, and is unable to have new valve inserts fitted at the factory, it should be noted that valve inserts can be obtained through the spares department, but are issued only on request and without liability.

During its production life the Type 405 model had three different ratios in its differentials:

a) On the early models, the differential unit was the same as that fitted to the 404 model, but the ratio was changed to 4.32. (Part No. 405–1–30003).

b) On the intermediate examples of the 405, the taper roller races were altered, which in turn changed the diameter of the pinion. Consequently, the crown wheel and pinion are not interchangeable with the previous type. (Part No. 405–1–30052).

c) On the later examples of the Type 405, there were many internal changes, including both crown wheel and pinion, and while individual parts are not interchangeable, *complete units* can be fitted as replacements. (Part No. 405–1–30071).

I have been asked whether an engine modified to 100C specification is suitable for general motoring, and I can confirm that such units are quite tractable, and do not call for any special treatment, other than for the driver to have an observant eye for the rev counter, and a sympathetic ear for the exhaust note. Such engines prefer to rev rather than to labour, as for example when taking a steep hill. A change to a lower ratio will enable the car to climb the ascent with the minimum of effort, and is far better than trying to remain in the same gear.

Fuel consumption may be a trifle higher, usually because the driver tends to use the higher performance more than might have been the case with a less exhilarating engine. Such units, if they are properly set up, with valve clearances, ignition settings and carburettors all to the maker's specification, should keep their tune for a very long period. But beware of the so-called expert, unless he can prove real Bristol experience. Otherwise there is a grave risk of falling into the hands of a 'bodger', which, in extreme cases, can lead to a heavy bill, and a sadly deranged engine.

I have never been able to understand why the 405 convertible was such a comparative failure. Its price in Britain was £3,188 12s 6d, including Purchase Tax, the same as for a 405 Saloon. Yet during its production life it is estimated that only forty-three of these Abbott-bodied dropheads were made. Abbotts were famed for their convertible bodywork, and one might have expected to pay much more, compared with the standard saloon. So what went wrong?

I suppose this seeming lack of interest by the home market, at a time when the saloon model was so popular, may have been a reflection of the rather grim state of the British economy, so that while money might be spent on a 'serious' car there was more resistance to one that was regarded as 'for amusement only'. Also, no doubt, the limited space in the rear compartment was a demerit, unless one had two small children, for whom the accommodation would have been both adequate and safe.

Lack of rear view, with the hood erected, was another fault. The rear window was really less than generous in area, and urban pollution tended to discolour it to a point where it became opaque. There were two large areas on either side that were well-nigh invisible to a driver using the small mirror set at the top centre of the windscreen. I found that a second one, of oval shape, set on the offside quarterlight, was a partial solution, though it did nothing to assist the driver with the blind spot on the nearside.

With the hood stowed away in its bag, things were quite different, and, most years, I had the car in its open state from early April till late October, unless the weather was unseasonably cold and wet. One thing I do know is that after one summer of such al fresco motoring my daughter's car sickness ceased, as abruptly as it had begun!

Though I have read many reports on the 405 saloon Bristols, I have yet to see one on the drophead version that was written when the model was current. However, in its April 1989 issue, *Supercar Classics* published an account of a test drive of a recently restored example. Amongst the comments, were two that I felt did reflect some of the model's characteristics and personality: 'The Bristol is a relaxing tourer, able to maintain a good average on country roads' and 'The 405 isn't a car that strikes you immediately, but one that insinuates its charm on you. An elegant refined grand tourer that's lovely to drive'.

Hints for a Potential Purchaser

Wood rot in the saloon version was covered in an earlier part of the chapter. In my experience, it is less common on the convertibles, not only because of the lack of the large timber canopy, but also because, for obvious reasons, a drophead is more likely to lead a rather more pampered existence, being stored in a garage and perhaps mainly used in the summer.

The most vulnerable area is in the vicinity of the windscreen; the massive timbers in the stowage spaces under the front wings seem almost impervious to rot, possibly because they are well ventilated. The boot lid is of steel, and is unlikely to have a problem more serious than hinge distortion, due to the much greater weight when compared with the wood and alloy used on the saloon.

Quite recently I have seen three dropheads, all badly neglected over long periods, and all with rear chassis, from just above the differential, that are little more than metal fragments to some extent bonded by rust. While a new rear section can be built up,

Front view of a Type 405 saloon Bristol. It was taken while the owner was on his honeymoon in Italy. The car is very original except for the wing mirrors.

such work has to be performed by expert restorers, and their charges are high, since much time and skill must be devoted to such a vital task.

A simple way of deciding whether an engine is an early or late example is to check the type of air cleaner. Up to Chassis No. 4036, the Vokes dry element air cleaner was used. It is contained in a circular housing, the two halves secured by a wing-nut. It requires cleaning every 10,000 miles, the procedure being to remove the element from its container, turn it grubby-side down, and to tap it, so that the particles of dirt are detached and fall away.

When quite clean, replace in the housing, and tighten the wing-nut.

On cars from Chassis No. 4037 and upwards, the AC combined air cleaner and intake silencer was fitted. It is a long metal cylinder, with a mesh window at one end. It requires cleaning every 5,000 miles, the complete unit being detached and the window end swirled in a shallow pan filled with paraffin. After draining the latter, the mesh window should be lubricated, using engine oil, and the surplus drained away. The unit is then ready to be refitted to the engine.

15

The Loner

Type 406E

The appearance of a new model on the Bristol stand at the 1957 London Motor Show seems to have aroused little interest in the contemporary motoring press. To date I have found only two references, both in copies of the same journal. Known as the 406E, it was for export only.

In its issue of 27 November 1957, *Motor* included a photograph of the Duke of Edinburgh in a Bristol, the caption reading: 'The recent visit of the Duke of Edinburgh to the Bristol Aeroplane Company was made the occasion to reveal this special-bodied prototype of the new Bristol 406. This model, which will be available on the British and Overseas markets next Spring, has the same chassis and 2.2-litre engine as the Beutler-bodied 406E which was shown for the first time at this year's Paris Salon and Earls Court Motor Show'.

The same journal's issue of 2 October 1957 included a short article with an illustration that might have been a photograph or an artist's impression of the 406E. It showed the car facing right to left, and slightly sideways, and the treatment of the front wing suggested some sort of styling addition, possibly a separate panel. In the article, the car's weight was given as 'an estimated 22¾cwt, in comparison with the 24½cwt of the Type 405 saloon'. I find this statement puzzling, as the weight of the 406 that succeeded the export-only model was shown by *Motor* in its issue dated 27 August 1958 as 'dry weight 26⅞cwt'.

It would seem likely that the autumn of 1957 was hardly a propitious time to introduce an expensive new motor car that was for export only, for the British economy was faltering, hard currencies were in short supply, and it almost looked as if the clocks were back to the austerity of the immediate postwar period.

Yet the 406E had many new features, and its chassis was to serve as the basis of a new generation of Bristol models, though the type of body and capacity of engine might vary. The 'one off' body was by the Swiss coachbuilders: Gebr. Beutler of Thun. Recently I was informed by a BOC member living in that country, that at one stage, another firm: Graber, was also considered.

Appearance

Externally, the 406E appeared utterly different from any previous Bristol model, and I remember one of the old guard grumbling, 'The only things I recognise are the wheels'. If the 405 Saloon was often called 'lean and hungry', I suppose the best one-word description for its immediate successor was 'bland'. It was of all-metal construction, the composite timber/metal techniques seen on the 404/405 models having been abandoned. Critics complained that the distinctive Bristol look, combining speed with elegance, had gone too. I feel this is rather too sweeping, for in fact the 406E was a handsome car, it is just that it seemed so much larger, yet its wheelbase was actually only 9ft 6in, as on the 405.

The frontal aspect of the new model might be described as modern orthodox, and had no trace of

Side view of Type 406E Bristol, with saloon bodywork by the Swiss coachbuilders Beutler. Only one example is known to have been made. Note narrow kick plate, and side 'embellisher.'

the aero-engineering legacy of the earlier Filton cars. The front bumper was of the single blade type, and a sensible and practical innovation was the use of small rubber insets in the over-riders. One relic from the past was the hole for the starting handle, just below the radiator grille. Large headlights jutted from the wings, with small circular flashers below them. The radiator grille was of slightly rounded shape, with pass lights at both corners, and a circular badge, possibly a Bristol roundel, in the centre. From it a pair of stylised wings sprouted.

I thought the bonnet treatment very pleasing, with the wide front sloping gracefully to merge with the apron, and a shallow air duct set into the top to feed the triple Solex carburettors. From the side view, one could see that the rear body overhang was not balanced by the forward section. Yet this did not spoil the general appearance. Rather it served to emphasize the considerable luggage-carrying capacity of the boot.

Front and rear bumper blades extended so as to afford some protection to the wings, and a chromed rubbing strip was attached to the lower edge of the body sides. The two wide doors were fitted with quarter-lights, and the roof pillar, just to the rear, was extraordinarily slim. With the door and side windows, plus windscreen and rear window of generous proportions, the car's interior was light and airy.

Front view of Type 406E Bristol saloon. Note the wide oval air intake with auxiliary lamps set into the grille and with Bristol badge and wings set between them. The wide shallow air duct in the bonnet top should also be noted. This is the only known example and is now in France.

The solitary Type 406E Bristol saloon, with Beutler bodywork. Note the Reutter fully reclining seat mechanism, tan leather upholstery, high set gear lever and typical Bluemel steering wheel, with the instruments in a 'pod' in front of it. This is the only known example.

A rear view of the Type 406E Bristol with bodywork by Beutler. Note simple treatment of lamps, the recessed number plate, wide rear window and finned rear wings. This is the only known example. It appeared at the Paris and London Motor Shows in 1957, and is now located in France, near Paris.

The rear view of the car could only be described as massive, and there was a hint of the contemporary American about it. From the wide and very slightly oval rear screen, the tail section curved gracefully over the boot lid, and down to the narrow bumper that had no over-riders. Oval rear light clusters were recessed into the edges of the wings, and there was just a trace of Bristol influence in the vestigial fins that were a feature of the 404–405 models. The road wheels were the standard Filton type, being discs with ventilating holes and chromed nave plates.

The interior was finished in tan leather, the steering wheel was the large Bluemel, standard since the 401 Bristol, and a typically comprehensive set of instruments were displayed in an oval console, taking up most of the dashboard space on the driver's side. The steering was left-hand drive, with the remote gear lever to the right, and with the handbrake between the seats. The latter were fitted with the fully reclining Reutter mechanism.

The exterior colour scheme was a lightish shade of blue for the main body, silver-grey for the roof and screen surrounds, and silver wheels. It suited the car well, I thought, and the appearance was quiet and dignified. It may be the colour scheme that is responsible for the optical illusion that the car is much bigger than is actually the case.

It has taken both time and good fortune to piece together the 406E story so far. My Swiss contact is confident that there was just the one example made, and since we know it was exhibited at the Paris Salon, which is usually held a few weeks before the Earls Court Motor Show, it appears not unlikely that the car had already found a buyer before it was shown on the Bristol stand in London.

This might seem to be confirmed by the fact that the car's home has been in Paris for most of its life, and that its long-term owner is stated to be a French Canadian artist who has lived and worked in the French capital for many years. It would appear that he does not welcome enquiries regarding his car, which is a pity, since from the photographs I have studied he would seem to maintain it in immaculate condition.

I would like to offer my sincere thanks to Hunter Rogers, a long-term member of the Bristol Owners' Club, who very kindly loaned me rare photographs, and also supplied background material that was most helpful, in researching the history of this enigma.

16

The End of a Line

Type 406 Saloon

The Type 404 coupe and the 405 in saloon and convertible forms continued in production until November 1958, when they were succeeded by the standard 406 saloon.

The new model was offered for sale in Britain as well as overseas, and the engine and chassis were both similar to those first seen on the export-only model of the previous year. However, the body was of Bristol design and was considerably different to other models.

The most obvious change was in the frontal treatment – the orthodox rectangular grille being replaced by an aero-type open inlet with a recessed wire mesh screen. The bonnet top was quite flat, the wide, shallow carburettor intake being omitted. The rear body section was more angular, the boot lid less curved, and though the vestigial fins were retained at the tops of the rear wings, the rear light clusters were quite different.

The bumpers, at front and back, were heavier and gave less protection to the bodywork, despite the equally massive over-riders, which helped to give the new model its appearance of a very substantial luxury motor car. As such it was far removed from the sporting good looks of many of the earlier Bristols, which had done so much to establish the marque's reputation.

The 406 weighed more than any earlier Filton-made car, and at 3,010lb was 288lb heavier than the 405 saloon. It was also the most expensive Bristol that had been produced to date, with an original British price of £4,493 17s including Purchase Tax; which was £1,305 4s 6d more than the 405. It was obvious that company policy intended to move the marque up-market, with a car to appeal to those for whom comfort was more important than sheer performance.

Yet despite the exterior differences, much of the old Bristol remained. The front suspension was still by transverse leaf spring; the light yet accurate

Three-quarter front/side view of a Type 406 Bristol saloon, with raised bonnet, waiting to be judged at the annual Concours of the Bristol Owners' Club, held on 3 September 1989, at Clifton Downs, Bristol. Note the rear edge of bonnet with ventilation vents, 'Pegasus' badge on grille, plus new style 'roundel' on bonnet.

Cutaway drawing of the Type 406 Bristol; note new type grille.

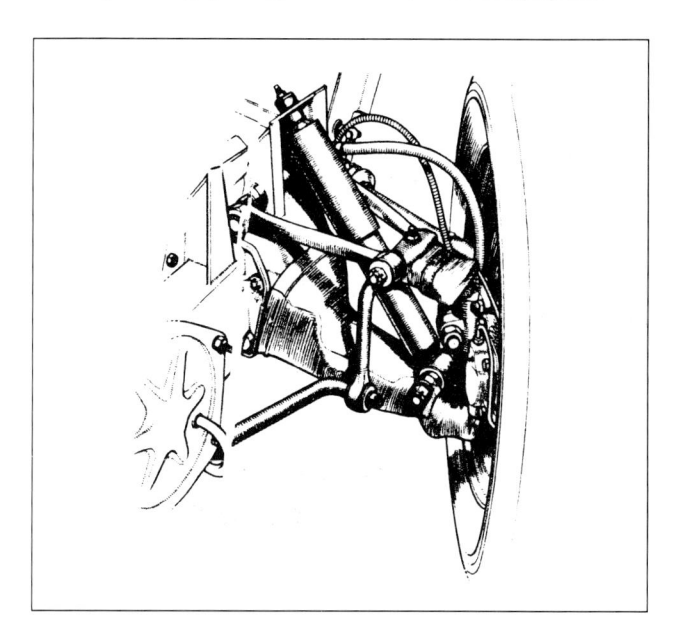

Showing front suspension details of the 406 Bristol.

Side view of Type 406 Bristol saloon. It is competing in Driving Tests held at the Patrick Motor Museum in 1988, which were organised by the Bristol Owners' Club. Note the non-standard kick plate, with 'Pegasus' logo just ahead of door.

Showing new rear axle location, as used on 406 Bristol, using Watt linkage pivoting on a central casting and anchored to chassis with mounting plates, a single fore-and-aft radius arm links axle to cross-member.

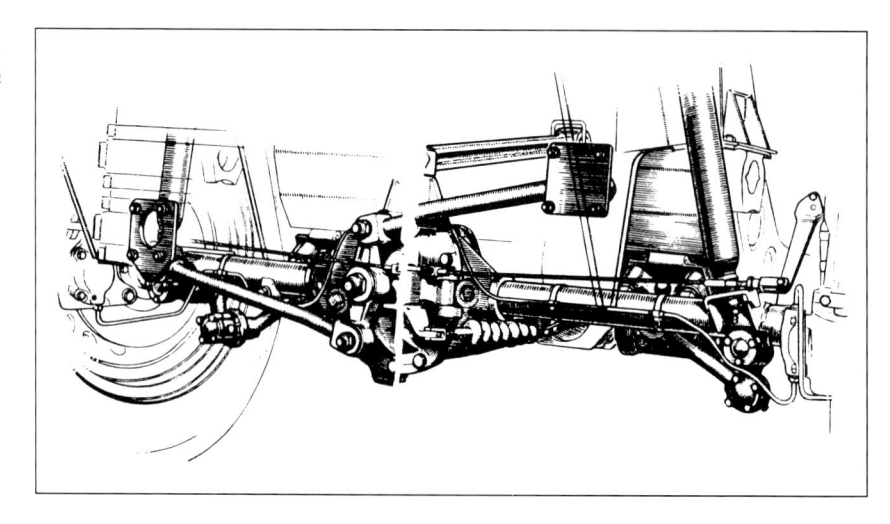

steering was still by rack and pinion; and at the rear, torsion bars were still employed. The manner in which the rear axle was attached to the chassis was different, and in *Motor* of 27 August 1958 was described as follows: 'Rear axle location is now by means of a transverse Watt linkage, pivoting on a central casting, and anchored to the chassis through mounting plates. A single fore-and-aft radius arm links the axle to a cross member' as in the above diagram.

A hypoid bevel rear axle (ratio 4.27:1) replaced the spiral bevel type (ratio 4.22:1) of the 405. This permitted a lower drive line, without the very high propeller shaft cover of the latter, facilitating entry to or exit from the rear compartment.

The Laycock de Normanville overdrive unit, first seen on the 405, was retained, but the gear ratios were lower:

	405	406
First gear – incorporating a free-wheel	15.24:1	15.42:1
Second gear	7.71	7.79
Third gear	5.46	5.52
Fourth gear	4.42	4.22
Overdrive	3.28	3.32
Reverse	12.20	12.34

With overdrive engaged, the road speed at 3,000rpm was 72.63mph, compared with only 56.8mph at the same engine speed but in fourth gear.

A New Engine

Just as the 406 was the heaviest and most expensive Bristol to date, so its engine had the greatest cubic capacity. From 1946 all Filton-made engines were of similar swept volume, namely 1,971cc; but the new unit, known as the Type 110, was of 2,216cc capacity. Both bore and stroke had been increased and were now 68.89 x 99.64mm compared with the 66 x 96mm of the earlier engines. Power output of the Type 110 was 105bhp, the same as the 100B engine, but this was achieved at only 4,700rpm, compared with the 5,000rpm of the earlier unit. As a result, torque was much improved and this, coupled with its flexibility and the lower gear ratios, enabled the new model to be driven in a more relaxed, less sporting fashion. Fewer gear changes were necessary, and in heavy urban traffic the freewheel on first gear remained a considerable advantage.

As regards the basic engine, with its complex valve gear, few changes had been made, though modifications were carried out on the triple Solex carburation. These were aimed at curing a slight hesitation that had sometimes been experienced with the earlier engines. Compression ratio was still only 8.5:1, as on the 100B engine, but there were new pistons of the truncated cone type. They improved the combustion space in the light alloy cylinder head, and there was a new tensioner for the chain from crankshaft to camshaft. It was of the rubber slipper

THE END OF A LINE

Side view of a Type 406 Bristol; the only standard series Bristol to use the 2.2-litre, six-cylinder Bristol engine. Note the wraparound bumpers, the very wide chromed strip from nose to door, and the kick plate along lower edge. The latter is non-standard.

type, using hydraulic pressure for its operation. The dip-stick had been repositioned in a more accessible location.

The Bristol policy of discreet innovation resulted in little publicity for the completely new braking system of the 406. It employed discs and calipers on all four road wheels, including the hand brake. Made by Dunlop, and assisted by a Lockheed servo, they were extremely effective. The diameters of the brake discs was 11¼in and the pads 2¼in. To accommodate them, the front track was ½in wider than the 405, and the rear track 2in more. The

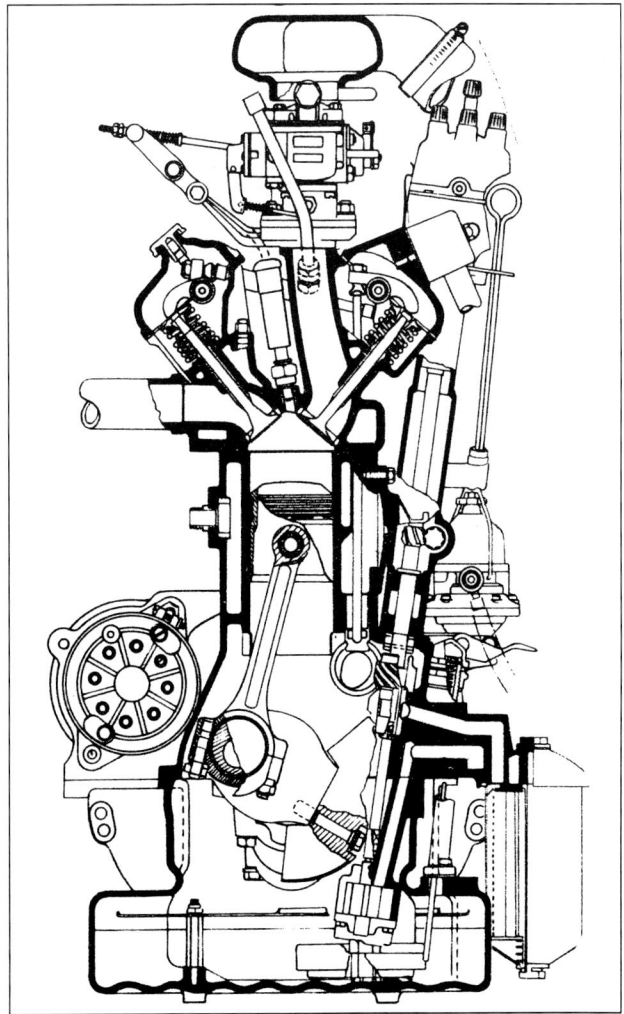

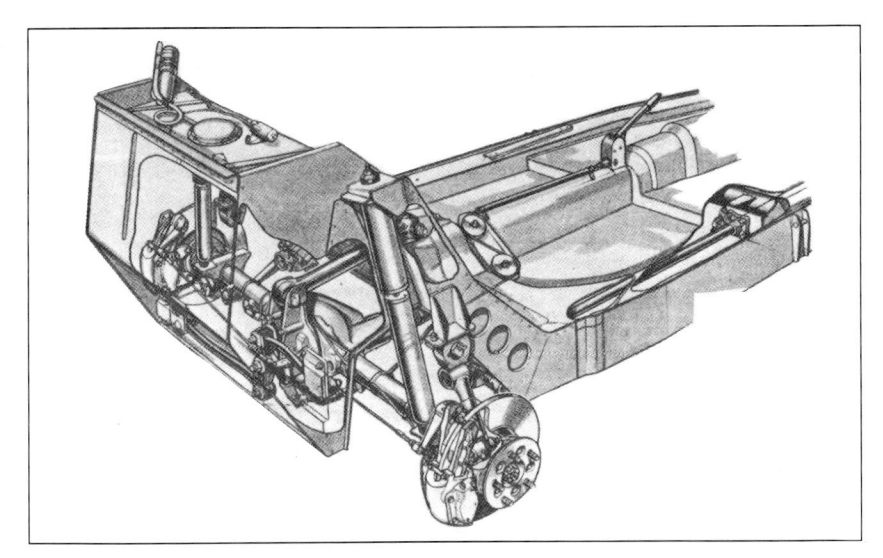

The Type 110 engine of 2.2-litre capacity, fitted to the Type 406 and also 406E and 406Z versions, using Beutler and Zagato bodies respectively. Note new type pistons of 'truncated cone' pattern.

Rear suspension of the Type 406 Bristol; note disc brakes.

151

figures being 4ft 5in and 4ft 8in respectively on the new model. The handbrake operated on the rear wheels only.

To compensate for the lower rear axle ratio, the 406 was fitted with 6.00 x 16 tyres, instead of the 5.75 x 16 covers used on the 405. The original equipment on the new model was either Michelin or Dunlop 'Gold Seal', but a customer might specify Dunlop 'Road Speed' tyres as an alternative.

Bought-Out Coachwork

In 1956 the Filton Car Division had become Bristol Cars Ltd, a wholly owned subsidiary of the parent firm, which coincided with an upturn in the fortunes of the Aero Division. As a result, the latter required additional personnel and accommodation. Much of this was at the expense of the former Car Division, and included the loss of its body-building facility.

So that the production of the 406 might continue, the new subsidiary company placed a contract with Jones Brothers, for the construction of the bodywork. This was to Filton design and, to maintain the traditional Bristol quality control, three inspectors were seconded full-time to the coachworks at Willesden in north-west London. The chassis and engines were driven up from Filton, and back again when the bodywork was fitted. The trimming, finishing and road-testing remained a Bristol responsibility.

The old guard criticised the new car, claiming it was too heavy, cost too much and was far removed from the spartan sporting image of the early Bristols. Yet the move up market proved a success, sales were buoyant, and despite its staid appearance, a 406 in good mechanical condition is still capable of a surprisingly high performance. The engine will rev willingly, though it must be admitted that above the 5,000 mark the valve gear does get a trifle intrusive. It is, however, a very strong unit, and from personal experience, I would say that the greatest danger lies in entrusting maintenance or repairs to a self-styled expert, without the practical experience of actually working on these very idiosyncratic vehicles.

Good examples are no longer easy to find, and even indifferent ones command prices that might have seemed absurd just a year or two ago. In a production life extending from November 1958 to September 1961, the estimated production was only 178 standard saloons, making the 406 one of the rarer models in the range.

Virtues and Vices

The Type 406 Bristol was fitted with an effective heating and cooling system, and an innovation – windscreen washers that worked at the touch of a tiny chromed button, set into the dashboard, just to the right of the steering wheel. Allied to a brace of

Showing cutaway details of body fitted to the Type 406 Bristol.

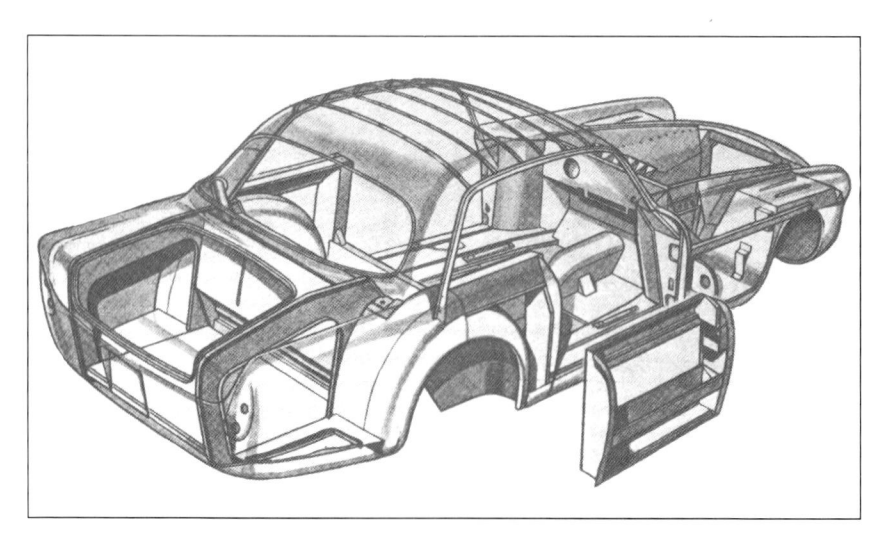

A sad sight! A Type 406 Bristol saloon in urgent need of restoration.

Rear view of the same Type 406 Bristol saloon, long-neglected yet still capable of restoration.

Close-up view of dashboard of a Type 406 Bristol saloon. Major instruments are all in a single 'pod' immediately in front of the traditional Bleumel twin-bladed steering wheel.

widely sweeping blades, with which the water supply was synchronised, the new system was especially valuable on those bitty days, when the weather seems unable to decide whether to rain or not. On a motorway, the muddy spume from other traffic bespatters the windscreen, and makes driving hazardous. Yet a touch of the button and, as if by magic, the jets begin, followed by the wipers, and all is clear again. Such a facility is commonplace now, but we are talking of over thirty years ago.

There was crash padding in strategic places inside the car, and the big two-bladed Bluemel steering wheel could be adjusted. Ample storage capacity was built into the car too – pockets in both doors and behind the front seats, plus a substantial cupboard (for it was bigger than a glove compartment), illuminated at night and with its own lock. As on the 404–405 models, the spare wheel was housed under a hinged flap on the nearside wing, with battery, servo and electrics in a similar position on the offside, and the boot could absorb an amazing quantity and variety of baggage.

The headlights by Marchal were able to throw a long enough beam on full to ensure that fast driving was safe at night. On dip, the light was spread in a fan-shape, useful without troubling other traffic. The pass and fog lights were especially valuable in mist or fog. Since the 406 was still equipped with that ultra-long starting handle, if one did leave the lights on all night, and was faced next morning with a flat battery, there was no need to call the garage, or bother one's neighbour. It was prudent, however, to retard the ignition, using the dashboard control. That 'stretched' engine can otherwise kick back quite viciously, and barked knuckles or even a sprained wrist can result, if the ignition is left fully advanced.

You ask: 'Surely this paragon must have the odd blemish?' Well, some early examples did tend to

Semi-front view of the Type 406Z prototype. It uses the Bristol chassis and Type 110 engine and a saloon body by Carrozzeria la Zagato of Milan. Note the shrouded headlights and the orifice for a starting handle.

overheat, though the repositioning of the auxiliary lamps seemed to cure this problem. And that handsome alloy body can be vulnerable to clumsy parkers, and possibly nowadays to the envious vandal too. After a couple of unfortunate incidents, I preferred not to use my Bristol, except for long cross-country journeys, or to friends with a drive or some other space where it might be left away from the road. Damaged alloy panels are usually repairable, but they call for specialist skills that are far from cheap.

This chapter, so far, has dealt only with the standard Type 406 Bristols that were made at Filton, but there were also some chassis-engine units that were sent to Italy. Here they were fitted with special bodies by the famous coachbuilders, Carrozzeria la Zagato, of Milan.

Two types of body were available: a Zagato saloon on the normal chassis, with the 9ft 6in wheelbase, or a Zagato hard-top coupe, for which a special short chassis was used. So far as I am aware, six of the saloons were built, but only a solitary coupe.

After so many years, it has not been easy to trace, or even to identify, these cars and I would like to record my thanks to Harry Wareham for the assistance he has given me. Not only is he the fortunate owner of the one Zagato coupe, but is a long-term enthusiast for the Italian coachbuilders, and possesses a fund of knowledge that must be unique in Britain.

The coupe is a regular visitor to the Bristol Owners' Club events, for Harry Wareham is the Chairman, and has organised several very successful events, including the Concours. The coupe has a wheelbase of only 8ft 6in, and its chassis is No. SP2.

A side view of the unique 406Z Bristol with coupe body by Zagato. Note the shrouded headlights, plexiglas air duct in bonnet, wraparound bumpers and generous window space. The wheels are the standard Bristol perforated discs, without nave plates.

The only similar short chassis has the number SP1, and will be dealt with later. The Zagato coupe, registered in Britain as 3 VPH, was exhibited originally on the Zagato stand at the London Motor Show of 1960, and not, as one might have expected, on the official Bristol stand. It was beautifully displayed, and attracted much favourable attention. The wide air duct is of Plexiglas, and it was specially fitted with an electric light, so that one could look down and see the immaculate Bristol engine with its three chromed pancake air filters.

Like so many interesting vehicles, the coupe changed hands several times, and when at last it was acquired by Harry Wareham, he found its handling far from perfect. As a long-term Bristol owner, he sought to find the reason, and discovered that someone had tried to improve the rear suspension. Large rubber blocks had been wired to the chassis and rear axle, though what the intention was for such action quite escapes me. Wareham lost no time in getting rid of the modification, and then, as he had hoped, the coupe's handling was all that could be desired in a no-nonsense sports car.

The engine was the extremely rare 110S, of which only a tiny handful were ever made. With a cubic

A front view of the Type 406Z Bristol, with coupe body by Zagato. It is the only example made, using a shorter than standard wheelbase (8'6" compared with 9'6"), and the very rare 110S engine, with a power output of 130bhp at 5,750rpm, and a cylinder capacity of 2,216cc. In the photograph, the car is cornering at speed during a hill climb. Note the shrouded headlights, wide shallow air duct in bonnet, and the way in which the body top 'dips' in the centre. It has been owned for many years by Mr Harry Wareham, Chairman of the Bristol Owners' Club.

THE END OF A LINE

Three-quarter side view of the unique Type 406Z Bristol, with coupe body by Zagato. Note oval air inlet, with twin fog/road lamps, starting handle orifice, plexiglas air duct on bonnet, and special nave plates.

The unique Type 406Z Bristol with coupe bodywork by Zagato on the right, with the 406Z Bristol saloon. Though its body is also by Zagato, the coupe is not similar as regards shape of bonnet top air duct, shape of grille and wheel base.

On the right one can see the unique Type 406Z Bristol, with coupe body by Zagato, and on the left is an Arnolt-Bristol, with open sports body by Bertone of Turin.

capacity of 2,216cc, a sporting camshaft giving valve timings of 40:80:80:40, and a very special twin-pipe exhaust system by the Italian specialist, Abarth, the engine developed 130bhp at 5,750rpm, with a compression ratio of 9.0:1. What the coupe's maximum speed must be, I do not know, but once, when I asked this question, he just smiled and said 'enough'. He is a very fast driver and has used the coupe for long continental tours as well as for many thousands of road miles in Britain. He had also campaigned the car in sporting events, including the Prescott Hill Climb, where it did not disgrace itself against modern opposition.

The car's interior is strictly functional, with simple bucket seats and slatted backs. The essential dashboard instruments are set out in typical Italian style, and the sprung steering wheel with its thin wooden rim is by Zagato, and quite unlike the big twin-bladed

Side view of unique Type 406Z Bristol with coupe body by Zagato. The car is competing in a speed hill climb at Prescott. Note low build, rear filler cap, shrouded headlight and standard Bristol road wheels.

Steering wheel on a Type 406Z saloon. This was a standard fitment. Note the 'Z' badge on the wheel boss. The 3 spokes are 'sprung'.

Bluemel of the standard 406 saloon. It is good to know that this unique machine is kept in superb condition by its enthusiastic and knowledgeable owner.

The Zagato Saloon Models on 406 Chassis

According to the BOC Register, just six of these models were made:
 1958–1959 Chassis Nos 5255 and 5256
 1959 Chassis Nos 5284, 5298, 5299 and 5300

Chassis 5255 Until recently the only knowledge I possessed of this car was that it had been registered in Britain as A 88, and had once been seen by a BOC member in the East Molesey area of Surrey. However, in September 1989, I received additional information confirming the car's existence, though now located in California. The body had been resprayed white, with cream upholstery, and the owner was stated to be Mr P R Schroeder. I am most grateful to Dr B J Cuddigan for this new data, and I know he is endeavouring to research the car's early history, when, for a time, it appears to have been re-registered in Britain as SPC 156. Its engine number is given as 5057.

Chassis 5256 Like the coupe, it was exhibited on the Zagato stand at the London Motor Show in 1959, and was subsequently purchased by a Mr McKechnie who lived in Cheshire. After being acquired by a Newcastle-under-Lyme garage, it passed into the hands of Messrs Bradburn and Wedge who were Bristol agents. It was loaned to Harry Wareham for some three months after which it was purchased by his friend, R F Brooks.

Following an accident, it was resprayed chocolate brown, but when spares proved hard to locate the car was sold to an antiques dealer from Moreton in Marsh, Oxfordshire. The next owner was Tony Mitchell, a great BMW and Bristol enthusiast, who sprayed the car purple, and changed the colour of the upholstery from its original white, using new Connolly hides. Its current owner is a BOC member, W Hunt of Stanford-in-the-Vale, in Berkshire. It is not often that one can trace a car's history for so long a period and with so many owners, and I am grateful to all those BOC members who have helped in this research.

Chassis 5284 I have not been able to find anything about this car, except that after being involved in a serious accident 'it was broken up on the instruction of Mr Crook'.

Chassis 5298 This car also suffered damage in an accident in Britain, but was later exported to New Zealand, completely restored, and has been owned for many years by BOC member, B R Flegg.

Chassis 5299 This car was registered on 12 May 1981 as 120 NPK, and was purchased by another enthusiastic BOC member, R D B Robinson. An engineer, he maintains the car in a really immaculate condition, and brings it to most Club events, where it is usually surrounded by enthusiasts with their cameras. At the Birmingham Classic Car Show (28 April to 1 May 1989), I remember one foreign visitor who remained on the Club stand almost all one afternoon. The Robinson car seemed to fascinate him, for he took many photographs, and asked innumerable questions about it. Just before he left, he turned to me and said: 'You know, this has really made my trip worth while. To me this is the finest car in the entire show. And to think, I very nearly didn't come!'

Chassis 5300 The last of the mini-series of Zagato 406 saloon, it was registered as 138 WPJ, and like the Robinson example was owned by a BOC member, L J Brownhill, and often appeared at Club events, always in superb condition. After keeping it for many years, during which he used it mainly for long-distance Continental tours, Brownhill sold his car to another Club member, L J K Setright, a motoring journalist, and a former Chairman. Afterwards, the car changed hands several more times, but is now being fully restored by J Hamshere who is also a BOC member.

Three-quarter side view of a Type 406Z Bristol, with bodywork by Zagato. Note the registration painted on bonnet, the grille below with twin fog/spot lights. The overriders and alloy road wheels are non-standard.

Rear view of Type 406Z Bristol with Zagato saloon body. Note high wide rear window, the very long boot lid extending to the concealed bumper. Note how latter extends to protect the wings. Zagato 'signature' on lid, and simple rear lamp treatment. The rear screen is fitted with a defrosting element.

Zagato Policy – and Practice

It appears likely that it was the Zagato intention to fit the 110S engine as standard. When John Dennis, later foreman at the Chiswick service depot, visited Milan to inspect progress, he found that owners were specifying the 110 unit instead. Presumably they feared that so highly tuned an engine might be unsuitable for their motoring needs. No one, except Mr Crook, now seems to know the precise number of 110S units shipped to Italy, or what their eventual fate may have been.

The bodywork which was fitted to the 406Z models had much less overhang than that of the standard Bristol 406, so that, apart from the badge and Bristol road wheels, there were few external points of resemblance.

One might describe the cars as close-coupled four-seaters, yet in fact they were astonishingly roomy, even if the luggage boot was smaller than on the Bristol 406. Compared with the latter, the interior was rather spartan; one felt the intention was to build a high-performance car that could take four adults and a limited quantity of baggage on long touring holidays, at high average speeds. Even when fitted with the standard Type 110 unit, the car was fast, due to its light weight and good aerodynamic efficiency.

A 'trick shot' of a Type 406Z saloon, taken through the back window of a Type 403 Bristol. It took place along the Mulsanne Straight of the Le Mans 24 Hour circuit, at a speed of 90mph!

Three-quarter side/front view of the prototype 406Z Bristol with saloon bodywork by Zagato. It bears a strong resemblance to another design used on the Lancia Zagato, though the road wheels are standard Bristol.

Three-quarter side view of Type 406Z with saloon bodywork by Zagato. It was exhibited on the Zagato stand at the London Motor Show in 1959. Note the shrouded headlights, starting handle orifice, shallow air duct in bonnet and large windscreen and side windows. The fake wire wheel nave plates are special; standard saloons usually had the Bristol pierced disc type.

A Type 406 Bristol saloon, side view. The wing mirrors and kick plate are non-standard, but the dark colour suits the rather heavy lines of the car very well.

The frontal aspect was not unlike a Lancia, with the smallish rectangular radiator grille recessed into the surround, and still with a hole for the Bristol starting handle. Large shrouded headlights were set into the tops of the wings, with flasher trafficators just below. The bumper treatment was very subtle – just a narrow chromed blade that from the front seemed part of the body, though its ends curved to protect the front wings to some extent.

The exterior was quite plain, except for a single chromed strip that extended rearwards, from the front wing to the edge of the door, doubling as a rubbing strip. The windscreen was rectangular and, combined with a generously proportioned rear window, made it a light and airy car. The roof pillars were slender as were the windscreen supports, yet there was neither rattle nor shake, even after a very considerable mileage.

The only styling quirk was the way in which the beading that ran along the edge of the windows at waist height suddenly turned at right angles, then became straight again, running below the side window. It seemed to serve no useful purpose unless it was intended to represent the 'Z' logo. The rear view was good, through a wide rectangular screen, and, like the Zagato coupe, the saloon had a most practical and purposeful appearance. As one BOC member said: 'There's something of the old "lean and hungry" look about them. How I wish they'd gone into series production'.

But that never happened, and there were just this half a dozen of those superb motor cars, which, for many enthusiasts, represent the very zenith of the Bristol-engined Bristols.

A rather different opinion was expressed by Mr Crook who explained that the short series was to allow an assessment to be made of post-war Italian coachwork 'build'. This was found not to meet the 'Bristol Standard' of quality, and much rectification was needed both at the Filton factory, and at Hersham where Anthony Crook Motors Ltd was then based.

17

The Bristol Racers

Although the Bristol Aeroplane Company had been building the FNS model engines for AFN Limited since 1949, it was not until November 1952 that an announcement was made that a works team would compete in the next year's Le Mans.

Since the event was due to be held in June 1953, the assumption has been made that, starting from scratch, the cars were built in seven months. In fact a Racing Department had been established by 1 January 1952, in a section of the Service Department. I knew the latter well, and marvel that so small an area could have been sub-divided. But this was typical of the fashion in which the infant department would be run, both as regards finance and staff.

A small team of experienced mechanics was seconded from other sections, and T V G Selby was moved from the Sales Department to look after general administration. Before the war he had driven Bugattis successfully, but lacked practical experience of team management. To assist him, S C H (Sammy) Davis was engaged, a journalist and racing driver, with tremendous experience, which included a spell with the Bentley team in its Le Mans heyday.

Other outside appointments included Percy Kemish and Stanley Ivermee. They were both development engineers of long standing: the former would be responsible for engine development, the latter with a more general remit. It was typical of Kemish that one of his first acts was to find out the octane rating of the French petrol that would be obligatory for the practice and race at Le Mans. Having done so, he next sought an English equivalent, for use in the engines he was to work on, and which would be supplied to him by the Engines Division.

They were delivered, with an alleged power output of 150bhp, but Kemish, who had never worked on a Bristol engine before, preferred to make his own judgement. Using a dynamometer, he spent 200

Front/side view of the only Type 450 Bristol extant. Note shrouded head lights and metal tonneau cover. The driver is Mr Anthony Crook, Chairman and Managing Director of Bristol Cars Ltd.

Side view, left/right of the only Type 450 Bristol racer still in existence. Note the large door (to facilitate entry after the traditional 'Le Mans' running start), the wide plexiglass screen and flush filler cap on wing, huge rear fin and inset rear light. A half-shaft might be replaced during a race without affecting wheel or brake if the circular hub plate is removed. It was never used in the three years 1953–1955, when the cars competed at the Le Mans 24 Hour and Reims 12 Hour races.

hours, increasing the engine speed in 500rpm stages, from 1,000 to 6,000rpm, and making adjustments where required. At the end of this long session, his engines would produce a maximum of 140bhp @ 6,000rpm, with complete reliability. The latter element was essential on engines that would have to survive twenty-four hours near the limit set for their revolutions per minute.

Discoveries and Misgivings

Kemish, who kept immaculate power curves and detailed notes, had found the optimum settings for the ignition systems, and the mixture of air and fuel that gave the best results. The ignition had to be set just 36 degrees before top dead centre, and the fuel mixture consisted of one part petrol to thirteen parts air. Both were critical, the slightest change resulting in an immediate loss of performance.

Kemish told me that he had sustained some criticism, on the grounds that he had wasted so much research time to obtain 140bhp, when other engines of basically similar BS type already produced more power at lower engine speeds, and had been used successfully in other makes of car, notably Cooper-Bristol and Frazer Nash. He rebutted such criticism by pointing out that he was using a much lower octane fuel, with a corresponding fall in compression ratio, and that his engines were to race for twenty-four hours, and not for the much shorter duration of the usual Formula 2 events in which the BS units had done so well.

Kemish was beset by fears concerning the manner in which the balance weights were secured to the massive crankshafts, and discussed this with Stan Ivermee. Both men considered it likely that, under race conditions, there was a grave danger of the weights detaching themselves and wrecking the engine. No notice was taken of his warning, but when

> **Percy Kemish**
>
> Though his primary responsibility was the development of the BSX engine, it would seem that he may also have been involved in the final stages of construction of some of the other types of racing engines. Ray Williams describes how he and Alfie Freke would wait outside the building in which their engine was being checked on the test bed. Only when the resultant power curve was to Kemish's satisfaction would their joint responsibility end. After that point, Kemish would attend to any further tuning. It is not clear if this referred to the BS engines, or only to the BSX series. It would seem that Kemish was not inclined to reveal his methods, or even the exact timings he used, preferring to keep such hard-won information to himself. I recall once asking him to complete a questionnaire, by just ticking a series of boxes. But it was never completed, and his vast store of knowledge died with him.
>
> Each engine was subjected to almost constant inspection, with the responsibility for building the unit 'up to the cylinder head' belonging to Ray Williams, and for the preparation of the cylinder head to Alfie Freke.
>
> Williams describes the quality of inspection as follows: 'I have never seen such exacting standards before or since, and I used to say the engines were good enough to fly.' He mentions how long the inspectors had been at Filton, most of them having been AID inspectors and so used to aero-engineering standards.
>
> Williams ends with an amusing description of the only two occasions when he actually accompanied a test-driver. The first was a rush down the two-mile-long Brabazon Straight, when over 100mph was achieved. On the second, with Dave Williams as the test-driver, the car was acting as 'pace-maker for the Police patrol'. The car took to the grass verge at over 80mph, and, though the driver had the car under complete control, the passenger said: 'I was glad to go home in my Fiat 500.'

he thought he had found an ally in Stuart Tresilian, he felt more hopeful that action would be taken, as the latter was a celebrated engineer.

Tresilian did mention the matter, but not, it would appear, with enough conviction, despite his vast experience of racing cars and their weaknesses. So nothing was done, and Kemish could only hope his fears were groundless, and await a suitable chassis into which the engines could be installed for road testing. He was well aware of the difference between the reliability on a test bed under near-ideal conditions and the behaviour of the same unit when subjected to the often rough and unsympathetic treatment of an average racing driver.

At the end of the Second World War, Raymond Mays founded British Racing Motors (BRM) and also Raymond Mays & Partners Ltd. Mr T A D Crook became a director of the latter while still in the Royal Air Force, and explains: 'This is how I became part of Bristol from Day One!'

The remnants of the pre-war English Racing Automobiles Ltd (ERA) were sold to Leslie Johnson, a successful racing driver. It was his intention to build up a 'G' type ERA of very advanced design. The chassis was both innovative and effective, but the venture was plagued with mechanical problems. Johnson wished to build an engine of 2,000cc capacity, based on the overhead camshaft Norton racing motor cycle unit. In the interim, he used Bristol engines, and, to reduce their height to fit his chassis, converted them to dry sump lubrication. In doing so, he appears to have spoiled their reliability, much to the disgust of his works driver, Stirling Moss.

With only the one chassis, and six unreliable engines, development was neither consistent nor effective, and when Johnson suffered a heart attack the chassis and blueprints were acquired by the Bristol Aeroplane Company. A well designed and race-proved chassis was now available, on which the team cars might be based.

Testing

One of the features of the 'G' type ERA was the extensive use of what in pre-war racing circles was referred to as 'trouble metal', rather than steel. Thus the chassis was of magnesium-zirconium – light, strong and very expensive. Selby used thin-wall steel tubing, yet 'his' chassis weighed just 3½lb more, including an additional cross-tie.

The next step, much to the relief of Percy Kemish, was to install the engine and the gearbox and then commence practical road-tests. 'Road' is perhaps a euphemism for the torture that was inflicted, by the 'pavé' section of the test track that forms part of the facilities at the headquarters of the Motor Industry Research Association (MIRA). At its first attempt, the car failed to complete even one lap – those uneven stone setts causing the entire collapse of the rear suspension.

When this had been corrected, a second attempt was made, and this time it was the engine bearers that failed, the engine crashing to the ground, fortunately without serious damage. Nothing daunted, Selby tried again, and with improved engine mountings the car completed three full laps without disaster, a distance that was judged the equivalent of a full Le Mans race.

The bodywork was supplied by the Aircraft Division, and the design had shown an excellent drag coefficient when wind-tunnel tested. It was a hard-top coupe, and when the cars were taken for road testing at Silverstone all appeared well, so far as the vehicles were concerned, though some of the taller drivers were less than enthusiastic.

Since at their first appearance at Le Mans only two Bristols would be competing, a team of five drivers was deemed sufficient; two pairs, plus one spare – all had previous experience of the French long-distance race.

Not only the chassis of the 'G' type ERA had been used as a pattern by Filton; the road wheels were also accepted, and much of the braking system too. The wheels were little more than rims, plus five lugs for attachment to the car. At the front this took the form of a five-pronged spider, while at the rear each half-shaft extended past a similar spider, so designed that in the event of failure during a race a faulty half-shaft might be withdrawn and another fitted, without removing the wheel.

The ERA had used 12in diameter drum brakes of ultra-orthodox type, yet they possessed a power of retardation so great that the car's designer, David Hodkin, had recorded a G stop @ 100mph, more than three times the theoretical efficiency of the 'Hundred Percent' formula on which the Tapley performance meter was based.

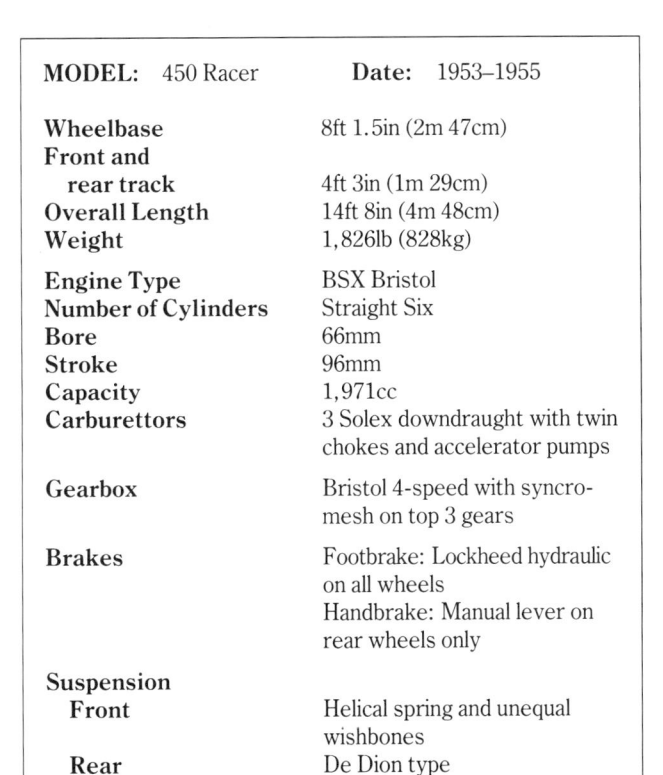

MODEL: 450 Racer	Date: 1953–1955
Wheelbase	8ft 1.5in (2m 47cm)
Front and rear track	4ft 3in (1m 29cm)
Overall Length	14ft 8in (4m 48cm)
Weight	1,826lb (828kg)
Engine Type	BSX Bristol
Number of Cylinders	Straight Six
Bore	66mm
Stroke	96mm
Capacity	1,971cc
Carburettors	3 Solex downdraught with twin chokes and accelerator pumps
Gearbox	Bristol 4-speed with syncromesh on top 3 gears
Brakes	Footbrake: Lockheed hydraulic on all wheels Handbrake: Manual lever on rear wheels only
Suspension Front	Helical spring and unequal wishbones
Rear	De Dion type

Road wheel on a 450 Bristol Le Mans racer. The design is similar to that used on the 'G' type ERA, the chassis of which formed the basis for the Type 450 Bristols. The 'wheel' is just a rim with five lugs to attach it to a 'spider' on the rear axle. An interesting Bristol refinement was the manner in which, while in a race, a damaged half-shaft might be replaced without disturbing road wheel or brake.

To Le Mans

Selby, with 'Sammy' Davis's concurrence, had allotted one car to be shared by T H 'Tommy' Wisdom, another journalist-racer, and Jack Fairman, a professional test driver. The other pair were much younger, though almost equally experienced in long-distance events. They were Lance Macklin, who proved wealth was not incompatible with a successful racing career, and Graham Whitehead, who often drove in partnership with his brother Peter. The reserve driver was Peter Wilson, a pilot in the Fleet Air Arm, and at 6ft 4in the tallest member of the team.

In February, his height had rendered it impossible for him even to get into the mock-up body, which caused some consternation, with only four months before the race. The Bristol gearbox was attached to the differential, so that the driver was positioned between it and a chassis tube. To make it even more uncomfortable, a cross member just behind the driver prevented him even leaning backwards, which might have provided some small relief. It must be remembered too, that the wheelbase was only 8ft 1½in, just 1¼in more than the little 404. Unlike the standard models, its front and rear tracks were identical, 4ft 3in, while the turning circle of 39ft was 3ft more than the 403's.

The original bodywork had been notably smooth, but various modifications had been made as additional equipment and accessories had been added, including an external oil cooler and bonnet straps. Not only must these have had an ill-effect on the drag coefficient, but holes were cut to accommodate some items, seemingly with little regard for their effect. When practice commenced, drivers complained that their cars were overgeared, yet at Silverstone all was well, so the assumption must surely be that the smooth air-flow during the earlier sessions had been affected adversely.

Though Sammy Davis found difficulty in imposing his ideas of pit discipline on some younger drivers, the mechanics appear to have been co-operative, and they soon became a most efficient team. Kemish remained worried about the crankshaft balance weights, but the practices passed off without any mechanical mishap. Vivien Selby had misgivings regarding the brakes, and holes were drilled in the drums so that the linings might be checked during a tyre/wheel change.

In his excellent account of the races, entitled simply *Le Mans*, Anders Ditlev Clausager's sole reference to the 1953 team was: '. . . two Bristol 450 coupes with their exceptionally aerodynamic but not very attractive bodywork'.

The original body used on the Type 450 Bristol racers. Note oil cooler in air intake, poorly streamlined lamps and the twin filler caps for the fuel tanks set into the wings.

The Race

At 4pm on Saturday 13 June 1953 the race began. This year a special regulation had come into force whereby no one driver might cover more than eighty consecutive laps, or spend more than eighteen hours at the wheel. Both of the Filton cars made excellent starts – the drivers sprinting across on the 'go' signal, leaping into their cars, with first gear already engaged, so that with one press of the starter button they were away.

As the hours passed and the number of laps covered increased, Kemish began to feel that perhaps, after all, his fears had been groundless. But on lap 21 the balance weights on the Macklin/Whitehead car did detach themselves from their crankshaft, smashing through the crankcase and almost causing a fire. The second Bristol continued to circulate well into the night, and when a similar mishap occurred some of the debris punctured an exhaust pipe, and a fire resulted. Wisdom, who was the driver, suffered burns and a dislocated shoulder and, for the team from Filton, the race was over.

Wisdom went to hospital, and the cars went back to the factory. With such a total disaster – a fall at the very first hurdle – there must have been some temptation for the directors to abort the rest of the programme, but this did not happen. Instead, just one month later, the two coupes, in their dark green livery were on the start line for the Reims Twelve Hour Race. In less than thirty days new engines had been fitted, this time with no balance weights, while the bodywork had been brought back to its original smoothness, the oil cooler faired in neatly, and the bonnet straps deleted.

Unlike Le Mans, the Reims Twelve Hour event, which was really a curtain raiser for the next day's Grand Prix, began at midnight, with drivers standing on one side of the road and their cars on the other. Graham Whitehead leapt into his Bristol and pressed the starter: but because of the exhaust roar from the other competitors, he could not hear his own engine, and took his foot off the clutch. In fact the engine had started and, since the first gear was already engaged, the transmission had to cope with the sudden surge of power from a crankshaft turning at some 6,000rpm. Something had to give, and a key sheared in the heavy-duty rear axle, which was a bought-out item from Ford.

But, as a disconsolate Whitehead was left to face an irate Selby and a disappointed Macklin, the other Bristol was well on its way. Wilson had taken over

On the left, a Type 450 Bristol racer can be seen passing slower cars, during the Reims 12 Hour race in 1953. The front of the car is much neater than when it ran in the Le Mans 24 Hour race earlier that year.

A night stop to refuel and change drivers during the Reims 12 Hour Race of 1953. The car is one of the three Type 450 Bristols. The mechanic on the right is checking the fuel level in the wing tank. There were two, and the filler caps were magnetic.

A Type 450 Bristol coming into the pits to change drivers, during the 1953 Reims 12 Hour Race. Note the oil cooler and shrouded lights. The body had been 'tidied up' after its first event – the Le Mans 24 Hour Race, a month earlier.

from the injured Wisdom, and with Fairman had a trouble-free race, winning the class for engines of 2,000cc capacity, at an average speed of 92.65mph. Perseverance and courage had paid off. Kemish of course was delighted, not only because his balance-weight fears had been justified, but also because of his success in curing a cooling problem that had only manifested itself during the Le Mans race. In the latter event, the regulations were interpreted so rigidly that radiators could only be replenished at stated intervals, which meant that a car might have to be withdrawn for the sake of a gallon of water.

Kemish had located the hot spot during the interim between races, and, after relieving the immediate area, he fabricated an additional method to cool the cylinder head. This included an auxiliary external pump, of high capacity, driven by a belt from the fan pulley. No further problems were experienced.

Record Breaking

With cars and staff back at Filton, one might have expected some sort of hibernation, for it was already autumn, and so much effort had already been expended. Instead, there were further modifications to the bodywork in an effort to reduce the drag coefficient even further. The original bonnet top had included a power bulge, and this was eliminated in favour of an air duct reminiscent of the 'elephant's trunk' used so successfully the previous year on Mike Hawthorn's Cooper-Bristol.

Kemish continued development work on the engines, but was unhappy with the connecting rod design, based on the standard Bristol engine. His persistence resulted in new rods; their purpose, as Kemish explained, was 'to put the cranks in line with the bearings, and eliminate their offset'.

It must have come as a surprise to the personnel of the Racing Department when instructions were received for a car to be prepared for E-class record-breaking at the Montlhéry circuit, near Paris. It was now very late in the year for such an enterprise, but it proved successful, despite some problems. The weather was cold, and trouble was experienced when carburation icing occured. A rough-and-ready solution was the insertion of an oily rag into the induction duct, thus raising the under-bonnet temperature.

Soon after the car had resumed its run, the bonnet threatened to come adrift, because the catch had broken. This might not have happened if the bonnet strap had been left *in situ*, but it had been eliminated during the inter-race modifications, and emergency efforts using wire did secure the bonnet. However, the perfect fit that had previously been taken for granted could not be achieved, and a slight drop in speed resulted.

All through that chilly day, the dark green Bristol continued to circulate, with the engine as crisp as ever, while one after another the records were broken. The new times and distances were:

Times
i) Over a duration of three hours an average speed was maintained of 116.42mph
ii) Over a duration of six hours an average speed was maintained of 115.43mph

Distances
i) 200 miles were covered at an average speed of 125.87mph
ii) 500 miles were covered at an average speed of 115.74mph
iii) 500 kilometres were covered at an average speed of 116.10mph
iv) 1000 kilometres were covered at an average speed of 115.49mph

With the above E-class records safely in the bag, the car was sent out for one more lap – the average speed being 126mph – and to use a well-worn cliche 'the engine never missed a beat'.

1953 was a year of change: a new Racing Department had been started from scratch. Kemish had, through painstaking experiment, developed the BSX, as the engine was called, into a unit that was fast, reliable and frugal; for a race can be won or lost on the number of replenishment stops. The disasters at Le Mans had been redeemed at Reims, and, as one mechanic put it after the Montlhéry visit 'Those records are just the icing on the cake'.

The much neater and aerodynamically efficient body used in the 1954 Le Mans 24 Hour Race. Note the 'rim' type wheels, magnetic fuel cap on wing and poor headroom for the driver.

1954 Le Mans and Reims

Perhaps the most obvious visual difference apart from a new nose section was the change of body colour, from the dark shade often referred to as British Racing Green to a much paler shade which some call Apple Green. I recall other makes, including Alvis and, I think, Talbot, which also altered their racing colours, as Bristol were to find, with success.

Yet more modifications were made to the bodywork, including the fitting of a new and larger rear screen. This was a result of alterations to the twin fins that ran from the roof and down the tail. Though some advantage was gained in directional stability, it was found that this feature also resulted in a local vacuum between the fins. A drag reduction of 14 per cent resulted from the changes and, from a layman's view, the car's appearance was a little less futuristic.

Meanwhile Kemish continued his engine development, concentrating on both improving carburation and designing a new exhaust system. As the designers of racing motorcycles had found, mainly by trial and error, considerable improvements in an engine's efficiency can be obtained merely by using a different means of exhausting the spent gases, and encouraging better combustion. Kemish spent many hours altering the air tracts, in quarter-inch stages, in his efforts to find an optimum length.

Another problem that required a speedy solution before the racing season was the elimination of carburettor fuel-spray at engine speeds at or near 6,000rpm. Kemish had failed in his attempts to persuade the Engines Division to provide him with additional camshafts, which he had hoped might cure the problem, and so he had to try another approach. The one big disadvantage of the Bristol engine was its height, which was due partly to its long stroke design, but also because of its direct induction system, with three Solex carburettors immediately above the cylinder head.

The solution that Kemish used – so that the engine height should not increase, yet the induction should be more efficient – was to design and fit a cone into each intake to provide a surface on which the spray could be collected. At the same time the air speed would be increased. After proving the success of these experiments, the remaining engines were also modified.

In a similar fashion, the exhaust systems of the three team cars were altered, though the single six-port exhaust manifold was retained. Now the six pipes were paired; 1–6, 2–5, and 3–4. This was an improvement on the single big-bore exhaust pipe used in 1953. But an even greater change was the adoption of a new and very special cylinder head, commonly termed the twelve-port, because there was now a separate intake for each cylinder, with its own choke because the Solex carburettors were of the twin-choke type. As in 1953, accelerator pumps were fitted to the carburettors, and the butterflies were streamlined.

On test, the 1954 engines produced 155bhp @

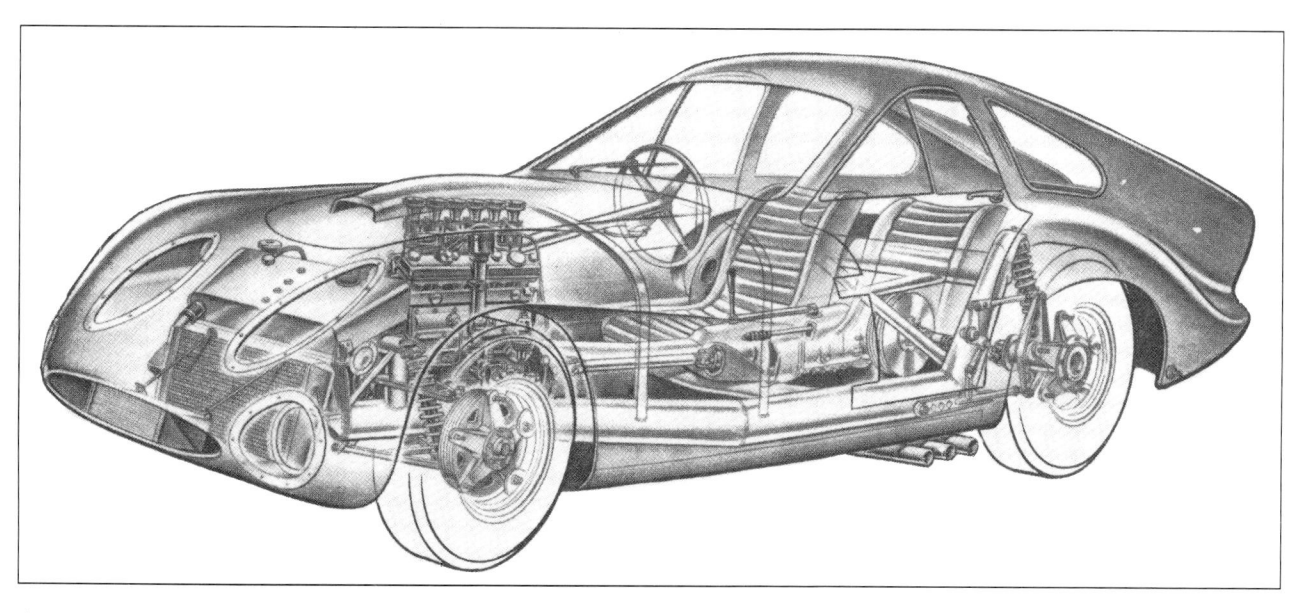

Cutaway drawing of the Type 450 Bristol racer. Note hammock seats, four spoked spring steering wheel, and six pancake air filters, indicating this is how engine was set up for 1954 Le Mans 24-hour race.

6,000rpm, which gave Kemish the perfect answer to those earlier critics, especially as he still used the same compression ratio of 8.5:1, due to the low octane value of the French petrol.

Now that Tommy Wisdom was available again, he was paired with his old running-mate, Jack Fairman. Peter Wilson now became a regular driver, with Jim Mayers, and the third car had a new pair: Mike Keen and Trevor Lines. The trio were members of a semi-amateur group called the Monkey Stable, and, to Sammy's relief, accepted his quite severe pit discipline without demur.

At Le Mans, the three Bristols ran faultlessly, despite atrocious weather. During one of his driving spells, Wilson lost his windscreen wiper blade, and knew his car carried no spare. Since no replacement would be permitted from the pits, he resolved to carry on despite the handicap. At one point conditions reached such a pitch that he could only see where he was going through a chink in the partly-opened driver's door.

To add to his misery, on the Mulsanne straight (the fastest section of the circuit) he was almost blinded by headlights on full beam. He learned afterwards that they belonged to the very fast Jaguar driven by Stirling Moss. He had turned off the course at a slip road, made a handbrake turn, and rejoined the circuit just as poor Wilson came in to view. Though the latter made light of it, it must have been a very nasty moment.

Perhaps to relieve the sheer monotony during one of his earlier driving spells, Wilson found that he could gain an extra 150rpm if the side windows were allowed to be sucked open by the wind pressure, to such an extent that he could insert his hand between the roof and the frame. Rather than lose this tiny advantage, he did not attempt to close them, though, since they were rear-hinged, this would have been both simple and a lot more comfortable.

Much to Selby's relief no brake problems had been encountered, though to facilitate any wheel changes he had fabricated an ingenious 'magazine' type wheel brace. As a wheel nut was unscrewed, it was retained in a spring-loaded tube, ready to be released when the new wheel was being fitted. Some years afterwards, a near replica must have made a lot of money for an enterprising accessory firm, since the design had not been patented either by the inventor or his employers.

The race ended with the three pale green coupes

The smiles of victory. The Bristol works team of Type 450 racers, just after the cars had gained the team prize in the 1954 Le Mans 24 Hour Race.

in seventh, eight and ninth places, and both the team and class awards were gained. Probably due to the weather, out of the original fifty-seven cars that began the race, there were just nineteen survivors.

Similar weather conditions prevailed at Reims three weeks later, and during the race problems arose because of rain water entering the air ducts and drowning the plugs. It seems strange that no similar trouble arose at Le Mans. Selby was content to allow a pair of fast Gordinis to forge ahead, as he was aware of their fragility, and doubted their likely survival. Towards the end of the race, there was a swift and reliable Ferrari leading the 2-litre class, with a Bristol only eight kilometres behind it. Perhaps it might have passed the Italian car to win its class for the second year, but Selby was intent on the team prize, and this was duly awarded to the Bristols, their finishing order overall being tenth, eleventh and twelfth. The Bristols were estimated to have covered a combined total of 10,000 miles in the thirty-six hours that the Le Mans and Reims races had lasted.

The only damage suffered by any of the trio had been at the very end of the race at Le Mans. Jack Fairman repeated in the latter event an accident similar to one suffered in practice. It was so close to the chequered flag that he just carried on, knowing that a pit stop to effect repairs would almost certainly have lost the team prize.

The Open Cars of 1955

Both Le Mans and Reims events had been marred by the humid weather conditions, and the drivers had found the confines of those narrow hard-topped coupes very trying. Whether it was because of this or for other reasons is not known, but for the 1955 races the cars were given open two-seater bodies. The passenger seat was blanked off with a metal tonneau cover, and behind the driver's head extended a fin of such proportions that it reminded me of something similar to that used on the Donald Campbell speedboat.

Like the earlier coupes, there were fitted carpets, and a set of instruments in a semi-rectangular panel in front of the driver. They included a rev-counter with a dial of 5in diameter, an ammeter and oil and water temperature gauges, an oil pressure gauge and the light switches. There was no speedometer, but there was an additional 'spy' needle in the rev-counter, so that the team manager could detect if his

Close-up view of Type 450 Bristol, the only example extant. Note the carpet, unusual on a racing car; also hammock-type seats and 'rear working' gear lever, as the gearbox was attached to the differential.

limit on engine speed had been exceeded. On one occasion, this involved a short conversation between Selby and Jack Fairman, as the spy was stuck very near the 7,000rpm mark, when the limit was still just 6,000.

As ever, Kemish was still seeking yet more reliable power, and he designed another exhaust system to this end. It consisted of the six pipes from the exhaust manifold merging first into a pair of larger pipes, and then blending into a single big-bore tail pipe. The crankshafts were completely polished, while the connecting rods were peened, to reduce the dangers of fatigue.

In a conversation with Percy Kemish many years later, he told me the open bodies were designed within the Racing Department, with one of the mechanics named Ken Evans holding up a large sheet

The Type 450 Bristol racer, with open bodywork, on test prior to competing in the 1955 Le Mans 24 Hour Race. Note the huge 'fin' behind the driver's head, the special 'rim' type wheels, inset filler cap on wing, and concealed door hinge. By unscrewing the rear hub cap, it was possible to change a half-shaft without disturbing wheel or brake. It was never needed.

of brown paper on which the shape was drawn. I did not ask where the bodies were made – probably by the Aircraft Division. Apart from the obvious advantage of no longer being cooped up in that confined coupe space, in an emergency a driver could steer by looking over the small curved aero screen that was mounted on a slightly raised scuttle.

The frontal area was reduced, compared with the 65 sq in of the coupes and it was found, during practice, that fuel consumption was improved to approximately 15mpg. At the rear, an ingenious modification had been made to the suspension, the object being to keep the wheels vertical under all types of road conditions. It was the brain-child of the chief engineer, David Summers. Though quite fragile in appearance, it proved most effective, and gave no trouble during the race. When asked to describe it, the reply was: 'Part Watt and part Summers'.

The 1955 Le Mans Twenty-Four Hours

Until now, nothing has been said of how the cars were conveyed from the factory to the venues and back again. Two trucks were used, each capable of carrying two cars, and fitted with body sides that could be let down to form either a counter or a shelter against the sun or rain. A full quota of hand tools was carried, with some simple machine tools such as a gantry for removing or fitting complete engines. Cooking facilities were included, so that the men could stop for a brew up, or a proper meal of eggs and bacon – and no doubt chips as well!

The one virtue those big trucks lacked was speed, and Kemish laughed when he told me of the consternation when the leading lorry found it had lost its fellow. It was a crowded road, and it seemed to take an age to turn and head back the way they had come, but the missing vehicle was found with, according to Kemish, 'a prop shaft that looked like a figure of eight'. The shame-faced driver admitted that 'he had been pushing it a bit', and with 35mph on the clock the truck had skidded to a standstill.

What to do? It was obvious that one over-loaded vehicle could not tow the other, and they were a long way from Filton. But the telephone can accomplish wonders, and in due course a small but powerful tug reached the scene, and the trek towards Le Mans resumed.

'And we didn't miss a practice session either,' Kemish told me, 'but the lads were a bit tired after they'd finished work, they'd had no sleep you see.' The team spirit was wonderful, and long hours and none too generous pay were taken for granted; to be able to boast of being a racing mechanic was the real if intangible reward.

For the 1955 event, the same three pairs of drivers were fielded, and as in the previous year the reserve driver was Jack Brabham, a dark, taciturn Australian. He did not drive in any of the 1954–1955 races, yet was destined not only to be a World Champion twice over but to make his own cars. They were winners of the Constructors' Award, a double that is, I believe, unique in motor racing history.

The 1955 Le Mans was, so far as the Bristols were concerned, almost a replica of the previous year's event. The three cars again finished in exactly the same order, and the 2-litre class award was secured again. However, the team prize went to a trio of fast and reliable Porsche cars of 1.5-litre capacity. Wilson's car suffered a broken exhaust pipe towards the end of the race but he carried on.

The event itself was marred by the terrible accident in which a Mercedes, driven by the Frenchman Pierre Levegh, was involved in a collison that resulted in his own death and that of 94 spectators and officials. The Mercedes team chief immediately withdrew his remaining cars, but the race continued, probably because of the organisers' fears that any other decision would have resulted in panic, and an attempt at a mass exit, which could have involved more deaths and injuries, and have prevented medical assistance from reaching the pit and grandstand area.

The Aftermath

Because of the accident, the Twelve Hour event at Reims was cancelled, and the Bristol team returned to Filton. Later the same year, Mike Keen and Jim

Mayers died in racing accidents not connected with Bristols. Whether this may have influenced the directors as regards their future policy is not known, but the Racing Department was closed down, and the regular staff moved back to their parent divisions, with most of the rest paid off to seek other employment.

It was a sad end to a project that, with a tiny staff, limited premises and a shoe-string budget, had established the Bristol as a marque that could win its class in major events, gaining valuable publicity and recognition.

But what, I have been often asked, happened to the cars? Here I feel it should be emphasised that I have had it on the highest possible authority that there were just three chassis, and not the nine or even twelve I have heard mentioned. The same three cars were fitted with two coupe bodies and one of open two-seater type and a variety of engines, and were subject to considerable structural modification. How different from modern racing, with a new team of cars for almost every big event!

On a board decision, to avoid the cars getting into the wrong hands, they were broken up and, the task being entrusted to the top members of the apprentice group. That one survivor has remained the property of Anthony Crook ever since, and at the Birmingham Classic Car Show, held at the International

---

Type 450 Bristol Racers at the Le Mans Twenty-Four Hour Race and the Reims Twelve Hour Race 1953–1955

Le Mans

1953 – The Macklin/Whitehead car recorded a lap of 97mph (some 5sec faster than any other 2-litre car that year). Later the balance weights detached from the crankshaft, wrecking the engine and nearly causing a fire. The car was retired.

The Wisdom/Whitehead car. After completing twenty laps the balance weights detached from the crankshaft, debris punctured the exhaust pipe and a fire resulted. Wisdom suffered burns and a dislocated shoulder. The car was retired.

1954 – The Wilson/Mayers car won 2-litre class, was placed 7th overall, covering 3503 kilometres.

The Wisdom/Fairman car was placed 2nd in class, and 8th overall, covering 3463.13 kilometres.

The Keen/Lines car was placed 3rd in class and 9th overall, covering 2327.16 kilometres.

Team award won.

1955 – The Wilson/Mayers car won 2-litre class and 7th overall covering 2,270.678 miles at 94.6mph (a new class record).

The Keen/Lines car was placed 2nd in class and 8th overall.

The Wisdom/Fairman car was placed 3rd in class and 9th overall.

Reims

1953 – The Whitehead/Macklin car broke a key in the rear axle at the start and was immediately retired.

The Wilson/Fairman car had a trouble-free race and won its class.

1954 – The Keen/Lines car won its class and was placed 10th overall. (Average speed 93.79mph.)

The Wilson/Mayer car was placed 2nd in class and 11th overall.

The Wisdom/Fairman car was placed 3rd in class and 12th overall.

1955 – The race was cancelled after the Levegh tragedy at Le Mans.

Other Le Mans Experience by Team Drivers

Fairman shared 1½-litre class award in 1949 and was 8th overall.
Wisdom shared 1½-litre class award in 1950 and was 16th overall.
Shared 5-litre class award in 1952 and was 3rd overall.
Macklin shared 3-litre class award in 1950 and was 5th overall.
Shared a car that finished in 3rd place in 1951.
Whitehead shared a car with brother Peter, and was placed 2nd overall in 1958.
Wilson had gained pre-1953 experience at Le Mans, sharing a Frazer Nash which finished but was not placed.

Side view of the only Type 450 Bristol still in existence. Note the shape of the wing just behind nearside front wheel, to allow air to escape after cooling brake. Note single exhaust pipe just ahead of rear wheel, also air duct on bonnet, and the huge 'fin' behind driver's head. The cars had competed at Le Mans and Reims: as closed coupes in 1953–1954; and in this open form in 1955.

Exhibition Centre (28 April–1 May 1989), it was exhibited on the Bristol Owners' Club stand.

The real motor sports enthusiast is often accused of being too emotional, so far as old cars are concerned, and, if such sentimental feelings are a fault in a hard and materialistic world, so be it. But I am sure the other members who helped staff the Club stand felt as I did when we saw that lovely pale green car in all its glory.

I had seen photographs of it as it had been prior to its complete restoration, but had not realised its size, for, with the overhang fore and aft, plus that enormous fin, it looked far bigger than I had expected. It was beautifully lit, both artificially and by being placed immediately below a large skylight. When the sun shone, the car seemed to change colour, from a greeny-silvery shade called, I think, 'eau de Nil', to a

A rear view of the only remaining Type 450 Bristol. Note the huge wing or fin just behind the driver's head, also the flush-fitting boot lid. Its size was dictated by the fact that all tools had to be carried on the car, plus spares and spare wheel.

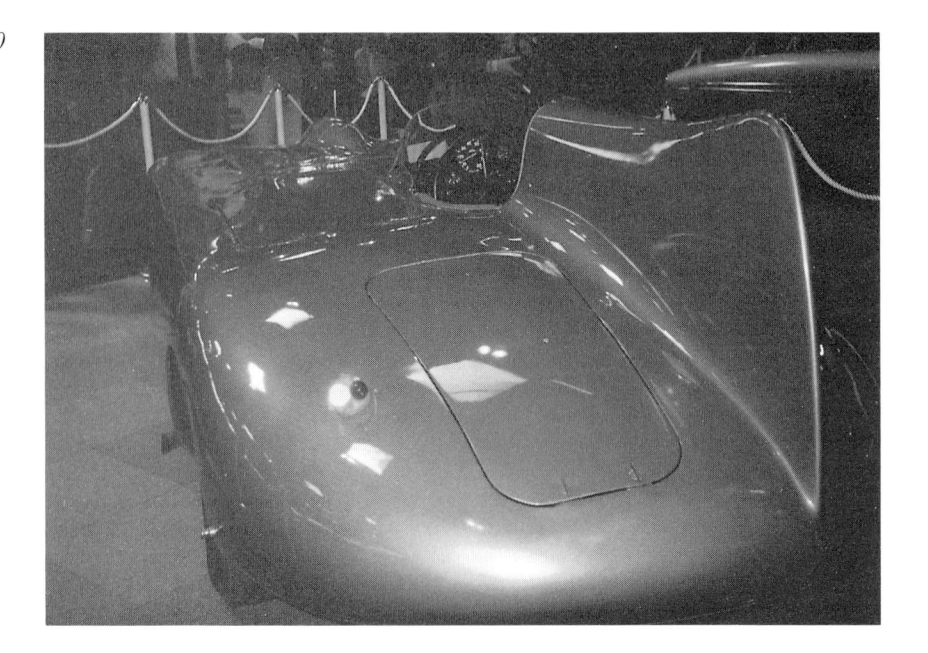

deeper hue, a trifle darker than the apple green, so often described.

The metal tonneau cover was in place, but the driver's seat was much more comfortable than many I have had the misfortune to occupy. The view ahead was reasonable, but then I'm short, and for someone of Peter Wilson's height it would have been much better. The door came up almost to my shoulder, and was slightly curved, with the catch neatly fitting into a depression on the inside, keeping the exterior quite smooth.

The carpets were fitted, and even piped (unusual on a racing car), and the short gear lever worked backwards, as it was connected to the gearbox mounted immediately in front of the differential. Clutch, brake and accelerator pedals all worked smoothly, and it was amusing, just for a few moments, to sit there 'doing a Walter Mitty' about competing at Le Mans.

Externally, there was plenty to see. Those pierced nave plates on the rear wheels for instance, where a faulty half shaft could be replaced without disturbing the wheel. Or the large rectangular panel concealing the space behind the driver's seat, where the spare wheel was stowed. It had a large empty area too, but that would probably have contained all the parts that could be required in the races, and which might not be stored at the pits.

On Sunday afternoon, 1 May 1989, Peter Wilson arrived at the stand, and stared for a moment or two at the car that he had once known so well. He climbed through the single smallish door, and settled himself behind the wheel, while the crowd watched, and asked such questions as: 'Who is he?' and 'Is it a Jag?'. The cameras whirred and the flash bulbs flared.

Much later, a harassed press photographer came and took a few pictures, while we hoped against hope that a journalist might interview Peter Wilson. After all, it cannot often happen that a man is reunited with the car which he drove, and won his class in, at Le Mans thirty-four years earlier. But no one came, and Peter had another appointment.

As he made a slightly difficult exit from the car, I asked him how he liked it, after such a complete restoration. He stared down at me for for a moment from his considerable height, and then said quietly: 'Oh it's all right, but what a pity they got the upholstery wrong, it was brown you know – not red . . .'

18
The Thief of Time

Despite its reliability and performance, the 2-litre Bristol engine suffered from one incurable problem, its limited capacity for further development. The Company's directors must have regretted their dismissal, back in 1945, of H J Aldington's advice to choose either the pre-war Type 335 BMW 3.5-litre unit or the 2.5-litre engine brought back from Munich on his second visit in October 1945.

By 1952, a demand for a bigger engine was growing, not so much because there was a lack of power (the FNS and BS series had proved their suitability as 'prime movers' in such successful racing cars as Frazer Nash and Cooper-Bristol), but because of the real skill which was required to get the best out of a long-stroke unit of a relatively small capacity.

Authority was given for Jan Lowy, a Czechoslovakian engineer in charge of power unit development at Filton, to begin design work on a new engine of advanced type, and with a swept volume of 3 litres. The Type number 160 was given this new unit, and the work progressed smoothly, until Lowy left Bristols for a job with Ford. His replacement was an engineer named Gerry O'Niell, from Rolls-Royce, and he increased the capacity of the 160 to 3.5 litres.

It was at this time that Stuart Tresilian became a frequent visitor to Filton, and began a working partnership with O'Niell as a consultant, with the detail design work still the latter's responsibility. Tresilian had had a long career, including involvement with the Schneider Trophy and Merlin aero-engines, and later with the Bentley 3.5-litre and the Rolls Phantom 3 cars.

Authority had also been given for work to commence on a new chassis, with the main responsibility given to Jack Channer, O'Niell's opposite number on the chassis development side. As he mentioned, during a talk to members of the Bristol Owner's Club in 1975: 'I became interested in rubber suspension. It was light, acted as the suspension pivot, had no static friction to spoil ride, and had inherent dynamic damping. Its disadvantage is that it settles, but this is a gradual effect, and can easily be overcome by adjusters, which we had anyway for the torsion bars of the later 2-litre cars.'

In his talk to the BOC members, Jack Channer described his design so clearly that I feel it should be quoted verbatim. The Code Number covering both chassis and the project as a whole was 220 initially, but this was altered to 240 in the later stages.

The Channer Chassis

'The 220 design became a skewed trailing arm type with the pivot axis crossing the axis of the wheels at 38 inches distance. This was done to avoid the jacking problems of the other swing axle designs which had a very bad reputation. We later had to lower the roll centre more, to put jacking completely to bed as a problem.

'The original front suspension design started by using coil springs. These changed to torsion bars, and finally to rubber. The reason for changing the front was a little different from the rear, which went to rubber first, for simplicity of layout and function. I found the proliferation of rubber pivot bushes at the front added a lot of spring rate without contributing to the supporting of load; they also gave rise to unwanted deflections.

'The twin wishbones using torsional rubber provided very large working bushes, with consequent small radial deflection. At the same time, there was fore-and-aft deflection or compliance – axial on the bushes, and this could assist in radial tyre thump reduction.

'The leading link design gave some braking anti-dive, and the links were convergent in front view, giving a slight swing-arm action. This gave better wheel camber angles when the body rolled, at the possible cost of gyroscopic kick. The roll centre was slightly raised to match the rear better than the 2-litre cars. There was, of course, an anti-roll bar, rack and pinion steering and disc brakes.

'We had earlier tried an aluminium road wheel, made in our 4 gauge, with a simplified peg-drive and knock-on fixing. This was a disaster. I used steel quick-release nuts, and they seized on the hubs – we never got them off at all. The wheel was not strong enough either. Dunlop went on with both these themes, and they and/or Jaguar eventually produced successful aluminium racing wheels with, more or less, my design of quick-release hub. Their wheels were much thicker, all credit to them.

'The 220 chassis frame was an improvement on the 400 or BMW/Budd frame in technical respects. The main members were 6 inches deep and 4½ inches wide rectangular sections in 14 gauge steel, that is 0.08 inches thick. This was lighter per foot and stiffer than the BMW. The front cross-member bolted to the BMW frame was welded into the 220. The centre cross-member was also 6 inches by 4½ inches rectangular, in place of 3 inch tube in the BMW. All joints were fully internally webbed, a very significant contribution to stiffness.

'The rear cross-member was formed by the fuel tank cavity, very large and stiff indeed. The seat pan and heel board formed the top and front. A skirt member mounting the final drive support casting formed the rear, and a detachable 'W' shaped bracing below the tank closed the member. This makes it advanced in concept even today.'

Work on the 220 chassis had now reached a stage when practical road-testing became possible. As the 160 engine was not yet ready, a 2-litre Bristol engine and gearbox were installed in an open chassis. The latter proved to be so stiff that it was possible to climb in, and rock it on its lightly set dampers in a 'rather boat-like fashion'.

A Change of Engine

After the chassis had covered 2,500 miles, a second-hand Jaguar twin-cam engine and gearbox were fitted. This was no reflection on the Bristol unit that had functioned in an exemplary fashion, but because it was necessary to discover how the chassis would behave with a unit of about the same capacity as the Type 160. The latter would now be of 3.65 litres.

Test drivers reported that they had experienced a 'very flat ride, with little roll'. During the subsequent road tests, another used Jaguar engine and two more gearboxes were driven virtually to destruction. It was found that while testing the chassis for maximum acceleration the hollow layshaft was split.

With winter approaching, some thought was given to the provision of a closed body, and a local caravan builder, Tom Clarke, was commissioned to build it, from a design by Jack Channer. He drew it quarter scale, with a sketch showing the front view, and another as seen from the side, and with this meagre data the body was built, from the dashboard rearwards, 'in a week or two'. Due to the lack of more sophisticated equipment, the only double-curvature was on the wooden members, for it was of mixed construction – wood frames and aluminium-skinned. Even the bonnet was without double-curvature, and the only other places where it was present were round the headlights, this work seemingly performed by one of the Filton fitters. The Jaguar engine 'sat in a rather untidy underbonnet, which never had any production design, of course'.

In place of the Enots pedal-operated One-shot lubrication system used on the standard Bristol models, there was a chassis lubrication pump, powered by pressure changes in the brake servo reservoir. It lubricated the rack and pinion steering, and the king-pins. The servo was by Clayton-Dewandre, a 5-inch VOM type. Channer reported that it caused 'brake response problems'. There was also an electric fuel pump (standard Bristol engines had mechanical pumps) and a vacuum tank for the braking system, using Dunlop multi-spot discs.

The steering column was of the jointed type and could be adjusted for rake, and the front seats were adjustable for height, as well as the usual fore and aft movement. This was of great advantage since the test driver, regardless of size, could obtain the ideal position both as regards visibility and control, and also comfort on the very long testing sessions.

The front springs, with trade name 'Flexitor', were of rubber, and made by the Spencer Moulton company. Alex Moulton was famous for his work on the rubber suspension of the Mini, and the various small and medium models then being made as either Austin or Morris cars. An interesting point was the fact that the treads on the tyres, which were prototypes, were cut manually and not by the usual commercial moulding techniques. To conclude, I will return to the Channer talk, as regards road-holding:

> 'On wet roads, on the tyres of those days, before the advent of hysteresis rubber compounds, the car could be drifted to very high yaw angles and easily recovered. Its first warning was a slight rear-endiness, or drift. This was followed by loss of steering feel, without front breakaway. The final break came on the rear. It performed in this respect, very similarly to the modern Mercedes 220 or BMW 2-litre. It was very safe.
>
> 'I remember looking out of the rear window as a passenger, when it was driven hard on a winding road. One couldn't detect any significant roll, by aligning the bottom edge of the window visually, against the road behind.'

Very precise requirements were given to the designers: the chassis was to have a traditional 9ft 6in wheelbase, but with the track enlarged to 4ft 10in. The weight of chassis, engine, transmission and bodywork was not to exceed 26.8cwt unladen. In fact, the wheelbase was originally 9ft 9in, and later lengthened to 9ft 10in, which was still not all that generous for a luxury full four-seater.

The Type 160 Engine

Mr Channer was not sure whether the the valve gear of the Lowy engine used the overhead camshaft type of actuation, but there was no doubt about the final version by Gerry O'Niell. This was in the classic tradition, with each bank of overhead valves possessing its own camshaft. The Type BSX engines that powered the Le Mans racers in 1954 and 1955 possessed what was known as the 'six-port' cylinder head, individual ports being cast into the alloy head, so that each hemispherical combustion chamber had an inlet and an exhaust port to itself.

This type of cylinder head was used on the new 160 engine, and since preliminary work on it began in 1952 it would seem that this predated the use of similar heads in the racing engines. An O'Niell innovation was the use of aluminium for the cylinder block, which was combined with the crankcase and ribbed for cooling and strength. With its classic 'Y' shape, narrow sump and block, twin valve chests and rocker boxes it was very handsome.

Carburation was by triple Solex instruments, each with two chokes – one for each cylinder. The crankshaft was fitted with a viscous damper, and the distributor was skew-driven, in contrast to the camshafts, which were driven by chain. Lucas equipment was used, including dynamo, starter and distributor. From photographs, it is impossible to tell whether there were separate pancake-type air filters, but a large oil filter was situated on the left-hand side of the block, just to the rear of the distributor.

The engine, in its later enlarged form, of 3.6 litres, produced 140bhp @ 5,500rpm. Maximum torque was 160lb ft @ 3,500rpm, suggesting a flexibility very suitable for a luxury car. The performance was excellent, considering that the only commercial fuel available was of very low octane value (70–74 RON).

The Transmission

This subject has been left until last because it was the main cause of the project's unhappy fate. Initially it appeared that the directors considered that a five-speed manual gearbox would be suitable, and one of the original conditions laid down was that the engine should be capable of giving the complete car acceleration in fifth gear at least as good as a contemporary 2-litre Bristol model enjoyed in top, i.e. fourth gear.

At that time, Dennis Sevier, the Chief Engineer, was designing a five-speed manual box with a direct top using a high degree of overdrive with a 3.45:1 axle. It was of a very sophisticated design, with a freewheel on first gear that would be virtually unburstable. Even when a fresh directive was issued to the effect that the new car should have automatic transmission, it is unlikely that anyone foresaw the long-term consequences. The Company had been building this type of transmission for large commercial vehicles for a considerable period, so that one might have considered it logical for a smaller version to have been designed, with little difficulty or delay.

This does not seem to have happened, with attention being focused on a design by the Smiths company, using a system which was originally American. This had relied on the magnetising of a metal powder held in a liquid in such a way that when the necessary electrical action took place the powder solidified, and was then capable of transmitting power. The Smith system differed from the American since no fluid was used, and the dry powder functioned just as well without it. This was modified by Filton, which produced a design that would allow the driver to use the transmission in manual or in automatic form.

Four years had now passed since the original authority had been given for the design and construction of the new model, yet it was still impossible for the car to be fully tested, though, individually, both chassis and engine had fulfilled expectations. Still the long-awaited gearbox was not ready, when seemingly to the surprise and consternation of all concerned, the order was given to abandon the project.

The reason for the decision was the accident to a Comet jet air liner, which crashed into the Mediterranean, under what at first were mysterious circumstances. The fault lay in the design of the windows of the fusilage, where cracking had resulted in what was termed 'implosion', with resultant loss of life. At the time, Britain led the world in the manufacture of jet aircraft, and the government panicked at the possibility that this market was in jeopardy.

The accident had occurred in 1954, but the research into its cause took almost two years. It resulted in a government order to the manufacturers of all British aeroplanes using jet engines that they should test every example made, in a most extensive, and expensive fashion. Bristols had no reserve funds to meet such an unforeseen contingency, and the only way it could be financed was by the immediate cessation of all development programmes.

This was the end of the 220/240 project, and in short order the junior staff were moved back to more routine tasks. A number of the senior members left for other fields, where their design talents might be better employed. One of these was Jack Channer, who moved to the Rootes Group, where his reputation grew until he was recognised as one the greatest experts in his very specialised field.

And what, I hear you ask, happened to the 240 chassis? After all, its innovations had been tested for more than 50,000 road miles, and found to be superior to any earlier Filton-made chassis. I found the answer in an account which included some 220/240 practical experiences, by Michael Newton, who had succeeded Channer at Filton. The relevant section reads: 'I think the 220 ended up in one of the draughtsmen's gardens, along with some other wrecks that the neighbours eventually complained about. It never actually ran with its own engine in it.' Newton also mentioned that 'about half a dozen of these engines were made, and they seemed to go quite well, though the aluminium blocks introduced some problems that were new to us'.

Conclusion

To an automobile historian, even an amateur, the unhappy conclusion of the 220/240 project and the 160 engine mark a watershed so far as the Bristol car is concerned. In 1956, the status of the Car Division was altered to that of a wholly owned subsidiary of the parent company, and in 1960 it was threatened with oblivion, when the government-inspired merger took place, whereby the Bristol-Siddeley Group, Vickers Ltd and English Electric Ltd were merged in a new consortium: The British Aircraft Corporation.

The marque was saved by the purchase of Bristol Cars Ltd, with Sir George White and Mr T A D Crook as co-directors, and it was they who made the policy decision to enter the luxury car market, with a series of Bristols using Chrysler engines of Vee-8 type, and their Torqueflite automatic transmission.

19
The Shape of Things to Come

With the cessation of the 220/240 project, it was obvious that some other engine and transmission system would have to be used if the marque was to survive. The first choice was the Star Sapphire unit used in the Armstrong-Siddeley luxury models, with its well-proved pre-selector gearbox. Some four Bristol chassis were tested with these units, before it was discovered that, since the Armstrong-Siddeley was being phased out of production, further tests of such obsolescent machinery would be pointless. At least one of these test cars has survived, and its BOC owner plans to restore it.

Now that it had lost the support of being part of the Bristol Aeroplane Company, it was essential that production should continue with as much as possible of the chassis and body used on the 406. Here the Chrysler package scored heavily, for, despite its greater cylinder capacity, the Vee-8 was compact enough to be fitted into the chassis frame used by the 406, and the Torqueflite automatic transmission required only minor adjustments to the chassis.

The front suspension had to be altered, coil springs replacing the transverse-leaf type used on the Bristol-engined models. The body design was altered very slightly: Dudley Hobbs, the Bristol Head of Design, proved a master in the art of obtaining the greatest visual change with the minimum of actual engineering.

The rear suspension was similar to that of the 406, using torsion bars as the springing medium, and when the new model – the 407 – appeared in September 1961, even the critics had to admit that, in appearance at least, 'it was still a Bristol'. But the demise of the Filton engine was deeply regretted by the old guard, who refused to admit that a big American Vee-8 could still give a car a sporting performance, or that an automatic transmission system was capable of being used to provide the driver with a means whereby he could still exercise some control of the intermediate gears.

Some test reports criticised the springing, as being too firm, but surely as a safety factor it is far better to have a car that may give a slightly bumpy ride over poor surfaces than to endure the 'wallowing' that was still not uncommon on many American sedans of that period.

Contrary to the gloomier prophets, the new model sold well, and it was obvious that the policy decision to move up market had been successful. A new type of customer was attracted to a car that combined exclusiveness with simple maintenance, since any local Chrysler agent should have been capable of routine servicing. Its mixture of luxury and performance was not lost on the businessmen who covered thousands of miles annually, and who appreciated such virtues, even if the price seemed high.

To the surprise of some 'little Englanders', the Chrysler engine proved extremely durable and reliable, so that six-figure mileages could be covered with just regular servicing, while the Torqueflite transmission gave very little trouble. Satisfied customers returned to buy the later models, confident that here was a make of car they could trust; one that believed in innovation and development.

As the years passed, model followed model, some with a close exterior similarity, yet each just that little bit more refined: a hold for the intermediate gears, power steering of the highest quality, a floor-mounted gear lever, and adjustable shock absorbers controlled from the dashboard. Such innovations received little publicity, though one did attract some brief press attention.

Mr Anthony Crook at Keevil Airfield after successfully testing the Avon safety wheel with a 144mph blow-out. He then announced that the Avon safety wheel would be fitted as an optional extra on all his cars.

The Avon tyre company had developed a safety wheel that was claimed to enable a car to slow down safely after a burst tyre, even at high speeds. Tests were carried out by Dennis Sevier, the Chief Engineer, who deliberately burst a tyre at 70mph, bringing the car to rest without mishap. Soon afterwards, Anthony Crook, the owner of Bristol Cars Limited, took another Bristol out and, with the speedometer needle steady at 144mph, pressed the button that would detonate an offside tyre. The car was brought to a halt with no fuss; one can but marvel at the cool courage necessary to carry out such a test, to make sure that even under the most extreme conditions the new wheel deserved its safety prefix.

The mid-seventies period was one of change in the British motor industry. Some much bigger car firms vanished. A few just went out of business, others fell victim to the sort of merger which can only end with a car that still bears a famous name, but is otherwise just a 'badge engineered' version of the standard model made by the dominant partner.

In 1976 the last of the second-generation Bristols was made. During the period 1961–1976 there had been six different models, one with a second mark, and one with no less than five, and technically only the 408(2) had a 'Mark'.

During the same period, three different Chrysler engines had been used, with various capacities and compression ratios. There were small changes to the dimensions of the bodywork, with the total length and height diminishing, and the weight increasing, as more and more equipment was added, making the cars ever more luxurious. Yet they were still capable of speeds and acceleration that were as good and sometimes better than the best of their continental rivals.

I have been asked to describe 'a typical buyer of a second-generation Bristol'. Not an easy thing to do! First one has to rule out what the economist calls 'ineffective demand', meaning the many who might wish to purchase the latest model, but lack the means. For some years such people were able to take advantage of the considerable difference between the price of a new and a used Bristol, though at the moment this appears to have diminished considerably.

So we must consider those fortunate few able to spend many thousands of pounds: mature businessmen in many cases. Then there are public figures who value the car's lack of ostentation, and those for whom the main attraction is its exclusiveness. Yet none would consider such a purchase if the car lacked its extremely high performance, or the perfection of its construction, equipment and comfort.

20

The Big Red Lump

The Chrysler Engine

In 1960, after Bristol Cars Limited had been formed as a private limited company, it must have taken a special kind of courage, faith and optimism to face a future that could only be described as bleak.

True, the actual factory building was still within the giant Filton complex, but the new company was no longer part of a giant organisation, and could no longer shelter beneath the umbrella image of what in 1939 had been recognised as the biggest manufacturer of aircraft and aero-engines in the world. Nevertheless, cooperation continued as before, on an agreed financial basis.

It was typical of the idiosyncratic manner in which the Bristol car evolved, that the two directors should have taken a view opposite to the popular one that 'bigger is better'. Instead they concentrated their efforts on a new hand-built motor car that would possess an unusual mixture of those qualities likely to appeal to discriminating motorists with the taste and means to appreciate them.

It must have been a relief that part of the bodywork of the Bristols was no longer made in-house, and for the new model a fresh contract was signed, for its panels to be made by Park Royal Vehicles Limited, at its works on the outskirts of north-west London.

But if the planned move up market was to succeed, it was clear that a new and more powerful engine was required – it would have to come from an outside source, preferably with its own automatic transmission. The company could no longer contemplate such new designs in-house.

The story is still told of how it was only because someone at the Chrysler plant at Windsor, Ontario, failed to detach the engine from its Torqueflite transmission that a Chrysler Vee-8 unit was even considered for the new Bristol. From my own practical experience of the controls common to American big business, I feel such a blunder most unlikely. What is certain is that a number of alternatives were under consideration, and that the final choice was the Chrysler.

In the late fifties and early sixties, the American foundry industry was famed for its skill in the manufacture of iron castings that were extremely thin and light, yet could cope with the output of very powerful engines. I have often noticed the harsh bark of a super-tuned American engine in some pursuit movie, compared with the high-pitched scream of its European counterpart.

That the choice of engine was right first time is indicated by the fact that from the original 407 in 1961 until the current range of models, every Bristol standard model has been powered by a Chrysler engine. A total of five different types have been used, each with a different cubic capacity, and with several changes in the compression ratio.

The basic design has not varied much, an oversquare type with the eight cylinders arranged in two banks of four, the valves actuated through short push rods, and a single chain-driven camshaft.

In standard form, a single carburettor was used, a Carter AFB 3131-5 4-Choke downdraught fitted with with an automatic choke, and drawing its fuel via a Carter mechanical fuel pump. Compression ratio was 9:1 (high by contemporary British standards) on the

Type 313 engine fitted to the 407, though on later models it varied from as low as 8:1 to as high as 10:1.

Some motoring writers have claimed that it is incorrect to refer to these excellent engines as Chryslers, but that they should instead be known as Plymouths – a make they appear to consider much inferior. For me, the basic criterion is that these engines have been designed to power models that may bear different names, but all of which are made and sold under the Chrysler banner, even if some dealers specialise in one variety, and others in another.

For this reason, I shall refer to all the prime movers in the series as Chryslers. In similar fashion I shall refer to the Torqueflite automatic transmission simply by its marque name, to avoid constant repetition. The system uses the hydraulic converter technique, as do several other American versions, yet many experts consider it as being their superior. I have no idea why this should be, but the changes from one ratio to another are made without jerk or snatch, and indeed are usually quite undetectable, unless one is watching the needle of the rev counter.

But enough on the history, background and choice of engine; let us now consider the various engines that have been used on Bristols.

Chrysler Engines

As mentioned above, the first model fitted to the Type 407 when announced in 1961 was the 313. Its bore/stroke ratio was 98.55mm x 84.07mm (hence the term over-square) and its capacity was 5,130cc.

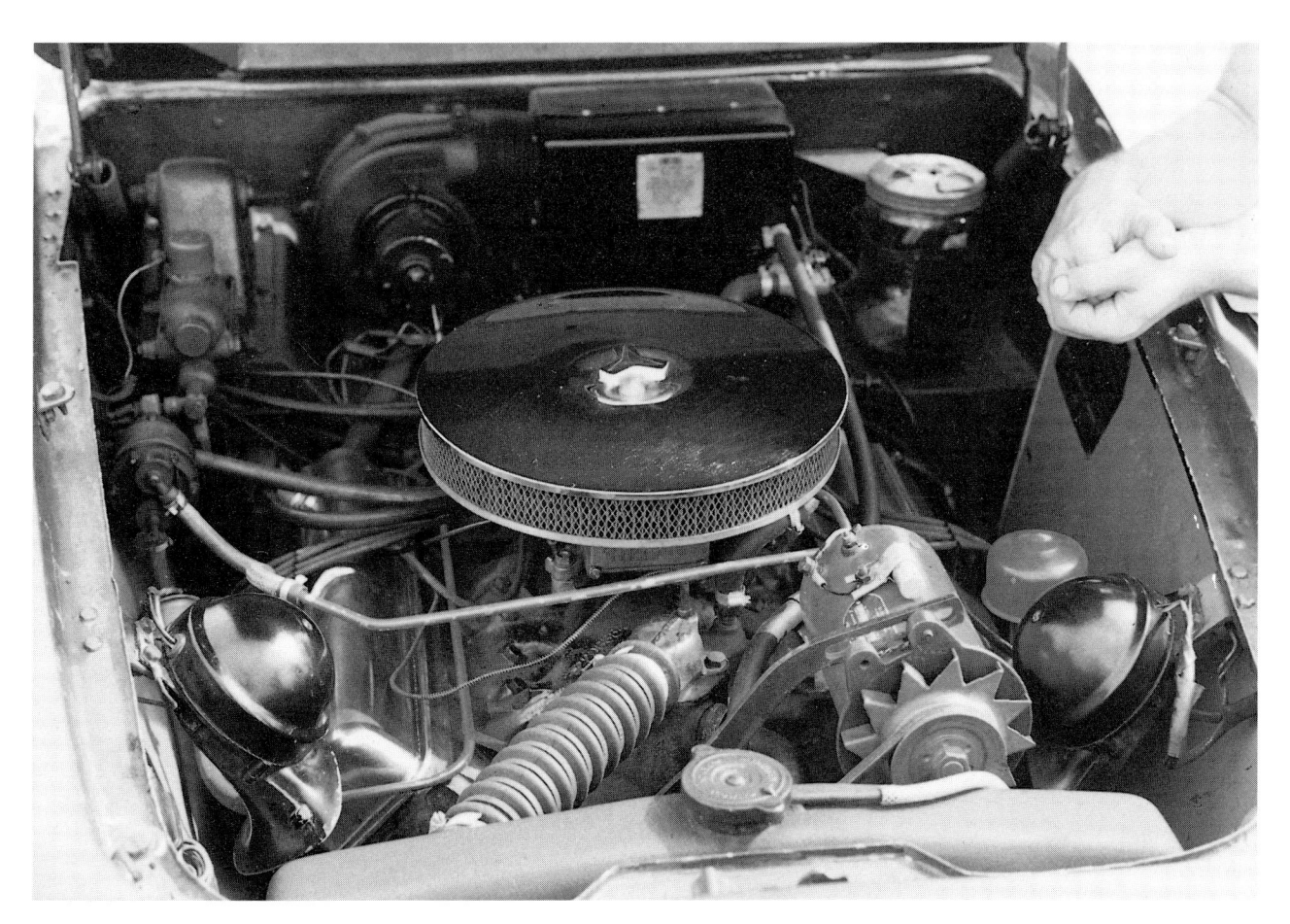

The Type 313 unit, with 5,130cc capacity. It was fitted to the 407 and 408 Bristols. Note dynamo.

THE BIG RED LUMP

If it lacked the pleasing aesthetic appearance of the tall, slim Bristol engine, it had a purposeful, almost brutal look about it, that was summed up in the nickname given at Filton of 'the big red lump'. Over the years I have seen other units, with the cylinder blocks painted black, blue and green. Whether this was some form of colour code, I have no idea. In the chassis, the most dominant feature was an enormous air cleaner, a fitment not unlike a frying pan, being circular, with a short tube handle, which was actually the air intake. Just to its left (looking towards the front) was the belt-driven dynamo, and the radiator, though large in frontal area, was notably shallow, considering that some thirty-six pints of water were in circulation.

The next type of Chrysler engine to be fitted in a Bristol chassis was the 318: its capacity was 5,211cc, and bore/stroke ratio 99.3mm x 84.1mm. Its compression ratio was 9:1, as on the 313, and it came into Bristol service on the Type 409 model in 1965. Like the earlier unit, the camshaft was chain-driven from the crankshaft, and located in the centre of the Vee between the two banks of cylinders. The combustion chambers were of hemispherical shape – hence the nickname of Hemi-head – as on the 313 – and the rest of the mechanical details were similar.

A Type 313 engine, modified by fitting an alternator replacing the original dynamo.

After seeing service, first in the Type 409 and then the 410 (announced in 1967), the 318 engine was succeeded by the 383 unit, fitted to the original Type 411 Bristol, and also to its Series 2 and 3

This is the Type 318 unit, fitted to the Type 408(2), 409 and 410 Bristols. Capacity 5,211cc. This unit was fitted to the 603E.

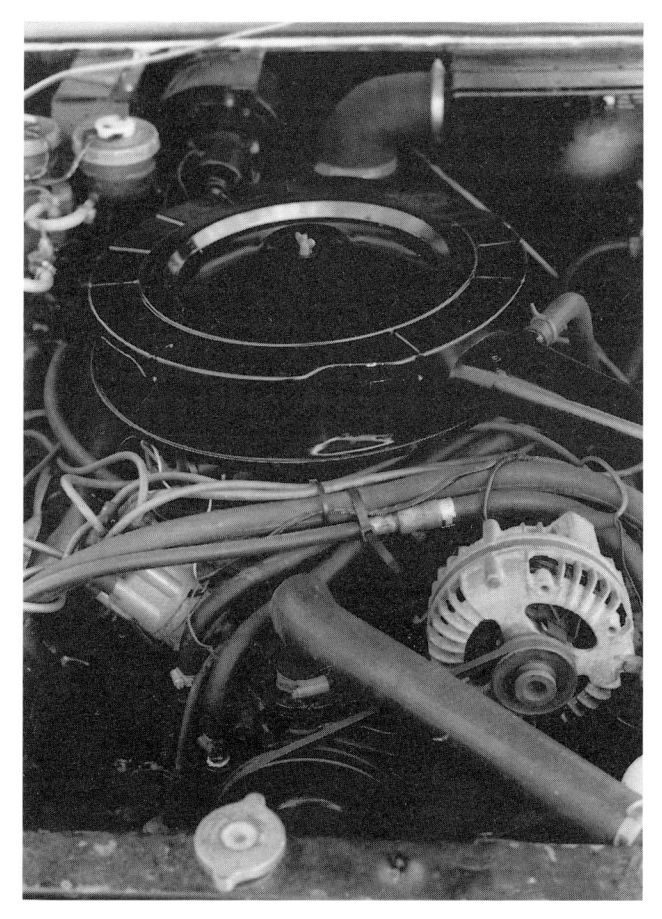

THE BIG RED LUMP

A Type 383 engine. Used on Type 411(1), (2) and (3) models: 6,277cc. (603S2 and Britannia).

This is the largest capacity (6,556cc) engine and was fitted to the 411(4) and (5) and 412(1) and (2).

A Type 400 Chrysler engine (capacity 6,556cc). Fitted to 411(4) and (5), 412(1) and (2) models.

versions, the dates of their appearances being 1969, 1970 and 1972 respectively. Not only was the cubic capacity greater, but the compression ratio was higher too. The new bore/stroke ratio was 107.9mm x 85.72mm, giving a capacity of 6,277cc with a 10:1 compression ratio. Its power output was an impressive 335bhp @ 5,200rpm, high revs for so massive an engine.

By 1973, when a new engine, the 400, came into service, and was first fitted to the series 4 Type 411 model, the anti-emission drive in the United States was beginning to be effective, and the compression ratio fell to 8.20:1. The cubic capacity was increased to 6,556cc which was to be the largest of any Chrysler unit used on Bristol cars. The bore/stroke ratio was now 110.28mm x 85.72mm, making it even more of an over-square unit. Cooling capacity was twenty-nine pints and the carburettor was a Carter Thermoquad. There was a manifold heat control valve to assist starting from cold. The engine also incorporated the American 'Cleaner Air System', which reduced the concentration of hydro-carbons and carbon monoxide in the exhaust gases.

The 400 engine continued unchanged in service with the 411 (Series 5) and the new Type 412 Bristol, with its convertible body, which appeared in 1975. The same year saw the phasing out of the 411 (Series 5) and in 1976 a new saloon, the Type 603S, was announced. This was powered by a new engine, the 360, with a cubic capacity of 5,898cc and even lower compression ratio of 8:1. The bore/stroke ratio was 101.6mm x 90.93mm. Unusually there was also an economy version known as the 603E, which used a new version of the 318 engine, last seen on the Type 411 (Series 3) Bristol. The capacity and bore/stroke ratio remained identical, and hydraulic tappets were used (the 313 and 318 had solid tappets).

In 1977, a new model Bristol appeared, a 603S2. There was no new version of the 603E (economy) model, however. Engine details were similar to the 603S, and it is this unit that is used to power the three models currently in production: the Beaufighter with convertible body, and the Brigand and Britannia saloons.

General Engine Details

The 313 engine had been introduced in 1957, to power the Plymouth and Dodge makes within the Chrysler group. Its distinguishing feature was the shape of its combustion chambers. These have been likened to a 'very shallow saucer, with no "squish" area'. To achieve this polyspherical shape, the exhaust valves were positioned vertically, with the inlet valves modestly inclined. The eight sparking plugs were located on the exhaust side of the cylinder heads, at an angle 'near 45 degrees to the bore'.

The tappets were of the solid type, and the engine was stated to have a power output of 240bhp. However, there was another version, known as the Power Pack, that used a 4-barrel carburettor (the standard only had a 2-barrel instrument) with appropriate exhaust manifolds. Other differences included a change in the ignition curve, and a camshaft with '20 thou more lift', plus a moderate increase in overlap. It has been stated that it was this Power Pack engine with Bristol-inspired modifications, that powered both the Type 407 and 408 Bristols in the period 1961–1964.

A turbocharged Type 360 unit, used in this form on both the 412(3) (better known as the 'Beaufighter') and the 'Brigand'. Capacity is 5,898cc, and the Rotomaster turbocharger can be seen to the left of the circular air filter/silencer. Without turbo the engine was used on 603S, 603S2 and Britannia.

A basically similar unit, though with its cubic capacity increased from 5,130cc to 5,211cc, known as the Type 318 has been stated to have been the engine used on the Type 409 and 410 Bristols in the period 1965–1968. The compression ratio of 9:1 remained unchanged.

In 1958 a new engine was produced, the 383, of 6,277cc; its most obvious difference being the use of hydraulic tappets instead of the solid version previously fitted. The changes of capacity, bore/stroke ratio and compression ratio have already been referred to above. In fact it was the result of 'Chrysler's next trip to the drawing board' in other words, it was a new design. The combustion chambers were now wedged-shaped, 'with slightly tilted valves', and the ancillary items differed, both as regards details and layout, from the earlier engine. The 400 unit was basically similar to the 383 apart from changes in the compression ratio, and of course the greater cubic capacity. This engine has proved to be popular with the tuners who tend to congregate mainly in the West Coast region, and in California in particular. The power they manage to extract from such big American engines is quite amazing, and the ability of the latter to endure such modifications as high-compression pistons and special overlap camshafts testifies to the quality of their materials, and the soundness of their original design.

Much of the later material in this chapter came from a Canadian member of the Bristol Owners' Club: the late Guy M Drummon QC. He owned a number of Bristols, including models with both Filton-made and American engines. I was somewhat amused when he wrote: 'However, in one way, owners of the 411 can be very snobbish . . . the big engine really is a Chrysler engine, the standard V8 for that car . . . I am perfectly accustomed to any gas station attendant looking at the 408 or 410 engine and saying: "Oh, a Plymouth" . . . They wouldn't do that to a 411, and some of my friends would have to learn not to enquire after the health of my "British Plymouth". See how every quarter of the globe has its own little snobberies.'

I have always felt it a pity that the American market is no longer considered suitable for Bristols. This is probably as much due to the demand for a number of Filton-made cars to be tested to destruction, as it is to the effects of the anti-pollution modification to the engines. As one indignant member observed: 'It's like taking a cracking good race horse, loading it down with lead weights, and still expecting it to win the Derby.'

However one may regard the use of the Chrysler engine and Torqueflite gearbox in a Bristol chassis and body, the fact remains that it has resulted in a long line of models, each just that bit (sometimes a lot) better than its predecessor.

The old guard still hold their inquests into the long-term results on Bristol design had the 220/240 project succeeded; but, as I tell them, even then, they would still have had to face up to the (to them) unpalatable fact that the transmission would have been automatic.

To my way of thinking, it is preferable for the Bristol to remain in production than for it to have lingered on a few more years, with various efforts to obtain yet more power from the original 2-litre engine, perhaps by supercharging. But that would not have accorded with the up-market image so keenly sought, after Bristol Cars Limited was established.

21

The Pioneer

Type 407

Recently, and quite by chance, I acquired a copy of the 1961 press release announcing the introduction of a new Bristol. It was shown as having the Type No 407, with the figures '5.2' immediately following, but there was no other indication that this was the first Bristol to use a Chrysler engine, or that its cylinder capacity was 5,130cc – or '5.2' litres for short. The announcement included the slogan: 'No other car in the world has *ALL* the features of the latest Bristol'.

Reference was made to the 'beautiful hand-made body, giving extremely roomy interior with the smallest possible exterior for today's crowded roads'. That was over thirty years ago!

The body, though based on the modified design already seen on the 406 Bristol-engined cars, was no mere replica. The then head of the Filton Design Department was Dudley Hobbs, and he had an ability to alter the appearance of a new model with the minimum of structural change. On the 407 the bonnet was flatter than on the 406, the number plate was no longer recessed into the tail, and though the rear wings were still crowned by vestigial fins they were

MODEL: 407 Saloon	**Date:** 1961–1963
Wheelbase	9ft 6in (2m 89cm)
Front Track	4ft 5in (1m 34cm)
Rear Track	4ft 6.5in (1m 38cm)
Overall Height	5ft (1m 52cm)
Overall Width	5ft 8in (1m 72cm)
Overall Length	16ft 7in (5m 5cm)
Weight	3,584lb (1,625kg)
Tyres	6.00 × 16in
Number of Cylinders	8
Bore	98.55mm
Stroke	84.07mm
Capacity	5,130cc
Carburettor	Carter 4-choke downdraught AFB 3131S
Gearbox	Planetary type: 3 forward speeds and automatic control
Ratios	High: 3.31 Intermediate: 4.80 Low: 8:10 Reverse: 7.28
Brakes	Dunlop discs, vacuum servo
Suspension	
Front	Wishbones and coil spring
Rear	Live axle, longitudinal torsion bars, central torque arm, Watt linkage lateral location

A Type 407 Bristol awaiting judging at BOC Concours, September 1989, at Clifton Downs, Bristol. Both hinged wing panels are 'up'. Note the battery under offside panel.

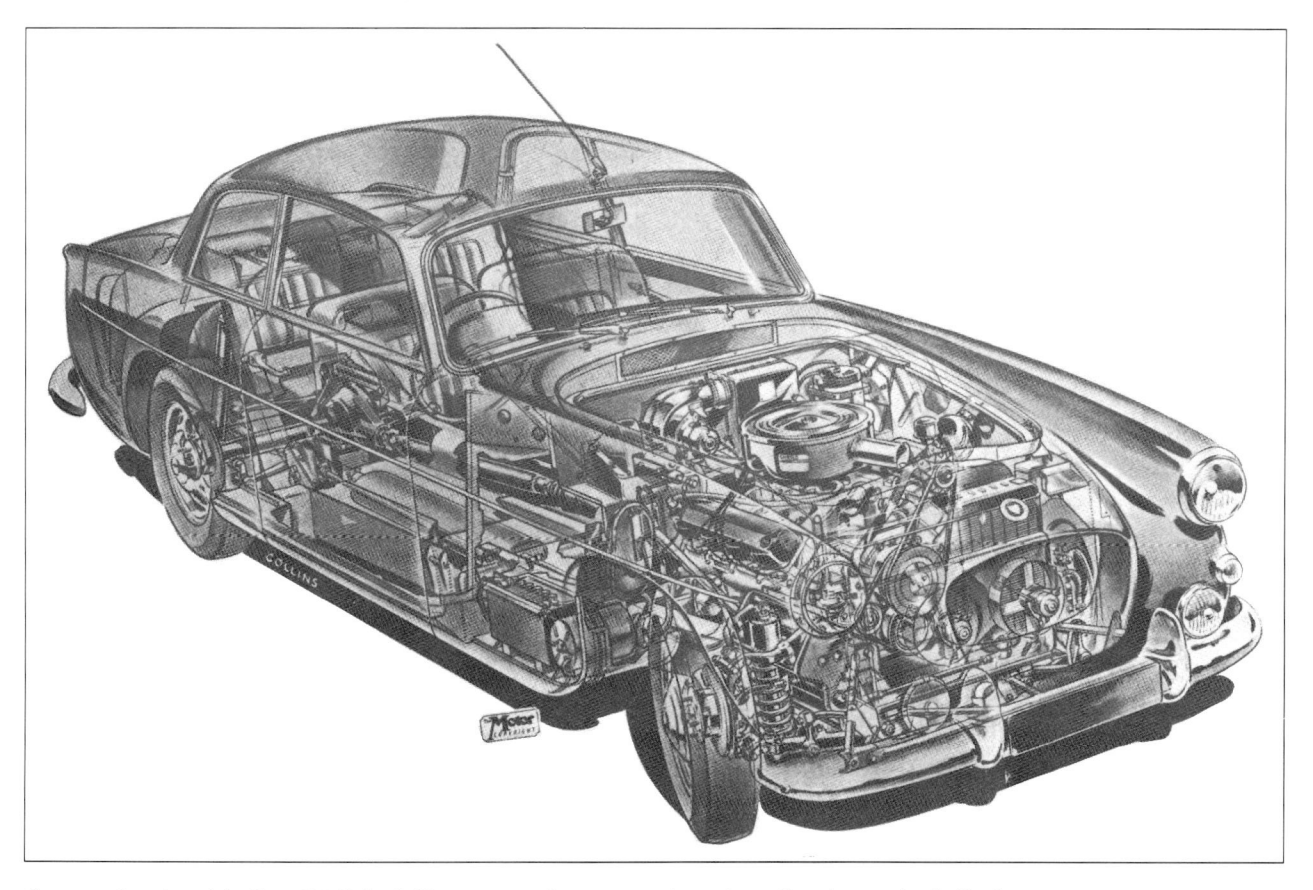

Cutaway drawing of the Type 407 Bristol. Note new type front suspension using coil springs and twin Kenlowe cooling fans to Chrysler engine.

Rear view of a Type 407 Bristol. Note the simple lamp arrangement and high-set boot lid.

Front view of red Type 407. Note 'Pegasus' emblem on grille, plus new bonnet badge.

treated in such a restrained fashion as to be hardly identifiable. Also the nave plates were bigger, and the boot lid appeared to be rather smaller than that on the 406, though this may have been just an optical illusion.

Following the example set by the 406, part of the coachwork was made by an outside firm, Park Royal Vehicles Limited of Acton, on the western outskirts of London. Bristol quality standards were maintained, and at the 1958 London Motor Show a gold medal was awarded for the bodywork. Even today, unless very badly neglected, the two big doors will still close with that delightful clunk one associates with hand-made coachwork.

The rear axle was of the hypoid bevel type, located by a Watt linkage for side reaction to steering loads. Rubber bushes were used at all location points, and a rubber-mounted arrangement replaced the lower mechanical ball joints. Front suspension had been redesigned, and was based on wishbones of unequal length, with coil springs seated on polyurethane pads surrounding Armstrong telescopic dampers, also used at the rear. Sealed ball joints on light stub axle carriers replaced the previous king-pin system. Front-end space was limited by the big engine, and steering was now by the Marles worm gear, with a three-piece track rod. This was sometimes criticised for vagueness at low speeds, compared with the rack and pinion system used on all previous Bristol cars. The Marles box was said to be the most expensive on the market.

The most novel feature of the 407 was its engine and transmission, both by the American firm Chrysler, though officially they came from its plant at

Windsor, Ontario, in Canada. Of typical transatlantic type, the engine was a Vee-8, with an over-square bore/stroke ratio of 98.55mm x 84.07mm, which provided a swept volume of 5,130cc, and its Type No. was 313. With a compression ratio of 9:1, a Carter 4-choke carburettor, solid tappets and high-lift camshaft, the stated power output was 250bhp @ 4,400rpm.

The valve gear had none of the complexity of the Bristol engine, consisting of angled pushrods operated by a single centrally situated camshaft. The engine was described in the previous chapter, and its specification is included at the beginning of this chapter.

Considering the criticism levelled at the use of an American engine, most press reports were favourable, and some enthusiastic, one comparing it with the fictional magic carpet. In fact it combined a number of virtues to an unusual degree – power, flexibility and a modest fuel consumption, if driven at reasonable speeds.

In its comprehensive road test report, published by *Autocar* in its issue dated 6 October 1961, the maximum speeds on the gears were given as: 49mph in low, 71mph in intermediate and 122mph in top. On testing the car's acceleration, it was found that from 0–60mph took just 9.9 seconds, while from rest to the 'ton' (100mph) took 26.6 seconds, but 0–120mph was much longer at 47.4 seconds.

Transmission and Braking

The Torqueflite was regarded by many experts as the best of contemporary American automatic transmission systems. It comprised a three-element torque converter with a stall rate of 2.2:1, and a planetary gear train giving three forward ratios, of 3.31, 4.80 and 8.10:1. Reverse ratio was 7.28:1. Under hard acceleration, the Torqueflite made automatic and very smooth changes; from rest to intermediate at 38mph; and from intermediate to top at 70mph.

The engine was extremely flexible, and, if the driver wished, would dawdle along in top gear without snatch or other protest. In top and at an engine speed of only 1,000rpm, the road speed was 23.8mph. On a motorway, a steady 70mph could be maintained at 2,942rpm, at which speed the fuel consumption was stated to be only 20mpg. This was excellent for so large an engine.

On a very long downhill section, if one wished to ease the disc brakes, the use of either bottom or intermediate gears would provide a very useful degree of retardation. The power in intermediate gear at a traffic roundabout could rather shock a following driver, anxious to demonstrate the superior acceleration of his own vehicle. I recall such an occasion, in a slightly later model with an even greater capacity engine, and when I glanced through the rear view mirror it gave the illusion that the other driver had changed into reverse.

On the 407, the propeller shaft was of the Detroit open type, with needle roller universal joints, the rear axle being of the 4 HA hypoid bevel type made by Salisbury.

For so heavy a car (its weight was 32cwt), an efficient braking system was essential and, like its predecessor, the 407 used Dunlop discs. The foot brake operated on all wheels, assisted by a Lockheed servo, and the handbrake lever, actuated by rods, on the rear wheels only. The adjustment of the latter was very simple, with adjusters accessible via the road wheels, which were of standard perforated-disc type. As on all standard Bristols since the 404, the spare wheel was stowed under a hinged flap on the nearside wing, with the servo, battery, and fuses under a similar flap on the offside. Original equipment tyres were of the Dunlop Road Speed type, with inner tubes, the size being 6.00 x 16.

Unlike the earlier Bristols, there was no provision for a starting handle, and a set of jump leads and a friendly neighbour, with a well charged car battery, can be very helpful if, on a cold winter morning, one discovers the lights have been left on all night.

Engine Cooling and the Car's Heating System

The Type 313 engine was water-cooled, the radiator being pressurised to 15lb per square inch, to raise

Three-quarter front/side view of Type 407. Behind grille, the twin Kenlowe fans can just be seen.

the coolant boiling point to 120 degrees centigrade. In addition, the car was fitted with a brace of Kenlowe electric fans, positioned just ahead of the matrix, and visible through the wire mesh grille. The latter carried a large new badge, with a representation of Pegasus above, and the Bristol City arms below.

The decision to fit the auxiliary cooling fans was only taken after extensive testing, and a factor in their favour, apart from their mechanical reliability, was their silence. The noise made by a conventional engine-driven fan would hardly have been compatible with the car's super luxury image.

The criterion was to maintain adequate cooling for the engine, with the car fully laden, on a gradient of 1 in 5, at a road speed of 15mph. This was typical of

Three-quarter side view of Type 407. Note aero-type air inlet, with 'Pegasus' emblem, new chromed 'roundel' on bonnet, and long chromed strip on side. The wing mirrors are non-standard.

the meticulous testing that was, and still is, a Bristol tradition.

It may be of interest to mention that the Jensen cars of the period used a similar Chrysler engine and Torqueflite transmission, but the auxiliary cooling was quite different. The fans were positioned between the matrix and the engine, so that cooling air was sucked through the honeycomb. On the Bristol, it was blown, and it would be interesting to obtain test reports on the relative efficiency of the two methods. The water capacity on the 407's engine, including the heater, was thirty-six pints. (On the 406, it was only sixteen pints). On some early models, the fan controls were unreliable, and if they failed to cut in correctly the water temperature could rise alarmingly fast, either in dense slow-moving traffic or when the car was driven for long periods at high speed. In extreme cases, the carburation could be affected, due to the excess under-bonnet temperatures. Happily my own car suffered no trouble, and proved to be a one-press starter, whether the engine was stone cold or had just been switched off.

The heating system was an improvement over that fitted to some early examples of the 406 model, and was really effective, with a fan-booster that was quite silent. But ventilation was a weak point, and on a long run in what I'd call muggy weather, the interior could become so stuffy that there would be a temptation to open a window. If one did so, it was quite amazing how much wind noise resulted, mostly from the hinged rear extractors. It seemed odd that such an obvious fault should not have been eradicated.

The Interior

As befitted a car of such luxury, and correspondingly high price, the quality of what the Victorians might have called the appointments was very high indeed. The walnut dashboard and door cappings were in the best British tradition, the upholstery was of top grade hide over Dunlopillo, and the extremely comfortable front seats were fitted with the Reutter fully reclining mechanism.

Interior lighting was also to a high standard, including an illuminated glove compartment, fitted with a stout lock, while safety padding was placed along the upper and lower edges of the facia. For stowing smaller items, pockets were provided on either side of the rear seats, with another pair on the backs of the front seats.

A full set of fine-quality (and accurate) round-dialled instruments were set into an oval console in front of the driver, with radio to the left and gear control buttons on the right. The big Bluemel steering wheel was adjustable, and there was plenty of leg room in the rear compartment. Entry and exit was facilitated by the two wide doors, and the ease with which the front seats could be moved and then reset.

Driving Impressions

As I had always preferred light cars, I approached my first Chrysler-engined Bristol, a 407, with some misgivings. When I lived in New York, I had owned several American cars, some with automatic transmission, but the press button controls on the Bristol dashboard were quite new to me. I suppose it was just the old dog's dislike of having to learn new tricks, but for a while I treated them with deep suspicion, and did not use the kick-down pedal facility either. I cannot say with any honesty that I enjoyed the thrills of some rather younger drivers, who appeared to play the control buttons almost like a piano, and to use the kick-down with little regard for engine speeds. Normally intermediate gear can be used on kick-down at speeds from 60mph, and bottom from 29mph, but the engine revs so freely and is so strong, it can endure much ill-treatment without serious damage. I would not recommend it, though.

As regards the car's general behavior, again I was favourably surprised and impressed. This may have been because from the driving seat the visibility all round was so excellent, and I could just see the top of the nearside wing, which was useful in narrow streets full of parked cars. When parking, I found the steering very heavy, but out on the open road it became progressively lighter, yet did not lose its accuracy. In some reports I have read, the Marles box is compared unfavourably with the rack and pinion system previously used, but, really, my only criticism was at low speeds.

The brakes with their 11¼in discs were superb, and would pull up all-square, regardless of whether the surface was wet or dry. The central handbrake lever could hold the heavy car on steep gradients without difficulty. Because of the engine's considerable power, I wondered whether wheel-spin from a brisk start on a wet road might present problems, but this did not happen.

I had been looking forward to some fast night driving, but found the headlights only adequate for local day-to-day (or night-to-night) use. One became aware of how quickly the eyes tired, peering into the darkness on a long cross-country journey. The fog light was useful in misty conditions, but the pass light was really too small, and set too low to be effective. I would have preferred one that resembled the big flame-thrower road lamp standard on the later 404 coupes.

In humid conditions, the rear window tended to mist up, so that the rear view mirror became ineffective. The electric rear window heater that is standard on so many popular cars today might have been a solution, but we are talking of a Bristol built thirty or more years ago.

Two Special 407 Bristols

In addition to the standard saloon models, there were two examples with special bodies. Until recently, both were owned by members of the Bristol Owners' Club.

The 407 GT Zagato (chassis No. 6151; engine No. PV 23862C)

It has been claimed that this very handsome body was built in just ten weeks after the chassis and engine had been received at the Zagato works in Milan. It arrived from Italy on Press day at the London Motor Show in October 1961. The 407Z was displayed on the Zagato stand, as it had been commissioned independently by Mr Anthony Crook then the Zagato concessionaire for the United Kingdom.

Some journalists reported adversely on the car's appearance, unaware presumably of the race against time to allow the vehicle to be exhibited. But only a few hours later staff members from Anthony Crook Motors had wrought a surprising change in the car's appearance. The ugly duckling had become an elegant swan, with glistening silver wheels complete with Bristol nave plates, while the steeply curving front section now had a Bristol badge, just ahead of the bonnet.

The travel-stained appearance had vanished, and the car could now be seen as it really was – a sophisticated coupe that really did warrant those over-worked initials 'GT'. Here was the epitome of the high-speed long-distance transport that could waft its fortunate occupants from chateau to five star hotel, before taking off again for some other exotic destination.

The engine was a standard Chrysler Type 313 unit of 5,130cc capacity with a bore/stroke ratio of 98.55mm x 84.07mm. Carburation was by a Carter four-choke AFB 3131S downdraught instrument, with automatic choke, and there was a high-lift camshaft. Power output was stated to be 150bhp @ 4,400rpm.

The car had Torqueflite automatic transmission and it has been claimed that special close-ratio gears were fitted, though I have been unable to substantiate this. Controls took the form of dash-mounted push buttons, as on the standard saloon. The rear axle used a 2.9:1 ratio, instead of the standard 3.31:1, and with a light aerodynamic body the performance must have been formidable, especially as regards acceleration.

In the usual Zagato fashion, the body combined light weight with great strength while still retaining the appearance of a true GT coupe. Unlike the Bristol Zagato 406Z, it used the standard Filton wheelbase of 9ft 6in, which enabled the new car to include occasional rear seats, as well as room for luggage. The glazed area was extremely generous, including a deep and steeply raked windscreen, and side windows that appeared to extend from front pillar to tail, with only the slimmest of roof supports immediately to the rear of the two wide doors. The rear screen was a most distinctive feature, for it was

The unique Type 407Z – with coupe body by Zagato and a claimed maximum speed of 140mph. Note the wide shallow air duct in bonnet top, wide oval grille, shrouded headlights and split bumper with registration plate between. The car is now in Tulsa, Oklahoma, USA.

virtually a perfect continuation of the roof line, extending well beyond the rear wheels, and wide enough to give the driver an excellent rear view on either side. In effect, it was that rarity – a car without any of those blind spots that make parking in a limited space such a nightmare.

The coupe bonnet was long and low without the air duct seen on the 406Z coupe, blending perfectly with the front section, including a very plain radiator grille. This was of the egg-box slatted type but in a very refined form. It extended almost to the shrouded headlights, and was curved at the top, yet square at the sides, and the lower edge was quite straight.

Bumper treatment differed at front and rear, the latter being substantial and extending as a wrap-around protection to the rear wings. By contrast, the front bumpers were vestigial – just a brace of chromed short blades, widely spaced, and affording little protection to the front wings, while the entire radiator grille was left quite vulnerable. A long narrow rubbing strip extended along the body sides and the doors, adding to the car's long, low appearance.

Standard Bristol road wheels were used and, with their chromed nave plates, suited the lines well. Unlike the standard 407 saloon, the spare wheel was not stowed under a hinged flap on the nearside wing, but in a separate compartment in the tail. A Bristol badge decorated the front apron, just ahead of the bonnet, and there were small circular trafficator lights immediately below the headlights, and on the outer edges of the rear wings, with the rear lights nearer the boot lid.

Luggage space was very limited, consisting of a shallow ledge above the spare wheel. A couple of soft-top cases of medium size might just have fitted, but little else. Most cars have at least one ugly angle, but this did not apply to the Zagato 5.2 GT – whether photographed from the front, back or sides, it remained a handsome and distinctive motor car.

As with other Italian coachbuilders, Zagato tended towards interiors that were practical rather than luxurious. The 5.2 GT was no exception, though the upholstery was in hide, and the front seats were very comfortable. However, they lacked the Reutter fully-reclining mechanism of the standard saloon 407. Either seat squab could be pushed forward, to allow readier access to the rear compartment. The space in the latter, while less limited than on the little Bristol 404 coupe, was hardly sufficient for a four-up holiday. It was quite adequate for short journeys and weight distribution was 50/50 front and rear.

A full set of instruments, with black circular dials and white needles, was housed in an arc-shaped panel that was recessed into the scuttle, but there was no tray for oddments under it. The steering wheel was not the big two-spoked Bluemel used on the standard saloons, but a thin-rimmed sports type with three spring spokes, so arranged that all instruments were visible to the driver. The head lining was in black leather and padded.

The push button controls for the Torqueflite automatic transmission were recessed into the facia, so the floor area was uncluttered by the conventional gear lever. Door furniture was simple and practical, and the floor carpet incorporated a rectangular heel mat just to the rear of the two pedals, one for brake and the other for the accelerator.

A simple yet practical touch, was the use of a small hydraulic ram on the boot lid making raising and lowering a simple matter, and so positioned that the scanty luggage, or the spare wheel, could be retracted (or stowed) with the minimum of difficulty. The lower lip was set at a slight angle, just above the twin exhaust pipes, allowing the spare to be slid in, without having to lift it.

The car was thus both handsome and distinctive, and it was a pity it never went into even limited production. The one example, registered as 160 PJ, was owned for many years by I W Hulbert, member of the Bristol Owners' Club. Present Club records indicate that it has been sold, the present owner being A Arutunoff, of Tulsa, Oklahoma, United States of America, who is a noted collector of fine cars.

The Viotti-Bodied Bristol 407 (chassis No. 6152)

Unlike the Zagato-bodied 407, this was a convertible and was an altogether more practical car. Using the standard Bristol chassis, with a wheelbase of 9ft 6in, there is considerable body overhang front and rear, making it very long vehicle, yet it handles well, and it is narrow enough to negotiate heavy city traffic without much difficulty.

A styling exercise by the Italian coachbuilders, Viotti, it attracted the attention of the late Peter Sellers, who was not only a gifted actor and comedian, but also a long-term Bristol enthusiast. At the time he was having a Type 407 saloon built, and saw the Viotti on one of his frequent visits to the Chiswick depot. He liked it so much that he bought it, and the saloon! But he rarely kept a car for long, and in due course the Viotti was sold; though how he could have parted with such a lovely convertible, I do not know.

It was bought back by Mr Anthony Crook, the sole proprietor of Bristol Cars Limited, and it was then fitted with a Type 318 engine similar to those used in the Bristol 410 saloon. As a result, the 407 type press button gear controls were deleted from the dashboard, and replaced by a floor-mounted gear lever, as on the 410 and all later Bristols. It had the very appropriate registration of AC1.

For a number of years it remained with Mr Crook, as one of his personal cars, and it was often driven by his daughter Carole. At that time, I lived in Cheam in Surrey, and often admired it when it was parked in the High Street. Whether the hood was up or down, the car always attracted attention, and in my personal opinion it remains quite the handsomest convertible I have ever seen, regardless of make or age. Its

A three-quarter side/front view of the Type 407 – with convertible bodywork by Viotti. It is the only example made, and is both handsome and practical. Note the unusual grille, wide flattish bonnet and massive bumper with overriders.

lines are simple, practical and timeless. For several years it has been owned by Miss Alexa Scott-Plummer, another Bristol enthusiast and member of the Bristol Owners' Club. The members' list shows its registration as HTW 696B.

Now finished in a colour scheme of dark blue bodywork, grey hood and late-type silver wheels, it is eye-catching whether in closed or open form. With the hood erected, it becomes a beautifully proportioned soft-top saloon, and with it down it is an open sports four-seater. The front seats are extremely comfortable, but there is a fair amount of room in the rear compartment too: it is a real four-seater, and not a two plus two. The door windows wind up to a height that keeps the wind at bay, and despite the very long bonnet forward visibility is excellent. As on most convertibles, with the hood up there is a small blind area. However, the rear window is wide, and the car has the unusual feature of windows recessed into the body to the rear of the doors, so that this blind spot is very much smaller than on the 405 convertible.

The engine now fitted is from the later 318 series, and the transmission has also been up-dated. However, the 318 Chrysler unit differed only in capacity from the 313 engine originally used in the Viotti – the swept volume of the latter being 5,130cc, and the former 5,211cc.

Other mechanical features that differed from the original 407 specification included a pre-engaged starter, an alternator instead of a dynamo and the replacement of the Dunlop braking system by the twin-circuit Girling. The gear knob featured a hold, so that if the driver wished the car could be driven as if it had a 3-speed manual gearbox, with quite shattering acceleration in the intermediate ratio.

The road wheels were the later type of 15in diameter, with Avon Turbospeed tyres of wider

Side view with hood lowered, of the unique type 407 convertible, with bodywork by Viotti. It has been brought up to Type 410 specification as regards engine and transmission. Note the protection afforded to the wings by the wraparound bumpers, the way the hood folds into the space behind the driver, and the very harmonious lines.

section, 6.70 x 15in, instead of the original 6.00 x 16 covers. Maximum speed would probably have increased, though with the hood erected there would be some wind roar, if full performance was used, with a possible maximum of 130mph. Again, because it was a convertible, the fuel consumption could vary, and one must set the wind resistance of the car in open form against the excellent aero-dynamic efficiency when closed. A range of 12 to 16mpg might seem likely.

In one respect the Viotti resembled the much earlier 402 convertible, since in both cases the lowered hood fitted into a well between inner and outer body skins. The result, with the tonneau cover in position, was a beautifully clean line from steeply raked windscreen to the sloping tail. Unlike the Zagato 407, the boot on the Viotti was practical, even if some space was lost because of the the fuel tank and spare wheel. Unlike the 402, raising or lowering could be done quickly and by one person – a big advantage when caught in a sudden cloudburst.

Both bumpers gave some protection to the wings, especially the rear one, which was curved round the lower tail section, and extended to the wheel arch. One-offs can present problems as regards body parts, and such protection is especially valuable for that reason. The exterior was devoid of chrome strips or other additions, the designer relying solely on the shape and proportions of the body. The result is truly satisfying and there isn't even a rubbing strip on the lower edge of the sides and doors.

But the car is far from being just a pretty face, and is used for fast journeys between the Scottish border country and London. The distance is approximately 350 miles each way, and has often been accomplished non-stop, apart from the usual difficulties posed by motorway delays. On such journeys, the Viotti really comes into its own, the engine keeping to a high average quite effortlessly, with no irritating noises from the tyres – just mile after mile of relaxed driving on those all too rare occasions when for long stretches the road is free of road repairs, contra-flows and towed caravans.

At the annual Concours of the Bristol Owners' Club, admiring spectators ask why such a delightful model never went into series production. I do not know the reason, but perhaps that is why, to me, this unique convertible will remain one of the jewels in the Bristol crown.

I would like to end with a quotation from a report on the Bristol 407 standard saloon which appeared in *Motor* in its edition dated 13 September 1961: 'Sheer performance is combined so well with quiet comfort and smooth controllability . . . that this English car with a Canadian power unit provides some of the best motoring that money can buy'.

22
Second Edition
The 408 Saloon

I have to admit that I have never found it an easy matter to distinguish a Type 406 Bristol standard saloon from its larger-engined successor, the 407. Unless it has some distinguishing feature I remember, such as an unusual colour scheme, I usually have to peer through the air inlet, to see whether it possesses the twin Kenlowe fans – a sure indication of a Chrysler engine within.

Fortunately the next model, the 408, presented no identification problems, since it possessed an orthodox slatted radiator grille, making recognition much easier. The new model went into production in November 1963, and its price in Britain then was £4,459 6s 3d, including tax. This was £199 7s 8d more than its predecessor.

There was a flatter bonnet, giving easier access to the engine compartment. On the 407, I felt the big Chrysler unit had been installed with a shoe-horn. Now the hot air did not concentrate and build up to ever higher temperatures, as it had done with some of the 407s, to an extent where performance could suffer.

The new rectangular grille was framed by a sharply defined apron, with the bonnet edge projecting very slightly forward. This was typical of Dudley Hobbs's design skills, for the result of this slight change was to give the car an eager questing air, that reminded me of a big yet amiable dog, straining at his leash.

Inset into the new grille were two large auxiliary headlights that operated on full beam only, with the two outer lamps able to use either full or dipped beam. They were recessed into the front wings, with

MODEL: 408 Saloon	**Date:** 1963–1968
Wheelbase	9ft 6in (2m 89cm)
Front Track	4ft 5in (1m 34cm)
Rear Track	4ft 6.5in (1m 38cm)
Overall Height	4ft 11in (1m 48cm)
Overall Width	5ft 8in (1m 72cm)
Overall Length	16ft 1.5in (4m 91cm)
Weight	3,584lb (1,625kg)
Tyres	Dunlop RS5 6.00 × 16ins
Engine Type	90 degree Vee-8
Number of Cylinders	8
Bore	98.55mm
Stroke	84.07mm
Capacity	5,130cc
Carburettor	Carter 4-choke downdraught with extra large air-filter/silencer
Gearbox	Torqueflite 3-speed and reverse automatic transmission
Ratios	Low: 8.1 Intermediate: 4.8 High: 3.31 Reverse: 7.28
Brakes	Footbrake: Dunlop hydraulic self-adjusting servo-assisted disc brakes on all wheels
Suspension	
Front	Independent by wishbones of unequal length with coil springs, telescopic hydraulic dampers and torsional anti-roll bar
Rear	Torsion bars, Watt linkage and electrically adjustable telescopic dampers

Three-quarter side/front view of a Type 408 Bristol. Note how sharp-edge grille is framed; also the twin chromed strips along the side, and the Pegasus 'logo' by door.

Front view of a Type 408 Bristol. Note the square edges to the grille.

oblong trafficators underneath, and the massive front bumper just below. It had no overriders, and by simpler attachment of the bumpers front and rear a reduction of 5.5in in the overall length had been achieved.

The roof was now a little more angular, and the car's height was 4ft 11in, which was just one inch lower than the 407. If the changes in dimensions were small, the effect was quite dramatic, for there was a more sporting air to the new model, compared with the somewhat staid and dignified look of its predecessor.

Bodywork was produced in the north-west London coachworks of Park Royal Vehicles Limited, but quite recently I was told that the painting of some cars had been sub-contracted to a Cheltenham firm. I have since learned that this is untrue. For instance, the bodies for those very pretty little sports Volvos, one of which featured as Roger Moore's faithful steed in the television series *The Saint*, were made in Coventry by a subsidiary of the Bristol Group specialising in plastics.

The engine fitted to the 408 was the Chrysler Type 313, that had already been used by the 407. Of

Three-quarter front/side view of a Type 408 Bristol. Note twin strips on side, and Pegasus 'logo', just ahead of door. Also square edges of the slatted grille. The badge bar is an 'extra'.

Side view (above) of a Type 408 Bristol. Note heavy kick plate along lower body, and the two chrome strips on side, Pegasus 'logo' inset by door. Three-quarter side/front view (below) of a Type 408 Bristol. Note the slatted grille with sharp corners, also the two strips on side, with 'Pegasus' logo by the door.

Vee-8 type, its capacity was 5,130cc, its compression ratio 9.00:1 and power production was claimed to be 250bhp @ 4,400rpm. I have always been surprised that the sump on this engine held only ten pints of oil; after all, on the 2-litre Bristol engines the capacity was twelve pints. On the other hand, the cooling system of the latter unit needed only eighteen pints (twenty-one with heater), compared with the thirty-six pints of fluid used by the Chrysler engine.

In the 408 Instruction Manual, the owner was advised to change his engine oil on average at 2,000 mile intervals, '. . . with an absolute limit of 4,000 miles between changes if the car is operating under good conditioins, i.e. mainly long runs'.

The owner was encouraged to check the sump level regularly, but was told not to add more oil 'until the level drops to the "add oil" mark on the dipstick at which time only two pints should be added'.

It may be the doctrine of perfection, but I have always changed the oil on my cars at intervals of 1500 miles, and usually with a change of filter every other change. I say usually because, for a while, the correct filter for the 2-litre Bristol engine became almost impossible to obtain. In desperation, I wrote to the Hon. Secretary of the Bristol Owners' Club of Australia, asking for details of their local conversion using Morris Minor filter bodies. I fear I did not get much help, and did not pursue the matter, having at last found a new source of supply.

The transmission used the same model of Torqueflite as had proved so satisfactory on the 407. However, the auxiliary dashboard controls had changed, from circular buttons with just an initial or number to indicate the relevant position, to rectangular metal keys with the details engraved in full. I found these rather easier to operate, and, as on the 407, one could hold bottom or intermediate gears until engine speed reached 4,700rpm, when it would change up automatically. In practice this was no hardship, the maximum speeds being quoted as 36mph and 70mph for first and intermediate gears respectively.

Braking was still by Dunlop, with Lockheed servo assistance. The handbrake used separate callipers of self-adjusting type, requiring little attention in normal use. They were operated via a lever set between the front seats, so that the floor space was unencumbered.

The difference between the 408 and the original 407 was the introduction of variable and electrically controlled shock absorbers on the rear suspension. Known as Selectaride, they were manufactured by Armstrong, who continued to supply their more orthodox dampers for the front suspension. Operated by a dash-mounted switch, the new shock absorbers gave a selection of four settings, from soft to hard, so that, if he wished, the driver might adjust his suspension to suit current road conditions.

In practice the handling was so excellent that some owners never bothered to alter their rear shockers, but this is not recommended. If left undisturbed for a lengthy period, the small valves on which the system relies can gum up and cease to function. Even more serious can be the occasion when a driver tries to adjust the suspension to cope with some especially rough surface, to discover that the damper on only one side obeys the instruction.

The Interior

This was fully up to the high standards set by earlier Bristols. Accommodation was provided for a driver and up to three passengers, but no attempt was made to cater for a fifth occupant, despite the space available. Leg room was generous, unless, as happened with one motoring journalist, the driver was six feet two inches in height, with very long legs. With the seat set to give him comfortable control, he found there was not too much room for someone sitting behind him, unless of rather more modest proportions.

All upholstery was in top-grade leather, deep pile carpets had sound-deadening underlay, and the dashboard and door cappings were in fine walnut veneer. Some reports criticised the front seats for lacking side support, but I found them excellent, and rather suspect that some drivers dislike leather, preferring a man-made alternative. Front seats were fitted with the Reutter fully-reclining mechanism, a standard feature of Bristol cars since the 2.2-litre models.

A view of the front seats, wheel and facia of a Type 408 Bristol. Note walnut veneer dash, with instruments grouped in 'pod' in front of Bluemel 2-spoked steering wheel. Note the buttons at extreme right, by which driver can exert manual control over automatic transmission.

Also as was usual on Filton-made vehicles, there was a wealth of stowage space – pockets in doors and on the backs of the front seats, cubby holes at either end of the rear seat squab, a lockable glove compartment on the left-hand side of the facia, and a useful shelf underneath it. The steering column was of the safety type, and there was plenty of padding both above and below the windscreen.

Instrumentation was comprehensive, and laid out in a practical, easy-to-read fashion. The minor controls and switches were set across the facia, with the major instruments in a rectangular console in front of the driver. Unlike some less carefully designed cars, the twin spokes of the big Bluemel steering wheel did not obscure any instruments, and at night road reflection was reduced by extending the scuttle slightly.

But if the Bristol 408 was extremely well-equipped, with a very high performance, it was a comfortable and restful car too. These qualities tended to attract a new type of customer, often men in early middle age who ran a business, and some covered an enormous annual mileage, visiting their factories and maintaining contact with customers and suppliers.

Such men had matured, admired the restrained lines and lack of ostentation of the Bristol, and appreciated its proven reliability. Some still preferred to drive themselves, and would use the car's performance to the full. One such had his base in London, and his main factory down in Devon. He thought nothing of making a visit to the latter, and still returning to his office the same day. He admitted that on the motorways 'If I'm in a hurry, as I usually am, I do press on a bit'.

The 408 (Mark 2)

As was to become almost routine with the later Bristols, a second version appeared in 1965, towards the end of the model's production life. Though outwardly virtually identical, the Mark 2 was fitted with the Type 318 engine that was to be standard on its successor. It was slightly bigger in capacity, its swept volume being 5,211cc compared with the 5,130cc of the Type 313 used on the original 408.

The Torqueflite transmission was of a different type too, designated the A 727. It was of more compact gear design, and the use of an integral light alloy torque converter/gearbox resulted in a weight saving of some 90lb. The Mark 2 version of the 408 was notably quicker than the original, and I have seen reports giving it a maximum not much less than the 132mph often quoted in road tests of the 409.

According to the BOC Registry, only fifteen of the

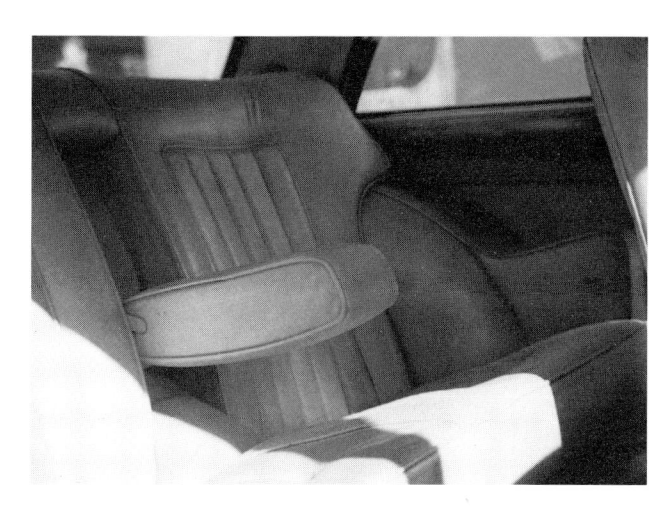

Interior shot of a Type 408 Bristol. Note retractable arm rest in centre, and shaped rest at end of seat. The ergonomic design of the seats hold each rear passenger securely.

Mark 2 cars were made, compared with an estimated sixty-six of the original 408. They are well worth seeking out, and, till recently, could often be obtained for much less than the 409, though possessing many of the latter's improvements, including engine, transmission and a new parking lock.

To my way of thinking, the greatest danger facing the driver of some automatic transmission systems stemmed from the ease with which a car so equipped could 'creep' if, for example, in getting into the vehicle, the driver should inadvertently touch the accelerator pedal. Many still left their cars in gear, and the usual parking brake might be over-ridden, unless of good design and correctly applied. Quite recently a typical such accident was reported, that resulted in the car, parked on the edge of a dock, creeping just enough to tip it and its four occupants into the water.

Under such circumstances, quite apart from the initial shock, it is extremely difficult to push a door open against the pressure of the water. Also, when electric windows are installed, it is all too easy for the system to be put out of action. Unfortunately, not all cars have any sort of manual alternative for emergency use.

The parking lock on the Type 408 Mark 2 Bristol was a very practical approach to the problem, for it worked on the transmission, and not on the braking system. I have a copy of the Mark 2 Instruction Manual, which reads: 'This provides a lock on the transmission to supplement the handbrake when the car is parked. The lock operates when the lever is pushed over to the right and it also automatically changes the transmission into neutral. Until the Parking Lock is disengaged by pushing it to the left, it is impossible to engage any button except neutral'.

A dire warning follows concerning stall tests, the term used if a motor car, with the engine at full power, is held stationary by its brakes, rather like a jet plane's run-up just before take-off. Evidently Filton had heard of such tests, for them to include this warning in the manual.

The lever mentioned above was very small, and was mounted on the dashboard. I found it rather fiddly to operate, and felt that something with rather greater leverage might have been preferable. But that might have upset the symmetry of the rest of the facia's lay-out, I suppose. Some new owners complained of the number of switches and instruments they had to understand and use. Perhaps it was because I had driven Bristols for so many years, but I never found it too difficult to familiarise myself, though I did prefer to take the first few miles along some quiet country road.

Driving Impressions

I was fortunate enough to borrow a Mark 2 Type 408 for a few days. It was in midnight blue metallic, which suited its lines very well. I parked it in the drive and spent some time looking it over. I noted the wide chromed kick plate along the edges of the body, and that there was now a second and shorter embellisher strip ending halfway across the door. The Pegasus badge had been moved to waist height, between the two chromed strips, just ahead of the windscreen.

The rear light clusters were simpler, the boot lid looked a little smaller, and the roof line was squarer, unless that was another of Dudley Hobbs's optical illusions. As ever, I admired the superb workmanship, and the way the two wide doors still closed perfectly, though from its overall appearance it was a long time since the car had received a good wash and polish.

As I sat in the driving seat, the sight of that dashboard control switch for the Selectarides started me thinking of the last time I had been in a car with dampers that could be adjusted while the car was on the move. It was a Ford special that I navigated through a pre-war RAC Rally. But then the 'shockers' had been on the front suspension as well, and there had been two sets of controls, big knurled wheels, with individual pressure gauges, as there were two circuits. Nothing electrical, just manual, but they worked well when bench-tested.

The engine was a big Vee-8, one of the American 30hp units, not the small one made in England. The bodywork was none too generous, a rather skimpy open four-seater, with fold-flat windscreen and cut-away doors. We had hardly left the start when a shock absorber pipe fractured, and John Whalley, who had had the car specially built, said the constant vibration was hardening the copper.

At the first control, we changed the defective pipe, and John purchased a small blow lamp. After that it was my job to anneal the pipes at every stop.

Of course it would have been much better to have used braided flexible piping in the first place, but this routine, though tedious, worked quite well. I gained a certain amount of cynical amusement by noting that when I was flaming the rear pipes, in very close proximity to the big fuel tank, all the rest of the crew vanished from the scene. After the event, we were taking a team member, a Swede named Poppe, to catch his ship when one by one the pipes failed. We had done quite well, and enjoyed lunch to celebrate, which I suppose was why I forgot to do the usual job with the blow lamp.

It was pouring with rain, and Poppe was scared that if we stopped for repairs he would miss the boat. With all four dampers out of action, the Ford's transverse suspension behaved most oddly; the ride was rather like a roller-coaster in a funfair. John's years of competing in the Monte Carlo rallies paid off then, and our last few miles to Tilbury Docks, over stone setts with tram lines in the centre, were quite spectacular. But we pulled up as the gangway was being taken aboard, and sat watching as Poppe trotted up onto the deck where he stood, waving his black Homburg, until the ship cast off and moved away. After which John and I set about getting the new pipes fixed, and then I drove on to Saffron Walden, at a rather more sedate pace.

So much for long forgotten memories: what about the 408? Mechanically it was excellent, a first-time starter hot or cold, and at night those four big headlights were a joy, compared with the 407 and its little fog-cum-road lamps. To me, though the handling was better than the earlier model, the steering was still very heavy at slow speeds, and parking it in a confined space was hard work.

The overall performance was excellent, and unless one indulged in too many street demonstrations of the car's tremendous acceleration, its fuel consumption was quite modest. I was disappointed that there was little difference whether the Selectaride switch was at the 'hard' or 'soft' setting, and I concluded that this was probably because the valves were sticking through lack of use.

I spent the weekend giving the car a thorough clean and, as I suspected, rust had already attacked the steel inner wing surfaces. Even the mountings for the seat belts were corroding. Yet another vulnerable point, where the dampers were mounted,

A front/side view of a partially dismantled Type 408 Bristol. Wing mirrors are non-standard.

was in excellent condition, and so was the underside of the chassis, once I had hosed off the hard coating of mud, mute evidence of long neglect.

On the Monday morning, I handed it over, and the owner was loud in his praises. A few days later, I heard indirectly that he had sold the car for a good price. Next time we met I raised the subject, just to watch his reactions. 'Well, you know,' he began, 'I'm not much of a spit and polish type, and felt now it looked so good I'd best get rid of it, before I let it get all mucky again.'

In its report on the 408, in its issue for December 1964, *Cars Illustrated* opined: 'It is tempting to enthuse over such things as polished woodwork, in the elegant shape and hand-made fit of the catches for the pivoting rear windows. However space only allows us to summarise it as being up to the best standards of London coachbuilders'.

High praise indeed, and it must be remembered that though part of the bodies for the 408 cars were made by Park Royal Vehicles, at their coachworks in north-west London, the traditional Bristol quality control was still maintained, by three inspectors seconded full-time from the Filton factory.

At the 1963 London Motor Show, a Type 408 Bristol was awarded the first prize for 'standard enclosed two door coachwork over £1,600 not exceeding £4,000 excluding Purchase Tax'. The prize was by the Society of Motor Manufacturers and Traders, who had awarded a gold medal to a 407, for its coachwork, two years earlier.

It would be interesting to know of any similar case in which a British make received two such awards for two successive models. Yet, for some reason unknown to me, the 408 often appeared the least regarded of the second-generation models. Even as late as May 1988, *Classic and Sportscar* stated: 'The 408 was perhaps the least desirable Bristol because of its awkward styling'.

I do not understand what this means; to me an example in reasonable condition still looks well balanced, and most owners seem to be pleased with them.

However, there were some motoring journals that took a rather different view, and I would like to end with a quotation that appeared in *Cars Illustrated* in its issue of December 1964: 'Although born of a fairly long line of cars whose appeal is in the connoisseur class, the Bristol 408 is comparatively unknown. In quality of manufacture, it bears comparison with the best products of other British manufacturers of luxury cars, while in performance it is surely sufficient to remark that it will hold a 250 GT 2+2 Ferrari over a standing half-mile'.

23

Great Expectations

The Type 409 Saloon

When, in the autumn of 1965, a new model – the 409 – was announced and many enthusiasts must have hoped for a Bristol of quite different appearance from its predecessor. If so, they may have been disappointed since the only visible difference between the two models was the slightly more rounded radiator grille. This was no mere cosmetic alteration, for it facilitated the air flow over the matrix immediately to its rear.

The British price, inclusive of purchase tax, was £4,849 which was an increase of £389 13s 9d compared with the original 408. As mentioned in the previous chapter, the Mark 2 version of the latter featured a new engine and Selectaride dampers, and both were standard equipment on the 409.

The engine, which was the Chrysler Type 318, had a swept volume only 81cc greater than the Type 313 used on the 407 and original 408, yet in its issue dated 23 October 1965 *Motor* included an article on the 409 called 'A lighter swifter Bristol'. There was a difference of some 56lb between the original 408 and 409 models, due to the alloy gearbox of the Torqueflite Type A727, and a maximum speed of 132mph was quoted. This was 10mph faster than the original 408, as recorded by *Autocar* for its issue dated 27 September 1963. In another test report, by *Cars Illustrated* (in December 1964), a 408 was given a maximum of 128mph, which puzzled me until I realised the car used was a Mark 2 car, with the same Type 318 engine as its successor.

A feature of the new engine that had something of a mixed reception was the automatic choke, to speed up the period between starting a cold engine and

MODEL: 409 Saloon	Date: 1965–1967
Wheelbase	9ft 6in (2m 89cm)
Front Track	4ft 6in (1m 37cm)
Rear Track	4ft 6.5in (1m 38cm)
Overall Height	4ft 11in (1m 48cm)
Overall Width	5ft 8in (1m 72cm)
Overall Length	16ft 1.5in (4m 91cm)
Weight	3,528lb (1,600kg)
Tyres	Avon Turbospeed 6.00 × 16ins
Engine Type	90 degree Vee-8
Number of Cylinders	8
Bore	99.31mm
Stroke	84.07mm
Capacity	5,211cc
Carburettor	Carter 4-choke downdraught
Gearbox	Torqueflite 3-speed and reverse automatic
Ratios	Low: 7.52 Intermediate: 4.45 High: 3.07 Reverse 6.75
Brakes	Footbrake: Girling hydraulic self-adjusting servo-assisted Handbrake: Separate clamps with automatic adjustment operating on rear discs
Suspension Front	Independent by wishbones of unequal length with coil springs, telescopic hydraulic dampers and torsional anti-roll bar
Rear	Marles worm type with external adjustment for mesh Sealed ball joints Watts linkage, with torsion bar springs, and electrically adjustable dampers
Note:	The last few Type 409 models also had power steering.

being ready to drive away. Some owners claimed that if they were in a hurry, and wished to start their journey as soon as the engine fired, the road speed was too high for safety. Perhaps it would have been useful to have fitted some form of override on the facia for such unusual circumstances.

By contrast, a new feature that met with general approval was the hold allowing an intermediate gear to be held, regardless of engine speed. The instruction manual might be quoted on this subject.

'The intermediate gears, particularly 2nd, may be found useful for special conditions such as climbing very steep hills of considerable length (more than ½ mile) with a heavy load where continuous heavy throttle is necessary, in dense urban traffic or in conditions where engine braking is desired, first gear may be used for similar conditions of even greater severity or for deep mud or snow. The lower gears reduce the possibility of overheating the transmission and torque converter under such conditions as these described above'.

Gear control might be exercised manually, via the facia-mounted buttons, or perhaps keys might be a better description since they were small rectangular plaques just large enough for each function to be engraved in full, rather than the numbers or letters previously used.

The parking brake, first seen on the 408 Mark 2, was continued on the 409 – an excellent safety feature.

Steering, Suspension and Braking

The 409 featured a new and more precise Marles steering box that included an external mesh adjustment. Considerable attention had been paid to the suspension, and by moving the engine further back in the chassis weight distribution was now 52 per cent on the front, and 48 per cent on the rear. Lower spring rating on the front suspension resulted in a softer ride, and to counteract any tendency for the car to lurch when taking an acute bend at speed the roll centre was raised by two inches. There were

Front view of a Type 409 Bristol saloon. Note the slightly curved grille.

revised settings for the dampers, and there was a torsional anti-roll bar.

The Dunlop braking system was replaced by the Girling version, still with servo assistance from Lockheed. The effectiveness of the self-adjusting handbrake was improved, plus the parking brake mentioned above. Prior to its acceptance by Bristol, the Girling system had to withstand thirty 'half G' stops from a speed of 70mph, with only a 30-second pause between each run. It is doubtful whether an ordinary driver would ever test his brakes to such an extent, even when crossing such Alpine passes as the Grossglockner or the Stelvio.

Side view of a Type 409 Bristol saloon. Note the very wide kick plate along edge of body.

The cooling system was claimed to be more efficient, and was sealed so as to require the minimum of attention. This was important now that the car's enhanced performance was being used to the full by drivers who tended, in some cases, to regard their Bristol as part of their business equipment, and expected it to convey them at consistently high speeds on their long-distance journeyings.

Road wheels were still by Dunlop, of the ventilated disc type, and were now shod with Avon Turbospeed tyres. These performed excellently under wet conditions and were very quiet, though their wearing qualities were sometimes criticised. Personally, I would prefer to buy a new set at rather more frequent intervals than to risk tyre failure. For safety, inner tubes were still fitted.

As on all previous Bristols, from the earliest Type 400, the 409 retained an immensely strong separate chassis frame, a prime reason for the marque's safety record. Anthony Crook, after his own very extensive experience of competing in Bristols, and Bristol-engined cars, such as Frazer Nash and Cooper, is aware of the risks attendant on an accident, even at quite moderate speeds, and has often stated that, so far as he is aware, only three people have ever been killed in a Bristol. He adds dryly: 'And one of those drove over a cliff, and you can't do much about that, can you?'

Until now, the company policy had been to regard power steering as a quite unnecessary added complication, but once it was accepted that, if the marque was to keep its up-market image, such a system was now inevitable, testing in the usual Filton fashion began. Virtually every system available was subjected to ruthless examination over a considerable period. Even when the German ZF power steering method was accepted, it was still subject to the Filton genius: 'to adopt, adapt and improve', to quote the late King Edward VIII when Prince of Wales.

The introduction of a later version of the 409 was the occasion for the ZF-cum-Filton power steering to come into regular service on a standard Bristol, and the majority of motoring journalists who tested it were loud in their praises, some even going so far as to call it the best system they had ever sampled.

There appears to be some confusion amongst Bristol enthusiasts on the use of 'Mark' or 'Series'. Only the 408 had a Mark 2, and the later version of the 409 remained just a 409. In cases where a later version was given a designation by the manufacturers, the word was series and not mark. In the past, some complaints had been made of rear screens that

Three-quarter front/side view of a Type 409 Bristol saloon. Note slightly curved grille and heavy kick plate.

misted in humid conditions, and frosted up in very cold weather. On the later version, there was an electrical element bonded into the laminated glass, and not merely 'stuck on', as still happens with some makes of car.

Silencers on a Bristol can be expensive, and owners of some 409s complained of the frequency with which they were forced to renew them. Other owners of 407 and 408 models criticised the shell noise, caused by vibration between the inner and outer silencer walls. As usual, the result was extensive testing, and the end product was a new type of silencer, made specially by the Burgess company for Bristol. The shell noise was completely eliminated by using a new sandwich method of construction. To increase the life expectancy, the opportunity was taken to make the internal components, the perforated tube, the baffle and the inner lining, all of stainless steel.

That a firm as large as Burgess should make a new silencer for Bristol is an example of the co-operation that was so often received by Filton. Even when the resultant order might be small, and subject to strict quality control, I doubt Bristol was ever told: 'We are not tendering, as the cost of retooling would make it uneconomic'.

Yet this attitude has increased within the British engineering sector, and may indeed be a prime cause of the demise of the country's once flourishing motorcycle industry. Though most of the big makes had ceased production by the late 1960s, there were signs of a new type of manufacturer, who concentrated on quality rather than quantity, but used off-site suppliers for many components.

A typical example was the Silk, a magnificent water-cooled two-stroke machine, made within George Silk's modest factory in Derby. He built his own engines, but relied on outside sources for such specialised items as the hydraulic front forks. After repeated delays and a general lack of interest by the suppliers, production of the machine ended, just as it seemed to be finding a niche in the highly profitable American market.

When I raised the question of small orders with a Chrysler executive, he assured me that what he called 'the Filton feed-back' was taken very seriously by his company. Bristol kept them informed of the various modifications made to engine and transmission, and where, after evaluation, they were found effective, similar alterations were often incorporated in later models. One of these, he told me, was called the Police Chief's Special, a model faster than the standard equipment, and sold only to 'reputable law enforcement agencies'. I almost asked him for details of the disreputable ones!

As an example of a Filton modification, he said that, prior to the 407 with a Chrysler engine being built, the standard Torqueflite automatic transmission had been subjected to high-speed running on the Filton test bed, to determine its suitability to meet the requirements of hard-driving Bristol owners.

When thermocouples, attached at various bearing positions, revealed localised overheating, the extension housing was modified, with a ball-bearing thrust race replacing the plain washer previously used. Chrysler incorporated a similar modification in a later transmission system.

The Gift 'Horse'

The Club's Annual Dinner was just over when the stranger approached me. 'I couldn't help listening to your conversation,' he told me, 'and I heard you say you are planning some research on Hadrian's Wall.' When I explained its purpose (to obtain the data for a paper I was writing on the Exploratores, the Roman army equivalent of our SAS), he offered me the loan of his son's Type 409. 'It would save you bringing your own car over, and a good hard week or so would do the Bristol good. It's far too big for me to drive, and it has been in the garage ever since my son's last leave. Now he's due back from Saudi next month, and I'd like it to be ready for him.'

I must confess I was a trifle dubious. I know to my cost, what can happen if a Bristol is left unused, but he assured me the local garage was excellent, and would give the car a thorough check-over. 'And at least I've kept the battery charged up,' he told me.

The trip up the M6 and on to Langholm, my base for the week, was carried out in pouring rain and a high wind, but the 409 responded well, thanks to its

Side view of a Type 409 Bristol competing in Driving Tests, Patrick Motor Museum, 1989.

late type Marles steering, and the power steering gave me plenty of feed-back as to road conditions. Also, later, it was to make parking the heavy car in confined spaces a simple matter.

I do not think the rain ever stopped, and as the hotel had no covered parking, the car was left out night after chilly night. But the new silent pre-engaged starter never failed me, and the new alternator kept the battery up to its task. The latter was smaller, with an Easifil top that would make servicing easier, and its extra supply of electrolyte provided the power required to spin that heavy engine after a frosty night.

Despite the weather conditions, I enjoyed myself, visiting the forts where the men had been stationed, and of which I had read so much. At Risingham I was accompanied by a trio of huge wide-horned Highland cattle, gentle giants who seemed sorry when I had to say goodbye. At High Rochester I stood gazing northwards, conscious that this was the most northerly fort in the Roman Empire, after the withdrawal from the Antonine Wall.

As I headed south to return the car, I pondered what were its essential differences, compared with the 408 Mark 2. Certainly it handled better, perhaps because of the repositioned engine. The springing was softer, yet there was only a very slight tendency to lurch, if a corner was much tighter than I had anticipated. That was about all, for the two cars had so much in common, as well as looking so alike. I wish I could be more specific, for there *was* a difference in feel, yet I cannot determine just what it was.

I broke my journey on the way south, and was rewarded next morning with the sun shining and dry roads. With a borrowed pail, sponge and chamois leather, I gave the car a much-needed clean, and, though I had no polish, the paint looked quite respectable as I reached the house, got out and rang the bell.

The little man looked confused and panicky, and then I realised the reason; his son had returned earlier than expected, and had not been pleased to discover his car had been loaned to a complete stranger. Just then he joined us, a big, grim, unsmiling man, who walked round the vehicle obviously checking for accidental damage.

I refused his half-hearted offer of a lift to the station, though with a heavy suitcase and a portable typewriter it would be quite a long walk. When I reached the gate, I looked back, but the father had scurried into the house, and the son, with the car's bonnet raised, was checking the engine.

As I walked to the station I thought about that week of temporary ownership with genuine pleasure, despite the sticky ending. The weather had been awful, yet the car had proved a faithful companion, the engine quiet and reliable, the heating and ventilation keeping me snug. On the evening runs back to the hotel, the lights had given adequate warning of abrupt corners, fallen rocks and the occasional sheep. And when I filled the tank just before handing the car over, I had calculated that, overall, the fuel consumption was in the region of 18mpg.

Despite its rather breathless style, I feel the following extract from the March 1983 issue of *Sports Car* is worth quoting: 'All that carpet, leather and walnut. The instrument panel designed by keen drivers for keen drivers. So much lazy power from the Chrysler V8. The ride as serene as a magic carpet. The faultless way in which this big luxury car responded to its steering and brakes.'

24

Evolution Not Revolution

The Type 410

In the autumn of 1967, a new Bristol, the Type 410 saloon, was announced. Its British price, inclusive of purchase tax, was £5,673 1s 10d, an increase of £824 1s, compared with the 409. But the economy was reviving, and there were enough discriminating motorists willing and able to pay what was then a considerable sum for the new model.

Dudley Hobbs had shown yet again how many variations were possible on a basic body style, and, though the exterior dimensions had not been changed, the car had a subtly different appearance. If one studies photographs, it is difficult to determine why the 410 looks different from its predecessor, but it does. The bonnet line was a little smoother, and the rake of the front and rear screens had altered a trifle.

More obvious were the new smaller 15in road wheels with their fatter tyres, and other recognition features included the extension of the lower embellisher strip, which now paralleled the upper one, with the two being joined at either end. There was also a small oval turn indicator repeater, which was set just aft of each outer headlamp. Vestigial fins still crowned the rear wings, but recently I saw a 410 which had had them eliminated. I thought a smoother line resulted, but it would seem this modification was quite expensive.

The smaller wheels had new and bigger nave plates, and the most popular tyre appeared to be the Avon Turbospeed 6.70 H15. Though sometimes criticised for alleged rapid wear, it was regarded as a quiet tyre that remained almost as tractable in the wet as in the dry. Professional testers as well as

MODEL:	410 Saloon	Date:	1967–1969
Wheelbase		9ft 6in (2m 89cm)	
Front Track		4ft 6in (1m 37cm)	
Rear Track		4ft 7in (1m 39cm)	
Overall Height		4ft 11in (1m 50cm)	
Overall Width		5ft 8in (1m 72cm)	
Overall Length		16ft 1.5in (4m 91cm)	
Weight		3,528lb (1,600kg)	
Tyres		Avon Turbospeed 6.70 × 15in	
Engine Type		90 degree Vee-8	
Number of Cylinders		8	
Bore		99.31mm	
Stroke		84.07mm	
Capacity		5,211cc	
Carburettor		Carter 4-choke downdraught	
Gearbox		Torque convertor 3-speed automatic	
Ratios		High: 3.07 Intermediate: 4.45 Low: 7.52 Reverse: 6.75	

owner-drivers agreed that the 410 was the best-handling second-generation model to date, but the reason for this still remains a mystery. Part of the credit should probably go to the traditional Bristol policy of continuous development, aimed at refining the good and eliminating the rest.

I feel that another reason may have been the result of a detailed suspension study carried out by the Chief Engineer, the late Dennis Sevier. His aim was to identify, and where possible to eliminate, those parasitic factors, including bushes, that could have a

A Type 410 Bristol saloon, on left, with Type 400 on right. Wing mirrors on latter are non-standard.

cumulative effect on the calculated performance of a suspension system. He was a multi-talented engineer, who, it may be recalled, was working on the design of a new manual gearbox when the 220/240 project began. Had it been made, enabling the new engine and chassis to be tested together, the later history of the Bristol might have been quite different. But this did not happen, and so we shall never know.

The 410 was fitted with the same Chrysler Type 318 engine as its predecessor. It was of Vee-8 type, with bore/stroke dimensions of 99.31mm x 84.07mm giving a swept volume of 5,211cc. The lubrication system incorporated an oil pump of rotor type, with an integral relief valve. There was full pressure feed to the camshaft, connecting rod and crankshaft bearings, and a reduced feed to the timing gears, chain, hollow valve rocker shafts and pushrod ends. Cooling was by a sealed and pressurised system, with a capacity of 32½ pints.

The Torqueflite automatic transmission system was also similar to that used on the 409, with the important difference being that there was a floor-mounted gear lever, instead of the facia keys used earlier. The lever incorporated a hold in its knob, so that if the driver wished an intermediate gear might be held, regardless of engine speed.

The lever, which was curved to be more convenient to use, was of the fore-and-aft type, with the various settings indicated at the side. The lever was enclosed in a high rectangular box, that made it virtually impossible for the driver to enter the car from the nearside, or the front passenger from the offside. It was impossible to retain the earlier method of button gear selection, with the new transmission system.

The braking system was by Girling, with Lockheed servo assistance, but now was of the twin-circuit type. In effect this amounted to two separate braking systems for the front and the rear, each with its own master cylinder, and a warning light on the facia in case of failure. Discs were used both for the foot brake operating on all four wheels and also for

Two Type 410 Bristols, note the chrome strip under headlights of front car, giving it the appearance of a smile. Note indicator repeater at extreme front edge of wing.

the separate callipers operated by the central pull-up handbrake between the seats. The latter applied to the rear wheels only, and there was also a parking lock operated by the gear lever through the transmission.

The suspension followed traditional Bristol fashion, with wishbones of unequal length, coil springs, telescopic shock absorbers and a torsional anti-roll bar on the front, and longitudinal torsion bars and Watt linkage at the rear, plus electrically adjustable dampers.

The chassis was of the box section type, with three cross members, and an open propeller shaft was used.

Bodywork and Interior

The methods used to build the bodywork of the 410 followed the techniques first seen on the Type 401 in 1948. Shaped steel supports were welded to the chassis, then the alloy panels were attached, an average of 1,100 welds being necessary. There were suitable insulation coatings between supports and panels to prevent electrolytic action, and the result of this technique was a body that was light yet immensely strong. It was also free of those creaks and groans one sometimes notes when riding in a modern car of monocoque chassis-less construction.

In 1967 Bristol customers still had a choice of any colour scheme they fancied. This was in addition to the fifteen or so official exterior colours, and the eight hues for the interior. Some choices appeared a trifle bizarre, and little regard seemed to be given to how they might affect the general appearance. We are told that 'beauty lies in the eye of the beholder', yet most shapes of car seem better in certain colours, and worse in others.

I recall once having purchased a 405 drophead in midnight blue, deciding on a 'bare metal up' respray, in what I think was called Rover Grey. A friend who was also a motoring journalist was horrified. 'But it's such a sad colour,' he told me; 'if you can change it to a lighter shade, please do.'

That evening I received a call from the coachpainters to say the 'pickling hadn't taken' on the bare

Three-quarter rear/side view of a Type 410 Bristol saloon. Note how twin side strips are joined fore and aft. Very simple rear lamp treatment, and lockable fuel flap, on a level with rear screen.

Head-on view of Type 410 Bristol saloon, competing in contest at Castle Combe, Wiltshire, June 1986.

alloy, and they would have to do the whole job again. I asked if they could change from Rover Grey to something else: 'the darkest white or the lightest grey you've got'. There was a pause, and then the man said: 'Leave it to me; I think you'll find Triumph's Dolphin Grey will suit you fine.' And it did.

At Filton, great pains were taken as regards silence, and not only were the carpet underlays of a special sound-deadening type, but an anti-drumming compound was used on some body panels, while the underside of the chassis received a full anti-rust treatment.

For the first time on a Bristol the traditional cellulose was replaced by acrylic, since in practice the latter kept its glossy appearance far longer. Using the latest drying methods, plus numerous applications of under and top coats, the result was a finish every bit as good as might be achieved by one of the famous specialist coachbuilders of the period.

There is nothing better than hand-fitting by a master craftsman, and even after a very high mileage, well over the 200,000 mile mark, the big doors of a Bristol saloon will still close with that solid clunk I find so satisfying. Incidentally, the lower door edges on the 410 were set high enough to clear most street kerbs. This was in contrast to the 405 saloon, the only standard Bristol with four doors. These were set so low that it was sometimes impossible to open them, as the kerb was too high. So one could neither collect or drop one's passengers – a potentially embarrassing situation.

The interior of the 410 was fully in keeping with Filton standards of quality and finish. The upholstery was in finest leather, cut and sewn in-house. An occasional application of the excellent Connolly leather food will keep it handsome and supple. If it is neglected, however, there is a risk that it may dry out and crack. To have even a single seat re-upholstered now is extremely expensive, yet a little attention can avoid it, and allow the leather to achieve that fine patina that shows the care it has enjoyed.

The steering wheel was still the big 17-inch diameter Bluemel, first seen on the 401 of 1948. In the brochure of the 410 the wheel is described as being of the deformable type, and there was safety padding above the screen and along the dashboard. A console of arc shape contained the major instruments, with the others, and also the various switches and warning lights, set across the facia.

A large lockable glove box occupied the left-hand quarter of the dash, and there were pockets in the doors, on the backs of the front seats and at either end of the rear seat squab. Though so lavishly equipped, a radio was still an extra, as were electrically operated windows. Front seats were equipped with the Reutter fully reclining mechanism, and could be slid forward to facilitate access to the rear. Yet they lacked headrests. Perhaps the high seat backs were deemed sufficient.

With its large front and rear screens, and generous glazed areas in the door and side windows, the 410 was a light and cheerful car. Its heating and ventilating systems functioned well, its boot was positively cavernous, and with its eighteen-gallon fuel tank (including a 2½ gallon reserve) here was a car that could function as a dignified town conveyance, or was equally suitable to take the fortunate owner and three passengers on the modern equivalent of the grand tour.

As was usual, the spare wheel was stowed under a hinged flap in the nearside wing, with the servos and electrical items in a similar position on the offside. This not only left the boot quite free, but allowed a puncture to be attended to without disturbing the luggage, and helped keep the weight distribution between front and rear as equal as possible.

Three-quarter side/front view of Type 410 Bristol saloon, with wing panels and boot lid raised. The spare wheel can be seen on the nearside. Note the wide kick plate and new nave plates.

Rear view of 410 Saloon Bristol. Note the horizontal rear lamp treatment, with reversing lamps either side of number plate.

Driving Impressions

Unlike the six-cylinder engines, with their mechanical fuel pumps, the Chrysler Vee-8 units were fitted with electric pumps, so that the engine is ready to start the moment the button is pressed. I found the borrowed 410 never failed me, even though I was forced to leave it out during a very cold winter.

These conditions allowed me to experiment with the heating/ventilating system, and I was most impressed. It is not difficult to obtain enough warmth for a car's interior to get very fuggy, and even for the rear window to become completely obscured. On the 410, fresh air was drawn in via openings just ahead of the windscreen, a position where the minimum of traffic pollution might enter the interior. At the base of the windscreen on the scuttle, four slots directed warm air onto the laminated glass, and even a well-frosted screen was soon clear. The electrical element bonded into the rear screen functioned equally well, as a demister or as a defroster.

I found the steering light yet accurate, thanks to the combination of ZF power steering (with Filton modifications) and the latest model of Marles cam and roller steering box. This was of especial value one night when the road glistened with a lethal mixture of new ice on old hard-packed snow. Yet I could sense the actual condition of the surface through the steering wheel, which enabled me to reach home safely, even when a number of other cars had slid off the road.

The lighting was excellent, with the two big inner headlamps operating on main beam only, while the outer brace could be used either on full or dipped beam. The control of the latter was via a foot pedal, which was what I was used to; yet several contemporary reports criticised it as being 'archaic'. I gathered that the writers much preferred the control to be via a stalk on the steering column. In fact this was available as an extra, costing, I believe, something of the order of £80, but most long-term Bristol owners preferred to stay with the pedal.

I found the brakes still needed a fair amount of foot pressure, if one's speed was reasonably high, but they were more progressive than the Dunlop system used on the 407 and 408 models. Even under the icy conditions described, they pulled up all square. The car's traction was beyond reproach, and one never had that nasty feeling that if one fed in the power a little too quickly the result might be either a sideways slide, or to be left sitting in a car with the rear wheels spinning uselessly.

Visibility was excellent to front, side and rear, and I liked the car's general feeling of safety and security. One was conscious of being in an immensely strong body, and I recall some publicity to the effect that 'a Bristol is built like a battleship'. A fair description, even though the Royal Navy has not possessed such a vessel for wellnigh half a century.

I liked the new floor-mounted gear lever, and soon found I could use it almost as an orthodox two-speeder. I would change down to the intermediate ratio at a wide traffic island, using the 'hold' incorporated in the gear lever, and let the engine speed build up until, with most of the traffic left behind, a swift change into top and one was back into one's normal cruising speed again.

At such times, the way in which the rev counter needle would swing round its dial seemed more in keeping with a peppy small sports car than a large saloon. Though I liked the appearance of the new smaller wheels and bigger tyres, I tended to agree with the BOC member who still pined for 'more rubber on the road'. If one wishes, there are alternatives; expensive alloys, or if one has some luck and a good car breaker, a set of steel wheels from an XJ series Jaguar may fit.

The snag is the close proximity of front wings and wheel arches, and I know of several cases where, having fitted the four new and very costly replacements, the owner found it impossible to turn the front wheels more than a few degrees without risking damage to the bodywork. It is wiser either to ring the Bristol Service Depot, to seek advice, or simply to put the replacements on the rear only. Never mix the type of cover.

I do not like this idea, however, unless the diameter of the new wheel and tyre is virtually identical with the standard equipment. Otherwise, in case of a puncture at the rear, a situation could arise in which

Front view of a Type 410 Bristol saloon; note wide screen and slatted grille.

the standard spare wheel is fitted, and the differential could then be trying to cope with two different diameters. This once happened to me, when I had taken my Tourist Trophy Austin on a pre-war visit to the Nurburgring. One of my large rear tyres 'blew', I fitted the small spare and reached home safely. But the 'diff' failed a few days later . . .

The parking lock proved its efficiency twice, when I had to park on an acute slope, and it was reassuring to know one was not having to rely on the hand brake only. The wintry conditions did not encourage driving of the 'press on regardless' type, and probably as a consequence the fuel consumption was surprisingly good. On average it was between 17½ and 18½mpg, including a long day's motoring in the Chiltern area. Many small hills and narrow lanes had to be negotiated and, though it never happened, I did wonder once or twice what I would do if I slid off the icy road and into the ditch.

Fortunately I did not have to find out, but I was all too conscious of the possibility, and that I was driving a borrowed and very expensive car. I am reminded of the amiable Dutchman who was once the Bristol agent in Sydney. While my 401 was being repaired, after its long voyage from Europe, he loaned me a very nice 402 drophead. When I thanked him, he grinned and said: 'But I am warning you, my friend, you bend her and you buy her.'

In due course the 410's owner returned from his long skiing holiday, and I met him, bronzed and unbearably healthy, at Heathrow and then drove him home, as he said he was mildly jet-lagged. He chattered away about the relative severity of various slopes, and of the joys of the après-ski evenings; and then fell fast asleep.

Only once in my life have I been present when a joke actually originated, and it was just after a blue 410 had won its class at the annual Concours of the Bristol Owners' Club.

A party of us stopped for a meal and a celebratory drink, and when we went back to the car a young man was waiting for us. Jerking his thumb at the 410 he said: 'I've never seen a car like that before – what's its make?'

'Oh?' said the owner airily, 'it's just a special we knocked together in a weekend or two.'

Just then a girl joined the man and remarked: 'Oh, it's got a badge – I can't make it out properly, but it looks like "Pistol".'

'Pistol', the man repeated, 'it looks more like a blooming great blunderbuss to me.'

I will end with a quotation from a report on the 410, by the late John Bolster, that appeared in *Autosport* on 8 December 1967: 'I must admit I have a great affection for hand-built quality cars. The modern quantity-produced car is an excellent vehicle . . . but for people such as myself, the pleasure of using a craftsman-built car is so great that it is a different kind of motoring altogether. To the man requiring a big, dignified car of very high performance, the Bristol brings a pride of ownership that abundantly justifies its considerable price.'

25
Advice to a Potential Buyer
Type 407–411 Models

Until recently, the earlier Chrysler-engined Bristols suffered very heavy depreciation, and as a result, some were purchased by people without the means or even the intention, of maintaining them properly.

This chapter is intended both to warn and to advise those who seek to become Bristol owners of second generation models, i.e. the 407, 408, 409, 410 and 411 types. Spare parts are easy to obtain direct from Bristol Cars Limited, at their Brentford depot. A well equipped service depot is on the same site, which could enable the purchaser of a used example, to have it serviced immediately, when any faults would be made known to him.

Because of their good design, top quality materials and fine workmanship, Bristols are excellent vehicles for restoration, but it will not be cheap. If possible, I would advise the potential buyer to opt for a car in better condition, even at what appears to be a much higher price. Anyone who has had a car fully restored, will tell you of the costs involved, also the time-scale, that may extend to years rather than months, since the top grade experts are usually fully booked.

I will deal with some of the individual items:

Rust With its alloy body and efficient undersealing, a second generation model may appear unrustable, but this is not so, and a potential purchaser should give careful attention to such areas as the lower edges of doors, sills and round the front wheel arches, the steel mountings in the storage compartments under the wing flaps, and also the rear wheel arches and around the headlights.

Paintwork On the 407–409 models, cellulose was used, but this was replaced on later models by acrylic, which explains why some of the earlier models have weathered less well. The use of T-cut may help restore some brilliance, but in a bad case, it could mean a total respray and that can cost well into four figures.

Body repairs Aluminium is a very forgiving metal, and an expert panel beater can often save a damaged item that may at first sight, appear beyond redemption. The massive separate chassis is immensely strong, but there are some vulnerable areas, the anchorage points for the suspension for example, and the mountings for the telescopic dampers. By contrast, the front suspension usually requires little more than maybe a new ball joint, or a replacement track rod. The coil springs can be re-tempered and re-set if the car has assumed a 'nose-down' appearance because the springs have settled.

Rear Suspension This is efficient and complicated. It is unique to Bristol, and includes many components. They include: a live axle, longitudinal torsion bars, a central torque arm, telescopic dampers and a Watt linkage. To check the condition of the rear suspension, the simplest test is to drive the car over a road containing numerous pot-holes, the deeper the better. If such treatment results in a number of sounds, resembling more a sharp crack, than a dull bump, be careful. Even to strip such a complicated system is expensive, due to high labour costs, while its reassembly and checking, are tasks for the specialist engineer. On the earlier models without electrically adjustable rear dampers, a rough and ready test of the shock absorber's efficiency, is to give each wing a good hard shove in turn, noting resistance and the eventual reaction.

Steering On the models with manual steering, check that there is neither vagueness nor wander, when driven reasonably fast on a smooth road. If there is, then it may merely require adjustment, but it could also indicate that the steering box is worn. Parts for the Marles cam and roller system are hard to find, and tend to be expensive.

Power steering Should be light yet positive, with instant response from road to steering wheels.

Heating and ventilation With the engine temperature at normal, the system should be tested for effectiveness, and if the rear window is fitted with the demisting and defrosting element, this too should be tried, also the radio and electric windows, both extras on early models.

Windscreen wipers and washers Should also be tested as the tubing or pumps may be defective.

Engine The big Chrysler engines used on the second generation Bristols (Type 313, 318, 383 and 400) were tough and reliable, but some of the later units tend to be handicapped by the power-sapping encumbrances of the anti-emission lobby. Their design is basically the same, apart from ever increasing cylinder capacity. Spares are plentiful and comparatively cheap. If the car has been garaged, a look at the floor may tell the potential purchaser whether it has been leaking oil from engine, transmission or rear axle. If the latter, check the oil seal. If a Chrysler-engined Bristol has been serviced and maintained correctly, a mileage of 200,000 is by no means excessive, and I know of engines with far more than this under their wheels. They belong to long-term enthusiasts, who make sure that the car receives regular attention. Take a look at the minor items, such as hoses, cables, belts, even the pedals, for they will tell how well or ill the car has been treated.

Lighting All lights both exterior and interior should be checked, including the instruments and rheostat.

Torqueflite automatic transmission Requires regular maintenance, including an oil change every 24,000 miles, and the belts adjusted. With proper servicing, it should be trouble-free, for at least 100,000 miles before major items need replacement. But neglect spells both trouble and expense. All gear changes, up or down, should be smooth, and any hesitation, judder or some untoward mechanical noise could be a danger signal. Distance from the Bristol service depot at Brentford need be no bar, as most garages specialising in American cars, should be able to service the Torqueflite transmission, and the Chrysler engine too.

Upholstery The advice is the same as for the first generation models with Bristol engines. Beware of leather that is dry or cracked, for nothing can be done to restore it. Small tears can often be mended with double-sided tape, but a seat with a wide rip in it, will require professional attention. Fading can often be restored with the excellent Connolly treatment, which is usually quite inexpensive.

Carpets Though perhaps less important than the leather upholstery it will still pay to check them for wear, and the condition of the underlay. Dirt and grease are less important than holes or tears.

Test run If possible, make sure the engine is started from cold. I would advise that, instead of taking the wheel straight away, the potential buyer should sit in the front passenger's seat, and watch the instruments, making sure they all function. A high reading on the oil gauge is quite normal in cold weather, and the needle should drop back to the normal reading as the oil warms. Keep an eye on the water temperature gauge, and when a stop is made, at a red traffic light perhaps, watch the behaviour of the oil pressure needle. It will fall back with the reduced engine speed on tickover, but not as far as the stop, though I have known this to happen. Then, when the light changes to green, note if the needle moves back to its correct position smartly, or is it sluggish, and maybe now showing a lower reading, indicating possible bearing problems. It is no bad idea to take a look at the dip stick prior to the engine being started, not only to check the level, but also the condition of the oil. In the bad old days of motoring, it was quite common for an unscrupulous seller, to fill the sump with much thicker oil to give a higher reading on the gauge. This is less common now, but one can quickly determine if the oil is comparatively clean, or is so filthy, as to suggest that neither it nor the filter have been changed at the correct intervals.

If having driven out on a very smooth main road, the seller suggests 'Now you drive it home', choose a different route, to take in some rougher and different surfaces, so that the car's handling and the probable condition of the dampers can be better judged. If the latter are of the Selectaride type (or later), turn the switch to various settings, observing whether there is any evidence that the adjustment valves are working.

Cowboys During my years as Hon. Membership Secretary of the BOC, by far the greatest numbers of woeful letters were from owners who had entrusted their cars to so-called experts, with no practical experience of Bristol cars. They are so unlike the ordinary mass-produced vehicle, that it is worthwhile seeking someone who really 'knows' the make.

Tyres Either before or after the test run, check the tyres, not just for the depth of tread, but for their general condition. Are the sides badly scuffed, are there cracks, and are the valve caps still in position? If the treads on the front tyres show uneven wear it may be advisable to have the steering checked.

Brakes Should be smooth and responsive, but do not worry if the pedal pressure is quite high, even with the servo. But if the pedal goes down almost to the floor, this may denote worn brake pads, not too expensive to replace, but they could be dangerous if left alone. Apply them hard in a suitably traffic free area: does the car pull to one side, or does it come to a full stop, all square?

Springs The front suspension depends on coil springs that can go soft. The most obvious sign is a nose-down position, which the seller may say is quite normal. But it is not, and though the springs can be retempered, the resultant labour charges will be considerable.

Self-levelling If the car is a late model, with this a standard fitment, try to ascertain it is working, by checking that the driving belt is at the correct tension, and that the car does remain level. At night a test would be easier, since the headlight beams should remain constant, regardless of surface or load.

Tools While the plug spanner is not as essential as on the first generation models, the comprehensive tool roll should go with the car. Often one finds, either that it is totally missing, or that desirable items have been retained. Have the two hinged wing panels up for inspection of the spare wheel, including the jack, on the nearside, and the electrical items, including the battery and also the servo and windscreen washer, on the offside. Check the latter is working, and the wipers too. Check behind the spare wheel for rust.

Log book and instruction manual Ensure both are present, and the car is owned by the seller.

How Bristols are Made

I am often asked why a Bristol costs so much and takes so long to build, and so perhaps it would be no bad thing to include a brief account of the manufacturing process. The manner in which a model is priced is very much a matter for the Company to decide. What is quite obvious however, is that the policy is based on the bespoke system, in which each car is made for a particular customer, rather than just being built for stock.

The body-building technique still used began with the Type 401. Shaped steel supports are first welded to

The Type 405(2). The dashboard and door cappings are walnut veneer and all the upholstery is leather.

the chassis, and afterwards the alloy body panels are attached, and insulated. The latter process is vital, to prevent electrolytic action between the two metals.

With the original system, the insulation was by means of a hessian-type material that was wrapped round the supports, prior to the panels being clenched onto them. Nowadays, the attachment is by welding, with some 1,100 spot welds being required on each body. The result is a structure that is very strong, and yet for its size, is still remarkably light. Hessian is no longer the insulating agent – instead both the supports and the panels are coated with a special compound, a first coat being allowed to dry, before a second coating immediately prior to attachment.

The chassis itself will already have received a full rust-proofing, so extensive in fact, that it usually takes four days to dry. The next step is to attach the suspension systems, the engine with its Torqueflite transmission, and also the self-levelling system. The engine still receives the detailed inspection considered necessary, the sump is still removed, bearings checked, and Bristol's own gaskets fitted to the cylinder head and the bell-housing. Prior to installation, the suspension will have been jig-tested for accuracy and alignment.

With all the body panels in place, the body receives an inspection, and any surface blemishes such as a bump or dent, are attended to before it enters the paint shop. Here the body shell is rust-proofed which is a lengthy process, and only when this has dried, can the undercoat be applied to the exterior, and rubbed down. If any cavities are discovered, these will be corrected, using a plastic filler, after which up to seven coats of polyester will be applied, and then flattened down.

The car is now ready to receive three surface coats plus a guide coat, and when these have been sanded down a further inspection takes place. Any exposed surface is treated, and at last four coats of the colour specified by the customer are applied. One more inspection, and if it passes, the car is ready for the trim shop.

Here the soundproofing and headlining are installed, along with the safety padding, and the walnut veneered facia and door cappings. Though the

The Type 409 Bristol. Fitted with a Type 318 Chrysler Vee-8 engine and Torqueflite automatic transmission. The car is a luxurious four-seater capable of 130mph.

upholstery will also be done at this stage, the front seats and carpets allocated to the car will be retained. These items will have been made up mostly by hand, the hides cut, sewn and fitted over Dunlopillo, while the carpets will be cut, stitched and fitted, together with their sound proof underlays.

Testing

The car, fitted with slave wheels and front seats, will be checked by two experienced testers, initially over a route of approximately thirty miles. Each will then submit a report listing any items requiring attention. Next comes a second check, over a twenty mile route, with similar reports, and corrective action where necessary. Then a final check, this time of only ten miles, and if no further faults have been reported, the car is ready to be taken to London. Although the wheels, seats and carpet allocated to the vehicle will have now been fitted, the nave plates will be snapped into position just prior to delivery.

Delivery

Every Bristol is driven to the London depot, either by Anthony Crook, a test driver, or by a chauffeur of long service and vast experience. They will keep engine speeds down to 2,000rmp, and have an ear cocked for the slightest untoward noise; which would then be rectified at the depot. The main functions of the latter, are the fitting of whatever accessories the customer has specified, and to give the car its final wash and polish before it is released to the doubtless impatient customer.

When one considers the time spent, first on the manufacture of the chassis and suspension parts, the assembly after checking, plus the frequent inspections during the painting process, and the individual road-testing, is there any wonder that each Bristol takes so long before it is ready for delivery?

Also, when one takes into account the sound design, top quality materials and the craftsmanship each car receives, it can be understood why Bristols are so rewarding to the owner, and why they last such an exceptionally long time.

The Type 411(2), fitted with a Chrysler Type 383 Vee-8 engine. The car could reach 138mph and was fitted with new self-levelling rear suspension.

A Spotter's Guide for the Chrysler-Engined Bristol Models

Type 407
1 No indicators on roof.
2 Air intake is different.
3 Bonnet is flatter.
4 No recess for the rear registration plate.
5 A twin exhaust system.

Type 408
1 Orthodox flat rectangular grille.
2 Roof line is rather more square.
3 No bumper over-riders.
4 An additional (shorter) chromed strip along the body.
5 A Pegasus logo on sides.
6 Wide chromed kick plate on lower edge of body.
7 Rear lamp clusters are simpler.
8 On the *Mark 2* examples, the facia gear buttons are different and there is a lever to operate a parking lock.

Type 409
1 Lower edge of air intake more rounded.
2 Demisting/defrosting element is bonded into rear screen.
3 6.00 ×16 Avon Turbospeeds fitted.
4 *Last few cars* – no visual difference, but power steering fitted and sometimes dual-braking systems.

Type 410
1 Two chromed embellisher strips on sides are joined at either end.
2 Side turn indicator repeaters fitted.
3 Front indicators protrude slightly.
4 Restyled hubs and rims.
5 6.70 ×15 Turbospeed tyres on smaller wheels.
6 Facia gear control buttons replaced by floor-mounted gear lever.

Type 411
1 Smaller kick plates.
2 No Pegasus logo, single side trim.
3 Turn indicator repeaters moved just ahead of doors.
4 Wings protected by bumpers.
5 Bristol plaque on boot lid.

Type 411 (Series 2)
1 Speedometer calibrated in both kilometres and miles.
2 Door lock inset into door.
3 Bumpers slightly higher.
4 Self-levelling system introduced.

Type 411 (Series 3)
1 Front and grille restyled.
2 Coachline replaced side strips.
3 Wider higher kick plate.
4 Direction indicator repeaters moved forward.
5 Four tail pipes introduced.

Type 411 (Series 4)
1 New type grille and logo.
2 Boot lid slightly flatter.
3 Simpler rear lamp clusters.

Type 411 (Series 5)
1 Grille now matt black.
2 Fog rearguard light.
3 Inertia seat belts fitted.

Type 412 Series
See specification – Chapter 28.

Type 603
'S' and 'E' visually identical.
Series S2 has ventilator aft of rear wheel arch.

Brigand and Britannia
1 Brigand has alloy wheels and bonnet bulge.
2 Britannia has pressed steel wheels.

26
Family Favourites
Type 411

For many years, one of the most important dates on the motoring journalist's calendar was the annual preview of new models that took place just prior to the London Motor Show.

In 1969 it was held at the Belgravia headquarters of the Society of Motor Manufacturers and Traders, and a model that attracted much favourable attention was the Type 411 Bristol saloon. At 4ft 9½in, it was 1½in lower than its predecessor, though its overall length of 16ft 1½in, remained the same. Dudley Hobbs had achieved another of his optical illusions so that the 411 looked longer and lower, and somehow more 'modern' than the 410 it had succeeded.

The car was now almost devoid of what *Classic and Sportscar* called chrome accents, with just one thin strip extending from front wing to midway across the door, while a second, even shorter, began above the rear wheel arch, to end just before the tail. The vestigial fins that had crowned the rear wings of every standard Bristol since the little 404 coupe were missing, and the resultant appearance was very harmonious.

A narrow kick plate ran along the lower edge of the body and door, and slightly ahead of the upper hinge there was now a turn indicator repeater. The long bonnet sloped gracefully to the wide front apron, with its slatted grille, the upper section shorter than the lower. Inset on either side were two auxiliary headlights. The traditional Bristol badge, last seen on the bonnet of the 410, was replaced by a narrow rectangular plaque in the centre of the grille, bearing the single word 'Bristol'.

The main headlights were recessed into the front wings in a very pleasing manner, with rectangular turn indicators below. The massive front bumper was curved at each end, to provide some protection for the wings. The rake of front and rear screens had been subtly altered, and the tail had been reshaped very slightly, in what L J K Setright called 'an

MODEL: 411 Saloon	**Date:** 1969
Wheelbase	9ft 6in (2m 89cm)
Front Track	4ft 6in (1m 37cm)
Rear Track	4ft 7in (1m 39cm)
Overall Height	4ft 9.5in (1m 46cm)
Overall Width	5ft 8in (1m 72cm)
Overall Length	16ft 1in (4m 90cm)
Weight	3,724lb (1,690kg)
Tyres	185–15 Avon Radial Ply tubed
Number of Cylinders	8
Bore	107.9mm
Stroke	85.72mm
Capacity	6,277cc
Carburettor	Carter 4-choke downdraught
Gearbox	Chrysler Torqueflite 3-speed automatic
Ratios	High: 3.07 Intermediate: 4.45 Low: 7.52 Reverse: 6.75
Brakes	Girling disc brakes with servo-assistance on all wheels, handbrake employs separate clamps operating on rear discs with automatic adjustment.
Note:	The Type 411 Saloon continued to be produced in four more series or versions, until 1976.

Close-up of front/side of a Type 411. Note the turn indicator repeaters in front of scuttle, single short chrome side strip, 'Bristol' name plaque on grille and wraparound bumpers.

artlessly graceful way that made the boot even more capacious'.

The lines of the 411 were now so simple and understated that as one journalist remarked: 'The Chrysler-engined Bristol has matured at last.' Here was a beautiful motor car that epitomised luxury and modernity.

The original price in Britain of the 411 was £6,997 (including purchase tax), which was £1,323 18s 2d more than its predecessor, yet when the model ended its production in 1976 the Series 5 cars cost £12,587. The demon of inflation was on the march . . .

The Type 411 occupies a very special place in the history of the Bristol car. It was the last member of the second generation, it was the heaviest and most expensive model to date, and it remains the only Filton-made car to have had five versions or series. It was in production from 1969 to 1976, a period only exceeded in length by the current trio of models: the Beaufighter, Brigand and Britannia.

Recently I was studying some production estimates prepared by the Chief Registrar Bristol Owners' Club. They indicated that a high proportion of the Second Generation Bristols consisted of the Type 411, in its five versions. *But I cannot stress too strongly that such statistics cannot be precise*; for they are based on chassis numbers. These apply only to the frames, which are not always issued in strict numerical order. This proviso applies to all the production estimates in this book, as for example those on page 17.

The weight of the Type 411 was 33.25cwt, which was 0.75cwt more than the 410. To cope with this extra weight, a new engine was fitted, the Chrysler Type 383. It had a swept volume of 6,277cc, which was 1,066cc greater than that of the Type 318 used on both 409 and 410 models. The compression ratio was higher too at 10:1 compared with only 9:1 on the earlier unit.

The new engine retained the high-lift camshaft and Carter 4-choke carburettor, but the solid tappets of earlier units were replaced by the hydraulic type, for easier maintenance. An extract from the original catalogue reads: 'The . . . engine developing 335bhp (S.A.E. gross), is very quiet and remarkably flexible throughout the range, from a crawl in top gear, to the extreme of acceleration. 0–70mph in 9.5sec., and 0–100mph in 19sec. can be obtained.'

The Chrysler Vee-8 was never a thirsty engine, despite its capacity, and for the Type 383 the fuel consumption was given as being 'in the range 13–17mpg'. Naturally, the way the car was driven, fast or slow, with or without maximum acceleration, had a direct bearing on the quantity of petrol used.

Such figures are all the more commendable, since already the anti-emission (some called it the anti-car) lobby in the United States was in full cry, and the engine was encumbered with what was known as a 'cleaner air system'. Its stated object was to reduce the concentration of hydrocarbons and carbon monoxide in exhaust gases. It must be remembered that this was long before the greenhouse effect had even been recognised as a threat to the world's environment.

To cope with starting the engine, even under semi-arctic conditions, there was an automatic choke, plus manifold heat control valve to enable the engine to reach its working temperature with as little delay as possible. The cooling system was pressurised at 13psi, and 29 pints (16.5 litres) of coolant circulated through block, heads and radiator. Additional cooling was provided by twin Kenlowe electric fans, normally using a thermostat, but with an 'overrider' switch on the dashboard.

The engine's full potential of 335bhp was produced at 5,200rpm, with maximum torque 425 (S.A.E. gross) lb ft at 3,400rpm. The latter figure indicates a very high degree of flexibility, which, coupled with an excellent automatic transmission system, was to appeal to a growing number of experienced motorists, who could afford an exclusive make combining exceptional performance with great comfort.

A limited-slip differential was standard on the 411, instead of an extra, as it had been on some earlier models. The suspension had received attention, though changes were small, and the pressed steel wheels by Dunlop, were shod with Avon Radial Ply tyres, 185 × 15, with inner tubes as standard equipment.

The disc braking system on all four road wheels, was of the dual circuit type, each circuit having its own master cylinder, and a warning light on the dashboard in case of a failure. In such cases, the driver should be able to control the car using just one circuit. The handbrake, of the pull-up type, located between the front seats, controlled a separate set of callipers on the rear discs, and there was a mechanical parking lock too. It was operated by the gear change, and worked through the transmission.

The first thing one noticed, when examining the 411's interior, was the new small (15in) three-spoked steering wheel. Gone was the big (17in) two-spoked Bluemel wheel that had been used on every Bristol since the Type 401 of 1948. With the excellent ZF power steeering system, as modified by Filton, there was no longer any real need for the leverage provided by such a large wheel. In the event of an accident, the steering column was collapsible.

The floor-mounted gear lever was welcomed by the sporting driver, though it meant less room in the front compartment. A 'hold' was incorporated in the gear knob, allowing the intermediate gear to be held, regardless of engine speed, as for example, when overtaking.

The dashboard had been redesigned, though it was based on the layout first used on the 410. But now virtually the entire space immediately ahead of the front passenger was occupied by a large lockable cupboard, still referred to as a glove compartment in the catalogue. The main instruments were grouped in a longer, narrower console, with the ancillaries set across the remaining space, with the addition of four 'face level adjustable ventilators'. These were of the 'eye-ball' type, and proved to be effective, even under tropical conditions, for Bristols are sold world-wide.

In the Bristol tradition, spare wheel, jack, electrical elements and servo were housed under hinged flaps in the nearside and offside front wings respectively, so that the boot was quite unobstructed, with an area of 19 cu ft. Front and rear seats were upholstered in top-quality hide, the pile carpet was on a soundproof underlay, and there were even two cigarette lighters!

In the catalogue, the heating and ventilation system is described as being '. . . very comprehensive . . . providing fresh air over a wide range of volume and temperature without opening windows. An air conditioning unit is available if required'.

The large rear screen incorporated electric heating and demisting elements.

In the issue of *Autosport* dated 20 August 1970, there was a detailed report on the Type 411 Bristol by John Bolster. It was entitled 'The fastest true four-seater touring car', and was lavish in its praise.

Bolster was never afraid to speak his mind, and could be very critical on occasion, yet the tone of his article on the 411 was almost euphoric, as witness his opening paragraph:

> 'The Bristol holds a unique position amongst cars of the highest quality. It is manufactured literally without regard to cost by the most painstaking craftsmanship. In a world where ostentatious appearance and flashy decoration are demanded by most wealthy car buyers, the Bristol relies on the custom of the few who prefer good taste. It is pleasant to record that there are enough discerning purchasers to keep the factory going at full capacity, who are happy to pay for intrinsic quality rather than outward show.'

Throughout his article, Bolster finds features he considers especially praiseworthy, such as the firm yet comfortable suspension, and the difference that three inches less width can make when threading one's way through dense urban traffic. He felt that the car's almost staid appearance concealed the fact that it was surprisingly aerodynamically efficient. He considered this to be a possible reason for its superior performance, when compared with other makes using similar power units.

Having made his usual speed and acceleration tests, he confessed he had relied on the efficiency of the Torqueflite automatic transmission, while admitting that 'It is possible that even more dramatic results could have been achieved by making manual changes'.

His one regret was his inability to reach 140mph, for as he said of the engine: 'it politely declined to be over-revved, and that was that'. The 411's ability to cover long distances made it equally suitable as a 'grand tourer' or as the town car of a city magnate. At night, he praised the headlamps thus: 'A carpet of white light makes fast night driving a pleasure.'

Such unreserved praise, from so outspoken a critic, says much for the quality of the car itself, and may account for the fact that in the Bristol Owners' Club, there are several members who bought their cars when they first appeared and have been content to enjoy them ever since.

Type 411 – Series 2

This version appeared in 1970, outwardly similar in appearance but possessing two new features.

Some owners of the original model had considered that the time had now come, as one member expressed it 'to get more rubber on the road', so that the tremendous power of the big engine might be enjoyed to the full.

On the Series 2, this criticism was rectified, for the wheel rims had been widened to 6in, so that they could accommodate bigger 205 VR 15 Avon radial-ply tyres.

The other innovation on the Series 2 model was an automatic self-levelling system, its purpose to maintain the handling and headlamp beam in consistent fashion, regardless of load. The original work on such a project was carried out by Armstrong, the damper specialists. Their system was self-contained, relying on the car's own movements to maintain the correct pressures to cope with varying loads. This worked well on rough going, but it was discovered that on a journey using smooth and level main roads the movement was insufficient, and pressures fell until the car was almost down on its springs.

Three-quarter front/side view of Type 411(2) Bristol saloon. The bonnet and side panels are raised, and the Type 383 Chrysler engine can just be seen. Note 'Bristol' plaque on grille.

But Bristol retained faith in the theory, if not the application, and evolved an improved version using an engine-driven pump, together with a reservoir for the fluid, plus two ride/height control units and a brace of hydraulic rams. This system was the one accepted for fitting to the 411(2), and the way it worked is described below.

With a normal suspension system, the effect of the driver entering his car is for the springing medium to be depressed, such depression increasing with the load, which might be in the form of several passengers, or a heavy case in the boot. But with the new system fluid would be pumped from the reservoir to the rams, which in turn would crank up the torsion bars to their normal predetermined height. Obviously less fluid would be needed if the driver was alone, more with additional occupants or if the boot was full.

In its fully developed form, the ride/height control units were sufficiently sensitive to compensate to some extent for even the effects of a well-cambered road. Since the two sets of valves worked independently, they were able to maintain the correct level, even when the load was assymetrical. Such a situation might occur when very heavy passengers occupied the nearside front and rear seats, while the driver had no one in the offside seat to his rear.

Despite its obvious advantages, and because of their usual aversion to all forms of publicity, Bristol made little of this innovation. In addition to such benefits as greater comfort, and a consistent headlamp beam, the system had the engineering merit that at all times the suspension was adjusted to suit the position on

Late Type 411(2). Note Bristol name plaque on grille, narrow bumper, but door mirrors are not standard.

which the steering and suspension geometry was planned.

Not unnaturally, in its early stages, the system was not faultless. Some owners complained of leaks that may have been slight but were persistent, and which, if ignored, could bleed the system of all its fluid. Other owners suffered the rather more dramatic experience of driving belt failure, and this occurred to a BOC member, just as he arrived at the annual Concours.

He spent much of the day seeking a replacement, but it was not until an hour or so before the event ended that a sister car arrived, and its driver not only carried a spare belt, but also helped to fit it. Though he had hardly enjoyed his day, the relieved owner remarked: 'Whatever else happens, I feel my membership of a one-make car club has been worth while.'

It is a pity that self-levelling is still relatively uncommon, for so often at night one meets a driver who dips his headlights, but seems quite unaware that either because his dampers are worn or there is a heavy rear load his car is so tail heavy that his lights are still striking the oncoming driver straight in the eye.

One problem that may have been peculiar to the 411 Series 2 cars concerned a too rapid tickover. With automatic transmission, this can be both annoying and even dangerous in traffic. The engine might also be difficult to restart when hot, if, for example, the driver stalled in heavy traffic.

Type 411(2) Bristol saloon heeling hard over during driving tests at the Patrick Motor Museum, Spring 1989.

With hindsight, it seems not improbable that both problems were interrelated, and stemmed from alterations to the ignition settings, and the use of a new 'cleaner air' carburettor. Cures for both problems were soon found, but some owners admitted that until they had been affected themselves they had tended to take the reliability of their Bristol cars rather too much for granted.

Type 411 – Series 3

This version went into production in 1972, and I remember the first time I saw one, at the annual Cavalcade of Motoring, held at Penshurst Place, Kent, the family home of Lord de L'Isle and Sidney.

As the Club's Hon. Membership Secretary, I had the task of bringing a representative group of Bristols, and was getting them into model order when my attention was called to what appeared to be a 'factory fresh' example of a type I had never seen before. It had been sent down by the Club's patron, Anthony Crook, and his kind gesture was much appreciated by the members present.

For much of the day, we were all kept busy answering questions from people who often looked puzzled, because they had been under the impression that 'Bristols went "phut" back in the early Sixties, didn't they?' By the time the event was over, I hope it had been made clear that the Filton factory had been in continuous production since 1946, and was still going strong.

In *Classic and Sportscar* for May 1986, the 411(3) was described as a 'decisive face-lifting exercise', for it differed from the earlier versions in several respects. The most obvious of these was a new grille, no longer of the familar slatted type but made up of a series of diminishing rectangles. It was small enough for a pair of 7in headlights to be inset at each end, and in the centre was a narrow oblong plaque bearing the single word 'Bristol'.

One member, whose spiritual home appeared to be Australia, expressed the belief that the grille was actually a griddle, designed for use in the outback of his adopted country. Blessed with a fertile imagination, he drew a vivid verbal picture of the jolly swagman, arriving at a eucalyptus grove at dusk. He would lower the griddle on an extended hinge, light a small fire below, then, having filled his billy from the nearby billabong, he would throw some tea leaves in, place it on the griddle, and wait for it to boil.

Somehow, I doubt that if the above flight of fancy had ever been recounted to members of the Filton Design Team they would have been amused. Various other ideas were floated by members as to how the grille came to be so shaped, one man assuring me that it was in fact 'a relief map of the Maze at Hampton Court'. Another said he had seen something very similar when visiting the so-called 'Treasury Building' at Petra.

For the first time, a second-generation body was without chromed side strips, and in their place there was now just a single fine coachline, so executed that its very simplicity accentuated the harmonious proportions and fine balance of the car. The direction indicator repeaters had been moved, from just ahead of the windscreen pillars, to the edge of the front wing, near where the coachline began, to end about midway across the door.

The chromed kickplate had been replaced by a more substantial version, set rather higher, so as to function as a buffer, preventing side damage, as for example when another car's door is opened in a crowded car park. The trafficators were now inset into the bumpers, with the top edges of the latter affording some protection, though I doubt if damage could have been prevented in other than a very slight 'coming together'.

On the 407–410 models, there had been just a pair of tail pipes, but now there were four, a feature that aroused comment, and even perhaps a little envy, from owners of the 'double-barrelled cars'. Beneath the bonnet, there was little external change. However, the compression ratio had been reduced to 9.5:1, which appeared to suit the Type 383 engine rather better. No more was heard of hot starting problems, or of too rapid tickover speeds. Yet overall performance had not suffered.

A change that worried a few of the old-style Bristol owners was the use of tubeless tyres on the pressed-steel ventilated-disc wheels. The latter were still of Dunlop manufacture, and with their full-width

Rear view of a Type 411(3) Bristol saloon. Note the two pairs of exhaust tail pipes, name plate on boot lid, reversing lights and retractable aerial.

chromed nave plates they suited the big car very well.

I have always wondered why the Bristol, so far as I am aware, remains the only make that stows its spare wheel and electrical elements under hinged flaps on the front wings. It has so many obvious advantages, and the argument that 'it'll only work on a car with a long wheel base' is not convincing. The only time I have seen a rather similar arrangement was on a Sebring model Frazer Nash belonging to Sir Clive Edwards, Bt, who once raced a very fast Cooper-Bristol. But in the case of his car the wheel simply dropped into a narrow slot, between engine bay and front wing. It seems significant that both Bristol and Frazer Nash used a separate chassis.

On the later examples, the battery is mounted on short legs, to allow cooling air to circulate, and perhaps to give a slight measure of shock absorbtion. Situated in the offside wing compartment, such batteries seem often to have very long lives, with anything from six to nine years being quite usual. On a large number of mass-produced cars, the battery is stowed within the engine bay, where it must endure high temperatures with almost no ventilation. It is perhaps because of this that on average such batteries seldom seem to remain effective for much more than two years.

Type 411 – Series 4

This version appeared in October 1973 and, though outwardly similar to the Series 3 model, was fitted with the Type 400 engine. Following normal Chrysler practice, the increase in cylinder capacity, from the 6,277cc of the Type 383 to the 6,556cc of the new model had been achieved by an increase in bore size, from 107.9mm (4.25in) to 110.28mm (4.342in). The stroke remained at 85.72mm (3.378in), so that the new unit was an extreme example of the then fashionable over-square type.

But if the swept volume had increased, the compression ratio was lower, and was now only 8.2:1, compared with 9.5:1 of the Type 383 unit. Power output was shown as being 330bhp, developed @ 5,200rpm.

For the first time, a Bristol was fitted with an electronic ignition system, and in the catalogue this is described as eliminating 'need for contact breaker points'. During this period, there was a spate of competing systems, some good, some tolerable, and some extremely unreliable. Added to which many of the smaller manufacturers soon ceased trading, so that supplies of spare parts dried up. Fortunately the system used by Chrysler proved a success, and to date I have not heard of a single case where the

Side view of Type 411(4) Bristol saloon. Bonnet and nearside hinged wing panel are up, and the spare wheel can be seen stowed in the wing compartment. The electrical items are under a similar flap on the opposite side.

owner of a Bristol with electronic ignition fitted as standard has had problems. I say fitted as standard, because some owners of earlier models 'modified' their ignition systems themselves, and a few told me they wished they had left well alone.

Three-quarter side/front view of a Series 411(4) Bristol saloon. Note the chromed grille of new type, indicator repeater at front end of wing, and small ventilator above rear wheel arch.

One of them enjoyed long-distance continental touring and, having reached Athens, stopped by what had been the royal palace to take some photographs. There were sentries on guard, in the exotic kilted uniforms of the crack Evzone Bodyguard. His photographs taken, the member returned to his car, which then refused to start. On raising the bonnet he realised the engine had overheated, and at that moment a hose split, sending a column of steam high into the air. Guards rushed over with bayonets fixed; they spoke no English, and he no Greek. It was obvious they thought he had been going to plant some infernal machine, and arrest appeared imminent when a passing motorist came to the rescue.

Having listened to the member's explanation, he gave the sentries a short resumé that appeared to satisfy them, but there was still the engine to repair. Fortunately the member always carried spare hoses, and as he opened the boot his wife called to him that a little box she had put with his tools, 'might come in handy'. Imagine his joy when he opened it, and there were all the parts he had removed when installing the electronic system, and had put on a shelf in his garage.

While the Good Samaritan fetched some water, the member, with jacket off and sleeves rolled up, set to work to put the Bristol's ignition back to

Side view of Type 411(4) Bristol saloon. Note there is a coachline instead of chrome strip, with indicator repeater at its front extremity. Note the ventilator above rear wheel arch and the wraparound bumpers.

'maker's original specification'. Despite the heat, the sightseers and, above all, the flies, the job was finished in time to carry on with the tour, though, as he said rather sheepishly, 'Of course we had to miss lunch, and my wife does love her food.'

Back to the Series 4 model, no doubt Sherlock Holmes would have no problems, but most people simply cannot see any differences in the external appearance of the Series 3 and 4 cars. But the rear lamp clusters are rather simpler, and the boot lid is a trifle flatter.

When I see the average popular car, with the rear screen obscured by an enormous spoiler, while on the tail are rows of letters and numerals testifying to the fact that it is turbocharged, has four valves per cylinder or possesses some other mechanical curiosity, I feel very glad that Bristols remain their efficient, comfortable and anonymous selves.

If the original 411 had created something of a sensation at its first appearance, in London, and the Series 3 had been 'christened' at the Cavalcade of Motoring at Penshurst Place, the launch of the Series 4 was almost an anti-climax. The Bristol Owners' Club had been invited to attend a vintage meeting on the airfield at Booker, where the cars would be accommodated within a special enclosure.

A representative collection of the various Filton models was duly assembled, and then, to the delight of the members, they were joined by Mr and Mrs Crook. It was only after several minutes conversation that it was realised that they had just arrived in the latest model. It was the Type 411, Series 4, but instead of parking amongst the other Bristols, as the cynosure of every eye, Mr Crook just left it where it was, out of sight beside a hangar. Somehow this was so very typical of the way all publicity is shunned, yet, as he has often remarked, 'The cars just sell themselves'. Shakespeare once observed that 'Good wine needs no bush', and in the same way the Bristol car does very well, without all the hype so dear to the hearts of some sales departments.

Type 411 – Series 5

The fifth series of the 411 appeared in 1975, and was to prove to be not only the last of the various versions of the 411 but also the end of the range of Chrysler-engined models from 407 onwards, generally called the 'second generation'.

This must have come as a surprise to many enthusiasts who had begun to regard the 411 not so much as a motor car, more of a way of life. After all, the original version had appeared in 1969, so it had

Front view of Type 411(4) Bristol saloon, with bonnet raised, revealing the Chrysler Type 400 Vee-8 engine, of 6,556cc capacity, the largest fitted to a Bristol as standard. Also note the plated circular air filter/silencer, and missing front bonnet support.

already been in production for six years, which was three times the average of the rest of the range.

Yet even this, the last of the line, had been given detail refinements, such as a slightly stiffer chassis and measures to reduce vibration and shake. At Filton the search for perfection never ceased.

Outwardly the only visible difference was that the grille on the Series 5 car was now matt black, while at the tail, there was a fog rearguard lamp. This can be a most valuable asset on a motorway in mist, fog, snow or even heavy rain.

Inside, the seat belts were of the inertia type allowing reasonable movement, but locking up to prevent any sudden forward motion, as for example when, because of a collision, the wearer might otherwise be hurled through the windscreen, or against the steering column.

In the catalogue it is stated proudly that 'A full programme of *Crash Testing* has been successfully completed to ensure compliance with the latest Department of Trade and European Safety Regulations'.

This programme was lengthy and extremely thorough, and was described by the late Dennis Sevier in a lecture he gave after the Annual Dinner of the Bristol Owners' Club in April 1976.

Suffice it to say here, that when a test car struck a concrete barrier at a speed of 30mph the steering wheel and column moved back only 0.9in, though the length of car was reduced by 24in. No visible movement was recorded on the toeboard or the engine compartment bulkhead. Other checks were made on the safety of the door locks and hinges, or whether the fuel tank was fractured, and the related subjects of noise levels and crankcase and exhaust emission.

On the 411(5) there were built-in head restraints in the rear compartment, and, to facilitate long-distance driving, and to reduce fuel consumption, there was now a 'cruise control'. It was called a 'Speed-hold' in the catalogue which stated: 'When switched on, provides electronic control of throttle, so that under cruise conditions, the car's speed is held constant, with the absolute minimum of correction being applied.'

This was a really worthwhile innovation, resulting in a useful fuel saving over a period. The system was pre-set by the driver, and could be over-ridden in an emergency, and would return to the pre-set pace as soon as normal conditions returned.

As the power of the Chrysler engines increased, so the Bristol designers had to ensure that the cooling system remained adequate. Unlike some other makes using similar power units, at Filton it was held that more effective results were obtained from the twin Kenlowe electric fans by placing them ahead of the radiator. In this way the cooling air was *blown* through the matrix, instead of being *drawn* through, as in other systems.

Considerable attention was paid to the development of a thermal switch to control the fans, and

Three-quarter side/front view of Type 411(5) Bristol saloon. Note two pairs of headlights inset either side of matt black grille with Pegasus emblem. Also the direction indicators below bumper.

eventually, in conjunction with Otter Controls, a simple bi-metal unit with a 'small differential and operating temperature tolerance' was produced. It was this type that was first fitted as standard to the Series 5 version of the 411 Bristol.

Close-up of offside front wing section of Type 411(5) Bristol saloon. Note that hinged wing panel is raised, revealing the servo, battery and electrical items. Tiny turn indicator is at extreme front edge of coachline above the wraparound front bumper.

Rather more general modifications, which also affected some of the earlier series, included adjustable dampers of a superior type to those first seen on the Type 409 cars. As a result of rig-testing, the damper mountings were improved. An idler-box of hydraulic damper type was fitted, in conjunction with the more robust power steering used by the 411 series. The steering arm and linkage arrangement was also redesigned, to provide a stiffer assembly.

Another more general modification concerned the size of the radiator matrix. As Sevier explained:

'With the larger engine, as used in the 411, the further points had to be considered:

1. At idle, with the same cooling arrangements as before, the larger engine would run 9 degrees C. hotter.
2. The low ratio of water in cylinder head to cylinder head mass would result in serious 'after boil' conditions, if the top speed cooling target was not reduced by 10 degrees C.
3. Emission controls increased the heat reject at idle by 200 Btu/hr.
4. Air conditioning was to be made available as an optional extra, and with the condenser in operation, the inlet temperature could increase by 8 deg C.'

Rear view of a Type 411(5) Bristol saloon. Note the lifeguard fog lights, two pairs of tail pipes, 'Bristol' plaque on boot lid, vertical lamp clusters, reversing lights and wraparound bumper.

After consideration, it was decided to increase the matrix, from 360 to 440 square inches, and this proved a satisfactory solution.

Since the American federal emission regulations were increasing, it was obvious that the time would come when the current generated by even a heavy-duty alternator would be unable to match the current consumed. As an alternative, it was found possible to increase the air-flow through the matrix by 40 per cent, for a current increase from 9 to 12 amps. Using twin 11in diameter 4-blade fans, it was possible to cool the engine at idle, from 105 to 95 degrees C., in approximately 2½ minutes.

High-speed cooling presented fewer problems, but each change to the front end involved reassessment of its effects on air pressure. Comparing the shape of

Three-quarter side/front view of a Type 411(5) Bristol saloon. Note the matt black grille, direction repeater at extreme front of coachline, Avon safety road wheels and twin headlamps. Behind it is a Type 405 Drophead with coachwork by E. D. Abbott Limited.

the 411 (Series 4) with that of the 410, it was found to have resulted in a drop in pressure from 1.2 to 0.9in @ 80mph.

It was during the later period of 411 production that the Avon safety wheel was tested by Bristol. Its Chief Engineer, Dennis Sevier, deliberately blew a tyre at 70mph, and brought the car to a smooth stop. Shortly afterwards Mr Crook carried out a similar test, at RAF Station Keevil. On this occasion the speed was 144mph when the button was pressed and the offside front tyre deflated. To make quite sure the cover would remain on its rim, he then threw the big car into a series of swerves, and found the new wheel amply justified its name. Such cool courage is rare, yet it is typical of a personality that combines steely determination with seeming diffidence.

Personal Impressions

My own experience with a Series 5 Type 411 was very limited, consisting of a single short run, so that I hope I may be forgiven if I am unable to do more than give very fleeting impressions. The car's quiet luxury impressed me as always, the more so with such items as electrically operated windows, the new Avon safety wheels (and the fatter tyres), and an effective and versatile heating/ventilating system. I had not sampled the Type 400 Chrysler engine before, and my somewhat gingerly use of the throttle provoked ribald comments from the car's owner, sitting beside me. I found his presence somewhat inhibiting. 'Don't just stroke it, give it a good hard shove' he shouted, and when I obeyed the effect was quite electrifying. But a busy urban thoroughfare was hardly suitable for an acceleration test, so I turned off onto a side road that I knew. It soon deteriorated into a narrowish lane, with plenty of potholes and a couple of fast open bends.

As expected, the roadholding was superb, and so were the brakes, for when a tractor and trailer came out of a field I was able to bring the big car to a halt with no drama, despite a road surface greasy with wet mud. With misplaced confidence, I took the next open bend a trifle faster than intended, and felt a slight lurch that rather surprised me. But it did not affect the power steering, the accuracy of which reminded me of the days when Bristols still used manual rack and pinion.

At the end of the lane I was quite happy to turn the wheel over to the owner, who then proceeded to demonstrate the car's performance, using the floor-mounted gear lever, and taking the revs up far higher than I had dared to do. When we reached home, I

Close-up view of driver's section of front compartment: Type 411(5) Bristol saloon. Note the large ash tray, heater and speaker vents inset into door, fine veneered facia and door furniture, Reutter fully-reclining mechanism on seat, eyeball type ventilators in facia, major instruments in panel in front of small three-spoked steering wheel. Note the large lockable compartment at far end of dashboard, with 'grab handle' inset on its lid.

then spent some time just studying the car, inside and out.

The smooth and silent action of the electrically operated windows was most impressive, the dashboard layout was both comprehensive and practical, and the heating and ventilating system effective. Outside, I liked the rear guard fog light, and the lack of chrome along the flanks; to me the simple coachline was very effective. When I opened the boot lid (which, like the bonnet, was of the self-propping type) it was so hot I backed away, thinking there was some fault in the wiring. But the owner merely laughed, and told me it had always been like that, and that he kept meaning to do something about it.

Whether it was due to the close proximity of the two massive silencers on their flexible mountings I do not know, and all I could do was suggest that maybe a sheet of insulating material in the boot might help matters.

But this problem did not affect my overall impression of a lovely car, hand-made, and equipped and finished in the true Bristol tradition. It is hardly to be wondered at that it appeals to an increasing number of businessmen, able to afford and appreciate a car that combines performance, comfort and practicality. It is significant that the 411 Bristol has been nicknamed 'The Chairman's Express'.

Though his comments were directed towards the original Type 411, I feel John Bolster was expressing views that are equally applicable to the other four versions of the model, and I will end with the following quotation from *Autosport* dated 20 August 1970: 'In the past, I have tested many costly cars that made me glad I am a poor man. The Bristol 411 is a car for the very wealthy but it has many special virtues which render it as desirable to the young sports car enthusiast as to the more mature and experienced driver. This is a modern quality car of traditional British excellence.'

27
In Pursuit of Perfection

It was at the 1976 Concours that I remember chatting with a group of members about the reasons for their very partisan approach to the Bristol car. While a few criticisms were expressed on minor points, the majority agreed that for them it was the car's performance allied with reliability, safety and comfort that most appealed to them. One or two also mentioned the distinctive styling, and one, a Scotsman, praised the moderate fuel consumption.

But the remark I remember most was when we were talking about the tremendous mileages that some cars had covered. There was the powder blue 400, 'Old Chassis No. 1', still in showroom condition after 330,000 road miles, and several of the group had covered well over 200,000 miles in their own cars. We were all put to shame by a visitor from Australia, who claimed he knew of a Bristol 'down under' that was still going strong after half a million miles.

Yet such phenomenal mileages were not achieved by luck or accident, but were the result of good basic design, supported by continuous and painstaking development. I was not amused when one man (our talk had moved to the later models) said rather loftily: 'Of course it was easy enough for them just to drop a Chrysler engine into the old chassis, and start a whole new series of Bristols.' A Concours is no place for a lecture, so I let the matter pass, but I feel maybe, just to set the record straight, I might give a few examples of the manner in which the second generation models were designed, or modified in the light of experience. In doing so, I shall draw on material provided by the late Chief Engineer, Dennis Sevier, who gave the annual Spring Lecture to the Club on the eve of the 1976 Annual General Meeting.

Reference was made to the unusually low drag coefficient of the Type 401 body, which at 0.32 allowed the 2-litre full five-seater to attain a speed of 98mph on the level, and more on a slight downslope. As regards the 450 racer, the scientific reasons for its unusual shape were given, and the part played by the fins, which were to be continued in increasingly vestigial form on many later production cars. Sevier described the Design Office philosophy at the time as being 'dominated by two principles; if it moved, we put a damper, and if it did not, we put a fin on it'.

He described the 2.2-litre Type 406 model, with its more flexible engine and all disc braking, as constituting 'the first real step away from the sports car image'. He added that from 1954 onwards, the need was recognised for an engine of greater capacity 'to enable the car to move into the super luxury bracket'.

Some time was spent discussing the Type 160 engine, of which three prototypes were made. Mr Sevier described it as:

'a light-weight unit of compact design, embodying an aluminium cylinder block with wet liners. Forged steel conrods (on which the caps were split at 45 degrees and serrated) were used with an alloy steel crankshaft with four 3 inch diameter main bearings. Twin overhead camshafts operated large valves inclined at 80 degrees, in an aluminium cylinder head, and three dual-choke 40mm Solex carburettors fed directly into six down-draught ports. The unit met all design specifications, and produced 160bhp @ 5,250rpm.'

The Car Division, as a part of the mighty Bristol Aeroplane Company, possessed at least one advantage over the Midlands factories of the period. Whereas the designers of the latter usually worked to a rigid deadline, at Filton the object to be achieved was considered more important than the time taken to achieve it. In the case of the ill-fated 220/240 Project, this philosophy was carried to a self-defeating extreme. Had the automatic transmission system been ready in time for road-testing with the new engine and chassis, the later history of the marque might have been quite different.

As we know, this was the final effort to produce a new 'all-Bristol engine', and within a year of the formation of the new private company in 1960 the first 5.2 litre model appeared as the Type 407 – a full four-seater, and capable of 122mph. The Chrysler engine was fitted with high-performance valve springs at Filton, in support of a special high-lift camshaft, and 4-choke carburettor. In this form, Sevier said the engine produced 'a net 200bhp'. He added: 'From the outset, it had been decided to fit the Torqueflite transmission with no manual alternative, a decision never regretted.'

Sevier then briefly reviewed the 408–410 models, praising the redesigned braking system and '. . . a superb power steering system, designed and developed over many years, to meet the most stringent demands of hardened Bristol "manual" drivers'. He added that one of the less usual variations of the Type 409 was ordered by an American with its 'sides in wickerwork trim'.

Oddly enough, a similar decor was chosen by the actor Peter Sellers, on a very special Mini-Cooper, with tiny carriage lamps at each side of its windscreen. Sellers was a great Bristol enthusiast, and was often to be seen at the Chiswick depot, as he changed his cars frequently, and kept them all in immaculate condition.

Sevier next turned to the subject of safety, which, along with comfort, had been 'the main requirements since 1962'. This was a prime reason why the massive separate chassis, first seen on the Type 400, was retained, though with considerably altered suspension. Examples of the safety measures included twin-circuit braking, collapsible steering columns, and a 'comprehensive heating and ventilation system'. As regards styling changes amongst the various second generation models, he mentioned 'deeper front and rear screens, modifications to front and rear of the body, and interior redesign.'

It was interesting to note that he called the Type 411 the 'Chairman's Express', and made the point that when an average fuel consumption of 15mpg was given for the 411 it was 'based on average figures obtained from approximately 5,000 miles running, on a development car used for normal routine tests'. He added that using the Speed Control, fitted to the 411(5) and the 412, the consumption might be improved to 'around 19mph'.

Reference was made to an experimental Bristol that was fitted with the Type 440 engine. This was of 7.2 litres capacity, and was capable of taking the heavy car from rest to 100mph in 14.5 seconds. It did not go into production, however, and one possible reason was because, in Sevier's words: 'It also rocked rather sharply, through torque reaction, when the accelerator pedal was lifted at 110 . . .'

Time was spent on some extremely technical matters, including the detailed requirements of the US federal legislation on exhaust emissions, the design of carburettors to meet these regulations, and the development of new exhaust systems. To ensure the interior of the car remained free of fumes, the engine of a development car was injected with a Redex-paraffin mixture 'from a screen-wash bottle into the engine, via a vacuum connection'. Observations from a following car showed that the worst condition occurred around 40–50mph '. . . when with normal straight outlets, the rear of the car occasionally became enveloped in smoke'.

Sevier concluded his description: 'With the final arrangements deflecting gases downwards at the outlets, the maximum CO readings recorded, within the interior and the boot, did not exceed 5ppm.'

It is interesting to note the similarity with testing methods used on some of the early 2-litre models. The engine was first dosed liberally with Redex, and then the car was driven along the Brabazon Straight, with a second car carrying observers and a cameraman. When the photographs were examined, it was seen that fumes were sucked upwards, and so into the car. The cure was to re-route the pipe from the silencer, to a new position that allowed the gases to be exhausted into the atmosphere.

Sevier next turned his attention to the subject of power steering, which he described as:

'... a mechanical gear with hydraulic power, and a hydraulic control system added to it. If something happens to the hydraulic part of the system, the driver can still manually control the car.'

Praising the system selected by Bristol, he said:

'... the exceptional standard achieved ... has been the result of close co-operation between ourselves and ZF, using sophisticated electronic equipment at Schwabisch Gmund, and extensive road and rig testing at Bristol.'

To give some idea of the strains imposed on a car's power steering, he mentioned that:

'when the wheels are turned with the car stationary, the maximum pressure in the system can reach 1,150 psi. Even negotiating roundabouts and high speed bends can produce pressures in excess of 400 psi.

I have always deplored the habit of some drivers when parking, of turning their front wheels with the car at rest, but I had no idea of the technical aspects of such driving methods.

Another feature of the power steering problem was the very high oil temperatures that can result from miles of high speed motoring on a level stretch of motorway. At such times, with the power steering not in use, oil in large quantities is released from the main circuit to flow within the oil reservoir. 100 degrees centigrade is the critical temperature, and trouble will result unless steps are taken to ensure that this temperature is not exceeded.

One field in which the ZF-cum-Bristol system excels, is the way that steering wheel 'feel' has been retained, so that the driver can be warned of the dangerous condition of the road. This may be caused by ice, mud, snow or some other adverse feature, and the lack of such sensitivity on some other systems made many experienced Bristoleers rather sceptical when power steering was introduced on the later Type 409 models.

A small but important point was brought to his audience's attention when Sevier observed that

'Drive belts must be tightened to a predetermined torque loading, to avoid occasional slip, and associated shudder, at maximum parking loads.'

Sevier next turned his attention to the Torqueflite automatic transmission, mentioning that on the A466 type the case was of cast iron, though the torque converter housing and extension were in aluminium die castings. After extensive testing, modifications at Filton included altering the extension housing and shaft, so as to incorporate a ball-bearing thrust race. The plain thrust washer was dispensed with, and Chrysler included this modification in later models.

A weight saving of some 90lb in the type A727 Torqueflite, first used on the 408 Mark 2, resulted from the substitution of an alloy gearbox, and when a hold was incorporated into the gear selection mechanism it worked so well that even hardened manual Bristol drivers finally accepted that the 'automatic camp' was worthy of their membership.

Further refinements included the substitution of an internal filter of Dacron felt for the in-line oil filter previously used. This enabled oil changes to be extended, so that they became necessary only after 30,000 service miles. This was very much in the tradition of the 2-litre models, in which routine servicing was reduced to an absolute minimum, encouraging ownership, even when the nearest garage might be hundreds of miles distant. Other modifications included induction-hardening the impeller hub, and increasing the diameter of the input shaft, and the number of shear points on each pinion shaft was doubled.

Suspension

Sevier referred to the substantial changes made to both front and rear suspension when the original Type 407 was being designed. Because of the weight of the new unit, and its power, which was more than double that of standard 2-litre models, the spiral bevel differential previously used was replaced by a heavier type hypoid unit. Another traditional feature, the A-bracket, was replaced by a forged light-alloy torque reaction link, with a Watt linkage for side reaction to cornering loads. Rubber bushes were used at all location points, and the outer lower mechanical ball joints were also replaced by a rubber-mounted alternative.

Front suspension no longer used the transverse spring first seen on the Type 400 back in 1946. Instead, a new system was designed, based on wishbones of unequal length, with coil springs seated on polyurethane pads. The dampers inside these springs were of the telescopic type by Armstrong – a firm that had supplied shock absorbers to Bristol since the little 404 coupe. The previous king-pin arrangement was replaced by sealed ball joints on light alloy stub axle carriers. Later, when power steering was inevitable, the front suspension was modified further, with substantial 'fail safe' inverted ball joints.

Despite further experimentation, it was found that the best seatings were of nylon. The forged type of hub previously used was replaced by the spheroidal graphite iron type, front and rear. Not only did this modification ensure adequate strength to the hubs, but a substantial reduction in machining costs resulted. For testing purposes, a Dunlop-Wohler fatigue test machine was used, with a 1.75 maximum cornering overload factor to 60,000 cycles. Yet there was neither failure not any signs of cracking.

Equal care was taken before the Armstrong Selectaride adjustable shock absorbers were adopted for the rear suspension, and it is said that Sevier spent more than a week down at the Armstrong works, testing a random sample of the new dampers, in all their settings, from soft to hard.

In 1964, the Filton design team was considering the merits of a rear levelling system that would enable a car so fitted, to compensate automatically when transversing less than perfect road surfaces. A proprietary system was kept under review until 1970, when it became standard on the Type 411(2) model. The system consisted of an engine-driven pump that supplied pressure to rams operating at the front end of each torsion bar, by way of control units connected by links to the rear axle. The result was an increase in the rear suspension travel, from 8 to 10.25in, making it possible to introduce superior damper settings.

Development work on the the adjustable dampers continued, and when the Type 411 was introduced in 1969 there was an improved mounting arrangement for the shock absorbers. The steering arm and linkage was redesigned, so as to provide a stiffer assembly, and a hydraulic idler box was fitted to help cope with the more robust power steering on the 411. By the time the 411(5) was ready for series production, in 1975, the proprietary rear suspension levelling system had been replaced by one of Bristol's own manufacture.

As an expert in his subject, Sevier explained that:

'The parasitic effect of the front suspension rubbers was eliminated to reduce the front wheel rate from 118 to 76lb/in, and with a rear wheel rate of 132lb/in, suspension frequencies in the cruising condition became 63 cycles per minute at the front, and 64 at the rear.'

Tyres and Wheels

Research had indicated that:

'the lateral frequency of the front suspension on early Type 411 cars was 39H, which was not ideally suitable for textile radial-ply tyres. To make the front suspension compatible with radial-ply tyres, and reduce thump around 40mph, it was necessary to lower the natural frequency to 20H. Subsequent testing on a sophisticated roller rig, with electronic acceleration attenuation assessment at the Dunlop tyre research department, showed considerable improvement from the extra compliance which was later confirmed by subjective testing. Careful assessment of compliance problems associated with the steering system ensured complete freedom from shake at the steering wheel.'

With typical modesty Sevier just mentioned his own testing of the Avon safety wheel. The purpose of the new design was to ensure that in the event of a blow-out the cover would remain on the rim, even at a high speed. So he took a Bristol fitted with the new wheels, and at 70mph deliberately blew a hole in the offside front tyre. The test was completely successful, but he was quick to add that the new wheel was

'. . . also tested with a burst at 140mph by the Chairman of Bristol Cars'.

So bald a statement robs both experiments of their dramatic aspect, but what cold courage must have been required to take out a car, attain such high speeds, and then press the button. It has been recorded that in fact, not only was Mr Crook's speed 144mph, but that, with the tyre blown, he then threw the heavy car into a series of violent swerves, to make quite sure that, even under such harsh treatment, the Avon safety wheel lived up to its name. From photographs I have seen of this incident, the amount of rubber shed on the track testifies to the violence of the various manœuvres, despite the offside front tyre being deflated. This test took place at the Royal Air Force base at Keevil, in Wiltshire.

Engine Cooling

For some years I lived in Geneva, and so was able to test my 2-litre Bristols under really severe Alpine conditions. Yet I cannot recall a single occasion when the engine overheated. In Australia it was the same. Even when the gauges for both oil and water had their respective needles way above the danger mark, the engine still functioned perfectly, and did not run on, when switched off at the end of a trip.

Yet when the policy decision was taken to use a big Vee-8 engine in the Bristol 407:

> 'tests on a typical US installation showed the low-speed cooling capacity to be very marginal. Previous development work with electrically operated fans led us to adopt them on a production basis. Apart from obtaining a superior cooling arrangement, the absence of general noise from an engine-driven fan was a worthwhile fringe benefit.'

Sevier continued:

> 'To obtain the most efficient installation, calculations were made to determine the air flow requirements to maintain adequate engine cooling on a 1 in 5 gradient, at a fully laden 15mph condition with no ram effect available.'

Just how thorough the further testing was may be judged from the following:

> 'From heat rejection curves for the engine, using a mean water flow at 1,500rpm of 18 gallons minimum and a calculated power requirement, a dissipation rate . . . was estimated, based on temperature drop over the radiator of 6 degrees centigrade. Wind tunnel performance checks on sections of the radiator core at a constant flow provided heat dissipation and air pressure drop related to matrix face velocity, and from this combined data an estimated 1,370sq ft min. was used as a design requirement for the fans.
> 'Subsequent tests on a fully laden car, over a steep three mile climb, in a 30 degrees centigrade ambient temperature at 15mph, proved the shrouded twin 10in diameter fans capable of pulling the water temperature down from 96 to 86 degrees centigrade. Further tests, with the front of the vehicle 1ft from a wall, were equally encouraging.'

Meanwhile work continued in the development of a thermal switch to control the fans, and eventually, in collaboration with Otter Controls, 'a small bi-metal unit with a small differential and operating temperature tolerance was produced'.

This was the unit fitted to the Type 411(5). The location of the fans was the opposite of that used by the Jensen car, in which cooling air was drawn through the radiator, with the fans placed behind the matrix. But further development at Filton took place:

> 'With the larger engine, as used in the 411, the following points had to be considered:
> 1. At idle, with the same cooling arrangement as before, the larger engine would run 9 degrees centigrade hotter.
> 2. The loss ratio of water in cylinder head to cylinder head mass would result in serious 'after boil' conditions, if the top speed cooling target was not reduced by 10 degrees centigrade.
> 3. Emission controls increased the heat rejection at idle by 200 Btu/hour.
> 4. Air conditioning was to be made available as an optional extra, and with the condenser in operation, the inlet air temperature could increase by 8 degrees centigrade.'

The solution was an increase in matrix area, from 360 to 440 square inches. In this condition, and with a suitably modified fan duct, the low-speed cooling capability was approximately half-way between the 407 and 409 standard.

One disadvantage in using an American engine was that it was subject to the US federal emission requirements which were being tightened at a consistent rate of 10 per cent per annum. Also, Bristol still saw America as a possible market for its super-luxury cars. The main problem was how to increase the fans' air flow, without a substantial current consumption. Even on the original Type 411, the alternator could not cope with the current consumed at idle. The solution was to increase the four fan blades to 11in diameter. With both fans, it took approximately 2½ minutes, to reduce the engine temperature at idle from 105 to 90 degrees centigrade.

It is not often realised what effects on engine cooling may result from alterations in the shape of the car's front end. If one compares the change from the Type 410 to the 411(4), a drop in air pressure was produced from 1.2in to 0.9in at 80mph. The tapping for the water gauge was inside the fan cowl.

The final portion of Sevier's lecture dealt with the regulations governing the design and function of motor vehicles, and the fact that the UK regulations were being replaced by directives from the ECE and EEC. They place an extra burden on the manufacturer to ensure that his products meet the standards required. These are extremely comprehensive, and cover such matters as steering, door locks, crankcase, exhaust emission, and vehicle noise levels.

Though perhaps it does not come strictly under the heading of development, I would like to mention that so jealous is Bristol of the inherent strength of its body construction that they insist, when a customer specifies a sunshine roof, that it be fitted in their own factory, by their own staff.

I realise that this has been a long and technically heavy chapter, but the object was to show, via extracts from Sevier's admirable paper, just how it is that a Bristol functions so well. It may also help explain its longevity.

28
From A to Zagato
The 412 Series

The relationship between the Milanese coachbuilders Carrozzeria la Zagata and the Bristol car was unusual. From the registry of the Bristol Owners' Club, we know that in 1948–1950 the firm made saloon bodies to be fitted to Type 400–401 used chassis, and in 1958–1959 there was a short run of 406Z saloons and the unique 406Z coupe.

There was also the 407Z, with a 2+2 coupe body, owned for many years by I W Halbert. I was talking to him recently, and he told me of the various modifications he had made. These included a stainless steel exhaust system, electronic ignition and power steering. The car is now owned by that well-known collector of classic cars Mr A Arutunoff who, Halbert told me, owns a car racing circuit near Tulsa, Oklahoma.

All the above bodies and cars were commissioned by Mr T A D Crook, in his capacity as head of Anthony Crook Motors of Hersham, Surrey, which was why both the 406Z and 407Z models were exhibited on the Zagato stand at the London Motor Shows.

It was not until production of the Type 411 series was drawing to a close that a contract was entered into directly between Bristol Cars Limited and Zagato. It called for a completely new design of multi-purpose coupe, using the traditional 9ft 6in Bristol wheelbase, and the Type 400 Chrysler Vee-8 engine with a capacity of 6,556cc. The transmission would be by Torqueflite, as on the Type 411(5).

The new car was announced in 1975, as the Type 412 convertible. Its most obvious feature was a double roll-over bar, so massive it might almost have been termed a girder. Designers of convertibles are

MODEL:	412 Convertible	Date:	1975–1978
Wheelbase	9ft 6in (2m 9cm)		
Front Track	4ft 6.5in (1m 38cm)		
Rear Track	4ft 7in (1m 39cm)		
Overall Height	4ft 8.5in (1m 44cm)		
Overall Width	5ft 9.5in (1m 77cm)		
Overall Length	16ft 2.5in (4m 90cm)		
Weight	3,780lb (1,714kg)		
Engine Type	Vee-8		
Number of Cylinders	8		
Bore	110.3mm		
Stroke	85.72mm		
Capacity	6,556cc		
Carburettor	Carter 4-choke 'Thermoquad'		
Gearbox	Chrysler Torqueflite 3-speed automatic		
Ratios	1st: 7.52 2nd: 4.45 Top: 3.07 Reverse: 6.75		
Brakes	Separate front and rear hydraulic systems. Self-adjusting servo-assisted Girling disc brakes on all wheels. Handbrake employs separate clamps operating on rear discs.		
Suspension			
Front	Independent by double wishbones, coil springs, adjustable dampers and anti-roll bar		
Rear	Live axle located by Watts linkage, longitudinal torsion bars and top link.		

Note: In mid-1978 the Convertible was succeeded by the Convertible Saloon.

The Type 412 – the first Bristol with convertible body since the Type 405 of 1954–58. In its series 3 (turbocharged) form it became the Beaufighter.

usually only too well aware of the need to reduce scuttle shake to a minimum, and on the 412 the bar served not only as protection to the occupants but also to brace the bodywork. In addition, a steel gusset was placed under the chassis, and, so far as I am aware, these measures eliminated scuttle shake completely.

There was a conventional canvas hood with rear screen, and also a removable Targa section that formed the roof, from the rear edge of the windscreen to the forward edge of the roll-over bar. In the brochure, it is stated: 'There is excellent visibility astern, because the hood practically disappears, unlike most convertibles whose bulky hoods protrude over the rear end. The huge luggage boot is unencumbered by a spare wheel. Note the rear guard fog lamps.'

Appearance

The 412 convertible looked quite unlike any previous Bristol, with an uncompromisingly square outline. The radiator grille was shaped like a narrow rectangle, its pattern not unlike the one used on the Type 411 Series 3–5. The wide flat bonnet sloped down very slightly to the top of the grille, and the bumpers were narrow blades faced with what appeared to be rubber. They gave no protection to the wings, and the filler cap on the near side was set

Type 412 Bristol, with convertible coachwork by Zagato. Note new elongated grille, with Pegasus badge, two large rectangular headlights, and narrow chrome-faced bumper.

behind the hood. Rear lights were in two rectangular panels, with the special fog lights set just below the bumper and above the four exhaust pipes. The boot lid resembled the bonnet in its width, and the latch was not recessed. Two large rectangular headlamps were inset at the extremities of the grille.

The production life of the 412 convertible was short, for it was announced that 'From 7th March, 1976, the Bristol convertible is discontinued, and replaced by the Bristol 412 convertible saloon'.

All the safety features of the original 412 were continued, and the announcement continued: 'The restyled coachwork incorporates a rear roof section with large electrically-heated glass rear window. The entire roof section may be removed in about one hour, with an ordinary tool kit, and replaced by the

Type 412(1), three-quarter rear/side view, with hood erected. Note the four tail pipes, Avon safety road wheels, horizontal rear lamp treatment, recessed boot lid release, narrow chrome faced bumper and rearguard fog lamps.

Rear/side view of driver's compartment. Note the leather upholstery, and the Reutter fully-reclining mechanism, small three-spoke steering wheel, veneered facia with circular ventilators, large lockable compartment on left, with 'grab handle'. The gear lever is of the curved type used on the earlier examples.

canvas hood with perspex rear window, when the car regains the appearance of the previous 412 convertible.'

The new rear roof section gave the car a rather less sporting appearance, the steeply sloping rear window matching the rake of the windscreen. Though there was neither chromed embellisher strip nor even a coachline along the side, there was a narrow ridge at the same height as the tops of both bumpers that extended across sides and doors. It added extra stiffness, and offered some protection in a crowded car park. With the Avon safety wheels, it was a handsome and purposeful-looking car, especially in side view.

Minor changes included the repositioning of the filler cap, now set at waist height just to the rear of the nearside wheel arch, and the 'addition of stainless steel bumper cappings front and rear, rear bumpers which extend further round the rear of the car for greater protection'.

There was little difference between the interiors of the 412 convertible and the later convertible saloon, and the brochure mentioned 'Fully adjustable and reclining front seats with individual centre arm rests and a safety locking device has been specially designed to reduce fatigue to a minimum on long journeys'.

There seems little doubt that the car was aimed, as a matter of company policy, at a new sector of the market. It was for hard-driving owners, who may previously have favoured a rather more exotic continental car, with less practical rear seat accommodation or luggage capacity. As the brochure said: 'There is ample head and leg room in the rear seats to provide good lateral stability. There are deep pockets either side of the seats. The front seat belts slide out of the way of the rear passengers entering or leaving the rear of the car.'

Though I have been unable to trace any reports on the 412 Convertible, there are several dealing with the version known as the 'Convertible Saloon'. Early examples were also known as the 412, and considerable attention was given to the safety aspects of its massive roll-over bar.

Much favourable attention was drawn to the versatility of the model for, as the brochure remarked, 'The Bristol 412 convertible saloon is to all intents and purposes either a full saloon or a full convertible with roll bar in either case, or a combination of both'.

As was usual with a Bristol, the customer had a very wide choice of colour scheme, both for the body and the interior, and it is interesting to note that it is when a light colour is chosen for the exterior that the

The interior – front compartment – of a Type 412 Bristol, with convertible coachwork to Zagato design. Note the leather upholstery, handbrake between seats, small steering wheel, circular ventilators in facia, large lockable compartment at far left, and major instruments in console ahead of driver.

wing panels, behind which the spare wheel and electrics are stowed, become clearly visible. With darker colours they seem to fade into the body sides, which then extend from front wing to rear, the only interruptions being the door lock and filler cap.

The boot latch was recessed, and the Pegasus badge in the centre of the grille was replaced by a large enamel plaque, showing the arms of the City of Bristol.

In a very handsome catalogue the choices open to the owner are shown as follows:

1. He could elect to drive his car with the rear section in place, when it was virtually a luxuriously equipped saloon.
2. He could remove the entire rear section, replacing it with the canvas hood with Plexiglas screen.

Front view of a Type 412(2) Bristol with convertible coachwork to Zagato design. Note the enamel badge on grille, the pair of large rectangular headlights and narrow chrome faced bumper.

Such versatility was not uncommon in the thirties, in the days of the great specialist coachbuilders, but is rare indeed today.

3. He could lower the canvas hood and, with the Targa top removed, enjoy al fresco motoring, yet still keep the big roll-over bar in place.

4. He could lower the canvas hood, and with the Targa top in position the car would be in what the brochure referred to as the 'de Ville' position.

This was indeed 'a car for all seasons'. It would seem that most owners, if the entire rear section had been removed for summer motoring, preferred to leave it in the garage till the autumn. By contrast, the Targa top was usually put in the boot, ready to be re-installed if rain threatened, or the weather turned cold.

In its issue of June 1977, *Car and Driver* gave the results of a series of competitive tests it carried out, using a Type 412 Bristol, a Ferrari 400 Auto and an Aston Martin Lagonda as guinea pigs. Referring to the roll-over bar on the Bristol, the writer commented: 'The superstructure may be light-weight, but it is far from flimsy. The roll-over bar adds such strength that the car can pass its tests roofless, one of the few openable tourers to survive.' Whether the owner of a 412 would really refer to his car as an 'openable tourer' seems doubtful.

Considerable attention was paid to the way in which the frameless door windows made a watertight

Close-up of a Type 412 Bristol, with convertible coachwork by Zagato. Note the narrow opening quarterlight on left, and the massive roll-over bar, with the 'Targa' top between it and the windscreen. Inside, the small three-spoke steering wheel can be seen together with a curved gear lever and instrument panel.

View of rear compartment of a Type 412 Bristol with convertible coachwork to Zagato design. Note the massive roll-over bar, that with a steel gusset under the floor prevented the scuttle 'shake' from which so many convertibles suffer. There are head restraints on all four seats. Note the leather upholstery and slightly opened rear quarterlight.

seal with the roof section. The latter possessed a lip, behind which the window top was located. If one wished to open a door from within, a pull on the handle appeared to have no effect, until one noticed that the electrically operated window had been wound down just enough to clear the lip. At which point, assuming one was still pulling on the handle, the latch would unfasten and one could open the door.

Having alighted, and wishing to lock the door, you simply pressed a small button in the lock plate whereupon, in uncanny silence, the window would slide up and under the lip, to keep the interior safe from the elements and thieves. Incidentally, the locks are burst-proof.

In the test report, it was remarked that with its standard Type 400 Chrysler engine the Bristol was

The rear section of a Type 412 convertible Bristol, from the nearside. The canvas hood is lowered and one can see the twin head restraints on the rear seatbacks, the massive roll-over bar and narrow rear quarterlight.

Side/front view of a Type 412, with convertible coachwork to a Zagato design. The canvas top is 'down', but the 'Targa' top is still in place, there are head restraints on all four seats. The road wheels are of pressed steel and the fuel cap is on the side above the rear wheel arch. The wide grille has large rectangular headlights at either end and an enamel badge in its centre.

the slowest of the trio, and also that its 205VR-15 tyres possessed less grip on the race track used for speed tests. On the other hand, out on the open road, the 412 came into its own, showing handling qualities 'astonishing for a car of this size'. The ZF power steering, with Filton modifications, was also praised, for though with its three turns lock-to-lock it was lower geared than the Lagonda and higher than the Ferrari, the response was quicker, and the feedback from the road was superior.

The combination of a comparatively long wheel base (the traditional 9ft 6in, as used on all standard Bristols except the little 404), a short rear overhang, and the low-set engine and transmission gave the car its outstanding controllability. The self-levelling system was also a factor making for a feeling of great security, even at very high speeds.

To some enginers of the new school, the Bristol 412 was very old-fashioned, with its box section separate chassis and live axle. Yet the first gave it a degree of safety impossible with the more popular monocoque body/chassis, and the live axle was controlled in a way peculiar to the Bristol. With longitudinal torsion bars to provide the springing medium, the axle was located fore and aft by drop arms attached to the bars. A torque reaction arm, with its rear end connected to the top of the differential housing, was a further means of locating the axle, and there was a

Rear view of the interior of a Type 412(2) Bristol, with convertible coachwork to a design by Zagato. Note the head restraints, massive roll-over bar, and small steering wheel with Bristol badge in centre.

transverse Watt linkage too. The end result of such a well-tried and developed system was a car that handled, in the expert's view, in a way that 'compares favourably with any car in the world'.

The Torqueflite automatic transmission was much praised for the unobtrusive fashion in which gear changes were made, up or down. The car could rocket from rest to 60mph in 7.9 seconds, and to 100mph in 21 seconds, without any drama, merely a 'throaty warble from under the bonnet'. It is this sort of performance that appeals to the mature motorist for whom the 412 was intended.

Some credit for such an unusual combination of high performance and lowish fuel consumption ought to be given, I think, to the Carter 4-choke carburettor, with its settings altered at Filton. Adjustments were also made to the ignition, and it can be a most exhilarating experience when the second bank of chokes make their presence felt. There can be such a surge of extra power, even when the car is already travelling fast, that I sympathised with the passenger who remarked, 'But you never told me it was turbocharged.' Though one did not know it at the time, this modification was to be a feature of the next model but one, the Beaufighter.

The Bristol Type 412/S2

Introduced in 1977, this model was visually very similar to its predecessor, but used the Type 360 engine of 5,898cc capacity. It remained in production until succeeded in 1980 by the Beaufighter. To facilitate licencing and registration, this was given the Type No. 412/S3.

The Bristol Type 412/S3

This model is still in production, under its better known title of Beaufighter, and, though in appearance it may have seemed very like its predecessor, mechanically it was very different. But the inclusion of a Rotomaster turbocharger boosted power by approximately 30 per cent. This in turn made it necessary for the transmission to be strengthened. This was carried out with typical Bristol ingenuity, by using the torque converter and internal clutches normally used with the Type 440 Chrysler engine, with its enormous capacity of 7,200cc. As a further precaution, a stronger propeller shaft was fitted, with universal joints larger than standard.

The Targa top had been superseded by a fixed roof with rectangular tilting panel that could function

MODEL:	412/S3 Beaufighter Turbocharged Convertible
Date:	1980–present
Wheelbase	9ft 6in (2m 89cm)
Front Track	4ft 6.5in (1m 38cm)
Rear Track	4ft 7.5in (1m 41cm)
Overall Height	4ft 8.5in (1m 43cm)
Overall Width	5ft 9.5in (1m 76cm)
Overall Length	16ft 2.5in (4m 94cm)
Weight	3,850lb (1,746kg)
Tyres	Avon tubeless radial ply 225 × 70 VR15
Engine Type	90 degree Vee-8
Number of Cylinders	8
Bore	101.6mm
Stroke	90.93mm
Capacity	5,900cc
Carburettor	4 barrel boosted by exhaust-driven turbocharger
Gearbox	Torqueflite 3-speed and reverse automatic
Ratios	1st: 7.06 2nd: 4.18 Top: 2.88 Reverse: 6.36
Brakes	Footbrake: Self-adjusting servo-assisted Girling discs Handbrake: Separate callipers operating on rear discs
Suspension	
Front	Independent by wishbones of unequal length with coil springs. Telescopic dampers and torsional anti-roll bar
Rear	Torsion bar springs with Watt linkage stabilisation and telescopic dampers. Sealed ball joints

virtually as a sun roof, or be removed completely. Other external changes included a restyled front end, incorporating four rectangular headlights, bigger rear quarter lights, and a power bulge in the bonnet top. This was necessary even though the engine and transmission had been set an inch lower in the chassis frame, because of the way the priority valve was interposed between the carburettor and the inlet manifold.

The choice by Bristol of the Rotomaster turbocharger was the subject of much comment, but proved to be a considerable success. The right-hand exhaust pipe is modified to provide a suitable mounting point for the turbocharger, and a secondary feed is taken from the left-hand pipe, under the oil sump, to the right-hand pipe.

By locating the turbocharger in a transverse position, just above rocker cover height, the compressor outlet points towards the carburettor, with the priority valve in between. To enrich the secondary choke circuit, the jets on the Carter 4-choke instrument are changed. At low throttle openings, the priority valve remains open, allowing all of the fuel-air mixture to enter the engine direct.

As the accelerator pedal is depressed, the pressure between carburettor and manifold begins to approach equality, and the priority valve starts to close. This action causes part of the fuel-air mixture to be redirected through the turbocharger's compressor, while the rest of the mixture still takes the direct route straight to the manifold. In the final stages, with yet wider throttle openings, the boost pressure increases to a point where the priority valve closes completely. This causes all the mixture to be compressed, prior to its entry into the engine.

On the normally aspirated Chrysler engine, a black box that was part of its electronic ignition system was responsible for the advance curve suitable for the 'lean burn' type engine. On the turbocharged unit, a modified bob-weight distributor replaced the black box. Since the fuel consumption of the turbocharged engine was greater than the normally aspirated version, a higher-capacity fuel pump was fitted, together with bigger-bore fuel lines, so that the engine might not suffer from fuel starvation, even when driven to its maximum.

Probably the most novel innovation on the Beaufighter was the new type front seat, which the occupant, driver or passenger, might adjust electrically for height, reach and tilt. All seats were fitted with head rests, 'specially offset at rear for lounging', to quote the brochure. To provide sufficient fuel for a reasonable cruising radius, the capacity of the tank was increased from the eighteen gallons of the convertible saloon to twenty-one gallons. In addition, and as an extra, a very hard-driving customer could specify an auxiliary tank of ten gallons capacity. The occupants, as a safety measure, were protected from the tank area by a strong steel bulkhead.

Despite their small numbers, the Bristol factory staff were capable of fabricating not only the massive box section chassis, but many of the other components too. These included the unequal-length wishbones and anti-roll bar for the front suspension, and the Watt linkage and top links for the rear. I have been told that the rear axle was also made in-house, except for the crown wheel and pinion, but have been unable to substantiate this.

A customer might choose to have either the 2.88:1 economy rear axle ratio, or the 3.066:1 performance ratio. Headlamp beams were no longer controlled by a foot pedal, but by a stalk on the steering column. A second similar stalk controlled the windscreen wipers. The tyres on the Beaufighter were different – 225-70VR15 Avons instead of the 205 VR15 Avon radial-ply covers used on the 412/S2 model. No alteration was made in the rim width of the 15in diameter Avon safety wheel, which remained at just 6in.

Although the Beaufighter's overall length is 16ft 2½in, it is only 5ft 9½in wide, and with its accurate steering, excellent visibility along the flat bonnet, and easily visible front wings the car can manoeuvre in heavy traffic in a manner one might only expect from a smallish sports car. Yet once it reaches open country, or a motorway without too many heavies, down goes the foot and what a transformation!

Driving Impressions

It was just before the 1980 Bristol Owners' Club Spring Weekend when we heard that Mr Anthony Crook would lend us two of his latest models, one of which was a Beaufighter.

This kind action was reminiscent of those other occasions when the Club had been given what I believe in film circles is called a sneak preview of a new model Bristol. Four of us collected the cars from the London showrooms of the Company at 368–370 Kensington High Street, and they looked absolutely immaculate, with full tanks, just awaiting our pleasure.

Front view of a Type 412(3), better known as the 'Beaufighter'. It is a multi-purpose convertible, designed by Zagato. The very slight 'bulge' on the bonnet denotes the presence of a Rotomaster turbocharger; the radiator is wide yet narrow in depth, with two sets of small rectangular headlights at either end, and an enamel badge in the centre. Note the wide apron with four ventilation slots, and direction indicators below the narrow chrome faced bumper.

The road was mercifully free of traffic, and as we headed westwards we were able to sample the joys of real thoroughbred motoring. After all these years, I can still remember vividly the instant response when one gave a good hard press on the accelerator. There was none of the throttle lag, that was then common with some turbocharged cars. The sensation was like a high-speed New York lift descending a skyscraper, only of course one was travelling

Liquefied Petroluem Gas and the Bristol Type 412.

I was checking some old press cuttings recently, and I came across one dealing with liquefied petroleum gas (LPG) and the type 412, and I felt it worth quoting.

It appeared in *The Daily Telegraph*, in its issue dated 2 January 1980, and was by its then motoring correspondent, John Langley. He had been testing what he termed 'a standard 412 modified to run on liquefied petroleum gas'. He considered that it was likely that such a conversion would attract the long-distance motorist, anxious to increase his cruising range, rather than for reasons of sheer economy. He added that it would be possible to give a 412 Bristol a 'total fuel capacity of 37½ gallons – 18 gallons in the original tank and 19½ gallons of LPG in two tanks installed in the boot'.

In effect, this would have provided a cruising range of 500 miles, and one might have extended this even further since there was an auxiliary fuel tank of ten-gallon capacity, available as an extra. In the above article, it was mentioned that because of the car's tremendous performance, under ordinary driving conditions, the difference between using petrol or gas 'is barely perceptible'. Langley had conducted some acceleration tests, comparing the two fuels and added 'a stop watch reveals that the 0–60mph acceleration takes about one second longer, at around 9 seconds, using LPG.'

The car under test ran smoothly and quietly on either fuel, but after some mileage had been covered using the gas cylinders, the engine commenced to stall on corners, and when negotiating traffic islands. The trouble ceased as soon as the gas was replaced by petrol, and later examination revealed that the trouble was due to 'dirt in the LPG system'.

During the test period, a careful record was kept of the fuel used, and the averages were estimated to be 14.3mpg on petrol, and 13.1mpg on gas. Since these figures included acceleration and maximum speed tests, one might consider them as being higher (i.e. more fuel used) than might be achieved by an ordinary driver, using his car for everyday motoring.

The threat of a shortage of petrol and the possibility of fuel rationing may have focused attention on the use of LPG as a practical alternative, but once the danger had receded, the attraction of LPG seemed to wane. One big advantage was the cleanliness of an engine using gas rather than liquid fuel, and it appears likely that had some system of cheap and reliable refuelling become more general, what was little more than an experiment might have had a much wider and more popular response.

---

horizontally not vertically. But at the same time there was the peculiar sensation of one's stomach momentarily losing contact with the rest of one's body, while the push in the back made one glad of the seat belt.

The trip to the Swan's Nest at Stratford-upon-Avon, which was where the Club stayed in those days, was all too short, and I persuaded the car park attendant to let us leave the two cars in a little space in front of the hotel. The official park was all gravel, and I shuddered to think of the damage that might be caused. The man did us proud, with a series of little white posts and chains, and it was not long before passers-by were stopping to look at these two magnificent Bristols. Several American tourists even wanted to buy them, and so I had to explain they were not for sale, and gave them the address and telephone numbers of the Bristol showrooms in London.

A Club weekend is always a crowded time, but by getting up early on the Sunday morning we were able to take the Beaufighter out for a short run over relatively empty roads. On the way back, we met a long line of fairground vehicles, and took a by-lane. It had been a wet spring, and the surface was greasy mud with plenty of potholes, but the big car rode smoothly, until a tractor came out of a farmyard. Firm pressure on the brake pedal brought us to a smooth stop, and with a cheery wave of his hand the tractor driver went on his way.

I remember one motoring journalist who criticised the Beaufighter for its 'heavy doors and high sills'. Speaking personally, I much prefer the protection of the one, and the convenience of the other. A low sill may facilitate entry or exit under normal conditions, but faced with a very high kerb one can find it impossible to allow one's passengers to enter or alight – which can be both time-wasting and embarrassing.

All too soon it was time to begin the trip back to London, stopping first to give the two cars a quick wash and polish, and then to top up their fuel tanks. We were surprised at the frugality of the big turbocharged Chrysler engine. Admittedly, we had never extended the Beaufighter, but a consumption of 14–15mpg seemed excellent.

Other Bristols

There were other versions of the 412 Bristol, that are perhaps less well known. The first was called the 412/USA Convertible and it resembled the original 412 Convertible very closely. The main differences were the headlights, for on the American version there were four smaller rectangular lamps, instead of the two large ones of the original. The bumpers had the chromed strips of the convertible saloon, and they were curved to protect front and rear wings. The filler cap was on the side of the body and not behind the canvas hood, and there was no detachable rear section. Also, direction indicator repeaters were fitted to the body sides, just above the curved bumper. If intended for the American market, presumably this model was fitted with left-hand steering.

Another version was named after the Beaufort, which was also an aircraft that saw service with the Royal Air Force, towards the end of World War II. It is much less well known than the Beaufighter, and tended to be regarded rather less favourably by the air crews. This may have been because the plane was so built that of the three-man crew, only one had a clear view.

The member of the 412 range known as the Beaufort is, to me, the most attractive of them all. With its hood electrically stowed under the tonneau cover, the eye is led from the low-set radiator grille with two pairs of headlights inset at the extremities, along the wide bonnet with the power bulge that indicates the presence of a turbocharger. The windscreen is very wide, its supports slim for a convertible, and they are joined at the top by a cross bar to which the hood is attached when erected.

The wide doors are slightly curved at the top, and both front seats have detachable headrests. Since the model is intended for export, it has the small three-spoked steering wheel on the left, with the straight floor-mounted gear lever to the driver's right.

With the hood in its lowered position, it rests in a shallow well, in such a way that it is scarcely visible from the driver's seat. This is quite different from the Type 405 drophead, in which the hood and its hood bag tended to obstruct the rearward view. Indicator repeaters are placed just above the bumpers, fore and aft, and are rectangular in shape.

The bumpers are very solid, with a chromed strip, and are curved to protect front and rear wings. Behind the front number plate is a wide apron, pierced with four wide ventilation slots, to help cool the sump. The sides are quite plain, but one deep ridge extends from the grille to the tail, while a

---

A Short History of the Bristol Beaufighter

Originally serving as a night fighter, to cope with the enemy attacks on British towns and cities in 1941, the aircraft was later modified to serve an ever-increasing variety of roles in all of which it was successful.

In May 1941 it began to function as a long-range day fighter in the Middle East, and in the autumn of the same year, with the addition of four 250lb bombs carried externally, it began a new career as a fighter-bomber. In this role, two squadrons of Beaufighters were based on Malta, from whence they became adept at intercepting General Rommel's air supply route to Africa. Direct support was given to the Eighth Army by attacking enemy land supply columns and depots.

In 1943, the Beaufighter was further modified, so that it might function as a torpedo-bomber with Coastal Command. In this role, it operated not only over the North Sea, Atlantic Ocean and the Mediterranean, but as far afield as the Indian Ocean too.

Later in the war, squadrons of Beaufighters were sent to support the 14th Army, and played a decisive part in driving the enemy out of Burma. It was during this campaign that new attacking techniques were developed, to such an extent that the enemy called the Beaufighter 'Whispering Death'.

The reasons for the aircraft's success were as various as the roles in which it was employed. An exceptionally strong air frame, twin Bristol radial engines sufficiently powerful to cope with an ever-increasing load, and an armament that included cannon as well as machine guns, all contributed to making it an outstanding warplane.

It could absorb punishment as well as give it, and many pilots and crews were able to reach a safe airfield, despite damage that on a less robust aircraft would probably have caused it to disintegrate. It seems to me that in calling the turbocharged convertible a 'Beaufighter', Bristol Cars Limited justly commemorated an aircraft that possessed the same virtues of performance, versatility and safety, that have contributed so much to the reputation of the Bristol car.

A 'Spotter's Guide' to the Type 412 Bristol Models

	Prototype	412 Convertible	412/S2 Convertible Saloon	412/S3 or 'Beaufighter'
Boot catch recessed	–	*	*	*
Bright strip on wraparound bumper	–	*	*	*
Filler cap on body side	–	*	*	*
Hard top as original equipment	–	–	*	*
'Pegasus' radiator badge	*	*	–	–
Enamel radiator badge	–	–	*	*
Headrests	–	–	*	*
'Grille' on roll-over bar	*	*	–	–
Glass sun roof	–	–	–	*
Engine fitted with Turbocharger	–	–	–	*
Fitted with Type 400 engine	*	*	–	–
Fitted with Type 360 engine	–	–	*	*

Note: a) There was also a *Type 412 (USA) Convertible* model. It was similar to the Type 412/S2, but lacked the latter's hard top. It was fitted with four rectangular headlights and turn indicator 'flashers' to meet American requirements. The engine was fitted with a 'Cleaner Air System', complete with catalytic exhaust.

b) A turbocharged convertible without a roll over bar was available. Known as the *Beaufort*, its flowing lines made it a very handsome vehicle. The canvas hood folded into a well in the tail – leaving the driver's rear view unobstructed.

c) The above list is only a guide, and there are some examples that possess features that in theory should belong to another type. This is probably either due to such changes being specified at time of original purchase, or because a later owner has wished to up date his car.

d) No prototypes were sold to the public.

---

second and much shallower one stretches from the front wheel arch, across the door, ending just ahead of the rear arch.

The hinged panels concealing the spare wheel on the nearside and the battery, fuse panel and servos on the offside are wide, extending from the front wheel arches to the edges of the doors. They are clearly visible, if the car has a light body colour, but might be less evident in a darker shade.

The road wheels are alloy of Wolfrace spoked type, suiting the car's lines very well. So far as I am aware, all the Beauforts produced to date have been exported except for the one that forms part of Anthony Crook's personal collection. Recently I saw it in the Kensington showrooms, and as I had my camera with me I took some photographs. I doubt any will do justice to such a lovely car, for taking snaps through glass is rarely successful.

In an earlier chapter, I said that I regarded the one-off Viotti 407/10 convertible as my favourite Bristol convertible, but the lovely lines of the Beaufort make it a worthy rival. It will be noted that no mention has been made of a roll-over bar, since one is not fitted.

I will end with a quotation that I feel sums up the ethos of the Beaufighter car rather well. It is from a report in the June 1981 issue of *Thoroughbred and Classic Car* and is as follows:

'. . . a breathtaking surge of power is the answer to pressure on the accelerator. Use this performance when passengers are not expecting it, and their white knuckles will suggest they don't share the confidence that the car undoubtedly gives the driver.

'When they have adjusted to the idea that a seemingly staid luxury barouche can move at this rate, in virtual silence, they will sink back into their leather armchairs, content in the knowledge that the Bristol is also very safe.'

29
Sleeping Beauty

Type 603

At the London Motor Show, in the Autumn of 1976, there was a new model on the Bristol stand that received much favourable attention. Known as the Type 603 saloon, its appearance was quite unlike any of the earlier Chrysler-engined models, and reminded some long-term Bristol enthusiasts of the first-generation cars, with their 2-litre Bristol engines

'It's as if Sleeping Beauty has woken up at last,' one man told me, and added: 'She may not be quite as pretty as my dear old 403, but the general impression is quite similar.'

Despite its flowing lines and delicate appearance, the 603 was some 10cwt heavier, and the capacity of its Vee-8 engine was more than three times that of the 403. All the same, the 603 did possess much of the grace and harmony that made those early Bristols so distinctive.

I am often asked why the model was numbered 603 and not 413, as might have been expected, and I usually give the same explanation that I received myself. I was informed that it commemorated the 603 years that had passed since the City of Bristol received its first royal charter from King Edward III, in the year 1373. Just recently I was checking the telephone number of the Kensington showrooms, and noticed that its local exchange was coded 603: an interesting coincidence.

Unusually, a potential customer had a choice of two versions. He could choose either the S model with a new Chrysler Type 360 engine with a capacity of 5,898cc, or the E model that was fitted with a modified version of the Type 318 unit, last seen on the 410 model, with a swept volume of 5,211cc. The

MODEL:	603/S2 Saloon	Date:	1978–80
Wheelbase		9ft 6in (2m 89cm)	
Front Track		4ft 6.5in (1m 38cm)	
Rear Track		4ft 7in (1m 39cm)	
Overall Height		4ft 8.75in (1m 43cm)	
Overall Width		5ft 9.5in (1m 76cm)	
Overall Length		16ft 1in (4m 90cm)	
Weight		3,931lb (1,783kg)	
Tyres		Tubeless Avon radial ply 205VR × 15	
Bore		101.6mm	
Stroke		90.93mm	
Capacity		5,900cc	
Gearbox		Torqueflite 3-speed and reverse automatic	
Ratios		1st: 7.06 2nd: 4.18 Top: 2.88 Reverse: 6.36	
Brakes		Footbrake: Self-adjusting servo-assisted Girling disc brakes. Separate front and rear hydraulic systems by tandem master cylinders Handbrake: Separate callipers on rear discs	
Suspension Front		Independent by wishbones of unequal length with coil springs, telescopic dampers and anti-roll bar	
Rear		By torsion bar springs with Watt linkage. Adjustable dampers front and rear	

'The Heavenly Twins'. On the left (WL0 956S), is a Type 603E Bristol saloon, and on the right (BWS 475), an example of the Type 603S, Series 2. The initials stand for 'Economy' and 'Super' or 'Sports' respectively, the main difference being that the 603E was fitted with the Chrysler 318 engine of 5,211cc capacity, while the 603S has the Type 360 unit, of 5,898cc capacity. The most obvious visual difference is in the type of head restraint; 'perforated' on the 'E' and 'solid' on the 'S'.

carburation was different too, with a 4-choke Carter instrument on the S, while the E used a 2-choke carburettor of similar make. Both engines shared a common compression ratio of only 8:1. This was lower than on the 412 models, reflecting the transatlantic obsession with exhaust emissions.

There are a number of reports on the model in the motoring journals, but they all appear to deal with the second series (i.e. the 603S2), introduced in 1977, and so it is on this model that I will concentrate.

The overall length of the 603 was 16ft 1in, just an inch and a half less than the 412, but it seemed longer and lower. In fact, the 603 was one quarter of an inch higher, and it would seem that the flowing lines of the new model created the illusion. A brace of round headlights were recessed at either end of the low-set

A close-up view of the 'Pegasus' emblem, on the offside quarter of a Type 603S Bristol saloon. Note the Arms of the City of Bristol on the lower section of the badge.

grille. The latter was quite plain, except for the new enamelled badge.

Immediately below was a narrow bumper blade, its chromed edge projecting slightly, with the ends curved to protect the wings. The registration plate was attached to a wide skirt, pierced by two long ventilation slots.

The bonnet was wide and flat, extending rearwards to a very large windscreen, with narrow pillars. The roof curved gracefully to an equally large, well raked rear screen, and then over the boot lid to the flat tail section. The rear light clusters were set into two simple panels, positioned either side of the number plate, with the bumper curving to afford some protection to the rear wings. The boot sill was low-set, making loading or unloading much easier than on some of the earlier models, and the lid was self-propping.

Front view of Type 603S Bristol saloon. Note oval grille with two pairs of large circular headlights inset, and enamel badge in centre. Also note absence of bumper, giving good view of direction indicators and the two large oval ventilation slots.

Three-quarter side/front view of a Type 603S Bristol saloon. Note the Avon safety wheels, narrow wraparound oval grille, with enamel badge and two pairs of circular headlights. Head restraints front and rear.

The side windows and those in the doors were very large, and the door pillar was so unobtrusive that the 603 was a very light and airy vehicle indeed. The body sides were quite plain, and a narrow ridge extended just above the wheel arches from nose to tail, and across the wide doors. There was no kick plate, but the lower six inches of body and doors on some examples were painted either black or a deeper shade of the body colour.

The wing panels, behind which, in traditional Bristol fashion, were stowed the spare wheel and electrical elements, were much larger, extending from the front wing back to the forward edge of the door. Even with a light colour scheme they were now indiscernable, and the effect was of a plain body side, its sole ornament being the chromed lock assembly, and a ventilator just aft of the rear wheel arch which was omitted on the original 603 models.

The method of stowing the wheel, under a panel in the nearside wing, is unique to the Bristol car.

Side view left/right of Type 603S Bristol saloon. Note the Avon safety wheels, very narrow wraparound bumpers and vertical rear light clusters. Also head restraints front and rear.

Rear view of a Type 603S2 on left, and the 603E on right. The latter has 'perforated' head restraints, while the former has the 'solid' type.

The Interior

The interior was fully in keeping with the Bristol traditions of quality and taste. The front seats were adjustable for reach and tilt, and there were detachable head rests front and rear. Upholstery was in top-quality hide, though if he wished a customer might specify another material, or even have cloth panels inset into the seats at no extra cost. Such individual tastes were catered for as part of the marque's bespoke policy.

Although all seating was within the traditional 9ft 6in wheelbase, there was plenty of leg-room, and, despite an external width of only 5ft 9½in, there was no feeling of constraint. The seat belts were of the inertia reel type, with the ingenious floor-mounted

Close-up view, offside, of the interior of a Type 603S Bristol saloon. Note the leather upholstery with head restraints, and arm rest between front seats.

Close-up of facia, common to the Type 603S and E Bristol saloons. Note the small three-spoke steering wheel, with major instruments in a console. Also the circular ventilators, and lockable glove compartment with 'grab handle'. The accelerator pedal is of the 'organ' type, the gear lever is curved, upholstery is leather and the carpet is top grade Wilton over sound proof underlay.

rail to prevent rear passengers risking entanglement when entering or leaving the car.

As was usual on a Bristol, there were small details that indicated the amount of care that had been taken with the design. There were arm rests front and rear, ample space for maps, guide books and all the other items that seem to accumulate in a car. There was a lockable cupboard in the dashboard, a concealed locker under the armrest, useful pockets in the doors and in the backs of the front seats, and what was described as 'a deep lockable cubby hole forming a picnic tray for each rear passenger when in the open position' on each wheel arch. There was also a 'full width rear parcel shelf, shaped to hold objects without sliding'.

Probably the most novel feature was the way the

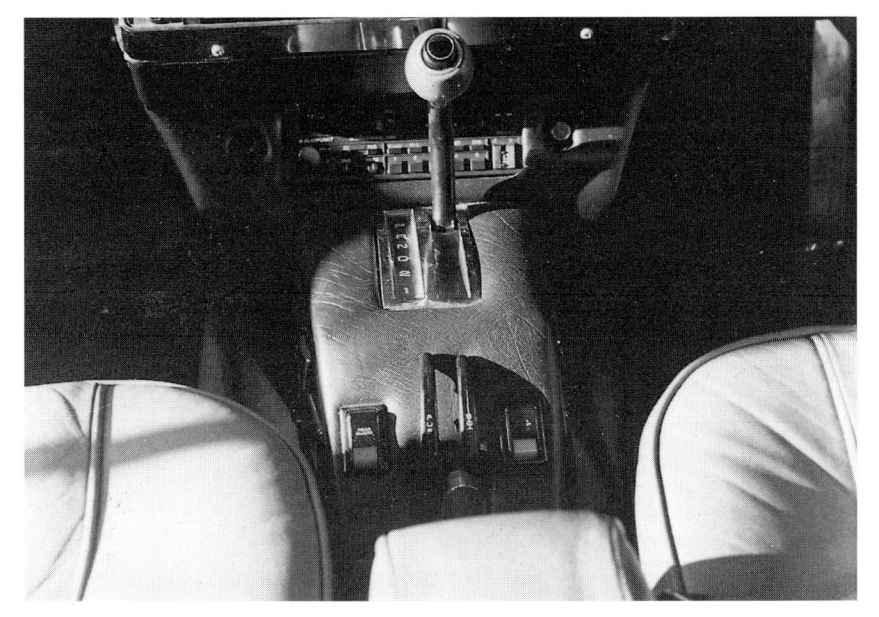

Close-up of curved gear lever and minor controls on a Type 603S Bristol saloon. Note the two small levers just behind gear lever; they release the boot and petrol filler cap. The upholstery is leather, and carpet is top grade Wilton with a sound proof underlay.

front seats could be adjusted electrically, or, to use the description from a report in *Motor* in its 2 September 1978 issue: 'Not just fore and aft and backrest tilt either; via a little joy stick on the side of the centre console, the seat can be raised or lowered, and moved backwards and forwards, while two further switches allow you to raise the front or rear of the seat individually.'

This sophistication was matched by its cost, for though the seats were original equipment on the 603/S2, they could be fitted to the 412, as an optional extra for £1,208.

Reminiscent of the anti-theft measures found on the 401–403 models, the petrol filler and the boot lid were both controlled from within the car. On the 603/S2 this was by means of small switches on the gearbox housing, but on the original 603S there were two levers behind the gear change.

Another identifying difference between the 603/S2 and the S and E versions was the shape of the gear lever. On the latter it was curved but on the former it was straight.

Mention has been made of the absence of a ventilator on the sides of the original 603. This was because a different system was employed for air extraction. On the early cars this was achieved by a series of slots on the shelf behind the rear seats, and into the open air via an opening under the boot lid.

On the 603/S2, ventilation was improved but it was criticised for too much wind noise.

The air-conditioning system was standard on all models of the 603, though it differed in detail. On the original version, there were two louvres, similar to the fresh air ones, immediately above the transmission tunnel. The theory was that the cool air would pass through the tunnel to the rear. But since it is only hot air that rises, some owners of the earlier versions complained that the interiors of their cars resembled greenhouses. A simple and effective solution was to install an evaporator of the type used on the Series 2.

One item of equipment that aroused much criticism was the fan. Up to the 411 this was of large size, revolved slowly, and the fitment was mounted on rubber feet. But the type fitted to the 603 was of the small high-speed type, and its mounting was different. The earlier model blew the air firstly into rubber bellows, so that at slow speeds there was a silent whoosh of air, but on the later model the noise was constant up to 50mph. At that speed it became inaudible, but, as one owner pointed out, 'You don't need it anyway'.

The 603/S2 had front seats with manual catches so that in an emergency crash stop the back of the passenger's seat could not fall forward. This had been a possibility on some 411 cars, and, unless

Nearside view of interior, front compartment of Bristol 603S saloon. Note circular air vents on facia, the curved gear lever, small three-spoke steering wheel and major instruments in console in front of driver. Also lockable glove compartment with 'grab handle'. Leather upholstery.

Three-quarter side/front view of Type 603S2 Bristol saloon. Note wide screens and windows, narrow door pillar, narrow bumper and pressed steel wheels with new type nave plates.

strapped in, a child sitting alone in the rear compartment might be flung over the lowered seat back and up against the dashboard. To prevent this, on the original 603 there was a catch on the front seat back, operated by a solenoid. The difficulty was that if the door was left open for any length of time there was a danger of the solenoid burning out. The manual operation on the S2 was simpler, and a lot cheaper.

Cruise control and self-levelling for the rear suspension were standard equipment on both the 603 and 603/S2 models, but some owners claim to have experienced problems. This seems odd, as on the later Type 411 cars both items had worked well. The cruise control has proved extremely useful when journeys of considerable length have to be undertaken.

A close-up view of rear nearside section of a Type 603S2 Bristol saloon. Note the small ventilator just aft of the wheel arch. This feature does not appear on either the 'S' or 'E' versions of the earlier 603 model. Note too, the narrow wraparound wing and pressed steel wheel.

A 603/S2 was the subject of *Motor* Road Test No. 38/78, and it was noted that central door locking was an option, and not standard equipment; that the external mirror could not be adjusted from within the car; the heating and ventilation fan had only two speeds; and there was no vanity mirror. Considering the arduous nature of this very complete test, I feel the list is not very serious.

The items in the test that were awarded top marks included the transmission, brakes, visibility, finish, and, rather surprisingly, the ventilating and air-conditioning system, despite the tester's earlier criticism of the fan noise.

There are some who would ask why air conditioning should form part of the original equipment, if the ventilation was so very adequate. But these cars are sold world-wide, and the latter can only offer ambient temperatures, fine in a temperate climate, much less so in a country of extremes. I recall once in Australia watching the twin needles of the water/oil temperature gauges climbing past the 100 degrees centigrade mark, and waiting for the engine to seize. In fact it functioned perfectly, but the interior of the 401 was like an oven. Air conditioning for cars was unheard of then except in America.

Driving Impressions

Mention has been made of the kind action by Anthony Crook, in his role of Club patron, in lending two factory-fresh cars for the annual Spring Weekend. One was the Beaufighter already described, and the other was a 603S. It was interesting to compare them, and the entire crew clamoured to try first one and then the other.

So we had a very early breakfast on the Sunday, and headed for a stretch of straight road where we could see what they could really do. It was raining, and there was much more traffic than I had expected, but I was impressed by the 603's excellent traction, acceleration and braking.

When we had all had a turn at the wheel, we realised it was much later than we had thought, and then, as we began the journey back to the hotel, we saw a shabby red Type 400 Bristol by the roadside, with its bonnet raised. We stopped to see what we could do, and the driver, an elderly man with a strong rural accent, explained the car had belonged to his late brother, and he was taking it to a garage to try to sell it, on behalf of his widowed sister-in-law.

It had been badly neglected, and even after we had cleaned all the plugs it took a very long push before it puttered off. There was no starting handle, and the battery was too feeble even to start a warm engine. Its exhaust note was most peculiar, and someone remarked, 'It sounds more like a lawn mower than a Bristol.'

Though no one said anything, I saw a few raised eyebrows when we trooped into the meeting, very late and with grubby hands. I must confess my greatest concern had been to try to ensure we did not leave any marks on the immaculate upholstery.

The rest of the Club weekend passed swiftly, and it was already dark when we commenced the journey back to London. The rain was still falling, but the wipers were excellent, and so were the headlights. We followed the 412, since it was the faster car, and I was quite content to occupy one of the rear seats, with the heater on, the radio playing softly, and the very quiet sound of the tyres on the wet road.

I must have nodded off, for when I awoke we were almost in London, and soon afterwards the driver stopped the car, and while three of us alighted, to make our ways home by public transport, the fourth man would return the car next morning, after filling up with petrol. Later, at a committee meeting, he told me he had worked out the average consumption over the weekend, and it was little more than 19mpg.

It was to be twelve years before I had the opportunity to sample another 603, this time the later S2 model. It belonged to a BOC member, unable to attend the annual Concours himself, but who had entered his car for the class award. Though it looked truly magnificent, he had warned us that it had been lying unused in his garage for a long time.

As we moved off, the steering made the most awful sound, and I feared the entire power-steering might seize, perhaps through a leaking hose.

Left to myself, I doubt I would have continued, but the driver was of sterner stuff, and as we headed west the noise diminished, and he told me that at

SLEEPING BEAUTY

Offside view close-up, of driver's seat, etc., on a Type 603S2 Bristol saloon. Note the gear lever is 'straight', not 'curved' as on the earlier versions. Also the circular air vents on facia, the large lockable glove compartment with well-used 'grab handle', small three-spoked steering wheel, with major instruments in a console in front of it.

last he was getting some assistance with the steering, so the ZF system was functioning after all.

We were running in convoy with a lovely Type 400 drophead, and I was glad I was not driving, as the pace was very hot indeed. The 400 is the only example this side of the Atlantic, but is driven without mercy, and the driver was adept at just beating a red traffic light. Once or twice, I was sure he had shown us a clean pair of heels, but always the superior acceleration and speed of the 603 enabled us to catch up.

Sitting there in the left-hand seat, I could enjoy the quiet luxury all about me, the superb leather upholstery and walnut dashboard: the excellent all-round visibility, quiet engine and self-levelling suspension. I watched the gauges, and noted oil and water temperatures were normal, the oil pressure steady, with the needle of the rev counter swinging round its dial in a way that indicated that the car's long hibernation had not harmed it. It was very pleasant, on an early autumn morning, to head westwards in so effortless a fashion.

The silver 400 drophead led us swiftly through Bristol, and up onto the Downs, where a large Bristol Owners' Club banner indicated the entrance to the Concours. Here we wished the 400's driver good luck, as he was defending the trophy won the previous year for the 'best in show', as they would say at Cruft's. Marshals waved us over to the area reserved for the 603 class, and soon we were hard at work, with chamois leather and polishing cloth, removing any signs of our journey.

After that, as in all Concours, there was a lengthy period of suspense, standing by the car waiting for the judges. At last they came, two men who probably knew as much about the model as the designers themselves. Each section – exterior, interior, engine compartment, boot and even the underside of the chassis – was inspected, with mysterious notations on their clipboards, and then they moved on, and we could relax.

The rest of the morning passed swiftly, greeting old friends, looking at unusual models, answering questions from new members, and finally it was time for lunch. Soon there were little groups sitting at picnic tables, in a most civilised fashion, while others were content to loll on a rug and share a packet of sandwiches.

It was a perfect day, the hot sun tempered by a cooling breeze from the Avon gorge, with the graceful Clifton suspension bridge in the distance. As usual, I made a head count of the cars, and arrived at the formidable total of 137 Bristols, the highest number to date. I wonder if as many had ever been assembled before, and what a magnificent sight they were, for even cars that were not competing were mostly in immaculate condition.

Just before four o'clock, the judges emerged from

the Club caravan, where they had collated the various marking sheets onto one large matrix, from which the various class winners were selected. The public address blared out its message that the awards were about to be presented, and soon a crowd had assembled in front of the marquee inside which Club regalia and publications were on sale.

As if by magic a large trestle table was set up, the trophies arranged in class order, and the distinguished guest and the Chairman stood ready. One by one the awards were presented, after which the cars were photographed, each with its trophy proudly displayed on the bonnet. To our delight, our borrowed 603/S2 had won its class, and the silver 400 drophead had retained the top award.

The next half-hour was spent collecting our possessions and stowing them in the boot, for judges do not like such objects, be they picnic baskets, coats or polishing kits. A last round of visits to say goodbye to old friends, before getting into the car and making our way out onto the main road, noting that zealous marshals had already removed the Club banner.

We stopped at a stately home, for a quick celebratory drink: after all, for two cars to win two awards is worthy of note. Then the journey home began, with still an hour or so before headlights had to be switched on. Driver and crew spoke rarely; this was a time to wind down, to let the tensions of the day gradually relax, and to savour silently the pleasure of riding in such a splendid vehicle.

It had been one of the happiest days of my life, one I shall not forget in a hurry. I recall that at Brooklands race track the slogan was 'The Right Crowd and no Crowding', not a bad description of a Concours.

Next day the 603 was duly returned to its delighted owner, with the addition of a handsome silver cup and a plaque, the latter to be retained after the cup was returned a year hence. It seemed a just reward for loaning us the car, and I felt that perhaps there was an additional bonus, since after that long Sunday journey the power steering was now restored to its original perfect state.

To end this rather personal chapter, I would like to use this extract from an article that appeared in *Autosport*, dated 14 October 1976: 'Like a good deed in a naughty world, the Bristol is built to the standards of the upper-crust cars of the good old days. There is no nasty pressed steel to rust, for the body is panelled in aluminium, and if some upstart in a cheap car is so foolish as to collide with the big machine, the immensely strong chassis will ward off the blow with contemptuous ease . . . the 603 is a very pretty car.'

30

The Paragons

The Brigand and the Britannia

In 1982, the 603/S2 was replaced by the Brigand and the Britannia. In effect, these were the equivalents of the S and E versions of the original Type 603 models. At first sight they appeared identical, until one noticed the different type of road wheels, and the presence of a power bulge in the Brigand's bonnet, indicating that it was turbocharged.

Both models shared a common engine, the Type 360 Chrysler Vee-8, but the Britannia relied on normal aspiration. Their original prices were £49,827.09 and £46,843.32 for the Brigand and Britannia respectively.

It was typical of the idiosyncratic Bristol policy that, just when some of the large volume continental car makers were using figures to distinguish their new models, the Filton-built cars should be given names. It has been suggested that one firm even attempted to patent the entire 400 series of numbers, but I have been unable to substantiate this.

In my opinion, both names were well chosen. The turbocharged Brigand's namesake was a World War II long-range attack monoplane, though it arrived too late for participation in the Far East theatre of conflict. By contrast, the Britannia was named after a post-war civil air liner. Like the Brigand, it was of Bristol manufacture, and soon gained the nickname of the 'Whispering Giant', because of the comparative quiet of its turboprop engines.

Some people find it difficult to distinguish a 603 from either of the later models, but in fact only the former's roof, doors and screens were retained, and the radiator grille on the earlier model was rather higher. It is said that the very different tail treatment

The Bristol Britannia Civil Airliner

The Brabazon Committee Type 111 was an airliner of 100,000 'TOW', but was not at first adopted by the industry. By 1946, however, the Constellation had proved its worth, and BOAC issued a requirement for Medium Range Empire Transport. Of the eight submissions, the Type 175 of the Bristol Aeroplane Company was considered the most promising.

The proposal was to use four Centaurus radial engines, with a passenger capacity of forty-four. BOAC opted for the Bristol turbojet unit instead of the radials, and the prototype so fitted was flown by the famous test pilot Bill Pegg. In its developed form the plane now grossed 140,000 lb, and could carry ninety passengers at the then considerable speed of 360mph.

During extensive route-proving, engine icing problems were encountered, and another test pilot, Wally Gibb, conducted an extensive and exacting test schedule and the problem was solved. The Britannia entered regular BOAC service on 1 February 1957, and their lead was followed by numerous other air carriers.

Some Britannias were built at Filton, others by Shorts at their Belfast factory, including some of the twenty-two examples ordered for the Royal Air Force. The aircraft soon established an excellent reputation for its reliability and economy. It was equally popular with passengers and crew for its comfort and the silence (by contemporary standards) of its Proteus turboprop engines. It was the latter feature that gave the aircraft its nickname of the 'Whispering Giant', though if one was set beside a modern Boeing 747 it would look puny indeed.

One of the last regular UK routes on which the Britannia flew was from the Ronaldsway airport in the Isle of Man, to the London airport at Heathrow. The front compartment became very popular with some Manx-registered companies, whose directors held board meetings while the flight was in progress.

on the new cars arose from an overheard conversation.

When the Company's Chief Engineer heard a critical remark, to the effect that the 603's rear-end resembled a van, he was not pleased, and lost no time in checking the facts. To his dismay, he saw what the critic had meant, and took steps to alter it on the later models.

One of the few reports I have read on the new models was in the 16 October 1982 issue of *Motor*. In it, the Company was praised for adhering to its policy of very limited production, comparing it with the dire consequences suffered by some other makers of super-luxury cars, who were left with numbers of unsold vehicles.

The author of the report admitted that his initial reaction was one of fear, since his first task was to negotiate a series of traffic-choked streets in an exceptionally powerful and expensive car. However,

---

The Type 164 Brigand

During the latter part of the war, the Bristol Aeroplane Company produced a trio of aircraft types which represented the logical development of the Blenheim-Beaufighter theme. They were the Type 160 Buckmaster, the Type 163 Buckingham, and the Type 164 Brigand. All were based on the versatility and performance of the Beaufighter, and in 1940 design investigations had led to a layout for a twin-engined machine, based on the Bristol Hercules engine.

A major problem was to provide a good view for pilot and navigator/air bomber, only one of whom had a good view on the Beaufort and Beaufighter. This was solved on the latter aircraft, and on the Buckingham, with each of the four crew members having free access between their separate sections. The Buckingham was not used on operations, but was developed and adapted for courier employment with Transport Command.

The Brigand was designed as a long-range attack monoplane, and as a faster replacement for the Beaufighter. The design took the wings and tail unit of the Buckingham, and the Hercules engines were replaced by the more powerful Centaurus units. The design was finalised with a three-man crew and became the Type 164 Brigand. It came into service too late to see action, either in Europe or the Far East, but was intended to become the standard torpedo-fighter-dive-bomber of the Royal Air Force.

The very rapid development of the Whittle-designed jet engine rendered the Brigand obsolete, and it seems a great pity that the slow-moving bureaucracy of the civilian side of the Air Ministry took so long before this excellent war plane was ready for effective action. Here is the technical description.

> 'The Brigand is a twin-engine long range attack monoplane powered by two Centaurus Type 57 engines, giving maximum power at low altitudes. With its crew of three, it can carry a 22in torpedo, a pair of 1,000lb bombs or sixteen rocket projectiles, in addition to its armament of four 20mm cannon. As a long range escort fighter it carries either a 200 gallon drop tank, together with rocket projectiles, or an additional pair of 90 gallon drop tanks, if the latter are not required. With the single drop tank, the range is increased to 2,375 miles, or with all three tanks, to 2,770 miles, compared with its normal range of only 1,980 miles.'

MODEL: Brigand and Britannia	**Date:** 1982
Wheelbase	9ft 6in (2m 89cm)
Front Track	4ft 6.5in (1m 38cm)
Rear Track	4ft 7.5in (1m 41cm)
Overall Height	4ft 8.5in (1m 43cm)
Overall Width	5ft 9.5in (1m 76cm)
Overall Length	16ft 1in (4m 90cm)
Weight	3,850lb (1,746kg)
Tyres	Avon Tubeless radial ply 215 × 70 VR15
Engine Type	90 degree Vee-8
Number of Cylinders	8
Bore	101.6mm
Stroke	90.93mm
Capacity	5,900cc
Carburettor	Carter 4-choke
Gearbox	Torqueflite 3-speed and reverse automatic
Brakes	Footbrake: Self-adjusting servo-assisted Girling disc. Handbrake: Separate callipers operating on rear discs only
Suspension	
Front	Independent by wishbones of unequal length with coil springs, telescopic dampers and torsional anti-roll bar
Rear	Torsion bar springs with Watts linkage and telescopic dampers. Sealed balljoints.

Note: Both models continue in production. Brigand is turbocharged. Britannia is normally aspirated.

Three-quarter side/front view of a Bristol 'Britannia' saloon. Note the big rectangular headlights on either side of the grille with enamel badge in its centre. Also the narrow bumper with direction indicators inset. Normally, the Britannia was fitted with pressed steel road wheels and nave plates. On this example, as an 'extra', the wheels are of alloy without nave plates.

his fears were quite unfounded, in fact he describes that first outing as 'an absolute doddle'.

He praised the driver's seat that could be adjusted electrically in every direction but rake, and he was able to make full use of this feature to improve all-round visibility, which is so vital in heavy traffic. He was also relieved to find the Brigand was not as wide as the average luxury car, enabling him to manoeuvre it in a way that he describes as 'a significant advantage in town traffic compared with a Rolls-Royce'.

Appearance

Whether Brigand or Britannia, here is an extremely handsome motor car. The long wide bonnet curves gently forward, and down to the low-set grille, with a large rectangular headlight inset at either end. The massive bumpers, front and rear, now incorporate the direction indicators. Behind the front number plate is a wide metal apron, pierced with ventilation slots to direct cooling air to the sump. The only clue to the car's identity is an enamelled badge in the centre of the grille.

The body sides are quite plain, save for a strengthening rib that runs from just above the wheel arches from nose to tail, and the wings are protected by the wraparound bumpers. Slightly aft of the rear wheel arch is a small ventilator, shaped rather like a parallelogram. The front and rear screens are of generous proportions, with very slender pillars, and with its wide side and door windows the car is light and airy.

Following the 603's example, the boot sill is set conveniently low, making it a simple task to load or unload even heavy articles.

The roofline is particularly pleasing, for it sweeps from the windscreen past the rear window, and across the wide flat boot lid to the tail section. This is quite plain, save for the number plate and a pair of rectangular panels containing the rear lights. There is a fair amount of overhang front and rear, and the boot is more capacious than it may appear at a casual glance.

The road wheels on the Brigand are of alloy, specially made by Wolfrace in a spoked pattern that suits the lines of the car perfectly. On the Britannia, the road wheels are of pressed steel, and while they are no doubt quite serviceable I much prefer the alloys.

Although the Avon safety wheel is no longer in production, the special Avon safety band is fitted to ensure, in the event of a tyre burst, that the cover will not become detached. The tyres on the Brigand

Side view of a Bristol 'Britannia' saloon. Note the ventilator panel just aft of the rear arch, also the tiny indicator repeater below the windscreen. The vertical rear light clusters can just be seen, and a very wide sloping rear screen. The alloy wheels are an 'extra', though standard on the 'Brigand'. But the 'Britannia' would normally have pressed steel wheels with nave plates.

This wheel is a light alloy version of the Avon safety wheel. The special feature was the way, in the event of a tyre burst, the cover would not leave the rim.

A late type pressed steel wheel and nave plate on a Type 411(5) Bristol saloon.

BRISTOL BRIGAND – Turbocharged Saloon

BRISTOL BEAUFORT – Turbocharged Drophead Coupe

BRISTOL BEAUFIGHTER – Turbocharged Convertible.

BRISTOL BRITANNIA – Saloon

Top right: *Three-quarter side/front view of Bristol Beaufort with hood stowed under tonneau cover. Note absence of roll-over bar. It is left-hand drive. Note the two pairs of small rectangular headlights, narrow grille and enamel badge.* Top Left: *Three-quarter front/side view of a Bristol 'Brigand' saloon. It is just possible to discern the 'power bulge' on the bonnet top, indicating the presence of a Rotomaster turbocharger.* Bottom left: *Three-quarter side/front view of Bristol Beaufighter with Clifton Suspension Bridge in background. Note the two pairs of small rectangular headlights, narrow grille and enamel badge.* Bottom right: *Three-quarter side/front view of a Bristol 'Britannia' saloon. Its bonnet top is flat, indicating its engine is normally aspirated. It is otherwise the same Chrysler Vee-8 Type 360 unit.*

are of the Avon Turbospeed ACR 18 type, their size is 215/70VR15. On the Britannia, the wheels have narrower rims, but are fitted with the same type of tyre, and also have the safety band.

The panels set into the front wing, behind which the spare wheel and electrical elements are stowed, are much larger than on some earlier models, and are virtually undetectable, even when the car is finished in a light colour. The panels are opened with a carriage key, which is normally retained in its own little holster, inside the car.

The Interior

With their graceful lines and large glazed area, both the Brigand and Britannia induce a feeling of relaxed ease. Though the width is only 5ft 9½in, as on the 412 and 603, the designers have managed to give an impression that one is sitting in a much larger vehicle. Upholstery is, of course, in top-quality Connolly leather, and the front seats are marvels of comfort and controllability. One's anatomy would have to be very odd if, using what a journalist described as 'a small joystick', one could not adjust the seat to give both comfort and control. It is even possible to raise or lower either end of the seat separately.

On a car that is well suited for long-distance touring, it is vital that there should be plenty of accommodation for all the impedimenta the occupants take with them, or may collect on the way. There is a large lockable glove compartment on the left side of the facia, pockets in the doors and on the backs of the front seats, and also some most ingenious fitments in the rear compartment that can also double as picnic trays. There is a wide parcel-shelf too, with a raised lip to prevent articles being displaced if a corner is taken a little too fast. There are armrests, one of which conceals a very useful hidey-hole beneath its lid. Detachable head-rests are fitted to all four seats.

As one would expect, the instrumentation is generous, the main instruments in a console in front of the driver, with switches and ancillaries arranged across the facia, and all show their functions clearly. Windows are operated electrically, there is central door locking, a separate and comprehensive heating and ventilating system, and the door mirrors are electrically operated and heated. A cruise control is also standard, operated by a master switch and a stalk on the steering column. At the required speed, the latter is pulled towards the driver, and that pace is then maintained, regardless of road conditions. However, if the brakes have to be applied, then the cruise control is over-ridden, and will only recommence its function when the accelerator is pressed or if the stalk on the steering column is again operated. Some of these cars are owned by businessmen who cover impressive annual mileages and several have told me how much they appreciate a control that renders unnecessary the constant adjustments of ordinary motorway travel.

Engine and Transmission

Both the Brigand and Britannia use similar engines, the Chrysler Type 360, with a swept volume of 5,898cc. The turbocharger selected by Bristol was neither of the two most generally used alternatives: the Garrett AiResearch or the KKK, but was the Rotomaster Rotocharger. As described earlier, this is interposed between the inlet manifold and the engine, with a wastegate so arranged that at small throttle openings the fuel-air mixture enters the engine direct, yet as the throttle is opened wider, the pressure increases progressively, allowing the two priority valves in the wastegate to close, until virtually the entire mixture passes through the turbocharger's compressor, prior to entry into the engine.

In practice the system appears to suit the Chrysler Vee-8 design extremely well, and fuel consumption can be surprisingly modest. At averages of less than 70mph, for example, owners have claimed figures rather above 16mpg; a few, indeed, mention 20mpg; but naturally, if the full performance is used much of the time, then the amount of fuel consumed will increase, and may be in the region of 12mpg.

The standard Torqueflite transmission is used on both models, but on the Brigand, where the power increase can be up to 30 per cent greater than on the unturbocharged Britannia, modifications are made accordingly. In effect these consist of using the torque converter and the internal clutches fitted as standard to the Type 440 Chrysler engine, with its huge capacity of 7,200cc. A stronger prop-shaft is used with universal joints of larger than standard type.

The suspension on both the Brigand and Britannia relies on the well tried Bristol system of unequal length wishbones with coil springs and torsional roll-bar at the front, and a live axle with torsion bars as the springing medium at the rear, plus Watt linkage stabilisation. Spax adjustable dampers are fitted fore and aft. Ball joints are sealed, and there are bonded rubber sleeves in mounting bushes for noise insulation.

Steering is by Marles cam and roller, power-assisted by the ZF system as modified by Bristol. The steering wheel is three-spoked, with a stitched leather rim, and a column which in the event of a head-on crash will collapse, avoiding the risk of chest injury to the driver.

Braking employs the Girling dual-circuit system, with Lockheed servo assistance and discs front and rear. In case of a failure, there is a warning light on the facia. A similar signal is given should the hand brake inadvertently be left in the 'on' position. There is a mechanical parking lock too, operated via the gear lever. The disc brakes are self-adjusting and extremely powerful, though firm pressure on the pedal is required to bring the car to a complete halt from a high speed.

The heating/ventilation system allows fresh air to enter the interior of the car with the windows closed, at varying volume and temperature. There are openings just ahead of the windscreen, through which the fresh air first enters, and then passes either through the heater to footwells, or it may act as demister/defroster via the slots set at the base of the windscreen. There are ventilators of the eyeball type, set into either end and in the centre of the dashboard, and others in the side panels of the footwells.

Included in the car's specification is an independent system of air-conditioning. At first sight this may not appear necessary in a temperate region, but such a system can be a boon in a really hot climate. A demisting/defrosting element is bonded into the rear window.

Lighting and Fuel Systems

The lighting on both the Brigand and Britannia is comprehensive. The big rectangular headlamps are of the halogen type, and are supplemented by parking lights, trafficators, stop lights, rear number plate lamps, and twin (automatic) reversing lights. For extra safety, there are also hazard lights, and twin rearguard fog lamps, plus reflectors. The interior lights are equally comprehensive.

Two fine Bristols, photographed at the Bristol Owners' Club annual 'meet' at the Albert Memorial, September 1988. On the left is a Beaufighter with turbocharger, on the right a normally aspirated Britannia, a convertible and a saloon respectively. The Beaufighter has two pairs of small rectangular headlights, the Britannia two much larger lights, also rectangular. On the Beaufighter the traffic indicators are set below the narrow bumper, on the Britannia they are incorporated at either end.

Front view of a Bristol 'Britannia' with the Albert Memorial as background. Note the very narrow bumper, with direction indicators at either end, the rectangular headlights and wide grille with an enamel badge in the centre.

Between the fuel tank and the passenger compartment is a strong steel bulkhead. The capacity of the tank is quoted as being eighteen gallons (82 litres). I would imagine that the owner of a Brigand, if of the hard-driving type, might specify the auxiliary ten-gallon tank too, for very long journeys.

A typically Bristol detail is the way in which both front wings have slightly raised edges at the top. These assist a driver of normal size to place his car accurately, and are useful in dense and heavy traffic, or when manoeuvering into a narrow parking place or garage.

Performance

Naturally, the Brigand with its turbocharger is rather faster than the normally aspirated Britannia; their maximum speeds being given as 150mph and 140mph respectively. In Britain such speeds may be impressive in theory, but can hardly be tested, at least not on a public highway. On the other hand, the smooth acceleration of the Brigand is there to be enjoyed. While not quite as exciting, the average speeds that can be achieved with a Britannia are surprisingly high, especially at night.

Front view of a Bristol 'Britannia' saloon. Note enamel badge in centre of grille, with rectangular headlights either side. Also the very narrow bumper of the wraparound type with direction indicators inset.

On a long cross-country journey, those huge headlights can cleave a way through the darkness, making even the bully boys with their rally-style auxiliary illumination 'dowse their glims', to use an old nautical phrase. I have noticed that such people pay scant regard to cars with more modest lighting, and I feel that some nocturnal accidents are caused by drivers being blinded by the oncoming vehicles. Under such circumstances the old advice, 'not to look at the lights, but at the kerb instead', is hardly practicable.

In the issue dated 23 December 1989 of the *Daily Telegraph* there was an article entitled 'Lights in our Darkness', which gave a brief description of two new lighting systems that might be adapted for use on motor vehicles. The first of these was the High Intensity Discharge (HID) tube, which is much cooler than the orthodox incandescent bulb. It can be manufactured to a smaller size, and there is a suggestion that a unit only one inch in height could provide illumination equal to that of a modern headlamp. Alternatively, it might be possible to have a form of strip light set across the full width of the car.

It seems likely that designers at General Motors are already interested, and apart from size, another claimed advantage is immediate full-strength power, compared with the warm-up period common to the street lights that use the same basic principle. It is also stated that such a system might function for an indefinite period without renewal. This would be a great advantage, when one considers the high replacement cost of the standard sealed beam units, or the planned obsolescence of the ordinary bulb.

The second system described in the above article, which also stated that it is receiving attention by designers at Ford, uses minute strands of fibre optics material. This too might be fabricated into a full-width headlamp, and proponents are confident that a height of 1cm would provide sufficient illumination. Such a narrow strip could be merged into the front of a car in so unobtrusive a fashion as to be virtually invisible except at night.

If either system proves a success, no doubt Bristol Cars will subject it to their usual very thorough testing, probably with some modifications, as has often been the case. Typical examples are the improvements and modifications made to the ZF power steering, and to the Armstrong self-levelling rear suspension systems.

Reports on either the Brigand or the Britannia are rare, but it is felt that the following quotation concerning the former is worthy of inclusion. It appeared in the August 1983 issue of *Thoroughbred and Classic Cars*:

> 'When you wish to use the other side of the car's performance spectrum, it is difficult to equate the rate at which the speedometer needle climbs and the other traffic falls away, like so many redundant rocket stages, with the quite imperturbable manner of its going. The gears slur one to the other virtually unnoticed, there is no turbo-lag, no kick in the back, just a smooth never-ending surge of power right up to the maximum speed.'

The Brigand and the Britannia saloons, together with the multi-purpose Beaufighter convertible, constitute the current Bristol range. Production seems likely to continue while there is sufficient demand, but what form a successor model might take is unknown.

31
The Club

Quite frequently, when helping to staff the stand at a Classic Car Show, someone will come up and say: 'What a good idea to have a club just for owners of Bristol cars, but why ever haven't you done it sooner?' In fact the Bristol Owners' Club was founded as long ago as 1964, so if people still have not heard of its existence, perhaps some of the Company's anonymity has rubbed off on us too. Here in brief is the Club's history to date.

On the evening of 6 November 1964, a small group of strangers met in the foyer of the Eccleston Hotel, near London's Victoria railway station, their only common factor being ownership of a Bristol car. We stood around, most of us with a drink in our hands, until we were taken to a room where a rather larger group were already seated. It transpired that they were members of the BMW Car Club, and that the intention was for the new body to have a very close connection with the latter.

A fair amount of argument and counter-argument ensued before we were satisfied that, though we might for a time work in tandem, the newly formed Bristol Owners' Club would be quite independent. In return for this concession, it was made clear to us that there would be no point in seeking financial help from the BMW Car Club: we had to stand on our own feet from the start.

What I did not realise until much later was the enormous advantage we enjoyed from having an experienced group of officials who had held, in most cases, similar posts in the other club. They included the first Chairman, Guy Machell; the Hon. Secretary, Ralph Hewitt; the Hon. Treasurer, Cecil Miller; and the Hon. Auditor, Harry Harrington. All were of the highest calibre, and it was mainly due to them that the new club was given such an excellent and business-like beginning.

Membership was slow to grow, however, and it

The Club's first Concours, held at Moore Place Hotel, Esher, 1966.

THE CLUB

The entire membership of the Irish Centre of Bristol Owners' Club, 1969.

seemed an age before the committee learned that we had passed our first century. Yet if our numbers were few, a full programme of events was soon organised, with speed events in the summer, and talks and film shows in the winter. We were unfortunate with our weather though, and I can remember the first Concours, in the car park of an Esher hotel, with Leonard Setright and myself acting as judges, while the rain dripped down our collars and up our sleeves.

Our second hundred members took a much shorter time to acquire, and amongst them was Dudley Rylett, who took over the post of Hon. Competitions Secretary. He was soon driver/manager of a team of Bristols that competed in quite major events, including the Prescott hill-climb, and managed, on occasions, to prove that a 2-litre Bristol saloon could still put up times equal to those of much more modern open two-seater sports cars.

From the early sprint meetings at Blackbush Airport, we moved to Greenham Common. With its enormous runways and hospitable American airmen, it was ideal, and timed runs were made that indicated just how good those Bristol engines were.

We were happy to welcome owners of other makes using 'our' engines, and a whole covey of AC Aces turned up at one meeting. With their small size and powerful 100D2 engines, they quite dominated the event, and I recall a Top Sergeant who took a lot of convincing that these lovely little two-seaters

Some of the cars competing in an early Concours held at Banbury.

288

The owner of the immaculate Type 400 Bristol, receiving his award from Lord King's Norton, at the Club's annual Concours, held at Ragley Hall, September 1981.

were 100 per cent British, and were not as he at first insisted, 'American Cobras all the way from California, US of A'. Even when I rolled back the carpet, and showed him the plaque reading 'AC Cars Limited, Thames Ditton, England' he was not really satisfied, and muttered that 'maybe that's where the body was made'.

The annual Concours seemed to change its venue almost every year, and including Esher, Banbury, Blenheim Palace, Weston Park, Warwick Castle, Trentham Gardens, Sudeley Castle and Ragley Hall. I recall a group of American tourists who took the wrong turning in a guided tour of Blenheim Palace, and thought the Concours was an auction. Cheque books were produced, and handsome offers made for 'these cute little English autos' before their harassed guide could shepherd them away.

At Ragley Hall the Marquess of Hertford became a firm friend of the Club and even presented the awards, and I was sorry when the venue was changed yet again. The argument was that it was unfair to expect the same members to have to travel so far, and that by moving it around all would have at least one occasion when the Concours would be held reasonably near their homes.

It seemed the Club was enjoying a Golden Age,

Bristols in France, one of the first official visits by the Club, May 1977.

with active competition in a wide variety of events. There were pageants at Penshurst Place, Booker and Sherbourne Castle; sprints at Topcliffe, Curborough, Duxford, Blackbush and Goodwood; hill climbs at Prescott and Gurston Down. There was even a series of affiliation exercises, with a group of members travelling over a pre-determined route so that a lone member who never saw another Bristol from one Concours to the next, might come to a convenient pub or just a crossroads, and spend a few minutes chatting with fellow enthusiasts.

It could not last, of course, and when things began to alter they did so with a vengeance. In a short time, the deaths occurred of the Treasurer, General Secretary and Competitions Secretary, and without them it seemed the Club might just disintegrate. No one is indispensable, and gradually things improved, a new committee took shape, posts were reallocated, and membership continued to grow.

At the end of 1989 the paid-up membership was just over the 800 mark, and enthusiasm for the Bristol car seems to grow month by month. For those unable to attend the annual Concours, there is now a meet by the Albert Memorial each year. It is quite unofficial – just an opportunity for members to come together, admire each other's cars and, as we say, 'talk Bristol fashion'. At the meet held in September 1989, there were fifty-seven cars of many models and ages, but the star of the show was the beautifully restored Type 450 driven by the Club's Patron, Anthony Crook. It is the only one in existence, and to drive it through London's West End on a Sunday afternoon is not a task I would relish, but there it was in all its glory, and I doubt there are many one-make clubs that are lucky enough to have as their supportive patron, the man who is also the owner of the Company.

An event that has always been popular is the Spring Weekend, originally organised by the Midland Centre, but now recognised as a full Club event. It takes the form of a dinner on the Saturday night, when there is a guest speaker who usually has much experience of the Bristol car. Over the years we have had the pleasure of listening to such experts as Jack Channer on suspension, Dennis Sevier on development, Percy Kemish on the 450 engine, Leonard Setright on 'Future Possibilities', Peter Wilson on his racing experiences at Reims and Le Mans, and Eric Storey on the service side of the Company's history. It is a great privilege to listen to such well qualified people, and is much appreciated.

On the Sunday morning there is usually some form

Of recent years, motoring journals have organised Classic Car Shows at various venues, though these have latterly been confined to London and Birmingham. These events have been supported by the Bristol Owners' Club, and the responsibility devolves on the nearest centre, to plan, organise and staff the Club stand.

It is by no means easy to arrange all the logistics of such an operation, so that the stand is dressed on time, with the various cars that members have loaned carefully placed to show off their immaculate lines to best advantage. The Club holds the various essentials centrally, such as the VDU, tables, chairs, the Club banner etc. These are drawn by the Centre, and returned afterwards.

Mr Anthony Crook, the Club Patron (and Chairman and Managing Director of Bristol Cars Ltd), inspecting the photographs on the Club stand at the Classic Car Show, held at the Wembley Exhibition Centre, December 1989.

of competitive event, driving tests are very popular, and in the afternoon there is the Annual General Meeting. It is well attended and, besides the official business, it is an opportunity to meet old friends, and also to purchase whatever items of Club regalia take one's fancy. From key fobs to sweat shirts, from ties to silk scarves – all in the Club colours and bearing the Bristol roundel.

In 1988 and 1989, there has also been a dinner at the Royal Automobile Club in Pall Mall. It is a most enjoyable winter event, and I hope it too may become an integral part of the Club calendar. Unlike some clubs, the BOC relies on its centres to organise their own events, apart from the few main ones such as the Concours, the Spring Meeting and the RAC Dinner.

The centres vary considerably in size of membership and enthusiasm. Thus, while some organise a full calendar of local events, sometimes with other clubs, there are others which provide little more than the occasional 'noggin and natter'.

Cutting the cake to celebrate the Club's 21st birthday: at Alveston Manor Hotel, 13 April 1986.

Bristols waiting for their owners during the Annual General Meeting, held at the Patrick Motor Museum, King's Norton, Sunday 16 April 1989.

Over the years there have been BOC stands at Classic Car Shows at Birmingham, Brighton, Bristol, London, Manchester and Woburn Abbey. A number of awards have been gained, including two first places, two seconds and four thirds in various categories based on membership.

Such shows have proved excellent recruiting grounds – lapsed members rejoin, other Bristol owners seek membership, and an increasing number seek to join in the hope of securing a good example at a reasonable price. The staff are usually kept very busy answering queries, selling books and regalia, and greeting a hard core of members from overseas who come year after year. We usually get a few 'wide boys' too, who seek information on rare models that they claim to have discovered, while keeping the locations very much to themselves.

The majority of members live within the United

An overall view of the Club stand at the Classic Car Show held at the Metropole Hotel, Brighton, December 1986, when four Bristols were exhibited.

THE CLUB

One of the Bristol cars exhibited on the Club stand at the Brighton Show, December 1986. (The car is a 1946 Type 400 convertible, and only two examples were made. This is chassis number 3.)

A long line of Bristols competing at a Concours d'Elegance at Chantilly, France, May 1977.

After the awards have been presented: the row of Bristols that have won their respective classes at the Club's annual Concours, held at Clifton Downs, Bristol, 3 September, 1989.

Kingdom, but the current list shows the Club now has membership world-wide. There are loners in Oman and Taiwan, and sizeable numbers in Belgium, France, Scandinavia and the United States. In addition, the Club has contacts with its namesake in Australia, and the very active Arnolt Bristol Registry in America.

From time to time, members of these other clubs get in touch while on a visit, and I recall one such occasion when a retired officer in the Australian Navy presented the Club with an ingenious gadget he had made, that greatly facilitated the often tricky task of synchronising the triple Solex carburettors on the 2 and 2.2-litre Bristol engines.

The main channel of communication is the Bulletin, normally issued as a quarterly, with supplementary news letters, as required. The main purpose of the latter is to advise members of any special happening, and it also indicates cars and spare parts that may be required by some members, and are available from others. Over the past two years, I have to say that the 'wants' have far outnumbered the 'for sales'. I mention this because so often when speaking to people on the Club stand at a Classic Car Show I gain the impression that they feel that to become a member is virtually a guarantee that in a very short time they will have acquired a good Bristol at a reasonable price. This was often true until the

Front view of a late Type 403 Bristol saloon at Tumut, New South Wales, Australia. A winner in classic car shows.

investment market began telling people how ridiculously underpriced the cars were, and that they would appreciate in value.

Most members deplore this attitude, for a Bristol is a car to be enjoyed, not something to be put away in the hope its value may increase. What is rarely mentioned is the fact that no Bristol thrives on inactivity. Even if a car is not taxed during the winter months, a wise owner will start the engine every week, and move the car at least every month, even if it is little more than to manoeuvre it out of its garage and down to the street and back. This should ensure that the clutch does not seize, or the brake cylinders become inoperable.

The Club has one member of the committee charged with responsibility as regards spare parts. He works in close co-operation with the Bristol Spares Depot at Brentford, and is a mine of information on his specialised subject. Spares are not cheap, but they are available.

A line-up of Bristols during a Club 'foray' to France.

A line up of Bristols of many types at a 'meet' organised by the Gundagai Antique Motor Club, at Talbingo, Australia, 23 April, 1989.

A word of advice to those optimists who advertise for a 'Bristol: any condition, for complete restoration'. If you are wealthy or are clever at such jobs as welding, trimming and painting, you may succeed. But all too frequently we hear of cases when a tyro buys what is a real 'basket case', and then, after spending a lot of money, has to admit defeat. Far better, in my opinion, to pay a higher price for a car in going order.

For those seeking more information about the Bristol Owners' Club, I would suggest that as a first step they contact the Hon. Membership Secretary. He is John Emery, and his address is

'Vesutor',
Marringdean Road,
Billingshurst,
West Sussex RH14 9EH.

32
The Others
Bristol 2-litre Engines

As recounted earlier, the Bristol Aeroplane Company made engines for AFN Limited, for use in the latter's post-war Frazer Nash sports cars. The engine was known as the 'FNS', the initials indicating it was built to 'Frazer Nash Specification'. The various models, especially the Le Mans Replica, proved tremendously successful; indeed I recall some of the major road races in the late forties to mid-fifties period, when they positively dominated the event. This was all the more remarkable, since the total post-war production at AFN Limited hardly exceeded 100 cars.

Another make that used the Bristol engine was the AC, with a small but very well equipped factory at Thames Ditton, Surrey. Three models were fitted with Filton-made units – the open two-seater 'Ace', its closed coupe counterpart known as the 'Aceca', and the very handsome 'Greyhound' saloon. Though a potential customer had a choice of either the 100B or the 100D2 engine, I have yet to see an Ace or Aceca with anything except the latter. In the case of the Greyhound, there was also a choice of engine – either the 110 or the 110S. Both were of 2.2-litre capacity, but the S model was very highly tuned, and it would seem most customers opted for the standard model. For a long time I was unable to ascertain the number of Bristol engines involved. AC Cars Limited had changed hands, the site at Thames Ditton was

This is a Targa Florio model Frazer Nash, fitted with a Bristol FNS type engine. It was originally delivered in April 1953, with chassis no. 421/200/185 and engine no. BS1/127. Note air duct in bonnet top, headlights inset into front wings, also fog/spot lights, but no bumper. Road wheels are ordinary bolt-on perforated discs.

Three-quarter front/side view of a Targa Florio Frazer Nash. It was delivered in April 1953, chassis no. 421/200/189, engine Bristol BS1/131. Note lack of bumpers, the knock-on wire wheels, bonnet top air duct, and head and auxiliary lights faired into wings and apron.

A Frazer Nash 'Le Mans' Coupe. It is a late model delivered in October 1954. Its engine is Bristol no. 100B/3564, and chassis no. 421/200/202. Note wire wheels, filler cap on tail, air duct in bonnet, ventilator in side, and headlights inset into front wings.

Nearside view of Mille Miglia type Frazer Nash. The open bonnet reveals the FNS engine made especially for AFN Limited by the Bristol Aeroplane Company. Note the peg-type knock-on road wheels, headlight and direction indicator inset into front wing, also the sloping windscreen and big filler cap behind passenger's seat.

A rare Le Mans Coupe model Frazer Nash, fitted with 2-litre Bristol engine. Note wire wheels but no bumpers.

Side/front view of Mille Miglia model Frazer Nash open sports/racer. Note air duct in bonnet top, and the 'pancake' air filters on the FNS type Bristol engine. The car was raced extensively by the late Dickie Stoop and is now the property of Sir Clive Edwards, Bt.

Rear view of a Mille Miglia model Frazer Nash, fitted with a Bristol FNS type engine. Note the big filler cap on left of tail, smooth flanks and tail without bumper. The car, after much racing by the late Dickie Stoop, is now owned by Sir Clive Edwards, Bt, in the Isle of Man: hence the NMN registration.

Three-quarter side/front view of an AC Bristol 'Ace' open two-seater sports model. Note the 'egg box' grille with AC badge. On the bonnet there is another AC badge with the small 'wreath' underneath incorporating the name 'Bristol', to indicate the power unit was a 100D2 Bristol engine. Note absence of bumper, just the overriders to serve as a buffer in a very minor 'shunt'.

Rear view of an AC Bristol 'Ace' open two-seater. Note how hood is stowed out of sight in the boot. On latter note AC badge with the additional 'wreath' with the Bristol name. The petrol filler cap is inset into top of nearside rear wing. The rear lamp treatment is very simple, with over riders but no rear bumper.

Three-quarter rear view of an AC Bristol 'Ace' open two-seater sports model. Note how low-set is the boot lid catch, with a circular AC badge with the semi-circular 'wreath' below bearing the name of 'Bristol'. The steering wheel is of the three spring spoke type, with major instruments ahead. Note large 'cupboard' on facia, with lock and a 'grab handle' on scuttle. The windscreen is wide, the doors flush-fitting, and with hood stowed in tail, it is a pretty yet practical car.

sold for development, and I was very fortunate when I contacted an official of the AC Owners' Club, at a Birmingham Classic Car Show. He promised to investigate, and let me have the results. Some time later he informed me that a total of 715 AC cars had been fitted with a Bristol engine, the majority, 465, being used on the 'Ace'; 170 on the 'Aceca', and 80 on the 'Greyhound'. I was interested to learn that some examples of the latter were fitted with the 100D unit.

Though the Bristol engine was used by a number of other makes, they were, in the main, manufacturers of hyper sports or out-and-out racing cars, in very small numbers. Probably Cooper Cars Limited were the largest, with two series of single-seaters, plus a few sports models, some of which had been converted from the racers. The Cooper-Bristol combined the reliability of the Filton engine with excellent road holding and light weight, and was very successful. The late Mike Hawthorn is often credited as having put the new model on the map by his victories at the Goodwood Easter Meeting in 1952, but I feel much of the credit belongs to Anthony Crook, who campaigned two examples in a much wider range of events, and for a much longer period –

Side view of Cooper Bristol open sports/racer. Originally a single seater, it is now fitted with late-type BS4 engine. Note the typical Cooper cast alloy road wheels, and twin-pipe exhaust system.

Hawthorne only drove a Cooper-Bristol in one season before joining Ferrari in 1953. Since reliable records now appear non-existent, I have used as my data base the autobiography of John Cooper, entitled *Grand Prix Carpet-Bagger*. By taking the figures he quotes for the first and second series racers, plus the handful of sports cars, I reach a total of twenty-five, but would assume that some owners might have had more than a single engine. I recall Hawthorn complaining because he was forced to use the same unit in race after race, and was unable to secure even additional road wheels. One cannot be certain just how many Bristol engines were used during the period 1952–1953, when the Cooper-Bristol was so successful.

At the Classic Car Show held at the Wembley Exhibition Centre 9–10 December 1989, one of the two cars exhibited on the Bristol Owners' Club stand was the second of the two Cooper-Bristols that were raced so successfully by the Club's patron. It looked very sleek with its immaculate magenta paintwork, and six-pipe silver exhaust system. I was surprised when Anthony Crook told me that it had begun life as an Alta-Cooper, using one of three engines loaned by Geoffrey Taylor, who made those fast but none-too-reliable four-cylinder engines in his tiny factory at Tolworth, Surrey.

During a race at Snetterton, dicing with Stirling Moss in a sister Alta-Cooper, Anthony Crook suffered the triple misfortune of a disintegrating gear box. I say triple, as in addition to the gearbox, the brake and clutch pedals were also put out of action. Down the Snetterton Straight he roared, with virtually no hope of taking the acute bend at the end. So he continued, until the track ended, and a field began. Still without any effective means of retardation, the car just carried on, mowing down a fine crop of cabbages standing in its path. Mr Crook is adept at telling a story against himself and ended by describing the reactions of his daughter Carole, then at boarding school, when she was shown a newspaper, complete with a photograph of her father, and the caption 'Racing Driver knocked out by a cabbage'! Fitted with a Bristol engine, the car was raced both as a single-seater and as a sports car, and was also supercharged successfully.

If John Cooper and his father Charles were the first small car makers to approach the Bristol Aeroplane Company for a racing engine, the late Leslie Johnson was not far behind. He had purchased the assets of the firm that made the very successful pre-war ERA racers, and had ambitious plans for its revival. In the meantime, he obtained six engines from Bristols, though he had only a single body/chassis. The latter was so wide as almost to be a two-seater, and was aerodynamically inferior to the higher, but much narrower Cooper. Probably the main cause for the G Type ERA's poor showing was because Johnson converted his engines to dry sump lubrication. This was so that he might bring the bonnet line rather lower, but it seems significant that, while the Cooper was a model of reliability, the G type was plagued by mechanical problems. Stirling Moss was the works driver, and complained bitterly, the more so since with just the one chassis/body development proceeded all too slowly, with little to show at the end but failure and frustration.

A much happier story can be told of the Lister Cooper, made at Cambridge by an old-established iron-working firm. The initiative was taken by Brian Lister who persuaded his fellow directors to let him make a small series of sports-racers, powered by the Bristol engine. Despite his lack of previous experience, the design by Lister was sound, and the workmanship so good that several examples are now being raced successfully in the many vintage class events that are so popular. I have been unable to obtain a reliable figure for the total number of engines involved, and will not hazard a guess. Later, the larger capacity Jaguar engine was used, and these models proved equally reliable and successful.

The Kieft was an unusual make for, though manufactured at Wolverhampton, Cyril Kieft always claimed that, since he was a Welshman, the cars he made must be regarded as Welsh too. Earlier the single-cylinder Formula 3 Kieft had been virtually the only serious rival to the Cooper, but his Bristol-engined cars were less successful. To emphasise that the Kieft was different, there was also a three-seater sports model.

When a Lotus Bristol was announced great things were expected, and the car, with its delicate lines and distinctive wing treatment, certainly looked the part. Unfortunately, Colin Chapman was deeply involved in the development and launch of his first road model that used glass fibre for the body work. Known as the Elite, the bodies were made by a Coventry-based firm, Bristol Plastics Limited, which was part of the industrial conglomerate of which the Bristol Aeroplane Company was the main component.

The Mark X Lotus racer was never developed fully, but did gain a fair measure of success, especially with the cars driven by Mike Anthony and P H G Cottrell. The latter was a Welshman, and drove a bright yellow Mark X with a red Welsh dragon prominently displayed.

Earlier in this chapter, reference was made to the very successful AC Ace – the basic design was by John Tojeiro, who specialised in building sports-racers, and sold the design to the Hurlock brothers who then owned AC Cars Limited. Tojeiro used Bristol engines in some of his other cars, and could be relied upon to produce a practical car with a simple straightforward chassis, even if it was sometimes clothed in bodywork of rather exotic appearance.

That really ends what might be described as the serious other makes that used the Bristol engine. However, there was also a handful of cars, built by enthusiasts, mostly as one-offs. A typical example was the quite handsome IRA, which its owner/driver, Joe Kelly, explained was short for 'Irish Racing Automobiles'. Another was the Warrior Bristol, that was basically a rebodied second-series Cooper Bristol, its name being due to the fact that the owner's family firm was called the Warrior Tap and Die Company. The car has long been in private hands in Australia, which supports the view that it scored some success in a Grand Prix held in the Portuguese colony of Macao.

In addition to the series 1 and 2 Coopers and the sports cars, there were two vehicles that do not fit into any category other than special. The first was the so-called Bobtail that was made by the talented driver, Sir Jack Brabham in 1955. It was built in the little Cooper factory at Surbiton in Surrey, where he had managed to obtain just enough space for this purpose. The other car was known as the

T44 – Cooper-BG-Bristol. In his autobiography, John Cooper states the car was built and raced by Bob Gerard in 1957. This was four years after the Cooper Bristol sports model had ceased production.

Though never recognised by the company, there was one car that competed as a 'Bristol Special'. It was designed and built by Brian Wingfield, using a chassis of his own design, and front and rear suspensions said to be of Lister derivation. The engine was a brand new 100D2 Bristol 2-litre, with a matching Bristol gearbox.

Though entered for most events by Wingfield, the car was usually driven by the late Jill Hutchinson. Her competitive career was of little more than two years duration, but she proved herself a talented driver, and the car to be fast and reliable. After her death, the car was sold, passing through many hands, including those of Peter Williams. He applied to have the car recognised, so that he might compete in it, presumably in vintage-type events. Though he did not succeed, his very detailed application has provided the data for the specification.

MODEL:	Wingfield Special	Date:	1958
Weight	1,344lb (609kg)		
Tyres	Dunlop 5.00 x 15 (front); 5.50 × 15 (rear)		
Bore	66mm		
Stroke	96mm		
Capacity	1,971cc		
Carburettors	3 Solex B32 PB1		
Suspension			
Front	Wishbone		
Rear	De Dion telescopic		

Three-quarter side/front view of the Wingfield Special. It was fitted with a new 100D2 Bristol engine. Note the twin-pipe exhaust system, knock-on road wheels with wide tyres, 'air box' in bonnet top, no doors or bumpers, lightweight wings and headlights. The car was raced successfully, but the original engine was missing when the latest owner acquired it. Even with a very tired engine, it can still give a most exhilarating performance on the road.

Front view of the Wingfield Special, a 'one-off' built by Brian Wingfield in 1958. It is of extremely low build, emphasised by the wide tyres on knock-on perforated disc wheels. Note the 'air box' inset into bonnet top. The nose section and grille are not original, but came from a Type 405 Bristol saloon. The car was eligible to compete in both racing and sports car classes, hence the very light wings and aero-screens, also the small headlights.

The view forward of the cockpit and bonnet of the 2-litre Wingfield Special. Note the plain facia with rev counter and speedometer on left. Also the small three-spring spoked steering wheel, remote gear lever and lack of doors. It is a spartan vehicle without a hood, and with only the two aero-screens for protection. The car was eligible to compete in both racing and sports classes, and was successful in 1961–62, usually with the late Miss Jill Hutchinson at the wheel. After her death the car was sold, and after many changes in ownership it now belongs to that great Bristol enthusiast and collector, Mr Brian May.

I am glad to say the little car is now owned by Brian May, a long-term member of the Bristol Owners' Club, and a collector of unusual Filton-engined models. Short and stubby, very low slung and with a raucous exhaust note, it is brought to most Club events, and arouses considerable interest. The original engine and gearbox were missing, but the 'cooking' unit that May has installed gives it an exhilarating performance. He still hopes one day to fit an engine more in keeping with the little car's potentialities. It is a trifle ironic that, though in its racing days, it was entered as a 'Bristol Special', it is now more often referred to as the 'Wingfield Special'. Whatever it may be called, it remains a splendid example of what can be achieved on a small scale by a talented engineer.

33
A Very Private Company

The Car Division was first created in 1946 as an integral part of the Bristol Aeroplane Company, then for the period 1956–1960 was a wholly owned subsidiary, and finally was hived off as a new company. In late 1973, the late Sir George White, Bt. retired, and since then Anthony Crook has functioned as sole proprietor.

Though Bristol Cars still occupied its site within the Filton complex, it was unable any longer, as of right, to use the facilities of the rest of the giant plant. The factory building was now held on a rental basis, and any other services had to be paid for.

The status of Filton itself had changed too, for with the formation of the giant British Aircraft Corporation, and the disappearance of the Bristol Aeroplane Company, it was now just one of several subordinate plants, each allocated its own sphere of activity. Henceforth Filton would be responsible for matters that tended to be covered by the single word 'Aerospace', which included the Bloodhound surface-to-air guided missile, the Skylark sounding-rocket, the vertical launch Seawolf anti-missile system, and also work in connection with special equipment for satellites.

Such a high degree of technical specialisation reduced the facilities that would have been of use to a car manufacturer, and as early as 1957 Bristols had been forced to sub-contract some of their body-building. For the 406 saloons, the coachwork was made partially by Jones Brothers of Willesden, but for the 407 model a transfer was made to Park Royal Vehicles Limited. In both cases inspectors were seconded from Filton full-time to ensure traditional Bristol standards of quality.

One of the policy decisions made when Anthony Crook assumed control was that bodywork should revert to in-house manufacture, despite an acute lack of space. The solution was to move the Spares and Service Departments to the London depot, while a large capital outlay was made to bring the machinery up to the highest modern standards. This enabled a small but highly skilled labour force to manufacture not only the bodies, but many of the components too. These included the massive chassis with its three cross-members, and much of the front and rear suspension. The hides for the seats were cut, sewn and fitted on site as were the carpets and roof linings. The company used its own castings and did its own machining in-house.

Another policy decision applied to the pricing of spare parts. Hitherto, these had been calculated on the basis of the original cost – now it would be on the more logical replacement cost system. In some cases, prices had scarcely altered since 1947. Yet even on those very moderate amounts there had been protests. I recall a man who wrote to me in my capacity of Hon. Membership Secretary to seek the price of a reconditioned propeller shaft for his Type 400.

After contacting the Spares Department, I was able to inform him that it would be ten shillings (50 pence), plus postage. I heard no more, until I received a furious letter to the effect that the postage had been fifteen shillings (75 pence), which he described as monstrous. He added that he held the Club responsible, and demanded that a refund of five shillings (25 pence) should be made to him by return. I am glad to say the Committee did not agree.

Over the years, Anthony Crook has almost literally sunk large sums in restocking the bins with new spares, even though some were required very rarely. I recall him telling me once that not one Type 403 anti-roll bar had been sold in the past decade; yet there they were, if they were ever wanted. Unlike the majority of large-scale car makers, there is no 'Ten Year Datum Line', so spare parts are available even for the Type 400 of 1947.

Because of the ever increasing militancy of OPEC (the Organisation of Petroleum Exporting Countries), in the late seventies and early eighties, petrol supplies became scarcer and dearer, and there was even a threat of rationing. Some newspapers began to criticize the large-engined cars, calling them 'gas-guzzling monsters', but it was typical of the Crook flair that a potentially disastrous situation resulted in some excellent publicity for the Bristol.

He had already experimented with the use of liquefied petroleum gas (LPG) in Chrysler engines, and found that the big Vee-8 units accepted it with virtually no mechanical alterations. Two big gas tanks could easily be accommodated in the boot, with plenty of room to spare, and, by a twin pipe system, a driver could switch over from petrol to gas, or vice versa, as he wished. This proved an excellent sales factor, at a time when some makers of cars with similar-type engines were faced with empty order books.

I once asked Anthony Crook why, having virtually pioneered the LPG system, he had not pursued it further, even when the threat of rationing had receded. He explained that, from his practical experience, supplies of various components were not always available, and so he just let it die on the vine.

So the company survived, when another rather larger firm had been unable to carry a comparatively large number of cars that had been built for stock. This contrasted with the Bristol policy of making cars on a bespoke basis only. Not only did this avoid storage costs and the loss in morale when staff saw unsold cars accumulate, but it also enabled a customer to specify exactly what he required, not only as regards the exterior and interior colour schemes, but also such mechanical details as the operation of dimmer switch by pedal or switch, the material for the front seats, and even the exact contours that would ensure a driver's comfort on a long journey.

A valuable if intangible asset was the quality of the middle management, and I have included a brief glossary, showing their names and functions.

A Glossary of Bristol Personalities

ABBOTT LTD, E D This firm built the convertible version of the Type 405 Bristol 1954–1958 at their coachworks at Farnham, Surrey. Also made the solitary example of a drophead body on the short-chassis 404 in 1953.

Random Examples of the Cost of Bristol Spares Prior to their Rationalisation

Part No.	Description	Price
312750	Cylinder liner	£1. 3. 1
–	Set of tab washers	6. 1
311370	Camshaft bearing – mid rear	10. 6
–	Camshafts – all types	£22
341710	Tappet – 100 type engines	9.11
360650	Insert assembly: Vokes	£1. 3. 0
361430	Oil pump unit – type 100	£7. 1. 4
422321	Brake drum – steel	£3. 5. 6
422661	Front transverse spring	£10
–	Wheel snap-on cap c/w medallion types 400 to 405 inclusive	£1. 7. 6

Serviced Exchange Units

Cylinder blocks	£30
Gearboxes	£60
Radiators	£10
Clutches – type 400, 401 & early 403	£7.10. 6

Manuals

Bristol type 401 Illustrated Spares Handbook	15.0
405 Driver's Instruction Manual	£1. 1.0
409 Driver's Instruction Manual	£1. 5.0
Bristol type 100 Engine & Gearbox Workshop Manual	£2. 2.0
85A Engine & Gearbox Workshop Manual, suitable for Type 85A Engine with Solex Service Sheets	£2. 2.0

Note carriage & packing charges are additional to all prices.

ABELL, Major George Was General Manager of the Car Division at Filton in 1946, and played major role in development and production of the original Bristol Type 400.

ALDINGTON, Harold J Played key role in negotiations with BMW post-war.

ARNOLT, Harold 'Wacky' Played leading role in the marketing in the US of the short-chassis Arnolt-Bristol, and led his own team of cars in the long-distance Sebring road races.

BERTONE, Nuccio Was responsible for the body design of the Arnolt-Bristol as Bolide sports/racer, de luxe roadster and a coupe.

BEUTLER, Gebr. A Swiss firm of coachbuilders, built bodies on 401 and 406 chassis. The 406E was an export-only model.

CHANNER, Jack A suspension specialist, helped develop the 220/240 chassis, and was responsible for design of 'the Bomb', from which the short-chassis 404 evolved.

CROOK, T A D Since 1973 has been the sole owner of Bristol Cars. After a distinguished and successful racing career, mostly driving Bristol-engined cars, formed new company with the late Sir George White, Bt, in 1960 to save the Bristol marque from oblivion. Has maintained early traditions of quality and continuous development, and is responsible for the Bristol car's up-market image, and success.

DAVIS, S C H 'Sammy' A celebrated racing driver and journalist, was responsible for training and discipline of the Bristol works teams that competed in the Type 450 cars at Le Mans and Reims in 1953–55.

DENNIS, John after long service as Mr Crook's racing mechanic, became foreman at the London depot, and was probably the finest tuner of the 2-litre Bristol engine.

DERHAM, F S Former Secretary of Bristol Cars Limited.

EBERHORST, Dr Eboran von Distinguished German engineer, responsible for design of G type ERA, from which the Type 450 Bristol racer was derived.

EVANS, Ken A member of the pit staff that supported the racing team, and later built and exhibited his own 'Delta' sports car.

FEDDEN, Sir Roy Famous aero-engine designer who in 1942 attempted to develop a road car for Bristol Aeroplane Company.

FIEDLER, Dr Fritz Pre-war Chief Engineer for BMW cars. Post-war spent a short time at Filton plant helping in further development of the 2-litre engine, used by Bristol and derived from Type 328 BMW unit.

GIBBENS, Syd Long-term head of the Spares Department, with encyclopaedic knowledge of parts for Bristols, from 1946 onwards.

GREY, Lt.-Col Was head of sales at the Kensington showrooms, and invented a number of useful devices, fitting them to his own immaculate 405.

HOBBS, Dudley The long-term Bristol Chief Designer, he was adept at creating the illusion of change, with minimum alteration to a basic body design.

HODKIN, David Co-designer of G type ERA which served as basis for the Type 450 Bristol racing car.

IVERMEE, Stan An engineer who assisted in the development of the Type 450 Bristol racer.

JOHNSON, Leslie Purchased remains of ERA Limited, with a view to its revival as a manufacturer of racing cars. As stopgap, used Bristol engines and later sold the single example made, the G type ERA, to Bristol, to serve as basis for the Type 450 racer.

KEMISH, Percy Was responsible for developing the BSX engine, used in the Type 450 Bristol racers. He extracted increased power, without affecting the 2-litre unit's reliability.

LOVESEY, Syd General production manager at the Bristol factory.

LOWY, Jan Czech engineer who commenced designing 2½-litre OHC engine for the 220/240 project. Left Bristols to join Ford Motor Company.

MARELLI, Brian Was for many years manager at the London depot.

MEAD, Richard Designed and built a convertible body on a damaged 401 chassis that was admired for its looks and practicality.

NEWTON, Michael Suspension specialist, who succeeded Jack Channer in development work on the 220/240 chassis.

O'NIELL, Gerry Joined Bristols from Rolls-Royce, to replace Jan Lowy, and designed 3-litre OHC engine for 220/240 project.
PERROTT, John A design engineer who worked with Dudley Hobbs in early development of the original Type 400 Bristol.
PININFARINA Italian (Turin) firm of coachbuilders, responsible for short run of handsome convertible bodies on Bristol chassis 1947–1949.
SELBY, T V G Managed the Bristol racing team: 1953–1955
SEVIER, Dennis Was Chief Engineer, Bristol Cars, and with Car Division previously. A very talented engineer, was designing advanced manual gearbox for the 220/240 project, when it was rendered obsolete by Board decision to use automatic transmission.
STOCK, Donald A long-serving member of the Filton staff, who later was manager at the London depot.
STOREY, Eric A qualified aeronautical engineer, who was later responsible for the Service Department at Filton. Maintained very high aero standards of efficiency and workmanship.
SUMMERS, David Was chief engineer with the Bristol racing team, and designed a successful suspension modification, describing it as 'part Watts part Summers'.
TOURING OF MILAN Famous Italian coachbuilders, allocated a few chassis on which they built their own bodies.
TRESILIAN, Stuart Distinguished engineer who was associated with the development of the BSX engine, and also the 220/240 project.
UNIVERSITY MOTORS LTD Was mainly a distributor of big-volume makes, but commissioned a single convertible body on 401 Bristol chassis. Novel feature was the electrically operated (and very heavy) windows.
VERDON-SMITH, Sir Reginald One of the two nominee directors during period 1946–1947, when there was a joint AFN board with the Aldingtons.
VIOTTI Famous Italian coachbuilder, who built solitary convertible body on a Type 407 Bristol chassis. Much admired for its proportions, but it did not enter series production.

WATT, James A member of the Bristol sales staff, credited with having interested the late Harold Arnolt in using a Bristol engine and short chassis in a sports car to be sold in America at a very competitive price.
WINGFIELD, Brian An automobile engineer who designed and built a sports/racer, that always competed as a Bristol Special.
WHITE, Sir George, Bt Responsible for implementing Board decision in 1945, for Bristol to enter quality car market. Later headed the Car Division and, with T A D Crook, hived it off in 1960, as Bristol Cars, so saving the marque from extinction. He retired in 1973.

Other Details

With the body-building programme organised, it was considered logical to ensure that the paintwork should be of as high quality as possible, and a de Vilbis infra-red dryer was installed. In appearance it is not unlike an illuminated arc, under which the newly painted car is passed slowly. It is subjected to a consistent temperature of 140 degrees fahrenheit, so that a uniform finish is achieved, with a degree of hardness that ensures the gloss will be retained for a very long time. Drying times are very short – just thirty-five minutes for a metallic finish, or twenty-five minutes if a plain coloured acrylic is used.

Another change in policy resulted in what I would call 'the second series syndrome'. It applied mainly to the second-generation models 407–411, and involved, with the exception of the 407 and 410 cars, the creation of a second version of the same model, using items that would be original equipment on its successor. Examples include the 409-type parking lock fitted to the 408(2), the power-steering of the 409 and the bigger section tyres on the 411(2).

The policy also applied to the Type 412 multi-purpose convertible, which passed through three stages: the convertible or 412, the convertible saloon or 412/S2, and the turbocharged Beaufighter or 412/S3. A different approach was used for the 603 saloon – in particular the engine, in the case of the S and E models, and detail improvements in the Series 2 model. Much the same policy may have been used with the Brigand and Britannia; the former, with its turbocharger corresponding to the S type, while the normally aspirated Britannia fulfilled the E type's role.

The continuous development that has been a basic tenet of Bristol policy is the opposite of that common to most large-volume car makers. At Bristols, it is possible to incorporate improvements into a model already in production. In a larger firm, such innovations would probably be held back, to be advertised as added incentives to purchase the next model.

Such flexibility of mix is of considerable advantage in a low-volume company such as Bristol, and I have been told that in case of need the change from one model to the next might be effected in little more than a couple of months. Yet in the big factories it would probably take as many years.

The close co-operation between the Company and Chrysler has been of considerable value, not only because this enabled Bristol to concentrate on the chassis and body problems, but also because, as the cars became ever more luxurious, there was a suitably sized engine and automatic transmission available. An enormous amount of time and money was saved against the cost if these components had been designed, tested and made in-house.

Unlike other motor manufacturers, Bristol Cars Limited has neither distributors nor agents. All the administration is centralised at the Kensington offices, and a similar policy applies to the Service and Spare Parts depot at Brentford. Publicity is almost shunned by the Company, and the continuous development, a company tradition, remains virtually unknown. Yet much pioneer work has been done: four wheel disc braking, modified power steering, turbocharging and rear levelling are some examples.

The cars are sold all over the world, and so an efficient spares service is essential. This, too, is centralized, and is most efficient. I speak from personal experience when I lived in Switzerland, Australia and the United States. The only occasion when things went wrong was the receipt of a set of brake linings, intended for my 405 drophead. In fact this model, unlike its sister the 405 saloon, used the brake parts of the little 404 coupe. A telephone call met with apologies, and the receipt of the correct linings a few days later.

Many Bristol owners take their cars for servicing to the Brentford depot, but if this is impossible it is usually possible to locate a garage reasonably near one's home with experience of American-engined cars. But the Bristol is so strong and so well built that, apart from accidental damage, the chassis and body usually require little in the way of attention, beyond a regular wash and polish. Ever since the very early models, with their Enots One-shot lubrication system for the front suspension and steering box, Bristol designers have aimed at making each model as simple to service as possible. Where there has to be a greasing point, it is placed in an accessible position, and where adjustments can be made – as, for example, the steering wheel, it needs little in the way of tools or time to accomplish the task.

On the other hand, regular servicing at the periods specified in the instruction manual will keep the car in top condition. Since most owners keep their cars for a considerable time, this rule is usually strictly observed, which may account for the increasing numbers of Chrysler-engined models that now compete at the Bristol Owners' Club annual Concours. They look so immaculate that it can be a shock to note the mileage covered.

It has always been Company policy to build cars to last, and indeed I recall one rare advertisement that said the 'Bristol is built like a Battleship'. Britain no longer has any of the latter, but it is still a way of suggesting great strength and integrity, both of which are still to be found in a Bristol car.

Recently I was crossing Pall Mall when I spotted a Bristol parked by the Royal Automobile Club. It was an early Type 407, but instead of the standard gear control by facia buttons it had the floor-mounted lever first used on the Type 410 model. Just then the owner returned and, though he was not a Club member, we were soon chatting about Bristols in general and his own example in particular. When I mentioned the gear lever, he laughed. 'Well you see,' he explained, 'the Old Girl had covered nearly 200,000 miles, so I bought her a new engine, and it came with the later model transmission.' It was simple enough, but I detected an affection for 'the Old Girl' one might not hear from the tycoon who changes his car to get the latest registration plate.

Goodwill has been called the most valuable yet intangible asset a business can possess. It can also be the most fragile, yet over the years the sheer quality and durability of the Bristol has converted mere car owners into Bristol enthusiasts. They speak of their cars with affection and of its makers with respect. They may voice the occasional criticism of some feature they do not like; but suggest a little mischievously that they might change to another make, and that usually puts them on the defensive.

But not all the visitors to the Kensington showroom are old Bristol hands – there is new blood too. I was sitting in the train opposite a man holding a brace of trade plates. When it transpired that he was a chauffeur on his way back from an auction, where he had sold an almost new limousine of a highly regarded and very expensive make.

'It was fine till we were on the M6 going to an important business meeting,' he told me, 'then it just faded on me. I managed to coast up onto the hard shoulder, and there was me with my head in the bonnet, and the boss fizzing like a firework. He's a lucky bloke, and soon got a lift, but he told me to get rid of the car, anyway.'

'What have you got now?' I asked, and he smiled.

'It's a Bristol Brigand, it's turbocharged and a lot quicker than it looks.' He paused, 'You see, the car he got a lift in was a Brigand, and the owner was full of praise for it – it was the third Bristol he had owned. So the boss decided that was the car for him.'

'And does he like it?' I enquired. The man's smile faded as he replied, 'A bit too much, if you ask me. In fact he hinted that he's enjoying driving it himself, so I might be getting my cards . . .'

In May 1985, a move was made from Filton to a new purpose-built factory of some 50,000 cu ft at Patchway, within sight of the Filton runway. About the same time, the Service and Spares departments moved from their former Chiswick premises to new ones at Brentford. But otherwise the routine remains the same, with Anthony Crook visiting the factory by air every week. He maintains a very complete control, and appears to fly in all weathers. I recall a meeting, one winter's afternoon – he arrived late, apologised and told me he had returned to London and had been diverted to another landing strip. He was very tired, but refused my suggestion that we might postpone our meeting. As ever, I was impressed by his dry humour and, above all, his ability to laugh at himself – a rare gift indeed.

History indicates that a country usually fares best when the monarch enjoys a long reign, and I feel Anthony Crook's near quarter century of control has enabled the Company to find, develop and retain its own niche in a very competitive market. There has been none of those palace revolutions that have bedevilled some of the bigger firms, including the disappearance of fine old makes such as Alvis, or badge engineering like the MG. Just a series of magnificent cars, combining the Bristol virtues of performance, reliability, and anonymity. There is nothing flash about these cars, and if they impress it is because of their air of quiet exclusive luxury.

An essential part of the Company policy is the protection of the identities of its customers, with the same quiet discretion that might appear more appropriate to a top-quality solicitor than a car maker. But if a list of such customers was ever to be made public it would probably resemble a small edition of *International Who's Who*. For this reason, it must have come as a most unpleasant shock when a newspaper reporter gleefully described how a provincial council had purchased a new Bristol for use by its chairperson and how the decision had been attacked by the opposition.

On the other hand it was cheering to note how vigorously the purchase had been defended, for it was claimed that in fact the Bristol was more cost-effective, since it would last twice as long as its predecessor – a limousine of imposing size and cost. If one might think it strange that a two-door model should have been chosen for use on ceremonial occasions, it has to be remembered that the doors are very wide, that the front seats slide forward to facilitate access to the rear, and that because of that ingenious floor-mounted rail there is little danger of feet becoming entangled with the safety belts.

Under Anthony Crook's leadership, the Bristol staff are a well-knit team, and I thought it typical when, in 1988, the Bristol Owners' Club held its annual Concours up on Clifton Downs outside Bristol, that some thirty members of the factory staff brought their families. I watched one man peering at the engine number of a handsome 405 saloon. He grinned, and beckoned for his son aged about twelve to look, and then said, 'Now you know what your Dad does for his living.'

In the autumn of the same year, I attended the funeral of John Dennis, foreman at the London depot, and once Mr Crook's racing mechanic. The service was at St Mary-on-the-Hill, Caterham, Surrey, yet the church was full of fellow employees who had come from Bristol to pay their last respects to a colleague and friend. Though I was unable to come over for the funeral of the Chief Engineer, the late Dennis Sevier, the Club Chairman told me it too was well attended by staff who had come just to say goodbye. I do not think that would happen at one of the huge plants that churn cars out by the thousand.

The deaths of two such key personnel must seem a dire warning, and it will not be easy to find replacements of similar quality. But the Bristol has now been in continuous production since 1946, and I have every confidence that it will pass its half-century in just a few year's time, and still, I hope, with Mr Crook's hands steady on the tiller, or perhaps I should say steering wheel.

It is due to Anthony Crook's devotion to the marque and his insistence that all its traditional qualities should be continued, despite its changed appearance, engine and transmission, that it retains its reputation as possibly the best made car in the world. Its anonymity and lack of ordinary publicity give it that special air of mystery that sets it apart from all other makes. Whether you own a Type 400 with a quarter of a million miles under its wheels or a factory-fresh Britannia, you know that you have an engineering masterpiece.

The following appeared in the August 1983 issue of *Thoroughbred and Classic Car*:

'The Bristol Brigand may be a very different machine from the first 400, but in its maker's striving to produce the best available for a small but discerning public, without compromising on cost, nothing has changed in these thirty-seven intervening years.

'And it says a great deal for the Company, that there are still a number of people working for them today, who were in at the beginning. These same craftsmen will lovingly restore any older Bristol . . . as easily as they will create a new classic Bristol.

'Despite the German, Italian and American genes in its heritage, today's Bristol is as true-blue British as could be.'

Bibliography

Anthony Crook Motors Ltd *Bristol Cars since their Origin: 1946–1966* (The Aycliffe Press)

Clarke, R. M. *Gold Folio – Bristol Cars* (Brooklands Book Distribution Ltd)

Clausager, Anders Ditlev *Le Mans* (Arthur Barker Ltd)

Cooper, John *Grand Prix Carpet-Bagger* (Haynes Publication Group)

Davis, S. C. H. *Motor Racing* (Iliffe & Sons Ltd)

Dymock, Eric *Post War Sports Car* (Ebury Press)

Jenkinson, D. S. *From Chain-drive to Turbocharger* (Patrick Stephens Ltd)

Lloyd, John *The Story of the E. R. A.* (Motor Racing Publications Ltd)

May, C. A. N. *Speed Hill-Climb* (G. T. Foulis & Co. Ltd)

Moss, Stirling & Pomeroy, Laurence *Design & Behaviour of the Racing Car* (William Kimber)

Nicholson, T. R. *Sports Cars: 1928–1939* (Blandford Press)

Scheel, J. H. *Cars of the World* (Methuen & Co.)

Sedgwick, Michael *Cars of the Thirties & Forties* (Beekman House)

Setright, L. J. K. *Bristol Cars & Engines* (Motor Racing Publications Ltd)

Slater, Don *BMW – the Book of the Car* (Ebury Press)

Stein, Ralph *The Great Cars* (Paul Hamlyn)

Thirlby, David *Frazer Nash* (Haynes Publishing Group)

Index

Abarth exhausts, 18, 100, 158
Abbott, E B Ltd, 12, 23, 114, 130, 139, 308
Abell, Major George, 309
AC Cars Ltd, 98, 99, 288–9
    Ace, 98, 99, 288–9, 297, 301–3, 304
    Aceca, 98, 99, 297, 303
    export to Australasia, 65, 66, 67
    Greyhound saloon, 100, 297, 303
Adam, Flt. Lieut., 11
addresses, current, 13
aero-engines, 11–12; *see also* Centaurus
AFN Ltd, 20, 21–2, 25–6, 310; *see also* FNS; Frazer Nash; Nash
aircraft, 9–14, 77, 277–8; *see also individual models*
Albert Memorial meetings, 290
Aldington, Donald, 15, 20, 21, 22
Aldington, Harold J, 12, 20, 309
    and BMW 12, 15–17, 180
    and British Aeroplane Co, 12, 21, 22, 25
    as driver, 17, 21, 24
Aldington, William, 15, 17, 20, 21
Alfa Romeo 2.5SS, 41
Alfin brake drums, 85–6, 114, 129
Alpine Rally, 15, 20
Alta, 101, 303
Alvis, 172, 312
Anthony, Mike, 304
Armstrong, 194, 206, 233–5, 248, 286
Armstrong-Siddeley, 184
Arnolt, Harold 'Wacky', 107, 118–19, 125–7, 309, 310
Arnolt, Michael, 116
Arnolt-Bristol, 12, 28–9, 118–29, 309
    appearance, 120
    basic data, 17, 18, 23, 119
    Bertone and, 12, 158
    Bolide, 119, 122, 123, 128, 129
    coupe, 123, 124, 128
    De Luxe, 119, 122, 123, 124, 128
    engine, 12, 103, 107, 120, 122
    exports, 128
    illustrations, 120–1, 123–4, 126, 158
    interior, 109
    modifications, 129
    prototypes, 119–20
    racing achievements, 125–8
    registry, 127–9, 294

Arnott superchargers, 91
Aruntunoff, A, 200, 251
Austin cars, 41, 42, 115, 222
Australia, 44–5, 63, 65–7, 77, 128, 294, 296
Autocar, 57, 58, 195
Autosport, 79, 83, 222, 233, 276
Avon safety wheel, 185, 243, 248–9, 253, 279, 280

Banks, J W E, 110, 44
Barnwell, Captain Frank, 10–11
Beaufighter (aircraft), 11, 13, 77, 263, 278
Beaufighter (car, Type 412/3), 13, 252, 259–62, 310
    basic data, 17, 24, 190, 260
    illustrations, 261, 281, 283
Beaufort (aircraft), 278
Beaufort (car), 263–4, 281
Belgium, 62–3, 294
Bertone, Carrozzeria, of Turin, 12, 118, 119, 158, 309
Beutler, Gebr, of Thun, 52, 53–4, 62, 145, 309
Blenheim aircraft, 11, 12–13
Blenheim Palace; BOC Concours, 289
Bluemel steering wheels, 47, 137, 154, 197, 207, 219
BMW, 12, 15–17, 20, 21, 22, 28
    Type 326, 25
    Type 327, 16, 24
    Type 328, 16–17, 21, 39, 92, 180, 309
    Type 335, 180
BMW Car Club, 287
'Bobcat', 66, 304
Boddy, William, 57–8
bodywork, 152, 194, 210, 307; *see also* coachbuilders
Bolster, John, 79, 83, 90, 117, 222, 233, 244
'Bomb, the', 105, 107, 309
Borg and Beck clutch, 78
Borg Warner, 43
    BW.CR gearboxes (CR/5), 83, 122
    (CR/7), 105, 112
    (CR/11), 30, 135
'Boxkite' aircraft, 10, 11
Boynton, Ted, 123
Brabazon airliner, 134
Brabazon Straight, 78, 166, 246
Brabham, Sir Jack, 176, 304
Bradburn and Wedge, 55, 159
Brazil-Straker, 11
Bridgehampton circuit, 127

INDEX

Brigand (aircraft), 278
Brigand (car), 13, 277–86, 312
  basic data, 17, 24, 278
  illustrations, 281
  turbocharger, 277
  for other details, see under Britannia (car)
Brimol valve inserts, 142
Bristol Aeroplane Company, 11, 12
Bristol cars
  Type 400, 11, 12, 27–38, 309, 310
    basic data, 17, 18, 23, 34
    convertible, 26, 28, 29, 31, 35, 275, 276, 289, 293
    engine, 17, 18, 95
    exports, 61–7
    illustrations, 26, 27–38, 90
    prototypes, 25–6
    purchase of used, 36–8
    rescued by BOC crew, 274
    Series 1/2 distinction, 34, 36
    shock absorbers, 78
  Type 401, 12, 39–60
    basic data, 17, 18, 23, 39
    clutch, 78
    engine, 17, 18, 23, 39, 95, 97
    evolution, 77–9, 80, 83
    exports, 61–7
    exterior, 39–43, 79, 245, 309
    illustrations, 26, 40–3, 45–54, 56–9, 61, 90
    interior, 45–8, 77–8
    non-Bristol bodywork, 50–5, 56, 62, 63, 64, 251, 309
    purchase of used, 58–60
    RDB Robinson and, 42
    Series 1/2 distinguished, 44, 48–50
    shock absorbers, 78
    and sport, 55–7
  Type 402, 12, 68–76
    basic data, 17, 18, 23, 68, 71, 74
    chassis numbers, 44, 71
    engine, 17, 18, 23, 95
    export, 67
    illustrations, 26, 69, 71–3, 75
    shock absorbers, 78
  Type 403, 12, 39, 80–93
    basic data, 17, 18, 23, 80
    export, 67, 294
    illustrations, 24, 26, 39, 45, 115, 294
    purchase of used, 92–3
  Type 404, 12, 28–9, 105–17, 309
    Abbott drophead, 114, 308
    basic data, 17, 18, 23, 105
    body building, 108–9, 117
    driving experience, 114–16
    engines, 18, 98, 99, 105, 112, 114, 116
    export, 67, 117
    illustrations, 26, 105–16
    purchase of used, 117
  Type 405, 12, 133–44
    Abbott version, 130, 308
    basic data, 17, 18, 23, 135

    convertible, 17, 67, 98, 114, 139–43, 311
    engines, 98, 114, 138, 142–3, 144
    exhaust modifications, 141–2
    export, 67
    illustrations, 26, 86, 133–7, 140–1, 144
    interior, 226
    low doors, 134, 219
    purchase of used, 143–4
    saloon, 26, 86, 98, 130–2, 133, 134–9
  Type 406, 12, 13, 148–63, 245
    basic data, 17, 18, 23
    braking system, 151–2
    engine, 18, 100, 150–1
    export, 67
    Jones coachwork, 152, 307
    overdrive, 150
    purchase of used, 152
    Zagato versions, 17, 42, 100, 155–63, 251
  Type 406E, 13, 17, 23, 145–7, 151
  Type 407, 13, 192–202, 246
    basic data, 17, 19, 24, 192
    bodywork, 194, 210, 307
    driving impressions, 197–8, 311–12
    engine, 24, 187, (cooling), 195–7, 249
    export, 67
    purchase of used, 223–30
    spotter's guide, 229
    suspension, 247–8
    Viotti convertible, 200–2, 264, 310
    Zagato GT version, 198–200, 251
  Type 408, 13, 203–10
    basic data, 17, 19, 24, 203
    engines, 24, 205–6, 207, 211
    export, 67
    production figures, 231
    purchase of used, 223–30
    Series 1, 203–7, 229
    Series 2, 207–8, 208–10, 211, 229, 310
  Type 409, 13, 211–15
    basic data, 17, 19, 24, 211
    engine, 24, 188
    export, 67, 246
    illustrations, 212–13, 214, 227
    Mark 2, 213–14, 247, 310
    purchase of used, 223–30
    spotter's guide, 229
  Type 410, 13, 216–22
    basic data, 17, 19, 24, 216
    engine, 24, 188, 250
    export, 67
    fitting larger wheels, 221–2
    illustrations, 39, 217–21
    purchase of used, 223–30
    spotter's guide, 229
  Type 411, 13, 230–44
    basic data, 17, 19, 24, 230
    engine, 24, 188, (cooling), 249, 250
    export, 67
    production figures, 231

INDEX

purchase of used, 223–30
seats, 272
Series 1, 13, 17, 24, 230–3, 250
Series 2, 13, 17, 24, 188, 228, 229, 233–6, 248
Series 3, 13, 17, 24, 189, 229, 236–7
Series 4, 13, 17, 24, 189–90, 229, 237–9, 240, 250
Series 5, 13, 17, 190, 229, 239–44, 246, 248, 249, 280
Sevier on, 246
spotter's guide, 229
wheels, 280
Type 412, 12, 246, 251–65, 272, 310
basic data, 17, 24, 251
Beaufort, 263–4
engine, 24, 190, 251
spotter's guide, 229, 264
Zagato and, 251
412/3, 310
412/S2, 253–4, 254–9
412/S3, see Beaufighter (car)
412/USA convertible, 263
Type 450, 12, 104, 164–179, 245, 309
basic data, 167
engines, 103, 164–6
open cars (1955), 174–5
restored model, 12, 26, 177–9, 290
Type 603, 13, 86, 229, 266–76, 277–8, 310–11
603E, 13, 17, 24, 229, 266–7, 269, 271
603S, 13, 17, 24, 190, 229, 266–7, 268–72, 274–6
603S2, 13, 17, 24, 190, 229, 264, 266–74
see also: Arnolt-Bristol; Beaufighter (car); Brigand (car); Britannia (car)
Bristol Cars Ltd; creation, 13, 183
Bristol Owners' Club, 34, 35, 127, 155, 274–6, 287–96
Anthony Crook and, 236, 261, 274
Irish Centre, 288
membership applications, 296
Bristol Plastics Ltd, 304
Bristol Tramways Company, 9–10
Britannia (aircraft), 277
Britannia (car), 13, 277–86
development, 311
engine, 190, 282–3
illustrations, 279–81, 283, 284, 285
spotter's guide, 229, 277–8
stowage, 110
British Aeroplane Company, 20, 21–2, 25–6
British Aerospace, 13
British Aircraft Company, 13
British Aircraft Corporation, 183, 307
British and Colonial Aeroplane Company, 9–11, 12
British Racing Motors, 166
Brividium, 77, 85
Brooklands race track, 20, 276
Brooks, R F, 159
Brownhill, L J, 160
'Brownie' aircraft, 11
Buckingham aircraft, 278
Buckmaster aircraft, 278
Burgess silencers, 36, 49, 214

Canada, 63
Cannes Rally, 55
Car and Driver, 256
Car Division, status of, 11, 152, 183, 307
Cars Illustrated, 210, 211
Carter carburettors, 186, 190, 192, 198, 259, 267
Castle Combe, Wilts, 219
Centaurus aero-engine, 12, 77, 83, 277, 278
Channer, Jack, 79, 180–1, 183, 290, 309
and 404 chassis, 105, 107, 119
Chapman, Colin, 304
Charlton, Bob, 66
'Cherub' aero-engine, 11
Chivers, E., 10
chronological record, 12
Chrysler engine
data, 13, 17, 24, 186–91, 224
introduction, 101, 183, 184
relationship with Bristol, 214, 311
see also under engines
Clarke, Tom, 181
Classic Car Shows, 291–2
Clausager, Anders Ditlev, 168
Clayton-Dewandre servo, 181
Clifton Downs, Bristol, 148, 294
coachbuilders, 62–3; see also individual firms
Coanda, Henri, 10
Comet air disaster (1954), 12, 183
Conibere, Ted, 122
construction procedures, 130–2
Cook (racing driver), 127
cooling of engine, 249–50
Cooper, John, 101, 303, 304
Cooper Cars Ltd, 101, 303, 304
Cooper-Bristol, 102, 165, 171, 180, 303
exports, 65, 66, 67
Corpus Christi circuit, 127
Cosmos Engineering, 11, 12
Cottrell, P H G, 304
Crook, Anthony Ltd
engine modifications, 18, 92, 98
and Zagato, 50, 198, 251
Crook, T A D (Anthony), 309
and Avon safety wheel, 185, 243, 249
and Bristol Cars Ltd, 13, 183, 307, 309, 310
and BOC, 236, 261, 274, 290, 291
customer relations, 227, 307–8, 311
driving, 55, 57, 227, (racing), 91, 113, 164, 303, 309
and 406Z chassis 5284, 159
on safety of Bristol, 213
and Viotti-bodied 407, 200
personal collection, 12, 177, 264
management style, 312, 313
Cuddigan, Dr B J, 159

Davis, S C H (Sammy), 20, 164, 309
Delco-Remy-Hyatt, 99, 102, 103–4
Delta sports car, 309
Dennis, John, 309, 313

Derham, F S, 309
development policy, 77–9, 80, 92–104, 151, 216, 310–11
DiCola, Mike, 128
'Dowidat Spanner Special', 66
Dowrick, N J, 55
Dreyfus, Rene, 125–6
Drumon, Guy M, QC, 191
Dunlop: braking systems, 151–2, 181, 195, 206
  wheels, 79, 181, 213, 232
Durbin, Ralph, 127

Eason Gibson, J, 43, 44
Eberhorst, Dr Eboran von, 309
Edinburgh, HRH Philip, Duke of, 145
Edwards, Sir Clive, Bt, 237, 300
Eifelrennan, 17
electrolytic action, 60, 90, 226
Emery, John, 296
emission controls, 190, 224, 232, 242, 246, 267
  and engine cooling, 249, 250
engines
  85, 17, 18, 23, 30, 31, 94
  85A, 17, 18, 23, 30, 31, 44, 49–50, 71, 94–5
  85B, 17, 18, 23, 30, 31, 96
  85C, 17, 18, 23, 30–1, 39, 44, 45, 49, 68, 71, 74, 82, 97
  100A, 12, 17, 18, 23, 36, 82–3, 85–8, 98
  100B, 17, 18, 23, 98, 105, (in AC cars) 98, 297, (in 400) 36, (in 401) 44, 50, 90, (in 404) 98, 112, 114, 116, (in 405) 98, 141
  100B2, 17, 18, 23, 98, 135, 138, 142 (in 401) 50
  100C, 17, 18, 23, 99, 105, 112, (in 405) 114, 142–3
  100D, 303
  100D2, 99, 129, 288, 297, 305
  110, 17, 18, 23, 100, 150–1, 161, 297
  110A, 45, 80
  110S, 17, 18, 100, 156, 158, 161, 297
  160, 12, 100–1, 104, 182, 245–6
  313, 13, 17, 19, 24, 194–5, 198, 205–6, 246, (basic data) 187–8, 190, 192, 203
  318, 13, 17, 19, 24, 200, 207, 211, 217, 266, (basic data) 188, 190, 191, 216
  360, 13, 17, 19, 24, 259, 266, 277, 282, (basic data) 190, 260
  383, 13, 17, 19, 24, 232, 236, (basic data) 188–9, 191
  400, 13, 17, 19, 24, 237, 251, 257, (basic data) 189–90, 191
  440, 246
  500, 17
  BS, 80, 83, 101–4, 112, 164–6, 180, (BS1) 102–3, (BS1/2) 12, 17, 18, 23, 103, 107, 119, 120, 122, (BS4) 103, (BSX (BS5)) 77, 103–4, 164–6, 167, 169, 171, 182, 309, 310
  see also: aero-engines; FNS
Engines Division, 13, 92–104, 130–1
English Racing Automobiles Ltd, 101, 166, 167, 304, 309
Enots One-shot lubrication system, 30, 36, 38, 44, 87, 311
Erikson, Ernie, 125–6
Esher, Surrey, 287, 288
Evans, Ken, 175, 309

exports, 61–7, 117, 191
  see also: individual countries

Fairman, Jack, 168, 171, 173, 175, 177
Falcon aero-engine, 11
Falcon Works, Isleworth, 15, 16, 20, 21, 22, 25
Fane, A F P, 16, 17
Farman, Maurice, 9
Fedden, Sir Roy, 9, 11–12, 309
Fiedler, Dr Fritz, 309
'Fighter' aircraft, 11
Flegg, B R, 160
Flexitor springs, 182
FNS engines, 99, 100, 101, 164, 165, 180, 297, 298–300
Formula 2 racing category, 101, 165
France, 290, 293, 294
Frazer Nash cars, 15–17, 20, 61, 297–300
  Frazer Nash-BMW, 22, (Type 327) 12, 24, (Type 328) 16, 17, 20
  Le Mans Replica, 297, 298
  racing, 123, 177
  spare wheel stowage, 237
  see also: AFN; FNS
Freke, Alfie, 122, 166

gas, liquid petroleum, 262, 308
Geddes, John, 120
Gerard, Bob, 305
Gibb, Wally, 277
Gibbens, Syd, 309
Girling, 90, 103, 122, 212, 217, 283
Goldich, Bob, 125–6, 127
Goldman, Max, 127
Goodwood (1952), 102, 113, 303
Gordini, 173
Gould, Horace, 122
Graber, 62, 145
Greenham Common, Berks, 288
Grey, Lt-Col, 309
Grier, Bob, 125–6, 126
Grossglockner Hill Climb, 17
Gurston Down, 290

Halbert, I W, 251
Hamburg Grand Prix, 12, 21
Hamshere, J, 160
Hardy Spicer, 83, 134
Harrington, Harry, 287
Hawthorn, Mike, 102, 125–6, 171, 303
Hewitt, Ralph, 287, 290
High Intensity Discharge tube, 285–6
Hill, Phil, 125–6
Hobbs, Dudley, 184, 192, 208, 216, 230, 309
Hoburn-Eaton oil pump, 82–3, 102
Hodkin, David, 167, 309
Holset viscous dampers, 99, 100, 103
Hulbert, I W, 200
Hunt, W, 159
Hurlock brothers, 99, 304

INDEX

Hutchinson, Jill, 305, 306

Inai, Walter, 125–6
Irish Racing Automobiles, 304
Ivermee, Stanley, 164, 165, 309

Jaguar, 181
Jensen, 197, 249
Johnson, Leslie, 101, 166, 304, 309
Jones Brothers, Willesden, 152, 307
'Jupiter' aero-engine, 11, 12

Keen, Mike, 173, 176–7
Keevil RAF base, Wilts, 243, 249
Kelly, Joe, 304
Kemish, Percy, 164–6, 168, 169, 171, 172, 175, 176, 290, 309
Kenlowe, 193, 196, 203, 232, 240
Kieft, Cyril, 101, 304

Laguna Seca, USA, 128
Lancia, 91, 162, 163
Langley, John, 262
Larkhill, 10
Laycock de Normanville, 137–8, 150
Layrub universal joints, 83
Le Mans, 12, 104, 161, 168–9, 173–4, 176, 177
Lear, Ron, 122
Levegh, Pierre, 12, 104, 176, 177
Leverol seat mechanism, 48
Lines, Trevor, 173, 177
Lister cars, 101, 304
'Longhorn' aircraft, 9
Lopez, Juan, 125–6
Lotus, 101, 304
Lovesey, Syd, 309
Lowy, Jan, 180, 182, 309
Lucas, 79, 94, 103, 104, 182
'Lucifer' aero-engine, 11–12

Macao Grand Prix, 66, 304
Machell, Guy, 287
McKechnie, Mr, of Cheshire, 159
Macklin, Lance, 168, 169, 177
Marchal headlights, 154
Marelli, Brian, 309
Marles, 194, 197–8, 212, 215, 220, 283
May, Brian, 53, 54, 306
Mayers, Jim, 173, 176–7
Mays, Raymond, 166
Mead, Richard, 52, 55, 64, 309
Mercedes racing team, 176
'Mercury' aero-engine, 11
Messerschmidt 'Taifun' Bf 108, 20
MG cars, 91, 118, 312
'Military Monoplane', 10, 11
Mille Miglia race, 12, 17, 21, 22, 78
Miller, Cecil, 287, 290
Mini, 41, 42, 246
Mitchel, Tony, 159

'Monkey Stable', 173
'Monoplane' aircraft, 10, 11
Monte Carlo Rally, 12
Monterey, USA, 128
Montlhéry circuit, 12, 57, 171
Morris, Jimmy, 122
Morris cars, 41, 42, 118
Moss, Stirling, 125–6, 166, 173, 303, 304
Motor, 27, 74, 76, 119, 145, 150, 202, 264, 272, 278–9
Motor Industry Research Association, 166–7
Motor Sport, 57–8
motorcycle industry, 20, 214
Moulton, Alex, 41, 182

Nash chain-driven cars, 15, 20, 22
New Zealand, 63, 65–7, 160
Newton, Michael, 183, 309
Newton and Bennett, 30, 43
Norwood, John, 125–6

O'Niell, Gerry, 180, 182, 310
Otter Controls, 241

paintwork, 60, 131–2, 219, 223, 310
Panks, John, 125–6, 128
Park Royal Vehicles, Ltd, Acton, 186, 194, 205, 210, 307
Park Ward, 55
Patchway factory, 13, 309, 312
Patrick Motor Museum, 149, 235, 292
'Pegasus' aero-engine, 11
Pegg, Bill, 277
Perrott, John, 310
personalities, 308–10
Pininfarina, 12, 25, 29, 310
  and 401, 50, 52, 63
Plymouth cars, 187, 191
Polish Rally, 12
Popp, Franz Josef, 16, 21
pre-fabricated houses, 14
Prescott Hill Climb, 158, 288, 290
Prier, Pierre, 10
production figures, 130, 231
Proteus turbo-prop engines, 277
prototype, Fedden's, 9, 12, 309
Pruett, George, 122

'Racer' aircraft, 11
Racing Department, 164–79
  see also Bristol cars (450)
Ragley Hall, 289
Raskin, Lee, 127, 128
Redex, 246
Reid, Fred, 122
Reims, 12, 169–71, 174, 177
Reutter, 147, 197, 206, 219
Riverley Motors, 52, 55
Robinson, R D B, 42, 160
Roe, A V, 13
Rogers, Hunter, 147

319

Rolls Royce, 11
Rootes, 13, 183
Rose, Bill, 122
Rotomaster, 190, 259, 260, 282
Rylett, Dudley, 288

Schieffelin, John, 128
Schroeder, P R, 159
Scott-Plummer, Alexa, 201
'Scout' aircraft, 11
Sebring race, 125–6, 126–7, 309
Selby, T V G, 164, 166, 168, 173, 175, 310
Selectaride, 208, 209
Sellers, Peter, 200, 246
Service Dept, 307, 311, 310, 312
Setright, L J K, 160, 230–1, 288, 290
Sevier, Dennis, 182–3, 216–17, 290, 310, 313
   and Avon safety wheel, 185, 243, 248–9
   on car design, 240, 241, 245–50
Shelby, Carol, 125–6
Shorts of Belfast, 277
Silk, George, 214
Silverstone, 33, 55, 167, 168
Smiths Electronics, 183
Snetterton, 303
Society of Motor Manufacturers and Traders awards, 210
South Africa, 63
Spares Dept, 295, 307–8, 309, 311, 312
Spax adjustable dampers, 282–3
Sports Car, 215
Sports Car Club of America, 123
staff spirit, 312–13
Star Sapphire engine, 184
Steib sidecars, 20
Stock, Donald, 310
Stoop, Dickie, 300
Storey, Eric, 290, 310
Summers, David, 176, 310
Summit Point, West Virginia, 128

T44-Cooper-BG-Bristol, 305
Tamplin, Bernard, 122
Taylor, Geoffrey, 101, 303
Thoroughbred and Classic Car, 264–5, 286
Tojeiro, John, 304
Tonkin, Ian, 66
Torqueflite, 13, 183, 184, 214, 224, 246, 282
   A466, 247
   A727, 207, 211–12, 247
Touring, 12, 25, 29, 39–43, 52, 310
   techniques, 40, 41, 43, 225–6, 286
Tresilian, Stuart, 166, 180, 310
Tufnol, 78, 90
Tulip Rally, 55

United States of America, 63, 65
   see also Arnolt-Bristol *and* individual places
University Motors Ltd, 52–3, 310
used car, advice on choice of, 79, 136–7, 296
   400, 36–8
   401, 58–60
   402, 74, 76
   403, 92–3
   404, 117
   405, 143–4
   406, 152
   407–411, 223–30
Uwins, Captain Cyril, 11, 12

Verdon-Smith, Sir Reginald, 21, 22, 24, 310
Vilbis infra-red dryer, 310
Vintage Sports Car Club of America, 128
Viotti 407 convertible, 200–2, 310
Vokes air filters, 103, 122, 144
Volvo sports cars, 205

Wacker, Fred, 123
Walters, Phil, 125–6
Wareham, Harry, 155, 156, 158, 159
'Warrior Bristol', 66, 304
Warsaw, Indiana, 126, 127
Waterford, USA, 127
Watkins, Bill, 128
Watt, James, 119, 310
Whalley, John, 209
White, Sir George Bt, 310
   and Bristol Cars Ltd, 13, 183, 307, 309
   and British and Colonial Aeroplane Company, 9–10
   and H J Aldington, 21, 22, 25
   and Type 404, 105, 107
White, Stanley, 9–10
Whitehead, Graham, 168, 169, 177
Williams, Dave, 166
Williams, Peter, 305
Williams, Ray V, 122, 166
Wilson, Peter, 168, 169, 171, 173, 176, 177, 179, 290
Wingfield, Brian, 305–6, 310
wings, stowage in, 110, 136, 138, 195, 219, 237, 269
Wisdom, T H 'Tommy', 168, 169, 173, 177
Wolfrace wheels, 279

Zagato, 13, 251
   and 401, 50, 51, 56, 251
   406Z, 17, 42, 100, 155–63, 251
   407GT, 198–200, 251
   412, 251
'Zebra' aircraft, 11
Zenith 36 VHG carburettor, 91
ZF power steering, 213, 215, 220, 232, 247, 258, 283, 286

RARITAN VALLEY COMMUNITY COLLEGE

3 3666 00098 0200

TL 215 .B76 O41 1990
Oxley, Charles.
Bristol

**RARITAN VALLEY COMMUNITY
COLLEGE LIBRARY
ROUTE 28
NORTH BRANCH, NJ 08876-1265**

GAYLORD